Religion:
Bane or Blessing

OTHER TITLES FROM NEW FALCON PUBLICATIONS

Cosmic Trigger: Final Secret of the Illuminati
Prometheus Rising
    By Robert Anton Wilson
Undoing Yourself With Energized Meditation
    By Christopher S. Hyatt, Ph.D.
Eight Lectures on Yoga
Gems From the Equinox
    By Aleister Crowley
Info-Psychology
The Game of Life
    By Timothy Leary, Ph.D.
Aversion to Honor: A Tale of Sexual Harassment Within the Federal Government
    By Thomas R. Burns, Ph.D.
Condensed Chaos: An Introduction to Chaos Magick
    By Phil Hine
The Challenge of the New Millennium
    By Jerral Hicks, Ed.D.
The Complete Golden Dawn System of Magic
The Golden Dawn Tapes—Series I, II, and III
    By Israel Regardie
Buddhism and Jungian Psychology
    By J. Marvin Spiegelman, Ph.D.
Astrology & Consciousness
    By Rio Olesky
Metaskills: The Spiritual Art of Therapy
    By Amy Mindell, Ph.D.
Beyond Duality: The Art of Transcendence
    By Laurence Galian
Soul Magic: Understanding Your Journey
    By Katherine Torres, Ph.D.
A Mother Looks At the Gay Child
    By Jesse Davis
Phenomenal Women: That's US!
    By Dr. Madeleine Singer

And to get your free catalog of *all* of our titles, write to:
New Falcon Publications (Catalog Dept.)
PMB 277
1739 East Broadway Road # 1
Tempe, Arizona 85282 U.S.A
And visit our website at **http://www.newfalcon.com**

Religion: Bane or Blessing

by

Charles Meister, Ph.D.

NEW FALCON PUBLICATIONS
TEMPE, ARIZONA, U.S.A.

Copyright © 1999 by Charles Meister, Ph.D.

All rights reserved. No part of this book, in part or in whole, may be reproduced, transmitted, or utilized, in any form or by any means, electronic or mechanical, including photocopying, recording, or by any information storage and retrieval system, without permission in writing from the publisher, except for brief quotations in critical articles, books and reviews.

International Standard Book Number: 1-56184-141-2
Library of Congress Catalog Card Number: 99-61060

First Edition 2000

We appreciate permission from Kappa Delta Pi, an International Honor Society in Education, to use quotations from Dr. Meister's article "The Concept of World Community" which appeared in *The Educational Forum*, March 1964, vol. 28, pp. 291-296, copyright 1964.

Cover by Studio 31

The paper used in this publication meets the minimum requirements of the American National Standard for Permanence of Paper for Printed Library Materials Z39.48-1984

Address all inquiries to:
NEW FALCON PUBLICATIONS
PMB 277
1739 East Broadway Road # 1
Tempe, AZ 85282 U.S.A.
(or)
320 East Charleston Blvd. • Suite 204-286
Las Vegas, NV 89104 U.S.A.
website: http://www.newfalcon.com
email: info@newfalcon.com

Table of Contents

	Preface	7
1.	Divisive vs. Unitive Religion	11
2.	Early Religions	34
3.	Religious Doctrine — Helpful or Hurtful?	53
4.	Religious Ritual — Humanizing or Inhumane?	102
5.	The Status of Women in Religion	120
6.	Unitive Religion — A Solution to Jewish-Moslem Discord	139
7	Mysticism	155
8.	Interfaith Dialogue, Ecumenism, and Syncretism	186
9.	Violence in Religion	212
10.	Contemporary Divisiveness — Religion as Bane	236
11.	World Law and Order	261
12.	Bill of Spiritual Rights	277
13.	Contemporary Unitiveness — Religion as Blessing	290
14.	The Unitiveness of Modern Science	317
15.	Religion — Bane into Blessing	340
	Bibliography	359

PREFACE

What is the matter with the world? Religion seems to be trying to drive us berserk. A young Jewish terrorist, Yigal Amir, killed Israeli Prime Minister Yitzhak Rabin in November 1995. Asked why he did it, Amir replied, "God told me to do it!" Amir resented Rabin's efforts to work for peace.

In Bosnia, Eastern Orthodox Christian Serbs kill Moslem Bosnians, and Roman Catholic Croats kill Serbs. Beneath the nationalistic rivalries lie deep religious hatreds: each of the three groups considers itself to embody the one "true" faith.

Willy Claes, the Belgian Secretary-General of NATO, said in 1995 that "Islamic fundamentalism is at least as dangerous as Communism was." In Egypt, Pakistan, and Turkey Moslem extremists seek to overthrow Moslem rulers.

"One million Arabs are not worth a Jewish fingernail," Rabbi Yaacov Perrin told an Israeli audience at the funeral for Dr. Baruch Goldstein, slain by a Moslem terrorist. Perrin was seriously misquoting a passage from the biblical book of Exodus.

"Never will I say that I am not an anti-Semite," declared black American leader Khalid Abdul Muhhamad of the Nation of Islam. "I pray that God will kill my enemy and take him off the face of planet Earth," he continued. His tapes are sold under the title "No Love for the Other Side."

A three-month old boy was stabbed fatally in a cult ritual in Quebec recently because he was considered to be the Antichrist. To fulfill ritualistic demands, a wooden stake was driven through the baby's heart. Fifty-three persons in Quebec and Switzerland died through murder and suicide linked to this cult, the Order of the Solar Temple.

A modern version of the Romeo and Juliet tragedy ended on a bridge in Sarajevo in 1995. Bosko Brkic, an Eastern Orthodox Serb, tried to flee to safety with his Moslem lover, Admira Ismic. While the lovers were crossing over the Miljacka River, Serbian and Moslem snipers fired at the unfortunate pair. Their lifeless entwined bodies lay for six days on the bullet-riddled bridge before being retrieved.

Narrow religion daily reaps its ghastly toll. What can be done to divert religious activity from cruelty to caring love? The paradox of religion is that it is at once responsible for both the highest achievements and the cruelest inhumanity in human history. How can we understand this enigma? Why cannot a believer realize the truth of the judgment of the Apostle John: "If anyone says 'I love God' but hates his brother, he is a liar."

Divisive religion separates person from person, and sometimes people from God. In God's name many crimes have been perpetrated throughout history.

In A.D. 747 a Moslem general invited eighty rival Moslems to a unity banquet. Instead, the rivals were slaughtered, leather hoods were placed over their bloody heads, and the general and his cohorts enjoyed the feast. In 1486 Aztec leaders in Mexico cut out the hearts of 20,000 live victims, allegedly to please a god. In the St. Bartholomew's Day massacre in 1572, French Catholics killed thousands of Protestants, even smashing embryos which had been torn from the wombs of slain mothers. In 1830 in India a male child was beheaded every Friday to appease the goddess Kali. In 1985 Sinhalese troops in Sri Lanka killed 150 Tamil civilians. A teacher's wife was breast feeding her baby when soldiers killed her, and then shot off her baby's toes for target practice.

Divisive religion ends up in mutual self-destruction. In the Fourth Crusade Christian Catholics killed Christian Orthodox in a savage revenge of earlier killings. Moslems killed Moslems for years in the recent Iran-Iraq war—who can invoke the "holy war" in such folly? In modern Ireland Protestants and Catholics vie as to which can be more un-Christian towards the other. Is there no limit to the perversion of religious goals when divisive religion takes over?

On the other hand, unitive religion has produced unparalleled heights of love, compassion, and forgiveness. Churches, schools, hospitals, and orphanages have served mankind's urgent needs when religion is on the right track. Hindus and Buddhists agree that whoever lives a good life, no matter what his faith, is on the path to God. The great Jewish philosopher Moses Maimonides said that "everyone who ennobles his soul with excellent morals and wisdom based on faith in God certainly belongs to the world to come."

From the cross Jesus Christ forgave his slayers, as did the Sufi al-Hallaj in A.D. 922. The tenderness of St. Francis inspires persons of all faiths to love God's creation as a way of loving God. The medieval Catholic thinker Raymond Lully wrote three works in which Jewish, Roman Catholic, Orthodox Christian, Moslem, and Tatar points of view are presented with astonishing fairness, understanding, and tolerance.

Recognizing the brotherhood of all of God's children, Moslems refuse to discriminate against persons because of their race, and frequently permit African converts to retain tribal practices and beliefs. When Allied troops liberated a concentration camp in World War II, they turned the Nazi oppressors over to the freed Jews. Rather than seek understandable personal revenge, the Jews turned the cruel Germans over to the law courts for judicial trial. During a mass on Good Friday, Pope John XXIII stopped the ritual in order to have anti-Semitic references eliminated on the spot. In April 1963 the Italian press reported that when Fernando Cardinal Cento inadvertently retained the phrase "perfidious Jews" in the mass, Pope John made him restart his prayer, deleting the phrase. Unitive religion continues to show mankind God's nature in action.

The term "God" refers to "Goodness." When an alleged god is cruel, or wants humans to be cruel in his name, this is "goodness" being evil—a contradiction. This is divisive religion parading as true religion, which is the love of God and of human beings. Other terms referring to the Supreme Deity will be discussed in connection with each religion.

Most religions in time deviate from the pure ideals of their founders. How does this happen, what price is paid for the diversion, and how can religions get back in line with their fundamental tenets? This book will explore the answers to these fascinating questions. It will also show why types of mystical religion are popular nowadays, and how modern science lends yeoman support to unitive religion.

This is not a book on comparative religion, although it contains much information about the major world faiths. This book reviews religious history in order to delineate the difference between divisive religion, which says there is only one true way to God—"my" way—and unitive religion, which says that all of us, as children of One God, should love one another as God has first loved us.

A student of religious history might well be pessimistic about mankind's future, after reading of all the hatred, cruelty, and killing that has gone on in the name of a god. A civil war involving Serbian Orthodox, Bosnian Moslems, and Croatian Catholics shows how disastrous it is when religion underscores "ethnic cleansing" rather than seeks brotherhood and tolerance.

But this book will also identify many encouraging developments in the modern world, providing hope that perhaps crucial numbers of believers will come to realize that to love God is to love His creation, especially its crowning achievement, the human race. A Mother Teresa, in her grand simplicity, reminds us of the immense goal awaiting us when we redefine religion as love, inclusiveness, and service.

Chapter I
Divisive vs. Unitive Religion

Louie Armstrong's favorite song was "What a Wonderful World!" When reminded that white people would not let him stay in a room of the hotel where he performed, the famous jazz trumpeter replied, "All I'm saying is see what a wonderful world it would be if we'd only give it a chance. Love—that's the secret. If lots more of us loved each other, we'd solve lots more problems. And then this world would be a gasser!"

Is religion man's best friend or worst enemy? Weighed in the balance, is mankind better or worse off because of religion? This book will summarize the highlights and low points in the human religious experience. It will also provide guidelines for determining when religion is in true service to humankind, and when it is a negative factor which mankind would do better to discard.

Raymond Panikkar says that "religion has been the place where the worst human passions and the most dangerous attitudes have occurred. At the same time, religion is the locus where the highest peaks of the human experience have been reached and where the most sublime quality of human life has been unfolded." "The fact that religion is the most glorious and the most cruel part of man's history," Paul Tillich felt, "is understandable only if religion is not a matter of wishful thinking but is a matter of powers of being which men encounter."

"Religion," Tillich continued, "is the state of being grasped by an ultimate concern, a concern which qualifies all other concerns as preliminary and which itself contains the answers to the question of the meaning of our life." Religion serves fundamental human needs. People prefer assurance to uncertainty. Ashamed of failure, bereaved by loss of loved ones, aware of sin, and fearful of death and punishment, they find that religion helps them to feel cleansed, relieved, and saved for eternal bliss.

In this world human beings are in a constant state of alienation. The separation can be from God, from other people, or from oneself. Since separation is painful, humans make continual efforts to acquire a feeling of belonging. Believers find God working steadily to overcome the alienation, through scripture, ritual, human fellowship, and answer to personal prayer.

Sociologist Peter Berger thinks of religion as "a human attitude that conceives of the cosmos as a sacred order." The sacred is a non-human influence of immense significance to human beings. Occasionally at a great turning point in human history a hierophany occurs, causing a special manifestation of the sacred. Thus are great religions born, giving whole civilizations moral and spiritual parameters for their value systems.

The word "religion" comes from the Latin *religare* (to bind). Aldous Huxley defined the good as that which makes for unity, and evil as that which makes for separateness. Plotinus, the Neoplatonic philosopher, declared that "everyone hath all things in himself, and again sees all things in another, so that each is in all."

Religion is the key to history. We cannot understand the central purpose of a society unless we perceive its religion. Its faith structure underlies and predetermines the society's art, literature, legal system, politics, and economic life. To change the society radically one would have to alter its belief system.

Most religions profess to be revelations of divine truth. Many times the revelation is alleged to be an exclusive one from God. This assists the faith in acquiring adherents but generally builds barriers against non-adherents. Thus the force building internal unity is often a factor causing divisiveness in the outer world. The purest form of religion (that binding humans to God, and humans to humans) is that which provides both internal and external unity.

Unity of Mankind

After a lifetime spent studying world mythologies, Joseph Campbell affirmed that his chief finding was to discover "the unity of the race of man, not only in its biology but also in its spiritual history." The same motifs he found appearing in every period and in every culture. "The inaudible 'music of the spheres,' which is the hum of the cosmos in being," Campbell said, "becomes audible through music. It is the harmony, the meaning, of the social order; and the harmony of the soul discovers therein its accord. This idea is basic to Confucian and Indian music, and was the Pythagorean belief, and the fundamental thought of our own Middle Ages, whence the continuous chanting of the monks, diligently practicing in accord with the choir of angels."

Universal ethical principles undergird mankind's leading religions. All of them admonish believers not to kill, lie, steal, lust, or amass goods beyond strict needs. Moreover, they all state that the way to conquer evil is through love.

"Religions diverge at the existential level," Ken Wilber states, "but converge at the level of mind." The transcendental unity of religions is a doctrine advanced by A.K. Coomaraswamy, R. Guenon, and Frithjof Schuon. It has been experienced throughout history by Christian mystics, the Hindu Shankara, and the modern physicist Erwin Schrödinger.[1]

Wilfred Cantwell Smith points out the essential agreement among leaders of five different faiths. These medieval contemporaries were the Christian Hugh of St. Victor, the Jewish Judah ha-Levi, the Moslem al-Ghazzali, the Hindu Ramanuja, and the Chinese Buddhist and Neo-Confucian Chu Hsi. All five agreed on the supreme importance to human life of spiritual transcendence, but not one said that his view of spiritual reality was the only viable one. Their views thus unwittingly coincided not only with one another, "but with virtually all other reputedly wise and respected thinkers in every culture known to man."[2]

Smith further reveals that, despite differences among religions, there has been only one religious history of mankind. All world religions, he says, are historically interconnected, and have influenced one another—at times grown out of one another or into one another, and thus any one religion can be understood "only in terms of a context of which the other forms a part." Not only are the basic scriptures interrelated but so are the emerging concepts of God. "God has not altered," Smith points out, "whereas the idea of God has never been unchanging, in Christendom or elsewhere."[3] Even the great Christian theologian Thomas Aquinas got some of his basic ideas from the Moslem thinkers al-Ghazzali, Ibn 'Aqil, and Ibn Rushd (Averroës).

Adrio König quotes Ephesians 1:10 that God's eternal plan of salvation is "to unite all things in Him, things in heaven and things on earth." Peter Hinchliff has a warning for terrorists, such as those in the Middle East and in Ireland: "If God is expressed in all creation and especially through human beings, then how we treat creation and other people has to be seen as part of the way we treat God."

The Arabic-Persian word for man, *insan,* means "the friend of all." The Sanskrit term, *arya,* means "he who helps others." In Romans 12:13 Paul admonishes Christians to practice hospitality. The Greek word he employed for hospitality means "love of strangers." Hence one test of a religion could be, how does it treat strangers?

Evelyn Underhill suggests a further test: how does one's faith impel one to serve life's unfortunates? Disgusted at the sight and smell of lepers, St. Francis, through love of God, brought himself to even kiss them. Other saints who loved and served the sick and the unclean were St. Catherine of Genoa, Madame Guyon, and St. Elizabeth of Hungary. Modern saints in this tradition include Mahatma Gandhi, Albert Schweitzer, Thomas Dooley, and Mother Teresa.

The American politician Barry Goldwater said, "I've never been in a place on earth that I would call ugly, because when you talk to the people there it begins to be a little beautiful. I have a strong feeling that when this world eliminates the social, language, and religious barriers, there will be peace. I think that's the way the Lord wants it."[4]

Bhagavan Das finds that all great religions describe the Ultimate Principle as triune, having the principal attributes of Being, Joy, and Knowledge. In Taoism there are Hsing, Chih, and Ch'i (form, substance, and spirit). Chinese religion says that in the beginning was the One. From the One came a Second, and the two produced a Third. Hinduism has the Trimurti: Brahma the creator, Vishnu the savior, and Siva the destroyer and recreator. The Christian Trinity is well known. Trinitarian concepts in even such rigidly monotheistic faiths as Judaism and Islam will be discussed later.

In Christianity the Holy Spirit is often depicted as a unifying force. St. Ambrose found the Holy Spirit at work in all religions: "All that is true, by whomsoever it has been said, is from the

Holy Spirit." Bhagavan Das sees the Holy Spirit as the conscience, or the joint-science of the Universal Self in all people, thus serving as the divine unifier of mankind

Paul Tillich, though a Protestant, felt that Roman Catholicism "rightly called itself a system which unites the most divergent elements of man's religious life," for it incorporates material from the Old and New Testaments, as well as from Hellenic mystery religions, individual mysticism, classical Greek humanism, and the scientific methods of the Middle Ages. For the apostle Paul, faith meant for a person to be grasped by the Holy Spirit, the spirit of love, justice, and truth.

When the Roman Catholic Church lost its splendid union of the elements of the ethical and the mystical, the Protestants reformers complained correctly that the moral strain was being submerged by the sacramental. In trying to avoid this error, the Protestant leaders made the opposite error, Tillich said, and stressed the ethical at the expense of the sacramental. Thus both main Christian branches have forfeited the Pauline concept of the Holy Spirit as the divine unifier. Christianity can regain its primitive strength, Tillich feels, only by regaining the unity originally provided by the action of the Holy Spirit.

Catholic theologian Hans Küng believes that there will be no world peace without religious peace, since now the basic world economic and political problems are global, and religious interface is inescapable. At best, world religions cannot solve all of these problems, but they can lessen hatred and discrimination, and increase understanding and reconciliation. They can at least eliminate the conflicts for which they themselves are to blame. "The most fanatical, the cruelest political struggles are those that have been colored, inspired, and legitimized by religion," Küng says. He feels the world needs the peaceful religious approaches of the Hindu Mahatma Gandhi, the Christian Dag Hammarskjöld, the Moslem Anwar Sadat, and the Buddhist U Thant.

Alfred Loisy believes that never before has the world so urgently needed the Christian ideal, which is "the reign of justice, realizable by the law of love." Christ, Tillich reminds us, prefers the representative of a rejected religion who practices love to the Levite and priest who fail to do good works. What is unique about Christ, says Tillich, "is that he crucified the particular in himself for the sake of the universal."

Bhagavan Das says that a corollary of the Golden Rule is to refrain from fault finding, back-biting, and slandering. Das emphasized control of the tongue, as recommended by Manu, Krishna, Zoroaster, Mohammed, and the book of James in the New Testament.

Unitive Religion

The Hindu Ramakrishna noted that as long as the bee is outside the flower, it hovers and buzzes, but inside the flower it noiselessly drinks the nectar. So, he concludes, "as long as a man quarrels about doctrines, he has not tasted the nectar of true faith. When he has tasted it, he becomes quiet and full of peace."[5]

In the Bible John asks, If you do not love your brother, whom you have seen, how can you love God, whom you have not seen? Harry Emerson Fosdick noted the similarity in the moral teachings of the major world religions. Sectarianism may have been useful at one time, Fosdick states, but now we live in one world, not only for the nations but also for religion. If religion continues to be one of the most divisive and alienating forces on earth, then that aspect of religion must be universally condemned. "Our new era," says Fosdick, "urgently calls for a kind of religion which will make for unity, mutual understanding, and brotherhood."[6]

God's unity underlies all religious unity. In his letter to the Corinthians Paul states that "whoever is joined unto the Lord is One Spirit." Christ describes this unity: "That they all may be one, as Thou, Father, art in me, and I in Thee, that they also may be one in us" (John 17:21). Taoism speaks of the Primal Unity, the One without a second. The Upanishads describe everything as being in Brahma; Zen Buddhism states that all things occur in the One Mind.

Bhagavad Das paraphrases John's gospel: You shall know the truth (of the unity of the Self) and the truth shall make you free (of all sin, fear, doubt, and sorrow). "Man is man," said D.T. Niles, "because he reflects God, and only when he does so."

It is hard for a person to find a consistent community of interest with any one other person, let alone with many others. But once one realizes even a partial union with God, one automatically achieves a feeling of identity with all of God's creation, including every other person. Thus, through God we are all united in one common family—the family of God. The good family member is loyal to the entire family, not just to that part of it dwelling in his community or attending his church. When we make God the King of our lives, to say "Thy Kingdom come" implies to make "our kingdom go."

The Kingdom of Heaven, we have on good authority, lies within us. When we set aside our selfish Self, the Higher Self (or the Holy Spirit) takes over, and the Kingdom has arrived within us. This is salvation, a return to our divine source in God. Since the same Spirit dwells in all of us, we are unified in God through the Holy Spirit.

As the soul finds its inner oneness with God, it no longer feels alienated. "It is conscious," says Radhakrishnan, "rather of the universal life of which all individuals, races, and nations are specific articulations. We cannot escape from the secret solidarity of the human race." Despite national patriotism, he continues, which often advocates hatred or warfare, and despite priests who preach exclusivity and superiority/inferiority relations, humanity is now pressing forward towards asserting its fundamental oneness. This unity is best seen when there is a huge disaster; then people all over the world respond quickly with offers of help.

From a theological perspective, the heightened interest in space travel is a subliminal effort for the human family to overcome the limitations of space and time, those things which separate us from God. The experienced spiritual seeker learns to cease his quest, knowing that as he opens himself to God's love, God steadily seeks him and returns him to His presence.

"Heaven cannot contradict itself," says Frithjof Schuon. "A given religion in reality sums up all religions. All religion is to be found in a given religion, because Truth is one."[7] At the esoteric level, Schuon adds, all religions are one. It is therefore futile to ask, which is the "true" religion?

The function of mythology, says Joseph Campbell, is "to foster the centering of the individual in integrity, in accord with himself, his culture, the universe, and God. The structure of any completely unfolded mythological system—be it Byzantine or Gothic, Hindu, Buddhist, Polynesian, or Navaho— is harmoniously beautiful and of Apollonian clarity, and at the same time fully electrified with experienced life."[8] Each system, in its own way, justifies the ways of God to man.

Ken Wilber describes how myth serves as a unitive force. Grounded in the collective unconscious, myth deals with universals that all persons experience. Also, mythological language is associative and integrative, unlike ordinary thought which is analytical and dissociative. In line with modern science, mythological language reflects the physical reality of the seamless web of the universe—the mutual interpenetration of all things. Perceiving this, a person experiences a joyful feeling of belonging, a wholeness overcoming all alienation, an ecstatic awareness of unity with all of creation. When a person is at one with the universe, there is no longer any outside force to fear.

Universal archetypes are found at the mythological level. One is the Savior God, who dies in order to live in all of us. Examples are Christ, Orpheus (or Dionysus), Vishnu (or any of his avatars), and Osiris.

Symbols are used in religion, says Campbell, to convey deep truths in a clear and moving fashion. Although intended to unify, they can frequently divide adherents. Campbell sees Roman Catholicism as top-heavy with too many symbols, and hence internal wars occur between proponents of different symbols. On the other hand, Protestantism, constantly seeking for unity, breaks into hundreds of competing denominations because of its lack of unifying symbols.

Ernst Troeltsch, a leading German theologian, said that all religions tend towards a common goal, union with God. Since the absolute goal, God, is unattainable by humans, no one religion can claim unique verifiability, and hence it behooves all believers to be tolerant of other religious seekers.

Charles Wei-Hsun Fu feels that "the history of world religions has clearly shown that dialogical openness (mutual give-and-take) is one of the most significant factors causing the development of new and creative ideas within every tradition."[9] As an example, Fu cites how Chinese Confucianism was incomparably enriched by Taoism and Buddhism.

An innovative Roman Catholic theologian, John Dunne says that "by passing through what I call sympathetic understanding of other religions, one can appropriate those insights and return to one's own. In this way all the basic spiritual experiences of humankind can somehow be re-enacted in our own lives."[10]

Wilfred Cantwell Smith judges that in comparative religion people are simply studying themselves. Instead of learning about varying religions, they are basically studying human religiousness. One function of comparative religion is to make statements acceptable to at least two religious traditions.

British theologian John Hick states that God's revelation is progressive. God is constantly pressing His transcendence upon mankind, Hick believes. "When the developing human race produces a spirit who is able to respond to the Transcendent in a new and fuller way, his experience overflows his inherited system and he proclaims a new truth about God, bringing with it new demands for living."[11]

All world religions have both exoteric rituals, which serve the common believers, and esoteric beliefs, which are similar to those of all other religions. Evelyn Underhill explained that God's infinity permits Him to be approached in an infinite number of ways: "That Circle whose center is everywhere and whose circumference is nowhere may be approached from every angle with a certainty of being found."

The Kingdom of God as a religious concept is found in Hinduism, Buddhism, Zoroastrianism, Judaism, and Christianity. Rudolf Otto said that Christ's preaching about the Kingdom had elements not so much of Palestinian origin as from those associated with the Aryan and Iranian East.

Bhagavad Das finds a unique virtue in each major religious tradition. Hinduism provides duty to the all-pervading Self. Buddhism exhibits renunciation and compassion. Zoroastrianism stresses rectitude and purity. Judaism brings out God's justice, as well as His special protection to those who love Him. Christianity emphasizes sacrificial love, and returning good for evil. Islam features brotherly equality, and resistance to wrong in complete obedience to God.

Peter Hinchliff sees the need for a pluralistic society to practice toleration, and to formulate a deep underlying consensus. He postulates a code of political responsibility as seen from a religious perspective:

1. People are ends, not means.
2. Force, violence, and bullying must be avoided.
3. There is no place for deceit and dishonesty.

Joseph Campbell notes a difference between Semitic and Aryan concepts of God. Originating as a protective tribal god, the Semitic concept formulates God as exclusivistic and intolerant of outsiders. Aryans tend to believe in universal gods of nature, and thus they can quite readily recognize their own deities in other religions. This enables Aryan religions such as Hinduism and Buddhism to be tolerant and syncretistic.

Campbell also differentiates between types of polytheism and monotheism. Normal polytheism is the worship of many gods, but henotheism is the worship of one god, while recognizing the existence of others. There are two types of monotheism. Ethnic monotheism says that only one's own god is valid—all others are false. Syncretic monotheism asserts that all concepts of God are limited but refer ultimately to the one God.

Problems of Faith

Man is a believing being. *Homo sapiens,* says Wilfred Cantwell Smith, is really *homo religiosus.* Religious faith is a requisite for a healthy personality as well as for a humane society. It is easy for a dog to be a dog, Smith opines, but hard for a human to be human, that is, live up to the responsibility of treating fellow humans with dignity and respect. Though a necessity, religious faith is easily perverted. "The history of man," says Smith, "has been disfigured by the arrant stupidities, rigidities, and fanaticisms of faith."

Faith leads mankind into devious snares. When narrow sectarianism takes over, and the multi-dimensional aspect of faith is forgotten, the result is a tragedy like the Crusades, the Inquisition, or the Thirty Years' War. Correctional steps, such as those undertaken by the writers of the U.S. Constitution, can lead to the secularization of a society. But a society lacking a spiritual base, such as Nazi Germany, Soviet Russia, or Communist China, is morally bankrupt from the start.

Paul Tillich charted the many shoals threatening to founder the ship of faith. Its vagueness permits religious faith to serve as a disguise for opportunists, mountebanks, and confidence men. Had he lived to see James Jones, Jim Bakker, and Jimmy Swaggart, Tillich could well have asked, "Did I not warn you?"

"The weakness of faith," Tillich reported, "is the ease with which it becomes idolatrous. The human mind, Calvin said, is a continuously working factory of idols. Every type of faith has the tendency to elevate its concrete symbols to absolute validity. No church has the right to put itself in the place of the Ultimate. Biblical research in Protestantism has shown the many levels of Biblical literature and the impossibility of considering the Bible as containing the infallible truth of faith. The ultimate concern of the Christian is not Jesus, but the Christ Jesus who is manifest as the crucified."[12]

Reason is an essential part of faith, in Tillich's view. "A faith which destroys reason destroys itself and the humanity of man," he states. Reason and faith must interplay creatively, each reinforcing the other's limits. Religion gets out of balance when either factor attempts to exclude the other.

Another potential danger is the separation of faith from love. "The separation of faith and love is always the consequence of a deterioration of religion," Tillich believes. "When Judaism became a system of ritual laws, when the Indian religions developed into a magic sacramentalism, when Christianity fell into both distortions and added doctrinal legalism, the relation of faith to love became a stumbling block for people inside and outside these religions, and many turned away to non-religious ethics.

Faith as the state of being ultimately concerned implies love, the urge toward the reunion of the separated. Love as the unity of eros and agape is an implication of faith. The fanatic cannot love that against which his fanaticism is directed. And idolatrous faith is by necessity fanatical. The mediating link between faith and works is love. Mystical love unites by negation of the self. Ethical love transforms by affirmation of the self."[13]

Divisive Religion

Love unites, but sin separates. Jesus saw sin as a type of slavery. Early in his ministry he announced his mission as to set people free from bondage to sin. In Galatians 5:20 Paul lists the works of the sinful flesh as being divisive factors: enmity, strife, anger, selfishness, dissension, and party spirit.

Behind much modern terrorism, such as the bombing of the U.S. Marine barracks in Beirut and the sabotage of Pan American Flight #103 over Scotland, lies the theology of divisive religion. The illogical rationale runs like this: If you oppose my view of God, you are not only wrong—you are an infidel, an unbeliever; in fact, you do not exist in God's sight. Since my view of God is the only correct one, any enemy of mine is an enemy of God and must be destroyed. I love God so much that I am willing to kill anyone whose view of God differs from mine. This will prove how much I love God, runs this rationale.

Unitive religion, in contrast, states that you, as God's creation, are just as precious in His sight as I, another of His creatures. Thus you have as much right to your view of God as I have to mine. Since He is the God of love, I must love you if I assert that I love Him. A major proof of my love of Him is my love of you.

The dichotomy is clear. One says, because I believe in God, I hate you. The other view is, because I believe in God, I love you. Misguided religion has a handy talisman for differentiating itself from the authentic search for God.

Many devout believers, assuming they are "saved," refuse to accept supposed non-believers, feeling superior to them. Also, many efforts to gain "salvation" for one's neighbor involves gross violation of the sanctity of his personality and the invasion of his unique search for God. To call a Jew a "Kike" or a Buddhist a "pagan" is to take the first step towards divisive religion, religion which separates rather than unites.

The biblical book of Jude warns that those whose divisive acts split communities are completely devoid of the Holy Spirit. Evangelist Billy Graham tells us that we quench the promptings of the Holy Spirit within us whenever we ignore others, are unkind to them, or are unduly critical of them.

Every war ultimately degenerates into the inhuman condition of considering the enemy as non-persons, or sometimes as *God's* enemies. This makes it easier for us to kill others, if we first strip them of their human dignity as children of God.

Dr. Fritz Klein, an S.S. physician in the Nazi army, was asked how he, as a doctor, could kill Jews. His reply was incredible: "As a doctor I want to preserve life. Out of respect for human life, I would remove a gangrenous appendix from a diseased body. The Jew is the gangrenous appendix in the body of mankind."

Ken Wilber comments that absolute power leads dictators to imagine themselves to be gods. Alexander, Julius Caesar,

Napoleon, Hitler, and Stalin all had over-inflated egos. "Every separate self is mad," Wilber states, "in the sense that it necessarily feels itself to be cosmocentric."

Sometimes religion is more a part of the problem than a part of the solution. As Edward Cell points out, "religion often functions as a substitute for relationship with God, so that the term 'God' is then really being used to refer to some idol such as the interests of one's own nation, or one's concern to maintain something which elevates him over others. Religion, in effect, may itself be a leading expression of the death of God."[14]

Violence dehumanizes. Even when the use of violence seems justified (for example, to restrain a killer amok in a crowd), "there is something dehumanizing about it. It has an obscene quality, as a kind of rape, a violation of human dignity."[15] Violence debases both the user and the victim. It is all the worse when it purports to be in the name of God. To mutilate the body of one of God's creatures is like a physical assault upon God's own body.

As Alan Watts points out, ideological wars are the very worst kind. In wars fought for conquest, the aggressor is careful not to destroy what he wants to use. But "wars fought over principle will be wars of mutual annihilation. Men who have dehumanized themselves by becoming the blind worshippers of an idea or an ideal are fanatics whose devotion to abstractions makes them the enemies of life."[16] This description seems to fit such widely divergent groups as Christian Crusaders, Shi'ite terrorists, and the Hitler Youth.

Carl Jung has demonstrated how evil can be transformed into a positive force. Evil exists, he says, as a necessary counterbalance to our own positive tendencies. We can have, for example, too much love—at the expense of other requisites, such as justice, common sense, or intelligence.

This helps explain religious fanaticism, which does much harm in the name of alleged good. Jung says we are horrified by the evil we see in others, since we recognize it as the evil we so much despise in ourselves. So we foolishly try to project our own evil out onto others. But if we are honest with ourselves and accept the responsibility for our own evil, we then reintegrate the Shadow (or evil principle) back into ourselves, and are not likely to try to project our evil onto others. We can then stand the evil we find in other people, since it is so much like our own. Just as projected evil can be vicious (and in a religious sense, divisive), so integrated evil can become a positive force.

Hazrat Khan, a modern Sufi, says that persons with unlimited identity with others do not judge them, for they see all humanity as being within their circle of love. Narrow personalities, however, see everyone else as outside their circle of concern, and thus constantly judge other people, in a vain effort to be considered superior, on howsoever invalid grounds.

In perceiving the difference between unitive and divisive religion, a good test is to ask oneself, how would I feel to be on the receiving end of the act, be it hatred and discrimination or love and acceptance. The biggest fool of all, says Joseph Campbell, "asserts there is no God but mine."

Divisive Factors in Religion

Many elements crucial to religious unity can be perverted into becoming instruments of division. This includes such vital factors as creed, dogma, ritual, and scripture.

A sect (from *sectare,* cut off) is a group separated from the main body of a church. There is much value in religious diversity, as long as the spirit of love blocks hateful division. Many sects originate in a sincere desire to purify a blemished practice, but through narrow concentration on a single factor or two lose the broader fellowship so vital to a united witness.

Constant intellectual analysis can be a divisive influence in religion. Greek philosophers, evaluating the unity of Plato's eros as a synthesis of emotion, will, and intellect, soon had separated emotion from the intellect, and Plato's concept became sterile. Tillich showed how the early Christian church stressed faith so unduly that the Apostle Paul's *gnosis* (meaning both knowledge and union) was lost.

"Dogma" is the Greek word for "that which *seems* true," but once it is accepted by a church body, dogma is considered to be incontestably true to the adherents. The danger with dogma is that it too easily becomes dogmatic; the trouble with doctrine is that all too often it becomes doctrinaire.

Adolf von Harnack, in *The History of Dogma,* said that dogmas are conditioned by the circumstances of their origin, and thus cannot possibly claim universal authority. John Henry Newman, however, in his study of the development of Christian doctrine, asserted that Christian dogma, particularly as it evolved in the Roman Catholic Church, was a valid organic whole which had retained essential beliefs even while incorporating new insights from outside religious sources.

Most American political leaders have had deep faith in God but have questioned particular churches whose creeds have led to divisiveness and acrimony. Thomas Jefferson said that "on the dogmas of religion, as distinguished from moral principles, all mankind from the beginning of the world to this day have been fighting, burning, and torturing one another, for abstractions unintelligible to themselves and all others. Every church is to itself orthodox—to others, erroneous or heretical. The care of every man's soul belongs to himself."[17]

Abraham Lincoln's position on religion was similar to Jefferson's. "I cannot without mental reservations," said Lincoln, "assent to complicated creeds and catechisms. If the church would ask simply for assent to the Savior's statement, 'Thou shalt love the Lord thy God with all thy heart, soul, and mind, and thy neighbor as thyself'—that church would I gladly unite with."[18]

Religious rituals can be unitive. As Joseph Campbell points out, "Not all of us are philosophers. Many require an atmosphere of incense, music, vestments and processions, gongs, bells, dramatic mimes and cries, to be carried beyond themselves. And for such the various styles of religion exist."[19]

Symbols are often an effective part of church ritual. A burning candle may stand for God's love in a dark world of sin, or the light of reason penetrating the night of ignorance, or the pious soul afire with the love of God. The mass dramatizes Christ's birth, life, death, and resurrection. The cross represents his sacrificial death to save believers from their sins.

But rituals can also readily become divisive influences. Campbell says that "the wicked thing about the 'collective faiths' is that they all, without exception, pretend to hold encompassed in their ritualized mythologies all of the truth ever to be known. They are therefore cursed with 'the error of the found truth,' or in mythological language, the sin against the Holy Ghost. They set up against the revelations of the spirit the barriers of their own petrified belief."[20]

Paul Tillich warns against the dangers of literalism in religion. Symbols and myths, the language of faith, point beyond themselves to the thing symbolized. Literalism strips symbols and myths of their rich meaning. Then, says Tillich, "the character of the symbol to point beyond itself to something else is disregarded. Creation is taken as a magic act which happened once upon a time. The fall of Adam is localized on a special geographical point and attributed to a human individual. The virgin birth of the Messiah is understood in biological terms, resurrection and ascension as physical events, the second coming of Christ as a cosmic catastrophe. The presupposition of such literalism is that God is a being, acting in time and space, affecting the course of events and being affected by them like any other being in the universe. Literalism deprives God of His ultimacy and, religiously speaking, of His majesty. Faith, if it takes its symbols literally, becomes idolatrous. It calls something ultimate which is less than ultimate."[21] Confusing the symbol with the thing symbolized, literalism calls the *works* of God, God!

Henri Bergson differentiated between a closed religion, credal and ritualistic, which gave oversimplified answers to deep religious questions, and an open religion, which provided for spiritual growth as the individual reaches for an ever closer direct personal contact with God.

Most religions base their authenticity upon scriptures allegedly handed down from God. Abraham Lincoln was so fond of the Bible that he said that "nothing short of infinite wisdom could by any possibility have devised and given to man this excellent moral code."

But having been received by humans, all scriptures contain some human errors. Receipt of the divine revelation, oral and written transmission, editing, publishing, and translating are all done by fallible human beings, and so we frequently find the word of man imbedded in the Word of God. How can one detect when human error prevailed? St. Augustine replied that whenever the scriptural interpretation does not further the love of God and the love of humans, the passage is suspect. Further, when God is purported to have violated His nature, and recommended evil acts, such as the bashing of infants' heads against rocks. Here man's thumbprint clearly dirties the sacred lens.

The great religious historian Max Müller, inviting readers to read the sacred books of the Orient, advised them to read these scriptures sympathetically, overlooking obvious human blemishes in order to focus on timeless divine truths. "We must not forget," Müller said, "that there are portions in our own sacred books which many of us would wish to be absent, which, from the earliest ages of Christianity, have been regretted by theologians of undoubted piety, and which often prove a stumbling block to those who have been won over to the simple faith of Christ."[22]

Recent translations of the Bible vary widely, suggesting that many key theological concepts originate with the translator. Mahatma Gandhi, convinced that all life is one and that there should be no exploitation of one manner of life by another, pointed out the errors in Hindu scriptures which stated that the *harijans* (the untouchables) were less worthy in God's sight than members of the four castes.

Scriptures can be used divisively. For example, although both Jews and Moslems trace their lineage to Abraham, the Old Testament states that God preferred Isaac over Ishmael, but the Koran avers that Ishmael was chosen by God over Isaac. If each side believes that its concept of God is the "true" one, there are scriptural bases for quarrels or perhaps even wars.

A modern Moslem, Khalid Duran, almost regrets the Biblical background of Islam: "Some of us Moslems felt that God could have made it easier for us by dispensing with those many references to the Biblical past in the Koran, and allowing us to start with a clean slate. To me this Jewish/Christian legacy appears sometimes as if it were our 'original sin.' A large portion of the *shari-ah* is Hebraic and Biblical, particularly where it conflicts with our present-day notions of human rights."[23]

So-called "holy wars" are often fought due to a too literal interpretation of scripture. Ken Wilber says that "the fundamentalists especially are committed to literal interpretations of the Bible, i.e., they recognize only signs, not symbols. No wonder that fundamentalist Christianity (along with fundamentalist Islam) has historically been the religion most willing to actually consummate their pagan Great Mother rituals, and murder, in blood sacrifice, any who disagreed with them. Holy war is nothing but thinly disguised Great Mother worship, and the exoteric

Christians and Moslems, without any doubt whatsoever, have killed more people in the name of a 'divinity' than any other people in history. In Buddhism's 2500-year history it has fought not one single religious war."[24]

Was there really a good Samaritan? It matters not—Jesus here teaches us the importance of love and charity. Were there an Adam and a Jonah? It matters not—but what does matter is what the inspired writers are telling us about sin, disobedience, pride, and selfishness. "The author of Genesis couldn't let you in on the 'big secret' of the actual details of creation because he wasn't there. But the sacred writer wants to tell his readers that it is God who has brought all this creation into being. He wants them to understand their own special dignity, and that they brought sin into the world."[25]

Finally, the figure of Jesus Christ has become "both a unitive and a divisive element in Christendom. All Christians are united in their loyalty to him, even though they express their loyalty in a variety of doctrinal and liturgical ways. But doctrine and liturgy also divide Christian communions from one another. It has not been the official statements about Christ that have differed widely. What has become a sharp point of division is the amount of historical and critical inquiry that is permitted where the person of Christ is involved."[26]

Thomas Sheehan, in his book *The First Coming,* says that the real message taught by Jesus was "an invitation to live God's future in the present." Jesus sought to replace institutional formalized religion with a caring ethic, a life of justice and charity. Tillich adds that the doctrine *of* Jesus got watered down into being a doctrine *about* Jesus. Tillich sees the mission of Jesus as announcing the coming of the Kingdom of God, "a state in which God and the individual Kingdom members are in a relation of forgiveness, acceptance, and love."

Religion for Survival

Jung Young Lee asserts that the Yin/Yang way of thinking is an inclusive, complementary method for ecumenical theology, in contrast to the either/or dichotomy prevalent in Mesopotamian religions like Zoroastrianism, Judaism, Christianity, and Islam. In Lee's words, "Emil Brunner points out that the doctrine of the Trinity, an intellectual indulgence of the early Church, became the norm to test the validity of the divine nature. Thus the doctrine became the judge of the divine. The Word of God became the servant of human words. The absolutization of human words is characteristic of the either/or way of thinking. Thus God has been made an idol of intellectual display."[27]

The either/or approach says the body is evil and the spirit is good, rather than seeing a complementarity between body and spirit. This approach also says that Jesus is either man or God, but not both. In the Yin/Yang method Jesus can easily incarnate both God and man, since both natures can exist in him in a complementary relationship.

Planetary inter-religious understanding is a survival necessity. The oversimplification of religion into the binary classification of true/false must go. Religion is too complex for such simplistic thinking. Even modern science rejects facile dichotomies of this sort. At one time in human history people felt threatened unless they approached the good in the true/false oversimplification. Now mankind is threatened if we continue its use.

In India if two widely divergent views are held, it is not assumed that one is true and the other false but rather that both are partly true and partly false. "The intellectual problem of the modern world," says Wilfred Cantwell Smith, "is how to be a relativist without being a nihilist. We are a corporate global pluralist community pledged, through our several disparate loyalties to truth and our mutual respect for each other, to move closer to that truth and hence away from the grosser cacophony of that relativism."[28]

In the interpenetration of cultures in the modern world, one can be true to neither himself, his neighbor, or God if he understands only his own culture. To theologize today is to work in a comparatist perspective. To serve humankind in an age of survival divisive religion must be reconceptualized. God is one, and so is truth. Religions which would divide fundamental unities fly in the face of that transcendent love revealed in unitive religion.

All Christians have known Jews, Hindus, Buddhists, Moslems, or Native American Indians whom it would be preposterous to assume that God would not "save." "In the history of the Christian church," says Smith, "the ratio of the Holy Spirit's activity to that of human devilment has fluctuated widely." The same can be said for the experience of all major world religions.

"Yet," adds Smith, "cosmic salvation is the same for an African tribesman, a Taoist, and a Moslem as it is for any Christian. How do I know that: by what I find revealed to me of God in Christ. The God whom Christ reveals is a God of mercy and love, who reaches out after all persons everywhere in compassion, and who delights to save. It contradicts certain man-made formulations of Christian theologians, but it contradicts the central revelation of Christ to say anything else. If St. Paul thought that only Christians could be saved, he was wrong. Christ, and God who has given me faith through Christ, saves me from believing so blasphemous a doctrine. St. Paul had never heard of Buddha or Islam. If it had turned out that God does not care about non-Christians, or was stumped and had thought up no way to save them, then that would have proven our Christian understanding of God to have been wrong.

God is more imaginative than we Christians used to think. He has participated more richly in human affairs than we once knew. To do justice, to act morally, is one of the ways (and a highly important one) of being in communion with God, or participating in the life of God."[29]

For those to whom God has been revealed through Christ, Smith says, two consequences follow. On the moral level, those persons are impelled towards unity, harmony, reconciliation, and brotherhood. On the intellectual level, exclusivist doctrines must be surrendered. "Christ has taught us humility," Smith feels, "but we have approached others with arrogance." The idea "I am saved, you are damned" is "intolerable from merely human standards. It is doubly so from Christian ones. Any position that alienates rather than reconciles, that promotes segregation rather than brotherhood, is ipso facto un-Christian. It will not do to have a faith that can be undermined by God's saving one's neighbor, or to be afraid lest others turn out to be closer to God than one had been led to suppose."[30]

Hans Küng conveniently summarizes the differences between divisive and unitive religion, as found in all of the world's great faiths. Divisive, and thus a contradiction of religion, are "the Hindu caste system, the Shakti form of Tantric Buddhism with its sexual practices, and the 'holy wars' and cruel punishment in Islam. Also, such things in Christianity as the Crusades, the burning of witches, the Inquisition, and the persecutions of the Jews."

But Küng sees optimistic promise for a resurgence of unitive religion. "In the future all the great religions will foster a vital awareness of the guarantee of human rights, the emancipation of women, the realization of social justice, and the immorality of war. Whatever clearly protects, heals, and fulfills human beings in their physical, psychic, and social life (integrity, freedom, justice, peace) can with reason call itself 'divine'."[31]

The term "unitive" as used in this book has no necessary relationship to any organized religion or church, such as the Unitarian Church or the Unity School of Christianity. Instead, it means primarily any unifying religious group or action, particularly referring to unification with viewpoints outside one's own group and with the entire human species.

This book will show the great difference, in terms of human suffering and human happiness, between the all too frequent resort to divisive religion and the saddening few occasions when unitive religion prevailed in human history. Reading this at times sordid and at times inspiring record should help all readers to turn their attention into a determination to use religion as a positive factor in relations both human and divine.

References

1. Joseph Campbell, *Oriental Mythology* (Viking, 1971), p. 114. Ken Wilber has written widely on transpersonal psychology. Coomaraswamy was a well-known art historian. Guenon is an expert on the Perennial Philosophy. Schuon is a modern transcendentalist.
2. Wilfred Cantwell Smith, *Faith and Belief* (Princeton University Press, 1979), p. 161.
3. Ibid., *Towards a World Theology* (Westminster Press, 1981), p. 16. Smith is Director of the Center for the Study of World Religions at Harvard. König is Professor of Systematic Theology at the University of South Africa. Hinchliff is Chaplain of Balliol College, Oxford.
4. *The New Yorker* (25 April 1988) 64:73. Evelyn Underhill is a world authority on mysticism. Hindu scholar Bhagavan Das wrote *The Essential Unity of All Religions*.
5. Quoted in Carl H. Voss, ed., *The Universal God* (World Publishing Company, 1953), p. 296.
6. Ibid., p. 131. A prominent minister, Fosdick was also Professor of Theology at Union Theological Seminary. Loisy was a priest who led the Catholic Modernism Movement. Manu was a semi-legendary lawgiver from the time of Christ. Krishna is one of the forms of the Hindu savior God.
7. *The Essential Writings of Frithjof Schuon* (Amity House, 1986) p. 75.
8. Joseph Campbell, *Creative Mythology* (Penguin, 1984), pp. 6, 370.
9. Leonard Swidler, *Toward a Universal Theology of Religion* (Orbis Books, 1987), p. 160. Swidler is Professor of Theology at Temple University.
10. Richard W. Rousseau, ed., *Christianity and the Religions of the East*, vol. 2 (Ridge Row Press, 1982), pp. 25-26.
11. Richard Woods, ed., *Understanding Mysticism* (Doubleday, 1980), p. 432.
12. Paul Tillich, *Dynamics of Faith* (Harper & Row, 1958), pp. 97-98. Tillich was Professor of Religion at Harvard.
13. Ibid., pp. 113-16.
14. Edward Cell, ed., *Religion and Contemporary Culture* (Abingdon, 1967) p. 19.
15. Peter Hinchliff, *Holiness and Politics* (Eerdmans, 1983), p. 62.

16 Alan Watts, *The Way of Zen* (New American Library, 1959), p. 41. A scholar of Oriental religion, Watts was Professor of Philosophy at Northwestern University.

17 Saul K. Padover, *Thomas Jefferson on Democracy* (Penguin, 1939), pp. 109, 118.

18 David Rhys Williams, *World Religions and the Hope for Peace* (Beacon, 1951), p. 102.

19 Joseph Campbell, *Occidental Mythology* (Viking, 1971), p. 254.

20 Campbell, *Creative Mythology*, p. 389.

21 Tillich, *Dynamics of Faith*, pp. 51-52.

22 F. Max Müller, ed. & tr., *The Upanishads*, vol. 1 (Dover, 1962), pp. xxxvii- xxxviii.

23 Swidler, p. 217.

24 Ken Wilber, *Up From Eden* (Shambhala, 1983), p. 137.

25 "Wise Man," *St. Anthony Messenger* (July 1987) 95:49.

26 Jaroslav Jan Pelikan, "Jesus Christ," *Encyclopedia Britannica,* 1971, vol. 12, p. 1027.

27 Rousseau, p. 10. Brunner was a Swiss theologian who stressed revelation.

28 Wilfred Cantwell Smith, *Faith and Belief*, pp. 155-56.

29 Ibid., *Towards a World Theology,* pp. 171-72, 174.

30 Ibid., *Religious Diversity* (Harper & Row, 1976), pp. 13-15.

31 Swidler, pp. 241-42. Küng is Professor of Ecumenical Theology at the University of Tübingen.

CHAPTER 2

EARLY RELIGIONS

In reviewing the examples of unitive and divisive religion in human history it is useful to have in mind criteria for delineating these two religious modes.

In sum, unitive religion endeavors to unite humans with God, and humans with humans. Key concepts are unity, love, brotherhood, compassion, forgiveness, and tolerance. The highest form of unitive religion is agape, or selfless love, in which a person is willing to forego a good in order to advance the cause of God or one's fellow human beings. God is perceived as being synonymous with love, and hence only loving acts are acceptable to the Godhead. Measures which advance human well-being are considered to be pleasing to God, who is love.

Divisive religion, on the other hand, invariably causes human suffering. Ostensibly to serve a deity, humans are made to experience pain, to feel inferior, to be deprived of personal property, and in some cases to be put to death. God is perceived as being disinterested, or partial, and at times jealous, vindictive, and cruel. Mental gymnastics are employed to show that the more human beings suffer, the happier God becomes.

Primitive Religion — Unitive

Primitive people conceived of the world as a cosmos. Nature always has a sacred value to the primitive. The sky shows God's infinite distance from humans. The regularity of the heavenly bodies reveals cosmic order, unity, and harmony. The Indo-European supreme god, Dieus, means both sky and the god of the sky.

"The creation of the world," says Mircea Eliade, "becomes the archetype of every creative human gesture, whatever its plane of reference." Since the whole world is sacred, to the primitive mind there is no place where God does not exist. Like modern science, primitive logic made no distinction between subject and object, and thus the primitive person sought to identify himself mystically with his Creator.

Where one lives is a sacred place. "A sacred place," says Eliade, "is a break in the homogeneity of space. This break is symbolized by an opening by which passage from one cosmic region (heaven, earth, underworld) to another is made possible. Communication with heaven is expressed by an image, which refers to the *axis mundi,* which connects heaven and earth. Around this cosmic axis lies the 'world' *(our* world); hence, the axis is located in the Center of the World."[1]

Cosmic symbolism is found in the structure of a primitive home. Building one's house is to recapitulate God's construction of the universe. The four walls represent the four directions. The center pole is a form of *axis mundi.* An opening in the roof facilitates the entry and exit of spirits.

Sacred mountains also serve as *axes mundi,* connecting earth with heaven. The higher one ascends, the closer one is to God, who reveals Himself on Sinai, Olympus, pyramids and ziggurats, the San Francisco peaks in Hopi country, and Golgotha. Islamic tradition calls the Kaaba the highest place on earth, because "it faces the center of Heaven."

"Temples," explains Eliade, "are replicas of the cosmic mountain, and hence constitute the pre-eminent link between earth and heaven. The ziggurat was literally a cosmic mountain. The seven stories represented the seven planetary heavens; by ascending them, the priest reached the summit of the universe."[2]

Each primitive society adjusts its calendar to fit a holy cycle: planting, harvesting, the lunar rhythm, the solar succession. A system of periodic purifications is provided, making possible a cyclical regeneration of life. Each start is a new creation, as if *ab initio.* In this way profane time (history) is abolished, and one lives perpetually in the renewal of sacred time.

Myths recount the lives of the gods, and thereby provide models for human behavior. As long as one imitates the gods, one escapes profane time and lives in sacred time, which is "a succession of eternities." Festivals recount holy events which occurred in sacred time, and thus they restore the purity and sanctity of the original situation. Rituals reenact the primal cosmic events which established the divinely ordained cosmos.

Trees also become sacred symbols. Yggdrasil was a cosmic tree in Germanic mythology. The tree of life was used in Mesopotamia, the tree of knowledge in the Old Testament, the tree of youth in India and Iran, and the tree of immortality in Asia and the Old Testament. Mythology endows trees with sacred fruit which possesses great healing powers. Even modern humans are charmed by the beauty of nature, and feel guilty for desacralizing it—polluting the atmosphere, robbing earth of oxygen, and turning rain forests into wastelands.

The triune concept of God appears early in history. A three-faced god is depicted on a statue found at Mohenjo-daro in the pre-Aryan period in India. He may be a prototype of Siva, who in later Hinduism was often depicted with three faces.

Joseph Epes Brown states that native American Indians conceive of religion as an organic part of everyday life, rather than as a separate act to be done once a week. A Papago basket maker, as well as a Navaho blanket weaver, ritually recapitulates the entire process of creation. Circular tepees or hogans are models of the universe in microcosm.

A Navaho healing "sing" helps restore the health of a person who became ill by being in a state of disharmony with the universe. Aided by a shaman, the sick person engages in a vision quest, in which he tries to reconnect himself with his spiritual roots. Black Elk, the Lakota sage, declared that "we should understand well that all things are the works of the Great Spirit. When we understand this deeply in our hearts, then we will fear and love and know the Great Spirit, and then we will live as He intends."[3]

Among the Sioux smoking of the calumet had symbolic significance. The six directions (including up and down) represent infinite space, or God, into which, like the smoke, a person must again be reabsorbed. One fulfills one's destiny when the unreality of one's ego merges with the Reality of the cosmos.

Albert Schweitzer felt that the great turning point in human history occurred between the eighth and sixth centuries before Christ. This was the period when such prophets and sages as Amos, Isaiah, Zoroaster, Confucius, and Buddha lived. In Schweitzer's opinion they taught a common message: "The ethical consists not in submission to traditional national customs but in the active devotion of individuals to their fellowmen or to aims which produce an improvement in social conditions. In this great revolution begins the spiritual humanizing of mankind."[4]

Primitive Religion — Divisive

Ken Wilber points out that the period in human history from 10,000 B.C. to 3,000 B.C. was the epoch of the Great Mother, when various forms of the archetypal Mother Earth (also known as the Virgin Mother) were worshipped in many places.

Forerunner of the Christian Mary/Jesus relation were the figures of Damuzi/Inanna, Tamuz/Ishtar, and Osiris/Isis. In each case, says Wilber, the woman is the virgin bride of God, and is the mother of the resurrected God.

Woman's role as child-bearer bound her closely to earth and to natural functions. Conceived of as a goddess, she has a masculine partner, heaven, and thereby God becomes a masculine construct. Man's orientation was social and mental rather than natural, and so as the human mind developed, men could go to war over mental constructs, something women could never do until they become "masculine" enough to put mental constructs ahead of natural functions.

An imperfect knowledge of human physiology led to tragic consequences in the form of divisive religion. The primitive mind believed that since women do not menstruate when pregnant, it is the withheld menstrual blood which forms the new baby. The mother needs more blood in order to bring forth life, and therefore the blood sacrifice (first of animals, then of humans) is justified. "Civilization and human sacrifice came into being together," says Wilber.[5]

"Religious offerings, especially of the first born, are known from the Bible (Genesis 22) as well as from the histories of Egypt, Greece, and Rome. Up to the 19th century first-born sacrifice was almost universal in India. Here the motive was the offering of one's most precious possession to the deities.

No mother convicted of the murder of her child under one year old has been executed in England since 1849, nor has one been convicted of the murder of her child of any age since 1889."[6]

Although human sacrifice was relatively rare among the Mayan Indians, human blood was a desirable offering to the gods. Aloe thorns were passed through the tongue on a cord.

Blood drops were caught on a piece of bark and used as a sacrifice.

The Aztecs were not nearly so squeamish. The sun, they believed, was a young warrior born of the earth goddess Coatlicué. His daily journey began in battle and ended in death; he was then revived daily through blood sacrifice.

In 1486 the Aztec leaders Ahuitzotl and Nezahualpilli began a two-year campaign into northern Oaxaca in Mexico to get human sacrifices to dedicate a temple, amassing no fewer than 20,000 victims. "Human blood was the food of the gods, and Huitzilopochtli, god of the sun and patron of the ruthless Aztecs, fed on it insatiably." The captives stood in two rows, and Ahuitzotl and Nezahualpilli began the grisly process of tearing out the live victims' hearts. Lesser priests followed, eager to show their love of the god. "Down the blood-splattered steps of the pyramid of Great Teocalli sprawled the bodies of slaves and prisoners."[7]

Montezuma II, nephew of Ahuitzotl, followed this bloody practice, in the hope that the war god would give him continual success. "He approached his uncle's piety on one occasion when 12,000 captives from a rebel province in Oaxaca were delivered up to the war god."[8]

Tizoc, who ruled from 1479 to 1486, had carved the Sacrificial Stone, a monstrous-sized vessel for burning human hearts. The priests of Xipe, the Flayed One, "danced in the flayed skin of a sacrificial slave. The whole skin, even down to the face, was used in this repulsive ritual."[9]

The Toltecs practiced cannibalism and human sacrifice. "At the Temple of Quetzalcoatl individuals were buried under the corners as foundation deposits. Shallow dishes, cut from the top of skulls, testify to other rituals involving sacrifice and death."[10]

Among other primitive people, "sacred kings (considered to embody gods of vegetation) were sacrificed when their vigor declined in order to prevent reciprocal effects on soil fertility; or sometimes a substitute was assigned divine status for a period of time and then put to death."[11]

Among the Ashanti in Africa about 100 victims, usually criminals, were sacrificed as a first-fruit offering at the festival of new yams in September. In Nyasaland and Uganda some of the slaves of a dead person were buried alive with him. Human sacrifice was practiced sporadically among North American Indians, such as the Skidi Pawnee, the Natchez, the Iroquois, the Huron, and some Pueblo tribes. Infanticide, as well as other forms of human sacrifice, was practiced in Hawaii during the period immediately preceding the discovery of the islands by Europeans. Laborers in modern Borneo feel there must be a blood sacrifice, lest spirits take revenge on a construction job. Animal blood may be used, but human blood is preferred. "If one longhouse pole traditionally requires the blood of one human being, then how much blood from how many people is needed to construct a 30-story concrete building? People from the highlands refer to construction projects in terms of their cost in human blood: a 200-person hydroelectric dam or a 100-person bridge."[12]

A recent study finds three reasons for the practice of ritual cannibalism:

1. People believe they are what they eat.
2. "Internal order is maintained by incorporating anarchic outsiders.
3. Social boundaries are drawn symbolically by denigrating outsiders as having monstrous characteristics."[13]

Some of the unitive factors in primitive religion can lead to divisive reactions. For example, conceiving of one's home as a sacred place can suggest that outside the home live strangers, enemies, and chaos. If enemies capture one's city (the center of an orderly universe), the enemies have destroyed the unity, brought chaos, and thus must represent demonic forces. The pharaoh's adversaries were considered to be "sons of ruin, wolves, dogs." Hebrew prophets identified Gentile kings with dragons. Eliade showed that ritual, emptied of its symbolic content, leads to the desacralization of sacred time, leaving the empty cycles of nature meaningless and frightening.

Many primitive people conceived of the world as full of evil spirits who had to be appeased. Cults developed to specialize in the propitiation of the spirits. Cult members had in-group unity, but anyone outside the cult was evil, untouchable, lost. Divisiveness grew out of human mind-sets.

Once men took over as priests, prophets, and scriptural scribes, women became systematically downgraded as spiritual entities. Sita, wife of the Hindu god Rama, was never happy on earth but was finally made divine in heaven. Maya, mother of

Gautama Buddha, seemed forgotten in Buddhist doctrine until she was finally glorified as Tara, "Mother of all the Buddhas." The Virgin Mary was ignored by many New Testament Christians, and is still undiscovered by many Protestants. Fatima, daughter of Mohammed, was often given cool treatment by her father. Many modern churches, such as the Jewish, the Roman Catholic, and the Mormon, still see the sacerdotal aspects of religion as primarily a masculine affair.

Religion in Mesopotamia

A cosmic unity was perceived in the early Mesopotamian religion. Everything in the world—people, animals, inanimate objects, and even ideas such as justice and the form of a circle—all were thought of as members of a cosmic state. The sky commanded the broad plains of the land. One felt insignificant compared to the vast sky, and yet one felt a glorious harmony, a oneness with the cosmos, under the endless canopy.

Anu, god of heaven, presided. His son Enlil, god of the storm, carried out the orders of the gods. Anu and Enlil appointed Enki, god of the waters, to oversee Mesopotamia. The gods' grasp was firm: "Order in nature is seen exactly as if the universe were a large, smoothly running estate organized by a capable manager. The whole universe showed the influence of the essence peculiar to Anu. He is the force which lifts it out of chaos and makes it into a structure. So the Mesopotamian universe is upheld by, and reflects in its structure, a divine will."[14]

Religion provided a framework within which international law could develop. For example, a boundary dispute between city-states would be adjudicated by Enlil, working through his appointed deputy, the king. Both sides accepted the god's decision.

The culture was what Ruth Benedict called a high synergy one. The prime virtues were justice and obedience. The rewards for proper conduct were promotion on the job, and the respect of the community. Disobedience, since it broke the natural order and caused chaos, was punished as a sin.

As in Christian and Hindu mythology, there is a perilously narrow passageway past Hell. Eliade says that "in Iranian mythology the Cinvat Bridge is traversed by the dead in their post mortem journey. It is nine lance-lengths wide for the just, but for the wicked it becomes as narrow as the blade of a razor. Under the Bridge lies the mouth of the deep pit of Hell. The mystics always pass over this bridge on their ecstatic journeys to heaven."[15]

Early Babylonian religion had several sets of trinities: Anu, Bel, and Ea; and the sun god, the moon god, and the goddess Ishtar, the embodiment of a planet. Justice and equity prevailed under gods who were depicted as having great compassion and forgiveness.

Perhaps the chief drawback of Babylonian religion was that, unlike Judaism, it lacked the capacity for growth. Divisive elements were present, as they are in all religions. Sir Leonard Woolley's excavation of the royal tombs of Ur reveal that whole courts of people had been ceremonially interred alive as recently as 2350 B.C.

Egyptian Religion

Much of the religion of early Egypt was of a unitive nature. The earliest known religious writings are the Pyramid Texts (from about 2300 B.C.) found in the vast necropolis of Memphis. There one reads: "It is said of Ptah: 'It is he who made all and brought the gods into being.' He is in all gods, all men, all beasts, and whatever lives. And in this way all are at one with Him, content and united with the Lord."[16]

God's purpose is seen to be a creation in which all humans are equals: "I made the four winds that every man might breathe thereof like his fellow in his time. I made the great flood waters that the poor man might have rights in them like the great man. I made every man like his fellow. I did not command that they might do evil, but it was their hearts that violated what I had said."[17] Egyptian priests said, "The Light is within thee; let the Light shine."

The Egyptian moral code was based on pleasing the indwelling spirit of God. Love of God implied love of fellow humans. Sounding like Isaiah or Jeremiah, the Instruction for Merikere (dated about 2100 B.C.) says that "the good conduct of the righteous man is more acceptable than the sacrificial ox of the evildoer."[18] The Book of the Dead contains directions for the soul when it appears before the Judge of the Dead. At that time the soul should be able to say, "I have made no one weep by any wrong actions of mine."

John A. Wilson points out that the Egyptians were monophysites: there were "many men and many gods, but all ultimately were of one nature. There was a continuing substance across the phenomena of the universe, whether organic, inorganic, or abstract." The universe was seen as a spectrum, with colors shading off into one another. "To the ancient Egyptian the elements of the universe were consubstantial. It was very easy for one element to take the place of another."[19] Bread depicted on the walls of a tomb fed not the deceased's physical, but his spiritual, hunger.

The pharaoh was God's agent of justice and mercy. Like the sun god, he had divine magnanimity, and superior capabilities of perception and communication: "These are godlike qualities, the perception of something in integrated and constructive terms, and the consequent authoritative utterance which creates something new."[20]

A triune god concept, consisting of father, mother, and son, was found in the Egyptian pantheon. Sometimes the triad was expanded into an ennead, three groups of triads.

Ikhnaton (also known as Amenhotep IV) ascended the throne in 1380 B.C. He revolted against the concept of multiple gods, and attacked sacrificial rituals, temple prostitutes, and superstitious beliefs. The one god Aton, said this reformer, was not a lord of battles but a gentle and compassionate father. His attributes were love, joy, truth, and peace. He is the god of all nations, and all people are to serve him in a divine brotherhood.

Unfortunately, Ikhnaton declared every creed but his own illegal, and therefore he closed all the temples in Thebes. The dispossessed priests plotted to overthrow him, while the people at home secretly worshipped their many gods. He died at the age of thirty, frustrated and financially bankrupt.

At its best Egyptian religion displayed a catholic tolerance towards other faiths. People saw nothing incongruous in accepting the most reasonable beliefs from diverse religious sources. Even under Christianity the Alexandrian church was famous for the catholicity of its outlook.

Like many religions, however, the Egyptian at times employed human sacrifices. At Abydos a First Dynasty tomb discloses that numerous servants had been interred with a princess in order to provide her with a retinue in the next life. As Egyptian culture declined, the earlier spiritual earnestness which had reflected itself as a *joie de vivre* degenerated, in Wilson's words, into "a recourse to oracles and strict ritualistic observance, until religion became as empty as Herodotus saw it."

Zoroastrianism

Zoroaster (628-551 B.C.) at the age of thirty preached the revelation of a new religion. Its peaceful and unitive message was a sharp contrast to the animistic polytheism of the warring nomads of southern Persia.

Zoroaster recommended that his followers be like God, whom he called Ahura Mazda. The father aspects of god incorporated righteousness, power, and a right mind. The mother aspects encompassed piety, wholeness, and immortality. To remind believers of the divine spark within them, a sacred fire burned constantly in the temple. Ahura Mazda expressed his will through the Holy Spirit, called Spenta Mainyu.

The prescribed civic virtues are charity, chastity, compassion, education, justice, righteousness, self-help, and care of animals. Besides teaching the Golden Rule, Zoroaster advised making a friend out of one's enemy. For him religious merit was not the practice of ritual or austerity but the diffusion of merciful acts, for "a good deed is superior to ten thousand prayers."

Zoroaster had no intolerance towards other monotheistic faiths. In fact, he recommended them, albeit not in preference to his own. But nowhere does he say that only his followers are the children of God.

The Biblical book of Daniel expresses this tolerance of other faiths. When Daniel survives in the lions' den, King Darius admits the greatness of Daniel's God. When Daniel cures King Nebuchadnezzar of lycanthropy, he praises Daniel's God. When Shadrach, Mesach, and Abednego live through their experience in the fiery furnace, Nebuchadnezzar admits that their God has saved them.

King Cyrus of Persia was another tolerant monarch. Within two decades he "raised an obscure and secluded tribe to the mastery of an empire that stretched from the Mediterranean to the Indus. A major factor was the liberal and lenient treatment accorded by Cyrus to conquered states, a policy without parallel in the previous history of the Near East."[21] People everywhere welcomed him as a liberator. In Babylonia Cyrus presented himself as chosen by the Babylonian god Marduk to put down the heretic Nabonidus. He then restored the Babylonian temples and participated in their rites. He not only freed the Jews from their captivity in Babylonia but also gave them gold and silver vessels, and timber grants for the rebuilding of the temple in Jerusalem. Had kings throughout history possessed his unitive approach to religion countless human lives would have been saved.

Kings Darius and Artaxerxes confirmed the decision of Cyrus to help pay for the rebuilding of the Jewish temple with funds from the Persian treasury. Artaxerxes sent Ezra and Nehemiah to Jerusalem with funds for the construction. He also decreed that no tribute was to be paid by Jewish priests, musicians, or temple servants.

The influence of this tolerant religion spread widely. In Buddhism the battle between Buddha and the evil Mara reflects the struggle between Ahura Mazda and the evil spirit Angra Mainyu. Also the Buddhist savior figure Maitreya reflects the character of Mithra, the divine savior in Zoroastrianism. During their Babylonian captivity the Jews incorporated new ideas concerning the resurrection of the body, the immortality of the soul, and future rewards and punishments. Some of these concepts were carried over into Judaism's offshoot, Christianity.

Sometimes Persian tolerance backfired. King Yazdgard I was so tolerant of Christians that he was sometimes called "the Christian king." He helped set up a Christian hierarchy, and permitted free movement of Christian clergy. "But the Christians apparently abused their privileges, and were guilty of violent demonstrations against the Zoroastrian sanctuaries and clergy. In view of this attitude, the king was compelled to revise his policy."[22]

Zoroastrianism had its divisive tendencies. The evil spirit Angra Mainyu (later called Shaitin or Satan) grew in strength and importance until he came to be considered a formidable rival to Ahura Mazda. As for followers of Satan, believers were taught to "resist them with the weapon!" At the general resurrection at the end of the world, it was said that a huge fire would consume all evil people, but that good people would not even feel the heat of the flames.

As the religion became debased, Zoroaster started to be worshipped as a god. The original monotheism became polytheistic, while the doctrine of evil spirits grew. Soon, as in other religions, rites and ceremonies assumed magical dimensions, and the original religion of love and peace was lost forever to the masses of the people.

Christianity was tolerated in Persia until it became the religion of Persia's mortal enemies, Greece and Rome. When Constantine adopted Christianity as the Roman faith, Persians Christians were persecuted as being disloyal to Zoroastrian Persia. In A.D. 341 the Sassanian King Shapur II ordered the massacre of Christians, and during his reign 16,000 Christians were killed. Open strife between the two faiths lasted for nearly two centuries.

Manichaeism

Mani (A.D. 216-277) came forth about A.D. 240 as the prophet of a new religion which synthesized elements from Zoroastrianism, Buddhism, Christianity, and Gnosticism. Mani called himself an apostle of Christ, saying that he was the Paraclete that Christ had promised to send. To Mani, humans were in an eternal war between God's forces of light and Satan's forces of darkness. Christ, as the Spirit of Light, could redeem mankind from its slavery to Satan.

Downplaying the role of women, Mani preached a doctrine of celibacy, pacifism, and non-violence. His cosmology came from the Gnostics, but the basic teachings emanated from Zoroaster. The belief in transmigration of souls came from Buddhism. From Christianity came the concept of the Trinity and various Gospel passages. Manichaeans practiced baptism and communion, and received absolution and remission of their sins before death.

Favoring Mani, King Shapur I allowed him to make converts, perhaps on the assumption that it would aid his rapidly expanding realm to have a religion which was both Iranian and syncretistic. But when Shapur I died, Mani left Persia to preach in the Far East. Upon his return he was prosecuted as an infidel by Zoroastrian priests, found guilty, and executed.

Upon the conversion of Rome to Christianity, Manichaeans were persecuted in Rome as agents of the enemy, Persia. With no home now in either Zoroastrian Persia or Christian Rome, the faith spread to Turkestan and China, and through Syria and Egypt to North Africa. St. Augustine describes himself as one of its adherents when he was a young man. The scattered sect continued to have followers until the tenth century.

Religion in Classical Greece and Rome

The early Greeks did use human sacrifice as a part of their religious rites. A hecatomb was originally the sacrifice of a hundred persons, and later of any large number of victims. With their love of the physical, however, the practice became so repugnant to them that it was virtually abandoned by the sixth century B.C. At this time the pre-Socratic philosophers of the Miletus school believed that all things were made of a single mystical supersubstance, a surprisingly early version of the grand unified theory of modern science.

The Greek monotheist Xenophanes of Colophon was the reputed founder of the Eleatic school, which had a great influence upon Plato. Aristotle said that Xenophanes was "the first to believe in the unity of all things." Xenophanes stated that finite humans could not grasp God's infinity. The Ethiopians naturally depict God as swarthy and flat nosed, he said, and the Thracians as fair-haired and blue-eyed. Homer and Hesiod, he felt, incorrectly attributed to the gods human faults such as adultery, deceit, lust, and theft. The concept of the deity held by Xenophanes is close to that of the Hindu Brahma or the Taoist Void.

Pythagoras taught that numbers controlled the true nature of things. He called three the number of God, since it comprised the beginning, the middle, and the end. Later, St. Paul said that God is "above all and through all and in you all" (Ephesians 4:6).

The followers of Pythagoras, believing in the transmigration of souls, lived exemplary lives so as to be born higher in the hierarchy. They regarded the sexes as equal, treated slaves humanely, and showed tenderness towards animals. Because their practice differed from traditional Greek religious customs, many were forced to flee for their lives. Those who remained behind were killed.

In 371 B.C. at the battle of Leuctra the Boeotian leader Pelopidas felt that the occasion required a human sacrifice for victory, but his counselors said that "such a barbarous and impious obligation could not be pleasing to any Supreme Being; that typhons did not preside over the world but the general Father of gods and mortals; that it was absurd to imagine any Divinity delighting in the slaughter and sacrifice of men."[23]

Plato spoke of the trinity of the physical, the spiritual, and the divine. He said that a human being's mission was to be as much like God as possible. "To become like God," he said, "is to become holy, just, and wise. God is never in any way unrighteous. He is perfect righteousness, and those of us who are most righteous are most like Him."[24]

As he conquered much of the known world, Alexander the Great brought unitive religious concepts to the subdued lands. He expanded the Greek idea of the polis, or city state, into the concept of the cosmopolis, or world community. He found striking similarities between the new gods and their Greek counterparts: "Isis and Demeter, Horus and Apollo, Thoth and Hermes, Amun and Zeus, Krishna and Heracles, and Shiva and Dionysus."[25]

The Greek love of free thought encouraged an unprejudiced study of religions, which led to syncretism. Alexander, adopting the Persian policy of tolerance towards outside religions, decreed that no sacred objects should be harmed in conquered lands. If all persons were to be subject to a universal law, why should that not be God's law, Alexander reasoned. Plutarch said that Alexander felt sent by God to establish unity, peace, and brotherhood in the world. After encountering resistance from traditional religionists, Alexander died of a fever at the age of 33.

The Greek slave Epictetus (A.D. 50-138) believed that the human mind is so marvelous an instrument that only a Divine Creator could have fashioned it. Insofar as we possess reason, he said, we are a part of Universal Reason, or God. Because God is our common Father, we are all members of one human family, and should treat one another with love. Many of the teachings of Epictetus resemble those of Christ. Denouncing slavery and capital punishment, Epictetus wanted to treat criminals as sick people. His version of the Golden Rule was, "What you shun to suffer, do not make others suffer." If someone speaks ill of you, he said, you should reply, "Had he known all my other faults, he could have mentioned those, too." He advocated returning good for evil. St. Augustine and St. John Chrysostom praised the teachings of Epictetus, and his book on asceticism was used, with minor changes, as a guide to Christian monastic life.

The Roman empire easily lent itself to monotheism. Having one supreme earthly leader made it easy for people to believe in one supreme spiritual being. The only religion which could survive in Roman times was a universal one, one disengaged from particular cults or sects. For centuries Roman intellectuals earnestly sought for a spiritual marriage of East and West.

The Stoics believed that the universe is a gigantic organism of which God is the soul. Morality, they felt, was a willing surrender to the divine will, and goodness meant cooperation with God and His laws. Humans, though usually materialistic, were inherently divine, because they reflected their Maker's image. The masses needed popular religion, for they required a faith system to undergird the moral code. Many Stoics ultimately believed in the brotherhood of man under the Fatherhood of God. Their tolerant attitude led them to accept Etruscan, Italian, Greek, and Oriental deities.

Seneca brilliantly restated the Stoic thesis that the many deities are all aspects of one God. He and Cicero taught that humans bore the spark of the divine within them. A sign of this was human reason, a reflection of the Divine Mind. Unfortunately some of the classical Romans showed anti-Semitic tendencies. Included among these were Cicero, Juvenal, Seneca, and Tacitus.

The emperor Marcus Aurelius, when he persecuted Christians, was not living up to his own credo, for he believed that "there is one universe made up of all things, and one God who pervades all. We are made for cooperation. We are all working together to one end, some with knowledge and design, and others without knowing what they do."[26] In the view of Aurelius, "All things are intertwined, and sacred is the band. All things are marshalled in order, and constitute the one cosmos. There is one God, one law, one common reason, and one truth."[27]

The philosopher Plotinus, said Evelyn Underhill, was "as celebrated for his practical kindness as for his transcendent intuitions of the One." He and his Neoplatonic followers were the gateway through which Hellenic philosophy permeated and fructified Christian theology.

Plotinus found three aspects of God, "three distinct but not separate realities within the unity of the Godhead." They were the One, or the Good, which originated all of life; *nous,* or the Holy Spirit; and the Universal Soul. Each person, said Plotinus, has both a higher and a lower soul. The higher is united with *nous,* and thus can know no evil. Imprisoned in the body, the lower soul is subject to evil. A person's true way of life is through the higher soul, seeking beyond the *nous* to ultimate union with the One. A false way of life follows bodily impulses, and the result is like a choir singing out of tune, with no one paying attention to the Director, God.

The Mystery Religions

Among the excellent institutions given Rome by the Greeks, said Cicero, the most important of all are "the mysteries, by which we have been brought forth from our savage mode of existence, and refined to a state of civilization. We have gained the understanding not only to live happily but also to die with better hope."[28]

The mystery consisted of a dramatization of the life history of a savior god, including his struggles, suffering, and triumphs. The participant achieved a profound intuition of the Spirit of Love. After this arcane experience one was impervious to life's frustrations and trials, and was assured of ultimate salvation.

The most famous mysteries were those held at Eleusis. It is not known why the rites were secret, since there was no doctrine which had to be kept from the uninitiated. It is likely that the religious leaders feared that a sacred ritual might be profaned unless special care was taken to safeguard the ritualistic details.

The mysteries helped develop a unitary conception of the universe, along with Plato, Aristotle, and Posidonius, who unified Platonic and Oriental mysticism at the same time as he was synthesizing science and religion. As in modern science, the mysteries perceived that the subjective and the objective approaches to reality were complementary.

An authority on the mysteries, S. Angus, found many ways in which they prepared the way for Christianity. The mystery associations were harbingers of early Christian churches. They made religion a matter of personal conviction, and sin an individual responsibility, with a corresponding need for redemption. They made people hungry for immortality, which was to be achieved through a monotheistic framework. They also denationalized the gods, with the ultimate aim of a universal human brotherhood. Angus say that "by fostering religious interests, by antiquating exclusiveness, by bringing religious systems into comparison and competition, by predisposing men to accept salvation wherever most effectively offered, Greco-Roman syncretism not only made ready the way of the Lord, but assured the victory of His cause."[29]

Dean W.R. Inge said that Catholicism owes to the mysteries "the notions of secrecy, symbolism, mystical brotherhood, sacramental grace, and above all, the three stages in the spiritual life: ascetic purification, illumination, and epopteia (secret initiation) as the crown."[30]

Early Chinese Religion

In early China when strangers met they would ask each *other's* religion, and then go into a panegyric on the *other's* religion rather than one's own. Then they would repeat together: "Religions are many, reason is one, we are all brothers."[31]

"Fundamentally, the idea is that the individual (microcosm), society (mesocosm), and the universe of heaven and earth (macrocosm) form an indissoluble unit, and that the well-being of all depends upon their mutual harmony." As Joseph Kitagawa says, the Chinese make no distinction between the sacred and the secular: "The religious ethos of the Chinese must be found in the midst of their ordinary everyday life more than in their ceremonial activities, though the latter should not be ignored. The meaning of life was sought in the whole life, and not confined to any section of it called religious."[32]

The ancient Chinese did not believe in personal immortality. The only part of the personality that survived, they felt, was that which is a part of the undifferentiated esthetic continuum (analogous to the Holy Spirit). The Chinese therefore perpetuate memories of their ancestors in order to keep the personality alive. The modern person thereby becomes a part of the same continuum as the ancestor, and one can acknowledge gratitude to one's forbears. Keeping alive the memory of one's ancestors grants oneself immortality.

References

[1] Mircea Eliade, *The Sacred and the Profane* (Harcourt Brace Jovanovich, 1959) p. 37. Eliade was Chairman of the Department of the History of Religions at the University of Chicago.

[2] Ibid., pp. 39-40.

[3] Yusuf Ibish and Ileana Marculescu, eds., *Contemplation and Action in World Religions* (University of Washington Press, 1978), p. 253. Ibish and Marculescu are Islamic scholars.

[4] Albert Schweitzer, *Out of My Life and Thought* (New American Library, 1953), p. 142.

[5] Wilber, *Up From Eden,* p. 127.

[6] "Infanticide," *Encyclopedia Britannica,* 1971, vol. 12, p. 217.

[7] G.H.S. Bushnell, in Stuart Piggott, ed., *The Dawn of Civilization* (McGraw-Hill, 1961), p. 368.

[8] George C. Vaillant, *The Aztecs of Mexico* (Penguin, 1950), p. 112.

[9] Bushnell, p. 370.

[10] Vaillant, p. 76.

[11] "Human Sacrifice," *Encyclopedia Britannica,* 1971, vol. 11, p. 829.

[12] Tim Cahill, *New York Times Book Review,* 6 March 1988, p. 8.

[13] Deborah Gewertz, ibid., 3 May 1987, p. 39.

[14] Thorkild Jacobsen, in Henri Frankfort et al., *Before Philosophy* (Penguin, 1949), pp. 152-53, 175.

[15] Eliade, *The Sacred and the Profane*, p. 182.

[16] Wilber, *Up From Eden*, p. 108.

[17] John A. Wilson, in Frankfort, p. 117.

[18] William F. Albright, *From the Stone Age to Christianity,* 2nd ed. (Doubleday, 1957), p. 184. Albright was Chairman of the Oriental Seminary at Johns Hopkins University.

[19] Frankfort, pp. 71-72, 75.

[20] Ibid., p. 93.

[21] "Persian History, *Encyclopedia Britannica,* 1971, vol. 17, p. 656.

[22] R. Ghirshman, *Iran from the Earliest Times to the Islamic Conquest* (Penguin, 1961), p. 298.

[23] Will Durant, *The Life of Greece* (Simon & Schuster, 1939), p. 194.

[24] Sarvepalli Radhakrishnan, *Eastern Religions and Western Thought*, 2nd ed. (Oxford University Press, 1940), p. 146. Radhakrishnan was a professor at Oxford, and was President of India from 1962 to 1967.

[25] Campbell, *Occidental Mythology*, p. 240.

[26] Voss, p. 190.

[27] S. Angus, *The Mystery Religions* (Dover, 1975), p. 70. Angus was Professor of Religion at the University of Edinburgh.

[28] Campbell, *Occidental Mythology*, p. 268.

[29] Angus, p. 195.

[30] Ibid., p. vii. Inge was Dean of St. Paul's Cathedral in London, 1911 to 1934.

[31] Bhagavad Das, *The Essential Unity of All Religions*, 2nd ed. (Theosophical Press, 1966), p. 71.

[32] Campbell, *Oriental Mythology*, pp. 457-58.

CHAPTER 3

RELIGIOUS DOCTRINE: HELPFUL OR HURTFUL?

Religious doctrine can be unitive or divisive, helpful or hurtful. It can also be unitive within one's religion but divisive as a part of its milieu. Ku Klux Klan members no doubt feel a strong sense of brotherhood, but the lynched black person derives little value from that group feeling. In our shrinking world, to be truly unitive a religious doctrine needs to have beneficial effects for more than the group which adopts it.

All world religions have some doctrines that are unitive and some that are divisive. It is instructive to look at the various world faiths from this perspective.

Unity in Early Hinduism

Greeting another person, a Hindu puts his hands in a praying position, bows, and says *"Namaste!"*, meaning "I bow to the God who is in you." Hindus feel that this could work for all people, since God's Spirit is within every person.

A Hindu musician, about to play his *vina* (a stringed instrument), addresses it: "I greet you humbly. Elevate my soul. Stand by me as I play you." The musician feels a kinship even with inanimate matter, since all things derive ultimately from God.

Hans Küng points out that since at least 500 B.C. Hindu rulers protected all types of religious worshippers. Hindu theologians characteristically tend far more towards integration than towards confrontation.

For the Hindu, says Heinrich Zimmer, "the individual's consolation lies in knowing that behind and within his doom is the Imperishable, which is his own very seed and essence." To take the proper attitude towards one's condition involves a correct approach towards breathing, eating, thinking, and living. "The mystery of the oneness of all in the Divine Being will then be made manifest. Disregarding differentiating, discriminatory notions, which set conflicting individuals apart, each ego clinging avidly to itself in isolation, one no longer feels bound in by one's personal perishability. Such a realization transforms the view of the seemingly merciless course of life, and bestows immediately a boon of peace."[1]

"There is in Hinduism," says Joseph Campbell, "an essential affirmation of the cosmic order as divine. And since society is a part of the cosmic order, the social order is divine."[2] Swami Nikhilananda states that the cardinal principles of Hinduism are "the divinity of the soul, the unity of existence, the oneness of the Godhead, and the harmony of religions. As the soul is divine, everyone is entitled to respect. This is the true basis of democracy and of all decent human relationships."[3]

Transcendentalism means that the spiritual transcends the physical in importance. By this means apparent contradictions are unified. Behind the facade of antagonism, the contending forces are in harmony. As a person finds the One in the many, he comes to realize that in lasting terms there is really only the One.

Many ancient Hindu teachings sound like the latest pronouncements of science. "The Lord is so inconceivably small," says one Hindu, "that He enters into the heart of a particle, and controls it as the Supersoul. Although so small, He is all-pervading and by His inconceivable energy sustains all planets and systems of galaxies. A living entity is not the material body but is a spiritual spark of the divine fire of God, who is Absolute Truth."[4]

When Hindu scriptures call the savior god Vishnu "the Milky Ocean of Immortal Life, out of which the transient universe arises and back to which it again dissolves," the concept calls forth physicist David Bohm's implicate order, as well as the universal creative ocean of the quantum theory, which will be discussed more fully in chapter 14.

Hindu Scriptures

The Vedas date from about 1500 B.C. when the western Aryans invaded India and conquered the native Dravidians. The Vedas explain the origin of evil as a result of a battle among the gods, in which earth and heaven were separated, and *Sat* (existence, good) was rent asunder from *Asat* (non-existence, evil). In the Vedas the spiritual masters show humans how to regain *Sat* (which brings with it love, intelligence, and happiness) by returning to their original condition. "The function of founders of religion," says transcendentalist Frithjof Schuon, "is to give back to fallen man his primordial 'being'. The first condition of spirituality is to be 'reborn'."[5]

After ridding oneself of the selfish ego, one is left with this higher Self, which both transcends the universe and inheres in every particle of it. The One God is hidden within all beings, as the all-pervading Inner Self. Realizing this, one discards one's masks *(maya)* and basks in the unity of love. "Hatred arises only from an illusion of diversity," explains Heinrich Zimmer.[6]

The Upanishads ("secret teachings") tone down the ritualism of the Vedas in favor of knowledge and virtuous conduct. One Upanishad teaches that just as bees deposit their honey in one unified collection, so are we all at last absorbed into the blessed One. A person gladly surrenders his lesser self in order to be reunited with his Maker. "The wise behold the Self, the One, standing in their own being; hence to them belongs universal peace, and to no one else."[7] Other scripture, the Puranas, an offshoot of the epic Mahabarata, stress the idea of a personal God, the Divine Incarnation, and the path of bhakti, or divine love. The Vishnu Purana states that universal love is a necessary fruit of one's union with God. The Puranas teach that "he who lives pure in thought, free from malice, feeling tenderness for all creatures, has Vishnu ever present in his heart. The eternal abides not in the heart of that man who covets another's wealth, injures living creatures, speaks harshness and untruth, is proud of his iniquity, and whose mind is evil."[8] This, then, is the heart of unitive religion.

The Bhagavad Gita

This, The Song of the Lord, is the favorite Hindu scripture. In it Krishna, disguised as a charioteer, teaches that life's goal is the love of God. Even when we love other humans, what we really love is the spirit of God that exists within them. "He who never hates any being and is friendly and compassionate to all, who is free from the feeling of 'I', who is forbearing, self-controlled, and has consecrated his mind to me—he is dear to me," says Krishna.[9]

In the union with God, one does not lose oneself but one finds one's true Self, and sees it to be the same Self that exists in all other persons. "The Bhagavad Gita declares that all religions are strung on the Lord like pearls in a necklace. In whatever way people offer their worship to the Lord, He accepts it. All religions lead to the same truth."[10]

Krishna explains the four types of yoga, or paths to God. Karma Yoga is for the person who emphasizes good deeds. Bhakti Yoga is for the one who primarily wishes to love God. Raja Yoga is for the one who concentrates on ethical disciplines. Jnana Yoga is for the thoughtful philosopher. All of these yogas can be unitive, and one person can employ a combination of these paths. All, however, require good works. One is never free of the obligation to love one's fellow humans as a sign that one truly loves God.

Once a person wishes to penetrate beyond the boundaries of one's particular faith to seek the Universal One, he will find help from the One. Whenever world conditions grow unbearably evil, the Savior is reborn into the world to save it.

The Supersoul, also called the Holy Spirit by Bhaktivedanta, is present as my Self, your Self, and everyone's. Never divided, He binds us all together. The source of all light, He makes us one with the Godhead. He can be perceived through any of the yoga methods: service, worship, meditation, or knowledge. The individual soul is the same substance as God, but is no more coextensive with God than a drop of water can be said to constitute the ocean. Since there is only one divine principle, the Hindu does not consider himself to be a polytheist. The fact that there are many roads to the summit does not mean that there are many summits.

Divisive Hinduism

In Hinduism, says Heinrich Zimmer, the Supreme Being "is always represented as the creator of demons as well as of the gods. He is the source of everything, malevolent or benign."

The word "caste" translates the Sanskrit *varna,* meaning color. The light-skinned Aryan conquerors were determined to maintain their alleged superiority over the darker native Dravidians by creating religious sanctions against intimate contact with them. High spiritual authority was to be used to prevent contamination from inferiors. This early experiment in apartheid, an excellent example of divisive religion, led, as it always does, to tension, discord, and alienation in Indian society.

Since the priests set up the caste system, they made the Brahmins (the priestly class) the highest caste. To protect them came the next highest caste, the Kshatriyas (the warriors). Then came the working-class Aryans, the Vaisyas (merchants and farmers). Lowest of all castes were the Sudras, who were the non-Aryan workers. At the very bottom of the social order came the outcastes, who were treated as if they were subhuman. If one felt this system to be a contradiction of unitive teachings in the Vedas, the reply would be that Vedic doctrines apply only to the top three Aryan castes.

Even within castes there were strict lines of superiority and exclusion. "The main castes fissured into hundreds of subcastes, each forbidding intermarriage into other subcastes and otherwise restricting freedoms of association. In 1963 there were more than 2000 such subcastes." Alleging that one's color (and thus one's caste) depended upon rewards or punishments in a previous existence, the Brahmins quote religious sanctions for this highly discriminatory practice, and "any attempt to level up the inequalities of society and lay a broader basis for social justice now became either impious or morally wrong-headed."[11] The best route of escape for a low-caste Hindu was to become a Jain or a Buddhist.

Although Mahatma Gandhi got India to outlaw all forms of untouchability in 1948, fifteen years later there were still over 50 million outcastes in India. Technically, the person having no caste is supposed to live beyond the pale of Hindu society. An object of contempt, he is told that even his shadow pollutes a person of high caste. In some parts of India an outcaste had to loudly announce his arrival on a street, so people could flee from possible contamination by him. Certain areas, such as temples and some streets, were denied his presence. He could not use public wells or take merchandise from the hand of a merchant. His uncleanness was alleged to be punishment for sins committed in a previous existence.

Hinduism has other divisive features besides caste. They will be discussed in the chapters dealing with ritual, women, and violence. As in all religions, there is the inevitable disparity between theory and practice, between scripture that is unitive and scripture which is divisive.

Islamic and Christian Influences on Hinduism

A modern Indian writer, P.N. Chopra, says that "the belief in the brotherhood of man and the theoretical equality of all believers, monotheism, and absolute submission to the will of God, which are characteristic of Islam, made a profound impression on the minds of certain Indian thinkers from the 8th to the 10th centuries. Vishnuite and Shivaite saints founded schools of bhakti, and such men of learning as Shankara and Ramanuja formulated their personal systems."[12]

Shankara (780-820) described his version of Vedanta as non-dualism, or Advaita. It recommended that a person worship his/her *ishta-deva,* which is that aspect of the deity that has been revealed to you, e.g., in Christianity, Christ. Ramanuja (1017-1137) postulated a much more personal God than did Shankara. Through bhakti (personal devotion to Brahman, or God), the soul gains an intuitive awareness of the Divine. Being all-merciful, Brahman frees individuals of their accumulated karma, and rewards them with a direct experience of His own nature, Ramanuja taught.

Moslem mystics known as Sufis influenced Hinduism in the direction of universal brotherhood. Kabir (1398-1518) preached a doctrine of love. "He is unique in being revered by Hindus and Muslims, some of his hymns being included in the scriptures of the Sikhs. He spoke of God being present in temple and mosque, known by the name Allah and Rama. Like a Sufi mystic Kabir sought an identity with the Divine Being to such an extent that his own self would be absorbed."[13]

It took a long time for Christianity to influence Hinduism. At first, the contrast between Christian precept and Christian practice left Hindus cold. But in 1820 Ram Mohun Roy published his *Precepts of Jesus.* Roy said, "I have found the doctrines of Christ more conducive to moral principles than any other. His goal was to abolish caste, child marriage, idolatry, polygamy, polytheism, and suttee (the widow cremating herself on her husband's funeral pyre). Roy perhaps underestimated the superstition of the populace, and his movement is now virtually extinct.

Ramakrishna (1836-1886) was a saintly mystic who found God in every religion. By turns he was a Hindu, a Christian, and a Moslem. All religions are good, he said, for each is a way to God adapted to the mind and the culture of the seeker. To convert from one religion to another is unnecessary, for all rivers flow into the ocean.

Sarvepalli Radhakrishnan, president of India from 1962 to 1967, helped bridge the spiritual gap between the East and the West. He was skeptical of faiths which alleged, through their scriptures, that they had a monopoly on the way to God. "Those who believe in an immanent Logos," he said, "are obliged to admit the value of other faiths. For a religion like Hinduism, which emphasizes Divine Immanence, the chosen people embrace all mankind. If we have something to teach our neighbors, we have also something to learn from them."[14]

To show our loyalty to God, Radhakrishnan said, we should respect His creation. This means respecting all people, and their right to seek God in their own way. If we try to change a person's faith, we may do more harm than good, for we may destroy that person's best original anchor to God. Rather, suggest that the person purify his own faith by having it coincide more directly with what the founder of the religion had in mind. Above all, said Radhakrishnan, stress love, which is unitive, over ritual, which is frequently divisive.

Wilfred Cantwell Smith believes that Hinduism has some unique contributions to make towards the coming community of world faith. "The new notion," says Smith, "must be global enough to do justice to the multitude of diverse forms through which faith has kept appearing among humankind." Instead of providing a dogmatic creed, Hinduism will provide a concept of faith called *sraddha.* It means "to set one's heart on. The person of faith is one who cares." It is perhaps best seen in its absence: movie lovers who know nothing about real love; workers with no dedication to their jobs; bosses with no conscience about their workers; mates with no fidelity; and parents with little regard for their children. *Sraddha* addresses itself to all these forms of modern immorality.[15]

Unitive Buddhist Concepts

"No religion has given a greater emphasis to morality than Buddhism," avers Thomas Altizer. "The Buddhist practices non-injury to life, continence in action and speech, and compassion for the suffering of all living beings. The Buddha has compassion because of his realization of the ultimate identity of all creatures. The Bodhisattva voluntarily returns to the world of suffering as a means of mediating salvation to all."[16]

Buddhists envision three types of training: moral, for virtuous conduct; intellectual, for profitable contemplation; and spiritual, for transcendental enlightenment. Help in mastering one's passions comes from cultivating the right inner attitude, a result of paying heed to the "divine lingerings" of kindness, serenity, sharing of joy, and sympathy. The four sublime states are stages in the progress towards enlightenment. Kindness promotes the welfare of others by seeing loveableness in them. Serenity is the outgrowth of equanimity, the capacity of treating all beings alike. We not only share our joy with others, but more importantly rejoice at their success. Sympathy is built upon compassion, which means to suffer along with someone in pain.

The Eight-fold Path offers liberation from all of life's suffering: right knowledge, right thought, right speech, right conduct, right vocation, right effort, right mind control, and right meditation. The Bhikkhu Silacara teaches that "the one who obeys the behests of morality, to whatever form of faith he belongs, is on the Path. To that extent he may be called a Buddhist, for Buddhism is no mere creed. It is the *Dhamma,* the law of the worlds," without which there can be no happiness. Christmas Humphreys adds, "It is the path of morality taught by Confucius and Zoroaster; it is the Way of Taoism and the teaching of the Upanishads; it is the clear commandment of Christ which Europe never heard."[17] When Christ said, "I am the Way, the Truth, and the Life," he was showing the Path from separation to unity, Humphreys feels.

Mahayana Buddhism

Mahayana (or large vehicle) Buddhism developed as an outgrowth from and a reaction to Hinayana (or small vehicle) Buddhism. Whereas Hinayana tended to be aimed at the select few,

Mahayana was a dynamic growing faith that was ever more inclusive.

Mahayana is a religion of love. One of its main features is loving adoration of Avalokiteshvara, the Lord who looks down with compassion upon suffering human beings. Another feature is *upaya,* or spiritual adaptation to the condition of the hearer. Thus, Mahayana can flourish in many different cultures. A third feature concerns two levels of truth: ordinary believers can worship Buddha or Bodhisattvas, but the person of true insight sees beyond the images to the transcendental reality of nirvana.

In late Mahayana, Bodhisattvas came to be preferred even over Buddhas, for they were willing to forego nirvana and continue to live in a world of suffering in order to help others. This, the height of altruism, is seen in all Savior figures, such as Christ, Krishna, and the Lord of Creation in Hinduism.

Buddhism teaches that the Buddha nature is a human being's original nature, sinless, as it was before the Fall. Everyone has it within, and thus all persons have the potential for becoming Buddhas or Bodhisattvas. Christ taught that "the Kingdom of heaven is within you," and St. Paul added that there is only one Holy Spirit for all people.

Chinese Buddhism

China has shown a propensity towards syncretism in religion. Because neither Taoism nor Confucianism had much to say about death, Buddhism came in to fill the void. In the opinion of F.S.C. Northrop, the Chinese people tend to be Taoists and Confucianists when they are successful but Buddhists when they are confronted with tragedy or death. A Westerner might wish that Judaism, Christianity, and Islam could get along so well together.

Chinese nationalism, however, did its best to turn unitive religion into the divisive sort. In A.D. 845 Wu Tsung of the T'ang dynasty "destroyed 45,000 Buddhist buildings, melted down tens of thousands of Buddha images, and sent over 400,000 monks, nuns, and temple servitors back into the world."[18] Later, the Neo-Confucian movement also tended to retard the growth of Buddhism in China. Nevertheless even today the cause of the Buddha ministers to the needs of millions of Chinese believers.

Buddhist Tantrism has flourished in Tibet, where the ten positive precepts again illustrate unitive religion. They include compassion, "not to take life," and even more, to protect it. People are humanized, it is said, by being purged of hatred and desire. Positive traits stressed include helpfulness, humility, integrity, and kindness. There are also aid to the poor, patience in adversity, respect for elders, and tolerance for adversaries.

Tibetan Buddhist Gampopa (A.D. 1079-1153) taught that "we must always be aware of human dignity and so respect others as equally worthy beings. By this awareness we realize a thoroughly humane goal, and find the meaning of life. In this striving we are in need of spiritual friends. They may be found at any level, because whomever we meet serves as a guide to transcendence. Aware of being human, we must not betray human dignity, but express this dignity in benevolence and compassion."[19]

Japanese Buddhism

The entrance of official Buddhism into Japan was bloody. In A.D. 552 Shinto priests tried to outlaw Buddhism, but Emperor Kimmei permitted the priest Iname of the Soga clan to pay tribute to a golden Buddha. After thirty years of strife Iname's son killed all members of the Mononobe family of priests, and by 587 Buddhism had a foothold in Japan. Five years later this son killed Emperor Sushun, whose brother Prince Shotoku proved to be one of Japan's best rulers. Shotoku converted to Buddhism, and at his death was declared to be a Bodhisattva.

Further problems occurred when the monk Nichiren (1222-1282) founded the Lotus Sutra sect. Curiously intolerant of all other sects and faiths, it promised a future peaceful utopia to all of its adherents. One of its offshoots is the modern intolerant Soka Gakkai. Nichiren's "vehement adherence to one scripture brought him into sharp conflict with other teachers and groups. Their doctrines and practices he declared to be false and dangerous to the welfare of the country."[20]

Zen Buddhism

The doctrine of the World of Total Harmony underlies most Japanese Buddhist sects. It postulates three fundamental relationships: complementarity, correlation, and Common Virtue. Common Virtue means that a leader and his group work as a team, on the principle of one-in-all and all-in-one so that the only true whole is the product of the group's efforts. This helps explain modern Japanese business success. Two significant Buddhist values are needed to achieve this *kegon,* or harmonious totality: compassion and a sense of universal Buddhahood.

The priest Dogen (1200-1253) founded the Soto school of Zen Buddhism, which teaches that strenuous meditational exercises can give the believer illumination. According to Alan Watts, Zen grew out of a merger of China's Taoism with India's Mahayana Buddhism. Zen monks in Japan were also influenced by Chu Hsi and his brand of Neo-Confucianism.

"Taoism, Confucianism, and Zen are expressions of a mentality which feels completely at home in this universe, and which sees humans as an integral part of their environment. The insight which lies at the root of Far Eastern Culture is that opposites are relational and thus fundamentally harmonious."[21]

Zen and Taoism, says Watts, seem to be the only faiths which feel secure enough to lampoon themselves. "Zen deliberately uses laughter as a means to a spiritual end. Roars of laughter, cleansing, healthy, ferocious laughter, are part of a Zen monk's daily life and of those who practice Zen."[22] The American writer Norman Cousins cured himself of two deadly diseases by watching Marx Brothers movies. Dr. Bernard Siegel tells patients that a deep belly laugh produces healthful endorphins for the next 45 minutes.

To love we must communicate, Zen teaches, but we must always be skeptical of language. For example, Christ said, "My peace I give you," but he also said, "I come to bring not peace but a sword." The Western mind sees this as a contradiction, but the Eastern mind views it as an insightful paradox: Christ wants us to fight (non-violently, spiritually) for peace. Christ also said, "Blessed are the poor in spirit, for they shall see God." Zen stresses *wabi,* meaning poverty, or independence from worldly things. A simple and direct appreciation of nature's beauty makes one feel at home in the universe and at one with the great Power that produced all that beauty.

The Zen search is for enlightenment, a total emancipation from every type of bondage—physical, mental, and spiritual. The revolution of Zen is the reevaluation of oneself as a spiritual entity. One feels "born again" as one's consciousness expands to infinity. Enlightenment, says Humphreys, is seeing into one's own nature, and then realizing that this nature is not one's own. "It is a foretaste of Cosmic Consciousness, of the conditions in which I and my Father are one."[23]

The Zen student can use any scripture or philosophy which helps him achieve enlightenment. If a person were chopping wood when it happened, he could continue to chop wood, if he wished. He knows he has achieved enlightenment when he finds that his physical, mental, and spiritual life are integrated into a harmonious whole.

There are moral teachings in the Zen decalogue. "In Soto Zen there is emphasis on teaching ethical precepts and on Bodhisattva practice of charity, tenderness, benevolence, and sympathy, for the sake of saving others. In Zen study associations, lay folk are given the ten precepts of right conduct—not to kill, steal, commit adultery, lie, or sell liquor; not to speak of others' shortcomings or to praise oneself; not to begrudge charity; not to be angry, not to speak ill of the Buddha or his order."[24]

Buddhist Divisiveness

Like all religions, Buddhism has some divisive characteristics. Within 100 years after Gautama Buddha's death, monks in the Bihar province were warned about ten heretical practices to avoid. The dissident monks founded their own order, and a civil war ensued. Fundamentalists wanted strict observance of laws and rituals; liberals said that more important than law or ritual was to enable each person to discover and nourish his potential Buddhahood. There were 227 rules for monks to obey, leaving little time for meditating on the achievement of Buddhahood. There was also a tendency for the monks to look down upon the common people as being too stupid to engage in advanced spiritual exercises.

By 200 years after Gautama's death there were at least eighteen varying Buddhist sects. Ironically, Gautama, who was lukewarm as to the existence of a supreme deity, himself came to be worshipped as God in several forms of Mahayana Buddhism.

Doctrinal disputes engendered their typical divisive rancor and hatred. Within the Hinayana camp arose the Personalists about 300 B.C. They adhered to the heterodox belief that a personal self really existed. By the seventh century A.D. Personalists monks numbered 60,000 out of a total of 200,000 Indian monks.

When the Mahayanas split from the Hinayanas there was much bitterness and hard feeling. Called heretics, the Mahayanas responded by labeling the Hinayanas with elitist epithets. The Hinayana concept that there can be only one Buddha at any period in history was challenged by the Mahayana doctrine of universal potential Buddhahood.

Within Mahayana Buddhism a rift was evident when missionaries tried to convert Tibetans. Indian Mahayanas taught that enlightenment was a gradual process, but their Chinese counterparts, perhaps influenced by Zen, argued that enlightenment can come in a flash. Neither side seemed to even attempt to understand the other's position. Two Tibetan monks committed suicide rather than accept the Indian view, which ultimately prevailed. A Chinese Buddhist visiting India decried the sectarian narrowness, declaring that "their contending utterances rise like the angry waves of the sea."

Some Zen Buddhists added a further problem when they held that enlightenment freed one from normal moral obligations. One even said that "if you are a real man, you may by all means drive off with the farmer's ox, or grab the food from a starving man."[25]

Buddhism's Influence

Japanese Shinto took over many important features from Buddhism, such as curved-roof temples and the use of sacred images. Often Buddhist temples and Shinto shrines were built alongside one another.

Radhakrishnan states that "two centuries before the Christian era Buddhism closed in on Palestine. The Essenes, the Mandeans, and the Nazarene sects are filled with its spirit."[26] Many parallels between Christ and Gautama are pointed out by Radhakrishnan. Both had virgin births, were great teachers, and condemned empty ritual as hypocrisy. Other similarities include triumphal entries, transfiguration scenes, and earthquakes at their deaths. Both preached self-denial and love of one's enemies. Since a Bodhisattva is one who sacrifices himself for others, Christ could be so considered.

The trinity concept is common to both faiths. Humphreys says that there are "a thousand trinities, with the Buddha in some cosmic aspect in the center," surrounded by a love aspect of deity on one side and a wisdom aspect of deity on the other. One such trinity consists of the Buddha's three bodies. The fleshly body is useful in approaching beginning adepts, the joyful body helps those having some understanding, and the spiritual body is for persons capable of the purest mode of spiritual ascension.

Sir Charles Eliot in 1921 declared that Buddhism must have been a profound influence upon Roman Catholic Christianity. "It is hard to believe," said Eliot, "that a collection of practices such as clerical celibacy, confession, the veneration of relics, and the use of the rosary and bells can have originated independently in both religions."[27] Eliot found no such parallels in Jewish, Syrian, or Egyptian antiquity.

Many Buddhist teachings sound strikingly modern. The concept of *sunya* or the void, can be a forerunner of contemporary particle physics, since it says that everything is relative to something else, and hence is devoid of independent reality. Ninian Smart shows that there is no clash between the spiritual and the scientific in Buddhism: "A modern Buddhist can certainly construct a very scientific framework of belief—the interpenetration of processes in the organic universe, the difference between processes themselves and the constructs which we impose upon the world, and the extravagant dimensions of the cosmos as perceived, though mythically, from earliest times."[28]

Sri Lanka feels it must displace Western materialistic social and individual values with the moral values found in the Buddhist *dhamma*. Speaking for many Buddhists, Sri Lankans assert that "in a society whose motive force is the acquisition of wealth by fair means or foul, the incidence of violence, crime, drunkenness, and gambling is not a matter for surprise. The production of wealth for social use instead of individual profit, the measuring of an individual in terms of his moral stature and not of his economic power, and of the nation's greatness in terms of the peace and prosperity of its inhabitants and not solely in terms of its balance of trade—these are values embodied in Buddhist character."[29]

Unitive Concepts in Taoism

Lao-Tzu, the legendary founder of Taoism, was born in China around 600 B.C. His chief teaching is this: Behind all change in the universe lies the Great Tao (the Way). Slowly but surely the Tao unfolds itself in the course of the world's evolution. By simplifying your life you can become at one with the universe. The Tao, the moral order of the universe, is a continuous field in which all physical and moral contraries are reconciled, and thus life's anguish and tensions are eliminated.

The *Tao Te Ching* (Classic of the Way and Virtue) advocates a primal unity. "The sage clasps the Primal Unity, testing by it everything under heaven. He does not contend, and for that very reason no one can contend with him."[30]

"Taoism," says William Newell, "looks back longingly to a unity which humans enjoyed before the Fall. The Fall imposed a false personality on humans' natural selves." Thereby humans careen ever farther from their pristine simplicity. Taoism is "a religion firmly rooted in a boundless optimism in human natural goodness. The world has a built-in harmony. Let things alone, and, like water, the harmony will seek its level."[31]

Like many religions, Taoism has a triune Godhead. An early trinity was T'ai I (the Grand Unity), T'ien I (the Heavenly One), and Ti I (the Earthly One). A later trinity, influenced by Buddhism, comprised the Jade Emperor, the First Principle of the Universe; the Mystic Jewel, who was in charge of Yin/Yang relationships; and Lao-Tzu, who was given the job of expanding the Way (the Tao).

A cardinal tenet of Taoism is *wu-wei,* or non-interference. Its symbol is water, which is soft and pliable, but strong enough to erode mountains and sink ships. This philosophy states, Quit pushing people around, for the harder you push, the harder they resist. As a citizen, let your neighbor alone. As a nation, let other countries alone. As a government, let the citizens alone. The result is peace and concord at home, in the nation, and abroad. The *Tao Te Ching* explains this philosophy:

> "The more prohibitions there are, the poorer the people will be. The more sharp weapons there are, the more benighted the land will grow. The more contrivances invented, the more

laws promulgated, the more thieves there will be. So long as I 'do nothing,' the people of themselves will be transformed."[32]

It can be seen that Taoism is a pacifistic religion, saying that violence breeds greater violence, and aggression harms the aggressor. If attacked, you must defend yourself, but if in the defense you engender hatred or vindictiveness, you will spread future wars. By keeping a compassionate attitude, you can convert an enemy into a friend.

The Interior Gods school of Taoism says that the spirit of the gods within a person's body will not cooperate with him unless he is virtuous and public spirited. This creed led to many altruistic acts: road and bridge repair, construction of orphanages, care for the poor, and ministry to the sick. In sum, Taoism has given China a majestic conception of the Way, an affirmation of the sanctity of life, an ethical doctrine of simplicity, and a formula for ways to overcome evil with good.

Divisive Concepts in Taoism

As expected, there have been divisive movements within Taoism. The Emperor Wen Ti (180-157 B.C.) used the religion to keep his people in servile submission to him. One result was that for the common people, the faith degenerated into magic and alchemy, a short cut to an elixir of immortality rather than a determined pursuance of the Way of love. A later emperor, Wu Tsung, persecuted not only Buddhists but also ordered 3,000 Nestorian Christian and Zoroastrian clergy to return to lay life.

A danger growing out of the doctrine of *wu-wei* is that people will either not try to improve themselves and society, or will put up with forms of government that are clearly oppressive or corrupt.

Unitive Doctrines in Confucianism

Confucius (551-479 B.C.), disgusted by the constant warfare among Chinese states and by the venality and tyranny of the rulers, evolved a series of teachings designed to bring peace and good government to his people. He said that by the age of fifty he was conscious of the decrees of Heaven, and that by sixty he was obedient to them.

To Confucius there were five cardinal virtues: respect for human dignity, magnanimity, proper conduct, disciplined power, and a feeling for beauty. For Confucius even the ethical was grounded in the esthetic. Moral order in the universe depended upon righteous conduct by the individual: "If there be righteousness in the heart, there will be beauty in the character. If beauty in the character, there will be harmony in the home. If harmony in the home, there will be order in the nation. If order in the nation, there will be peace in the world."[33]

Scholars, not warriors, were at the top of Confucian society. The Book of Rites describes five key social relationships, each having tenderness in the wielder of power, and an appreciative response in the follower:

1. Kindness in the father, filial piety in the child.
2. Gentility in the older brother, humility and respect in the younger.
3. Righteousness in the husband, obedience in the wife.
4. Humaneness in elders, deference in juniors.
5. Benevolence in rulers, loyalty in subjects.

Mencius (370-289 B.C.) ranks next to Confucius in the hearts of many Chinese. Mencius was noted for his gentleness, optimism, pacifism, and love of wisdom. He believed in innate human goodness, saying that every person possesses a sense of mercy, righteousness, and respect. The sage is the only one fit to govern, said Mencius, for he understands "the unity of the ways of Heaven and men," and therefore bases his rule on righteousness and dignity.

Chinese Syncretism

Mo Ti (486-390 B.C.) preached a doctrine of universal brotherhood based upon persons doing the will of Shang-Ti, the heavenly sovereign, from whom redemptive love and benevolence flowed out to all people. If a man steals a pig, Mo Ti observed, we put him in jail, but if he steals an empire, we worship him as our ruler or even our god. Aggressive war is an offense against Heaven, Mo Ti taught, and thus hatred and discrimination, the causes of war, must be replaced by the all-embracing concept of universal love.

Following centuries of warfare, T'ai Tsung (A.D. 597-649), adopted an ascetic way of life and stopped making war. Instead of harsh punishment for robbers, he said, "if I diminish expenditures, lighten taxes, and employ only honest officials, so that the people have clothing enough, this will do more to abolish robbery."[34]

T'ai Tsung's outlook on religion was catholic. He supported not only the Chinese faiths of Buddhism, Confucianism, and Taoism, but also adherents of Judaism, Manichaeism, Christianity, and Zoroastrianism. He gave these adherents protection and freedom from taxes, at a time when Europe was stagnating in theological darkness. It is perhaps no coincidence that during this period China was the best governed and the most prosperous nation in the world.

Chinese syncretism achieved a unique unity. Many Chinese were at once Buddhists, Confucianists, and Taoists. Some believers felt that the Tao was the common element in all three faiths. Others said that the Tao was the middle way, steering the faiths into a course between asceticism and materialism. One Buddhist monk founded a sect which had images of Lao-Tzu, Confucius, and Buddha on the altar. Wing-Tsit Chan said that "Buddhist deities became Taoist gods and vice versa. Many 'temples for the Three Sages' were built. The masses frequented Confucian temples, Taoist shrines, and Buddhist temples without discrimination."[35] In this way unitive religion in China has been a source of concord.

Divisive Religion in China

Despite the unitive ideals espoused by China's three leading faiths, the nation experienced centuries of war, exploitation of the poor, mistreatment of women, and adherence to subhuman rituals. For example, the king's retinue was commonly buried with him, as human sacrifices, until the seventeenth century. Civil rights were commonly denied to prisoners, and there was no tradition of due process of law. Many of these instances of cruelty, however, grew not out of the application of the religious principles but rather out of a failure to apply them. This is vastly different from situations in which the religious beliefs themselves are the cause of the mistreatment.

Unitive Religion in Japan

The traditional Japanese religion is Shinto (from Chinese, Shen-Tao, the Way of the Gods). Unusual is the role played by feminine deities in Japanese religion. The typical male chauvinism is missing here. Also, the plurality of gods suggests that the early Japanese saw the divine in every aspect of their daily lives. The *kami,* or gods, were supernatural spirits who ruled over nature. They were pleased when humans practiced virtue and sincerity. Shinto showed a great reverence for nature. Since humans are nature's objects, and nature is inherently good, it follows that a human being in his deepest nature is divine. The three cardinal Shinto virtues are benevolence, courage, and purity.

To eliminate religious conflict Prince Regent Shotoku announced a synthesis: "'Shinto is the source and root of the Way; Confucianism, the branch, teaches humans the Middle Way; Buddhism, the flower and fruit, teaches humans the Final Way. To love one in preference to another only shows man's selfish passion. The introduction of another system of faith will add a new cubit to the stature of the nation's mind, for each new creed enlightens the old."[36]

Japanese religious toleration is seen in The Oracle of the Sun God (A.D. 1650): "The Japanese God of Heaven manifests himself in different forms in many lands. In India he was born as Gautama Buddha, and in China as the three sages: Confucius, Lao-Tzu, and Yen Hui. Why does one and the same God assume such varied forms? Because being one God, He desires to preach the selfsame truth, and takes differently appearing forms so that He may best adapt His teaching to the understanding of every person."[37]

Japan's defeat in World War II had far-reaching religious implications. The divine authority possessed by the emperor had little value in defending the islands against American atomic bombs. General Douglas MacArthur issued an order outlawing State Shinto, the form that drew upon public funds for support. Two weeks later Emperor Hirohito made a historic statement: "The ties between us and our people have always stood upon mutual trust and affection. They do not depend upon mere legends and myths. They are not predicated upon the false conception that the emperor is divine and that the Japanese people are superior to other races and are fated to rule the world."[38]

Thirteen separate sects of Shinto continue in force in Japan. Shinto's amazing survivability is probably due to its lack of a dogmatic scripture, its ability to draw positive aspects from other faiths, and its appeal to a people who love art, beauty, nature, and simplicity.

Divisive Religion in Japan

Japan's "Christian century" began when the Roman Catholic missionary Francis Xavier arrived there in 1549. Portuguese vessels brought silk and gold from Macao, and Christianity at first was given a cordial reception. But in 1587 the military ruler Hideyoshi, suspecting that the Christian clergy were forerunners of an external conquest, as they had been in Manila, issued an edict expelling all Christian missionaries.

Persecution increased when the first Tokugawa Shogun, Ieyasu, came to power in 1614. In the Shimabara Rebellion of 1637-38 many thousands of native Japanese Christians were killed. In 1639 all Christians were ordered to leave Japan.

Japanese claims of religious exclusivity had fed an incipient jingoistic nationalism. In 1369 Kitabatake Chikafusa had written: "Great Yamato is a divine nation. It is only our land whose foundations were first laid by the divine ancestor."[39]

In the 18th century several scholars led a Shinto revival designed to purify the faith of foreign accretions. Buttressing their position were two powerful myths: that the Japanese had a pristine state of nature before Chinese influence was felt, and that Japanese gods had made the Japanese people superior to all other human beings.

Motoori Norinaga declared that "from the central truth that the Mikado is the direct descendant of the gods, the tenet that Japan ranks far above all other countries is a natural consequence. No other nation is entitled to equality with her, and all are bound to do homage to the Japanese sovereign and pay tribute to him."[40]

The Way of the Gods (Shinto) fit in nicely with the Way of the Warrior (Bushido). The samurai, the feudal military class, observed this chivalric code, which included fighting to one's death to protect one's superior, and if one made a bad mistake, to commit hara-kiri. Kamikaze pilots in World War II were fulfilling a religious as well as a patriotic mission, an act understandable to those Moslems who believe in the *jihad,* or holy war.

Judaism's Evolving Monotheism

Like all great religion, Judaism is a syncretic faith. The Jews (named after Judah, great-grandson of Abraham), were greatly indebted to their neighbors for key religious concepts. When Abraham came to Canaan about 2000 B.C. he brought with him many of the stories recounted in the Bible. "The story of creation in Genesis 2, the story of Eden, the accounts of the antediluvian patriarchs, the flood story, and the story of the Tower of Babel were all brought from northwestern Mesopotamia to the West by the Hebrews."[41]

Conquest of Canaan by the Jews led to much borrowing from the Canaanites. Specific influences are found in architecture, arts and crafts, language, music, and religion. Rituals were borrowed from Canaan, as well as many of the names for God: Adonai (my Lord), El (Power), and Elyon (Most High).

When the Israelites took over parts of Canaan, said Professor Adrio König, their "Lord appropriated some of the functions of the Canaanite gods, and in this way revealed His own being and qualities more clearly to Israel."[42] One Canaanite function he took over was as president of the pantheon of Gods (Psalm 82). Like Baal, he makes crops prosper and gives fruitfulness. Psalm 29 was probably originally a hymn to Baal as the god of storm.

Many Jewish feasts derived from the Canaanite calendar of feasts. The Jews, however, put their distinctive mark upon the main elements of their faith. Yahweh was a term of Arabian origin, but as the Jews came to know Him His character improved. As God of the Jews, He took over Baal's good features but not his evil ones. Later, Yahweh also incorporated aspects of Greek deities, such as becoming the ground of reality. As Yahweh appropriated the functions of other gods, they disappeared. Also, God became personal. Whereas formerly people chose gods, Yahweh chooses people. And He is incomparable—He cannot be portrayed in images.

"The biblical idea of God," says Joseph Campbell, "must be clearly set apart, as representing a principle nowhere else exclusively affirmed: namely, of the *absolute transcendence* of divinity. There can therefore be no question, in either Jewish, Christian, or Islamic orthodoxy, of seeking God and finding God either in the world or in oneself. That is the way of the repudiated natural religions of the remainder of mankind. The mythic imagery of the Bible bears a message of its own that may not always be the one verbalized in the text. For this book is a carrier of symbols borrowed from the deep past, which is of many tongues."[43]

Judaism's contribution to world religion is inestimable. Directly, it can be seen as a revelation concerning God's nature (including the important concept of monotheism), laws of ethical conduct, and inspired religious prophecy. Indirectly, such other religions as Christianity and Islam are built upon a Judaic base.

Divisiveness as God's Chosen People

Are the Jews God's specially chosen people? Rabbi Arthur Hertzberg says this doctrine is both a mystery to the Jews and a scandal to all non-Jews. He feels that each notion of a "chosen people" has degenerated into some idea of a master race. Judaism, he says, is torn between two mighty strains: the Jews are God's chosen people, but God, being One, will accept all who sincerely accept Him and try to obey His laws.

The idea that God prefers one part of His creation over another part is demeaning to God. Can He lack elementary principles of fairness and justice? Peter did not think so, for he said (in Acts 10:34): "God shows no partiality, but in every nation anyone who fears Him and does what is right is acceptable to Him."

Who owns Palestine? God. Yet religious enthusiasts of several faiths kill one another to possess God's land, and then make matters worse by saying they are doing it to please God. This kind of arrant hypocrisy needs to be unmasked as the most flagrant brand of divisive religion.

One way of demonstrating chosenness by God is by loving all of His creation. A so-called chosen faith can be a light to other religions, showing how love can humanize religious practices, converting divisive religion into unitive religion. Kaufmann Kohler (1843-1926), a leader in U.S. Reform Judaism, saw chosenness as only one stage in mankind's moral evolution. He said that "it must be considered a divine call persisting through all ages and encompassing all lands, a continuous activity of the spirit."[44]

Unitive Forces in Early Judaism

Since humans are created in God's image, Judaism places great stress upon human dignity. Jews are taught that God loves mercy and justice, and that our job is to build a just and merciful society. We are to do this by hallowing all of life, so that every meal, every job, and every daily act reflects the divine unity of all being: "I the Lord practice kindness, justice, and righteousness in the earth, for in these things I delight" (Exodus 31:16-17). One is never justified in treating a fellow human as anything less than the image of God.

Rabbi Hertzberg quotes a series of rules of conduct taken from the Passover Haggadah: Avoid arguments, keep away from envy and hatred; do not be a drunkard or a glutton. Also, "distribute your money according to God's will. Belittle your good deeds and magnify your transgressions. Serve in love. Do not raise your hand against your neighbor."[45]

Hertzberg details other Jewish beliefs. One must atone for one's sins. One should do one's best not to be a burden to the community. This may involve hard work, self denial, and if need be, suffering. If you cannot help a beggar, soothe him with words, for he already has a heavy heart.

Divisive Forces in Early Judaism

At one time in their history the Jews adopted the Canaanite practice of sacrificing their children at the foundation of their important buildings (I Kings 16:34). Human sacrifices were offered in return for victory. "The practice of devoting a recalcitrant foe to destruction as a kind of gigantic holocaust to the national deity was apparently universal among early Semites."[46]

The Old Testament is replete with examples of Yahweh calling for a "holy war." In Judges 5 Deborah's song celebrates Yahweh's assistance in destroying Sisnera and his Canaanites. Deuteronomy 20:17 gives directions for the waging of holy wars: "Utterly destroy the Hittites, Amorites, Canaanites, Perizzites, Hivites, and Jebusites." Deuteronomy 7 orders the Jews, with Yahweh's help, to "utterly destroy the enemy, and show no mercy unto them." Orders allegedly from Yahweh went so far as to advocate the bashing of infants' heads against rocks! The "holy war" provided imagery for prophetic oracles, as in Joel 2 and Zephaniah 1. Frequently (as in Deuteronomy 30:15) the religious war is defined as one in which the Israelites represent life and goodness, while the enemy stands for evil and death.

Unitive Teachings of the Prophets

The prophets of Israel are without parallel as brave spokesmen for God against the worldliness and the narrowness of their people. Repeatedly they asserted that what God wanted was not ritual but justice and morality. It is surprising that more of them were not put to death for their frank condemnation of the Jews for forsaking their God. However, "the very nature of the spiritual communion between the prophet and his God led to the spiritualization of His relationship to man in general."[47]

Chapter 18 of Ezekiel is a great expression of the worth of human dignity under God, who promises to judge people according to their deeds. The righteous shall surely live, says the Lord, if they do not defile their neighbor's wife, nor oppress anyone, nor rob, nor fail to give bread to the hungry. The wicked, refusing to do these things, will surely perish.

Hosea called Israel a harlot for deserting the Lord. While defending Yahweh, one still had to observe certain humane rules of conduct. For his wanton cruelty, Jehu was destroyed. 'The Lord said, I will punish the house of Jehu for the blood of Jezreel, and I will put an end to the kingdom of the house of Israel" (Hosea 1:4).

Amos quoted God as saying, "I hate, I despise your feasts, and I take no delight in your solemn assemblies" (Amos 5:21). Amos shows God to be a universal deity, and not just Yahweh of the Israelites: "Did I not also bring up the Philistines from Caphtor and the Syrians from Kir? Am I not also the God of the Ethiopians?" (9:7). Amos was convinced that God was sovereign over "all the families of the earth "(3:2), and that Israel, by failing to live up to its part of the covenant, had dissolved its special status as the chosen people of God.

In the words of E.W. Heaton, "the moral obligation of which all persons are aware (later called natural law) is identical with the personal will of Israel's God, who exercises universal sovereignty and holds all people accountable for their conduct. Any crime against human decency is an affront to Yahweh's universal moral sovereignty and will be punished. Morality in

Amos' teaching is an index to the character of God, and the pursuit of goodness the primary way of knowing and serving Him."[48]

Malachi (in 1:11) says that the Gentiles' innocent worship of God is more acceptable to Him than the elaborate but careless Jewish worship. And he postulates a brotherhood of man under the Fatherhood of God: "Have we all not one Father? Hath not one God created us all? Why do we deal treacherously with our brothers, forsaking our fathers' covenants?" (2:10).

The prophets properly applauded Cyrus and other Persian rulers who were tolerant of monotheists such as the Israelites. Isaiah went so far as to call Cyrus a messiah (Isaiah 45:1). When Cyrus permitted them to return to Jerusalem, over 40,000 Jews returned to their homeland in 537 B.C.

Since he sought world peace, Cyrus respected the religious views of the people he conquered. He was conscious that "the ancient world, civilized cities and barbarian hordes, dimly obey inner forces which strive to merge in a common humanity. He was always magnanimous to his defeated enemies, to whom he extended the hand of friendship."[49]

The Diaspora

In the second century B.C. Antiochus IV Epiphanes, King of Syria, tried to get the Jews converted to the Greek religion. When Jewish women had baby sons circumcised, he had both mothers and sons killed. He attempted to get the Jews to worship Zeus in their temple in Jerusalem. His soldiers killed Jews celebrating the sabbath. He had a Jewish mother and her seven sons tortured to death for refusing to eat pork.

But the Jews also brought grief upon themselves. John Hyrcanus, a high priest who was the second ruler in the Hasmonean dynasty (c. 135 B.C.), extended the frontiers of Palestine at a great cost to Jewish values. "He converted the pagan Idumeans and Galileans to Judaism by the sword. From Idumea came one of the greatest scourges of the Jews, Herod the Great." The sons of Hyrcanus also ruled cruelly. Aristobulus murdered his mother and his brother. Janneus wrought vengeance on the Pharisees for inviting the Seleucids in to battle against his Sadducee reign. The revenge taken by Janneus against his rival Pharisees was "as bloody as any in history," said Max Dimont.[50]

Divisiveness among the Jews led to their being driven out of the land that had been their home for nearly two thousand years. Fearful that violent acts would cause Roman retaliation, moderate Jews drove the passionate Zealots out of Jerusalem. The Zealots countered by getting reinforcements from converted Edomites in Idumea. The combined forces butchered the moderate leaders, with no trials and no mercy. This Jewish civil war so weakened the Jews that Titus was able to capture Jerusalem in A.D. 70. Driven out of their homeland, the Jews had no resting place for the next 1700 years. They survived as separate enclaves in Christian and Moslem countries.

Their patience in enduring vicious and ubiquitous anti-Semitism is one of the great miracles of religious history. There were many causes of this religious animosity. Their spirit of freedom caused the Jews to revolt against tyrannical rulers. Their religious separateness kept them from being absorbed socially. They avoided public feasts, games, and the theater as being pagan influences. Their frequently successful proselytizing was resented by non-Jews. Their prowess in business made them marks of envy and jealousy.

How did the Jews manage to survive in the Diaspora? Through living in cultures where different gods were worshipped, Judaism absorbed some of the better teachings of competing religions. Also, living under the rule of various conquerors, they had learned to get by through separating their allegiance to church and state. They could observe civil laws insofar as they did not violate their sacred laws. By strenuous effort they learned to support two communities, the Jewish and the Gentile.

As their theology grew more tolerant, the Jews became more acceptable to the Gentiles. The Seder Eliahu Rabbah taught that "the spirit of holiness rests upon each person according to the deed that each does, whether Jew or non-Jew, man or woman." The Exodus Rabbah stated that "the Holy One does not disqualify any creature; He accepts everyone. The gates are always open, and whoever wants to enter may enter."[51]

Nevertheless the Jews had the problem of maintaining their religious and cultural unity, despite being widely spread through many lands. They accomplished this through a conscious effort.

The Hebrew language was standardized, for use in the same form by Jews everywhere. The synagogue liturgy was also made

Religious Doctrine: Helpful or Hurtful? 79

standard. Any ten male Jews living within commuting distance were asked to establish a religious community. As soon as they had 120 adult males they were to set up their own courts. Jews sold into slavery had to be ransomed within seven years by Jews in the nearest community.

Charity, with dignity, was to be provided to all needy Jews, who were told to never ask for help from the state. Generally the Jews were asked by their leaders not to proselytize actively. They agreed to obey all state laws, provided those laws did not arbitrarily forbid a religious practice, or compel them to murder, practice incest, or worship idols. They promised to fight to protect their nation (even against Jews on the opposite side), but not support an aggressive war.

Philo of Alexandria, a contemporary of Christ, was a Jewish philosopher who achieved a synthesis of Judaism, Christianity, and Platonism. He shaped Judaism around a metaphysical framework that he found in Plato and the Stoics. He said that the Jewish prophets had possessed the Holy Spirit, and he praised the Essenes for their high ethical standards. Philo said that humans found God in two ways: through prophecy, as in the Jewish experience, and through inner mystical meditation, a path which Paul developed in his Christian epistles. Philo spoke of the divine image in man as mediated by the Logos, "the firstborn Son of God" or "the second Deity."

The Jews were now busy codifying their scriptures. By A.D. 220 the Mishnah (Repetition) was completed. By this time the Torah, the law of Moses, was virtually inapplicable, so the Mishnah quoted the rabbis' interpretation of the scriptures. Another holy writing was the Gemara, which included the Halakah (study of the unwritten law) and the Haggadah (rabbinic historical and moral instruction). The combination of the Mishnah and the Gemara comprised the Talmud, which in 63 volumes was completed by A.D. 500 and has been a standard Jewish religious authority ever since. One of the quotations in the Talmud shows its unitive teaching. When the Israelites want to sing for joy over the Egyptians drowning in the Red Sea, they are admonished by God: "How can you sing songs, when My handiwork is drowning?"

Divisive Elements in the Talmud

The Talmud also contains elements of divisive religion. Max Dimont states that the anti-Semitic laws of medieval Christianity "were patterned after Old Testament and Talmudic laws against non-Jews." The Talmud said that Jews were not to be governed by non-Jews, and that they were not to socialize with non-Jews or sell land to them.

The famous historian Edward Gibbon, betraying a bias, reported that from the reign of Nero to that of Antoninus Pius the Jews broke out in "the most furious massacres and insurrections. Humanity is shocked at the horrid cruelties which they committed in the cities of Egypt, Cyprus, and Cyrene, where they dwelt in treacherous friendship with the unsuspecting natives."[52] Gibbon applauded the Roman soldiers for restraining this "race of fanatics."

In the period around A.D. 200 Christians were in a dilemma as to how to regard Judaism. Christians felt they needed the Old Testament as the foundation of their religion, but they found it hard to forgive the Jews for repudiating Jesus. They tried to depict the Jews as followers of Ahab, Dathan, and Manasseh rather that of Moses, David, and Isaiah. "A wall of misunderstanding and hate was erected by the narrow zealotries of the two faiths," said Jacob Agus. "In the turbulence of passion, the light of either faith became invisible to those whose eyes were accustomed from childhood to the illumination of the other."[53] The unity of the Judeo-Christian tradition was being lost.

Jewish Unitive Medieval Theology

Saadia ben Joseph (882-942), head of a Talmudic academy, wrote "The Song of Unity," telling of God's immanence and omnipresence in all of His creation. Bahya ibn Pakuda encompassed his traditional Jewish piety in a doctrine steeped in Neoplatonic and Sufi asceticism. Abraham bar Hiyya of Barcelona wrote of the Neoplatonic doctrine of the soul's ascent, in a work showing Christian eschatological influence.

The Jewish writer Pinchas Lapide said that "Mohammed was recognized by Jewish scholars as early as the 11th century as a prophet on a par with the non-Jewish biblical prophets, such as

Job." Perhaps some day modern theology will catch up with medieval theology.

Shlomo Itzhaki, also known as Rashi (1040-1105), was a pro-Christian rabbi. Fond of Christian songs, Rashi used their melodies in his synagogue. "Rashi's commentaries had a great influence on Christian theologians, especially Nicholas de Lyra, who in turn had a profound effect on the religious development of young Martin Luther."[54]

Moses ben Maimon, also called Maimonides (1135-1204), was one of the greatest of all Jewish theologians. His writings show the influence of Aristotle, Philo, and the Moslems Avicenna and al-Farabi. His *Guide for the Perplexed* rejected the literal anthropomorphism of the Old Testament for a more esoteric explanation of creation. In an Oriental mode he pointed out that any effort to define God would be foredoomed to failure as a limitation of His infinity. He said that the teachings of Christ and Mohammed tend to lead mankind towards perfection. Imagine this outlook in the modern Middle East!

A follower of Maimonides, Abraham Abulafia, had views so similar to those found in Hinduism that his works have been called a Judaized Yoga. The mind, he says, must purge itself of pressing everyday concerns, for "he who is full of himself has no room for God." At this time Isaac of Acre said that the person who enters into "the mystery of adhesion to God, called *devekut,* attains equanimity, and then loneliness, and from there he comes to the Holy Spirit and to prophecy."[55]

Jewish moral standards were very high in medieval Europe. Despite their ostracism, Jews were often put into positions of high financial trust because of their reputation for honesty. Seldom were Jews guilty of a violent crime. Jewish family life was exemplary, and sexual perversion was rarely found among their numbers. They took care of their own, with hospitals, orphanages, poorhouses, and aid to widows. Rabbis preached that it was much worse to cheat a Christian than a Jew. The Talmud recommended extending Jewish charity to non-Jews. Christians often tried to raise funds by citing the extreme generosity of the Jews.

Jewish Mysticism

Jewish mysticism provided a unitive response to the dreadful debacle of divisive religion as seen in medieval Christian anti-Semitism. Their unprecedented persecution did little to shake the Jews' deep faith in God. If materialistic Messianism was to be denied them, they sought it in the spiritual realm. A major effect of their expulsion from Spain and Portugal was to move the Kabala, the source of their mystical religion, from an esoteric to a popular doctrine. More even than the Old Testament, the Kabala gave the Jews deep consolation in a time of great distress.

Mysticism is as old as Judaism. It existed before Moses, but the Law tended to suppress it. It was kept alive by select mystics. "It fed on non-canonized prophecy, Zoroastrian resurrection mythology, numerology, and gnostic heresies."[56]

The word Kabala comes from the Hebrew *kabeil* (to receive) and hence it means "revelation" or "tradition." It has two chief books: *The Book of Formation* (8th century A.D.) describes the ecstatic experience of God, and the *Zohar* (Book of Splendor) of the 13th century has occult and metaphysical speculation on God, the universe, and science.

Merkabah mysticism had flourished among teachers of the Mishnah in the first and second centuries A.D. "In opposition to the radical dualism of heretical Jewish Gnosticism, however, it was careful to stress the unity of God. Its main concern was the mystical contemplation of the Merkabah (throne of God) described in Ezekiel 1."[57]

Rabbi Joseph Karo (1488-1575) wrote the Shulhan Arukh, the standard code of Jewish law. He left Turkey for Safed in upper Galilee, where he founded a school of mystics. He taught that suffering had cleansed the souls of individual Jews and had elevated the community of Judaism in the eyes of God and mankind. After all, even the Shekinah, God's Holy Spirit, had suffered exile because of human sin.

Continual suffering from persecution had given the Jews a strong sense of unity. This was now reflected in their theology. "In union there is redemption," said the Kabalists. They tried to point the way back to the original unity that had existed in the world before the Fall. The essence of Kabalist teaching is to explain how the present imperfect world came to be, and how its imperfection, which is really disunion or separation from God, can be overcome. To know creation is to know how we can backtrack to God. The mystical path is thus "a reversal of the process by which we emanated from God." The Kabalists did not feel that mystical insight was their private monopoly. The purer anyone's insight is, they said, the closer it is to the original common stock of mankind's knowledge.

The core of Kabalist teaching concerns the Sefirot, or divine sparks emanated from God. We can understand God because we contain within us channels of light (Sefirot) which came out of creation. One of these sparks is the Shekinah, the female presence of God. Unfortunately, the left side of the Sefirot rebelled and separated from God, bringing evil into the universe. The Shekinah is now in exile, appearing only in isolated places and persons.

The ten Sefirot form the world of union, as distinct from the world of separation, that is, the lower order of created beings. "The unity of the divine life is expressed in the union between the first and last Sefirot: the Supreme Crown and His Shekinah. The present unredeemed state of the world is explained due to rupture of that supernal union."[58]

Some day God will again be One, and further, we humans have the responsibility of hastening the coming of that great day by our virtuous conduct and by our attachment *(devekut)* to God. *Devekut* (being joined) is the goal of all religious searching. Pure action in this world strengthens the upper roots in the world above. By obeying divine commandments one prepares one's individual soul, giving it its celestial garment for its final eternal life.

The glory of God and His first creation is "the great radiance called Shekinah, and is identical with the *ruah ha-kodesh,* the 'holy spirit,' out of whom there speaks the voice and word of God. This primeval light of divine glory is later revealed to prophets and mystics in various forms, in accordance with the demands of the hour."[59] The Shekinah is God's communicator. A person cannot speak to God, but can to the Shekinah. In *The Book of Life,* the Shekinah is defined as the divine will, the Holy Spirit, the word of God (Logos), a spirit inherent in all creatures.

An anonymous book, *The Revealed Mysteries,* in 1552 said that Jewish suffering could help save mankind: "This is the secret why Israel is fated to be enslaved by all the Gentiles of the world: In order that it may uplift those sparks which have also fallen among them. Therefore it was necessary that Israel should be scattered to the four winds in order to lift everything up."[60] Thus, the Diaspora was God's design to bring about the salvation of all human beings.

Isaac Luria (1534-1572) was a leading Safed Kabalist. He taught that "the seven lowest Sefirot were unable to contain the awesome might of the light of creation. Like glass beakers they shattered. The sacred sparks of splendor became mixed with shells of impurity. Each person must help restore the holy shards back to their original Source. We do this through good deeds and meditative prayers."[61] The divine sparks are a unifying principle, since they are found in everyone.

It is no wonder there is religious diversity in the world, said Luria, for "the lights of the Sefirot each reveal God under a different aspect." Salvation, or *tikkun,* means restitution, or reintegration of the original whole by reuniting the scattered divine sparks. "The Lurianic Kabala from about 1630 onwards became the true *theologia mystica* of Judaism," said Scholem. "The doctrine of *tikkun* raised every Jew to the rank of a protagonist in the great process of restitution."[62] Cosmic harmony could be restored through the collective organized effort of individual Jews. Despite material suffering, the individual's concept of self-worth was enhanced at the realization that he had a role to play in the complete self-realization of God.

Partly to understand God's sense of justice, Luria believed in the transmigration of souls. Divine justice might be delayed for a new reincarnation. In almost a Hindu sense, whoever sins injures not only himself but also that part of him which belongs to another. One must love one's neighbor as oneself, because the other is oneself. Luria further taught that all souls that have fulfilled their respective moral laws (613 for Jews but other numbers for other faiths) are exempt from transmigration, and await reintegration into Adam's soul at the end of time.

One of Luria's concepts sounds intriguing to modern physicists. Luria believed in *Zimzum,* or contraction, meaning that after creation God withdrew Himself from the cosmos to make room for the world. The lower six Sefirot (minus the Shekinah) were separated at the Breaking of the Vessels. Modern superstring theory, believed in by many particle physicists, says that the world began with ten dimensions, six of which retracted after the Big Bang. Modern physicists, says Malcolm W. Browne, are willing to risk something like Kabalistic mysticism in order to try to explain the mysteries of the universe. Superstring theory assumes that if we could perceive the universe in its ten-dimensional totality, we would see a new symmetry, and the puzzling array of particles and forces would be revealed as varying facets of one cohesive whole.

Jewish mysticism led to improved ethical conduct. Rabbi Samuel Laniado of Aleppo said that "since the soul of each person and the soul of his neighbor are both carved out of the same Throne of Splendor, your neighbor is as you." Thus, to love your neighbor is to love God, for He made both of you. Rabbi Isaac of Worka declared that "in every person there is a spark of the divine soul. The power of evil in humans darkens this flame and almost puts it out. Brotherly love among humans rekindles the soul and brings it closer to its Source."[63]

Spinoza's Unitive Religion

A lens grinder in Holland, Baruch Spinoza (1632-1677) developed a high order of unitive theology. When he was asked if he believed in God, Albert Einstein replied, "I believe in Spinoza's God, who reveals Himself in the harmony of all being."

The center of Spinoza's religious thought came from medieval Jewish mysticism. He said that "as soon as the mind finds itself in living unity with the eternal Nature of things, and views all things from their center in God, it is led to its highest blessedness."[64]

Spinoza agreed with the Christian Scholastics that we can know God but not all of His attributes. He felt Thomas Aquinas was right in saying that it was absurd (however convenient) to use masculine pronouns in referring to God. He conceded, with Maimonides, that most qualities we ascribe to God are weak analogies based on human traits. "He who lives under the guidance of reason," Spinoza said, "endeavors as much as possible to repay hatred, rage, and contempt with love and nobleness." The Bible, he said, contains a moral code that has led many people to live good lives, but misused it has produced many bad effects. Spinoza conceded that the Jews had a special revelation from God. "No one except Christ communed with God mind to mind," he added. "Justice and charity are the surest signs of the true Catholic faith. Where these are found, Christ really is, and where they are lacking, Christ is not."[65]

The Syncretic Origin of Christianity

Evelyn Underhill, the great authority on mysticism, found a score of influences that helped influence early Christianity. She said that "it accepts and elucidates Greek, Jewish, and Indian thought, fuses them in a coherent theology, and says to all speculative thinkers, 'Whom therefore you ignorantly worship, Him declare I unto you.'"

Will Durant further traced contributing sources. He said that the Greek mysteries were absorbed into the symbolism of the mass. From Egypt came the ideas of a divine trinity, the Last Judgment, and mystic theosophy. From Phrygia came the worship of the Great Mother, as seen in the veneration of Mary. Salvation figures included the resurrection of Adonis in Syria and of Dionysus in Thrace. From Persia came millenarianism, the final conflagration, and the dualism of Satan and God.

Paul Tillich felt that Christianity was indebted to the Stoics for moral principles, to the Romans for legal concepts, to the Germans for feudal institutions, and to various pagan tribes for the concept of the veneration of saints.

Specifically, of course, Christianity was an outgrowth of Judaism. From the Jews came the belief in one God, creator and ruler of the universe, a loving but a demanding Father. Judaism also contributed moral and ethical precepts from the Old Testament, the Jewish scripture. The Christian church service was an adaptation of Jewish worship in the synagogue. Specific concepts from Judaism include Satan, evil demons, hell, angels, and the earthly millennium.

Christ as a Unitive Figure

Joseph Campbell said that "the recurrent mythological event of the death and resurrection of a god, which had been for millenniums the central mystery of all the great religions of the Near East, became in Christian thought an event in time, which had occurred but once, and marked the moment of the transformation of history."[66]

Christianity was unique in incorporating its ideals in a historic person. There had never been a Mithra, a Great Mother, an Isis, a Dionysus, or an Apollo. "Ideas must be incorporated in a person before they can effectively move mankind," said Angus. "Christianity could boast of a founder of unique holiness and power. The ethics of Jesus defied challenge. His character required no burnishing. He was and remained Leader to His followers."[67]

"Christ," said George Brantl, "realized perfectly the union of love between God and man. The commandment to love summons people to incarnate God in each human life, to unite the finite will to the divine. Christ is the model. The virtues of Christ are the measures of a person's perfection, and His sacrifice is the measure of a person's love."[68]

The core of Christ's teaching was the proclamation of the coming of God's kingdom on earth. All through his message the infinite worth of the human personality is extolled. Christ expanded the Jewish messianic kingdom into a universal kingdom of the Father of all human beings. And this kingdom is as much of the present as of the future. It exists here and now for all who accept God as the King of their lives.

When Jesus said, "I and the Father are one," he implied being one in spirit, in purpose, in will, and in love. Jesus revealed God's Spirit to be at the core of a person's true being. To realize this is to be saved: saved from our sinful nature, from ignorance, and from selfishness; saved for loving, for sacrificial giving, and for living in unity with God.

St. Paul understood that liberty can lead to unity. Quakers, who require no credal confession, are often more closely unified than churches with strict doctrinaire confessions. Division results in a church, Paul said, when believers abandon the Holy Spirit and deify their own sinful selfish preferences. Paul, in the words of John Noss, "demonstrated the power of the Christian religion to bring together Jew, Greek, and Roman; mystic, legalist, and rationalist—all under a common sense of their vital spiritual community in Christ."

Divisiveness in the Early Christian Church

"It was a miracle," said Max Dimont, "that the Christians survived their first 300 years. One schism after another within their ranks threatened to obliterate them." Divisiveness has characterized Christianity throughout its history. Here are a few examples.

In what way was Jesus Christ God Incarnate? An aged abbot named Eutyches in A.D. 448 said that Christ had been of two natures (God and man) before their union in the Incarnation but of one nature (Monophysite) thereafter. His view was condemned, reinstated, and then again condemned. Those who followed him split from Rome to form the Coptic Christian Church, found today in Ethiopia, Somalia, and India. Each side accused the other of being divisive heretics. The historian Edward Gibbon said that Christians split hairs rather than practice the love of Christ. "In the pursuit of a metaphysical quarrel many thousands were slain," Gibbon reported.

If Christ is God, is His mother Mary the mother of God? No, said Nestorius, bishop of Constantinople, explaining that Mary was the mother only of Christ's human nature. When Nestorians were declared to be heretical, they fled eastward to survive today in Iran, India, and China.

Roman Catholic veneration of Mary is a divisive element in Christianity. Most Protestants do not accept Mary as "conceived without the sin of Adam, the Mediatrix of all graces, Coredemptrix of man, and Queen of Heaven."[69] They would not accept her Immaculate Conception, declared by Pope Pius IX in 1854, or her physical Assumption, stated as a doctrine which all Roman Catholics must believe by Pope Pius XII in 1950.

The doctrine of the Holy Trinity has been one of the most divisive factors in Christendom. How are the three facets of God similar, how different, and how do they interrelate? It is unfortunate that the Bible has so little to say on this subject.

Holy scriptures could never serve as the sole rule of faith to Roman Catholics, as many Protestants later alleged they did for them. There were several reasons for this. For example, for the first several hundred years there was no authoritative scripture. The Bible also had some inconsistencies, such as the varying genealogies and birth stories of Jesus. The census of Quirinius took place ten years after the death of Herod, who persecuted Jesus. Further, most believers were illiterate, and thus had to rely on someone else to read the Bible for them.

Papal infallibility leads to Christian division. Bishop Cyprian (200-258) said that the Holy Spirit was carried in the bishops, in their inheritance from the apostles. He then concluded that "there is no salvation outside the Church," a dogma that no first-century Christian church would ever have asserted, said Paul Tillich, since the earliest churches were not institutions of salvation but rather communities of saints.

Christianity became increasingly intolerant of every other avenue to God. Forgetting the forgiving spirit of its founder, the Church vigorously persecuted Jews, pagans, and heretics. Heretics were those who strayed one iota from accepted dogma. Thought control was the goal of overzealous and thus divisive Christians.

Gibbon said that Christianity (along with Germanic invasions) had led to the fall of the Roman empire. Gibbon said that first the Church stripped Rome of its native faith, and then, becoming dominant itself, outlawing all other churches. Gibbon also accused Christianity of diverting Rome's interests from worldly to spiritual matters, and thus the worldly defenses crumbled.

Unitiveness in the Early Christian Church

The first churches expected Christ to return soon. When the Second Coming failed, it was replaced by faith in the invisible presence of Christ within each believer's soul. Justin Martyr (100-165) said that Christ is the Logos who dwells in every person. The Logos, he explained, is the power of reason which preserves the unity of God. Justin called "Christians before Christ" all who lived in accordance with the Logos before Jesus was born. This included such Greeks as Heraclitus, Plato, and Socrates. The Logos is the universal principle of the divine self-manifestation. It stands behind all religious expression, so that persons in every religion have a moral sensitivity, a love of beauty, and at least a partial grasp of the truth. Truth, being universal, incorporates Christianity, Greek philosophy, and Oriental mysticism, Justin said.

The Christian church in Alexandria was outstanding for the catholicity of its outlook. People like Clement, Origen, and Pantaenus made Christianity acceptable to deep thinkers. Clement said, "If anyone knows himself he shall know God, and by knowing God he shall be made like unto Him." Origen found three levels of scripture: the literal meaning, the moral application to the reader's life, and the spiritual level, known only to those capable of perceiving the symbolic and the mystical. Heaven, said Origen, is not a place but a spiritual condition, for God has no space or time limitations. In the end all souls, some cleansed by fire, will share in universal salvation, he believed.

"Church Fathers tried to show the convergent lines between the Christian message and the intrinsic quests of the pagan religions," Tillich said. Early Christianity did not see itself as exclusive, but rather as all-inclusive, Tillich felt. St. Augustine believed that salvation was for everyone, not just for Christians. He said that "from the beginning of the human race, whoever believed in God in any way, and led a just life according to His commandments, was undoubtedly saved by Him. The true religion, although formerly practiced under other names and with other rites, is one and the same in both periods. Thus, true salvation was never wanting to any one who was worthy of it."[70]

Divisiveness in the Medieval Christian Church

Christianity had a hard time surviving in Africa. At the Council of Carthage in A.D. 411 there were 286 Roman Catholic bishops and 279 Donatist bishops. Donatists were those who insisted that for a bishop's actions to be consecrated, the bishop had to lead a holy life. When the Donatists, like the Monophysites, were declared to be heretics, the Church lost much of its strength.

Islam swept quickly through north Africa. The centuries-long Christian battles over heresy so confused Africans about which was the "true" Christianity that when a simple sincere monotheistic faith came along in Islam, Africans flocked to it. Islam was color blind as to race, and also permitted more survival of native African rituals than did Christianity.

The use of icons, or religious images, led to further division. To humanize the faith, statues and pictures of Christ became popular, but the strong Judaic undercurrent against graven images opposed this trend. A compromise was reached at the Second Council of Nicaea in 787 with the ruling that icons deserved reverence but not adoration, which was to be reserved for God alone.

Farther north, in the original home of the Normans, divisive Christianity was still in force. In 996 King Olaf Trygveson of Norway invited all persons in a northern region called Viken to accept Christianity. "Those who opposed him he punished severely, killing some, mutilating others, and driving some into banishment. Thus all Viken was made Christian."[71]

The great schism between the Eastern and Western branches of the Church had long been in the making. Constantinople and Rome differed on such matters as the use of icons, celibacy of the clergy, and the power of the papacy. The triggering action in 1054 was the phrase *filoque* (and the Son) inserted into the Nicene Creed. Did the Holy Spirit proceed from the Son as well as from the Father? The Council of Toledo ruled so, in 589. But the Eastern church, fearful of polytheism and trying to protect God the Father as the source of all deity, rejected the phrase. In 1054 the pope and the Eastern patriarch excommunicated each other. The schism existed until 1965, when Pope Paul VI and Patriarch Athenagoras rescinded the rash action.

In the words of Frithjof Schuon, the Roman Catholic Church by now had become more Roman than Christian. "The World of the Gospel was Oriental and Semitic and plunged in a climate of holy poverty, whereas the world of Catholicism was European, Roman, imperial." To Schuon some of the Roman signs were the juridicism, bureaucracy, and militant spirit of the Church, as well as its use of parades, pageantry, and ostentatious art. Jesus washed the feet of his disciples, Schuon said, but popes preferred to have their subjects kiss their feet. "If the Church of the West had been such that it could have avoided casting the Church of the East into the 'outer darknesses'—and with what manifestation of barbarism—it would not have had to undergo the counterblow of the Reformation," Schuon felt.[72]

The Crusades are a glorious example of divisive religion. Built on the notion that all non-Christians (as well as some Christians) were infidels, the Crusades succeeded in splitting Christianity, until Christians were killing Christians. Thousands of Christians had been exposed to the superior culture and superior tolerance of the Moslems, a blow to Christian assumptions of superiority. Many serfs refused to return to their semi-slavery in Europe.

The divisiveness of the Crusades did not end with the last Crusade. When the Knights Templars returned to France, King Philip the Fair considered them a threat, since they reported directly to the pope. So he charged them with heresy. "Some of the leaders were tortured and confessed. The Inquisition treated them as relapsed heretics. Fifty-nine were burned at the stake in Paris, including the Grand Master, Jacques de Molay. The order was suppressed, and the pope acquiesced. This is an example of the use of the Inquisition as an instrument of national policy."[73]

Unitiveness in the Medieval Christian Church

While Christian practices degenerated, Christian doctrine flourished. St. Bernard of Clairvaux (1090-1153) said, "The greater thou art, the more humble thyself in all things, and thou shall find grace before God." He criticized monasteries for their extravagance. In an effort to spread understanding between Christians and Moslems, Peter the Venerable distributed a book in Spain in 1142 explaining the basic beliefs of Islam.

Influenced by Peter, Francis of Assisi sent work missionaries to Morocco in 1219. To show deep love of God, love His creation, Francis recommended. In his great prayer Francis asked believers to replace hatred with love, discord with union, and injury with pardon. His followers practiced unitive religion at its best. They repaired the homes of the poor, cleaned sewers, and nursed the sick and the aged.

Emperor Frederick II of Sicily created a dialogue of Christian, Jewish, and Moslem representatives at his court, leading to his reign becoming very humane and tolerant. Throughout Europe the Church installed programs to help the poor, the sick, widows, orphans, and lepers. Finally Christianity was beginning to practice the teachings of its founder!

Just as Francis united the beauty of nature with Christ's spirituality so did Thomas Aquinas synthesize Aristotle's philosophy with Christ's love. Aquinas unified ideas from many sources, including Maimonides and Moslems like Avicenna, Averroës, and al-Ghazzali. At last the medieval mind had found what it had long sought—a synthesis of reason and revelation. Since both have their source in God, Aquinas said, they could not possibly be contradictory.

Raymond Lully (1232-1315) wrote three works in which Jewish, Roman Christian, Eastern Christian, Moslem and Tatar points of view are presented with astonishing fairness, kindness, and tolerance. But in 1315 he openly preached Christianity in Tunis and was stoned to death by a Moslem mob.

Thomas à Kempis (1380-1471) wrote *The Imitation of Christ,* a classic of spiritual contemplation. His highly unitive work points out that philosophy avails nothing unless one loves one's neighbor: "Our Lord says, I am not God of dissension and strife, but of unity and peace, and peace stands rather in true humility than in pride and vainglory."

Nicholas of Cusa (1401-1464), member of the papal court, wrote a book *The Peace Between the Different Forms of Faith,* in which Christ convenes an imaginary council representing many religions. After extensive discussion, "the King of Kings decreed that under the names to which they were accustomed all should hold one faith in perpetual peace." Christ then explained the unity among the world religions: "There is only one religion of all who live according to the principles of Reason, which underlies the different rites. The cult of the gods everywhere witnesses to Divinity. So in the heaven of Reason (Logos), the concord of the religions was established."[74]

The Great Schism

For decades the papacy served as a political toy, being dominated by the leading civil ruler in Europe. Bullied by King Philip IV of France, Pope Clement V moved the papal court to Avignon in 1309. Pope John XXII spent 64% of his budget on warfare, 21% on personal matters, and only 7% on charity. After a quarrel with King Louis of Bavaria, John excommunicated Louis. Louis got himself appointed Holy Roman Emperor, declared John deposed, and had antipope Nicholas V elected.

In 1377 Pope Gregory IX returned the papacy to Rome. At Gregory's death the College of Cardinals selected an Italian, Urban VI. Under pressure the College of Cardinals rescinded its appointment and selected as pope Clement VIII, cousin to the French king. Urban VI responded by setting up his own College of Cardinals. Clement VIII moved his papal court back to Avignon. Now there were two popes and two colleges of cardinals!

"Half the Christian world held the other half to be heretical," said Will Durant. Each side considered the other's sacraments to be worthless. "Expanding Islam laughed at disintegrating Christendom," Durant remarked.

In 1409 cardinals from both sides declared both Gregory XII and Benedict XIII to be schismatics, and elected a third pope, Alexander V, who died in 1410. The new pope, John XXIII, had seduced, according to his secretary, over 200 virgins, nuns, matrons, and widows. In 1415 the Council of Constance deposed all three popes and installed instead Martin V. To show its orthodoxy, the Council burned at the stake Bohemian reformer John Huss.

Unitive Christianity in the Renaissance

Marcilio Ficino (1433-1499), in an effort to reconcile Plato with Aristotle, studied Zoroaster and Confucius. In Plotinus he found the mystical cord that bound Plato and Christ in a unity. In his synthesis he asserted that God is the soul of the world.

Giovanni Pico della Mirandola (1463-1494) was the perfect Renaissance scholar. His ecumenical approach synthesized Plato, Aristotle, Judaism, Christianity, and Islam. Writing on human dignity, he said that, by being made in God's image, humans have almost limitless potential. He said, "Let us enjoy the desired peace, the union indissoluble, the friendship in which all souls accord not only in that one Mind which is above every mind, but in an ineffable manner are fused into one. We shall no longer be ourselves, but rather He who made us."[75]

The Dutch theologian Desiderius Erasmus asked for Christian peace. "Christians," he said, "behave more cruelly in battle than non-Christians or wild beasts. None among them is ashamed to start the war that Jesus so execrated," He called nationalism a curse to mankind. He wanted Anabaptists to be treated humanely. His goal was to clean up Church immorality without destroying the Church in the process.

A god who predestined some to eternal damnation would be a monstrous tyrant, Erasmus taught. "The sum of our religion is peace and unanimity," he said, "but these can scarcely stand unless we define as little as possible. By terrorization we drive men to believe what they do not believe. That which is forced cannot be sincere, and that which is not voluntary cannot please Christ."[76]

In Sir Thomas More's *Utopia* there was religious tolerance. The only persons banished for religious reasons from the fictional paradise were those who tried by unfair or violent means to convert people to their religious outlook. In the utopia, More said, "there are diverse kinds of religion. But the most and wisest part believe that there is a certain Godly power, unknown and everlasting, dispersed throughout the world in virtue and power. Him they call the Father of all."

Michel de L'Hospital, chancellor of France from 1560 to 1568, was a strong force for religious toleration. Supported by the regent Catherine de Medicis, he composed edicts tolerating the Huguenots. For trying to be fair to both Catholics and Protestants he was of course attacked by extremists of both sides. "While he favored unity of religion," said Robert J. Knecht, "he did not believe that persecution was the best way to achieve it."

Henry IV of Navarre was a model unitive king of France. As he converted to the Roman Catholic faith, he said, "Perhaps the difference between the two religions is great only through the animosity of those who preach it. Those who unswervingly follow their conscience are of my religion."[77] Henry sought no heretics. On the contrary, he granted amnesty to dissidents. He ended the French religious wars, and taught Catholics and Protestants to live together in peace.

In 1598 Henry issued the Edict of Nantes, a landmark in religious liberty. Protestants were permitted to worship freely in most French cities, and they could now hold governmental offices. Protestant churches would now receive governmental support, as had Catholic churches for centuries. Protestants would be admitted equally to all schools, hospitals, and universities. To ensure equal justice, Protestant judges would sit with their Catholic counterparts. Many Catholics complained. Pope Clement VIII said that the edict was "the most accursed thing imaginable, granting liberty of conscience to everybody, which is the worst thing in the world."

Matteo Ricci (1552-1610) was a unitive force as a Christian missionary to China. He dressed in Confucian garb and accepted Confucian ethics He quoted passages showing similar thoughts in Confucius and Christ. Chinese converts were permitted to continue ancestor worship. Ricci shared Western science and thought with the Chinese. Had there been more like this tolerant Jesuit, Christianity might have received a more cordial welcome in China.

Francis de Sales preached a doctrine of universal love. He said, "It is as images of God that we are capable of being united to His divine essence. The same love extends to God and to our neighbor. To love our neighbor with a charitable love is to love God in man."[78]

Another unitive Christian was Vincent de Paul. Captured by pirates and sold as a slave in Tunis, he escaped and founded the Vincentian order, which has become famous for its good works. His beneficence extended to Moslems as well as Christians. His order mediated rivalry among competing Catholic orders. Everyone agreed when he was made a saint in 1737. Even today in Tunis he is remembered as a good *marabout* (Moslem saint).

Religious toleration paid off for Cardinal Richelieu. After a Huguenot revolt, he was very lenient towards them. He observed the Edict of Nantes, and added the Edict of Grace, which assisted Huguenot laymen and clergy. From that time on, Huguenots became a positive force in French life, and both they and France flourished because of the amity.

Unitive Christianity in the Enlightenment

Voltaire, although only a nominal Roman Catholic, helped make many monarchs more tolerant towards religious differences. "The shameful quarrels of divided Christians," he said, "have done more mischief under religious presences, made more bad blood, laid waste France and Germany under presence of maintaining the balance of Europe." He added that savages could not have done a better job of dividing Europe. Voltaire's deism influenced many of America's Founding Fathers, as they drafted documents guaranteeing religious tolerance. "After him," said Will Durant, "no tribunal in Europe would have dared to break a man on the wheel."

Influenced by Voltaire, Joseph II of Austria used unitive religion in his approach to government. In 1781 he issued an Edict of Toleration which allowed Protestants and Jews to be students and teachers in public schools. Under his tolerant government the number of Protestant communities in Hungary grew from

272 to 758. But he suffered a loss of popularity among his subjects, many of whom were not ready to treat non-Catholics as equals.

Divisiveness in the Orthodox Christian Church

The Eastern Orthodox Church comprises one-sixth of all Christians. It considers itself to be the true original church of Christ. Its doctrine derives from the seven church councils held from 325 to 787, all of which were convened by Byzantine emperors. As Rome fell to the barbarians, Constantinople came to be regarded as the second Rome. When the Moslems captured Constantinople in 1453, Moscow considered itself to be the third Rome.

Barriers separating the Orthodox Church from the Roman Catholic Church are many. Doctrinally, the Orthodox refuse to accept the doctrines of Purgatory, the Immaculate Conception, the Bodily Assumption of Mary, and the papal infallibility. None of these doctrines existed at the time of the early Church Fathers, and thus they are considered to be inauthentic additions. The Orthodox accuse the Roman Church of juridical scholasticism, saying that logic and reason do a disservice to the divine mysticism of God.

The Orthodox Church places little stress upon the social gospel, feeling that one's chief concern in life should be spiritual. Monasticism and asceticism are important parts of the Orthodox heritage.

Unitive Elements in the Orthodox Christian Church

The goal of religion, say the Orthodox, is for the individual to achieve a mystical union with God. The Christian does this through acquiring and nurturing the Holy Spirit in one's life. In Christ, God became man that humans might become divine. Humans become "partakers of the divine nature" (as described in II Peter 1:4) without ceasing to be creatures of God. The Orthodox feel that it is futile and dangerous to dogmatize over doctrines that lie beyond human reason, including such concepts as original sin and divine grace. Russian intellectuals, however, have been given spiritual sustenance, whether suffering under czarist or communist tyranny, by the challenging world outlook of such Orthodox mystics as Vladimir Solovyov, who will be discussed later.

In the modern world the Orthodox Church sees itself, like the Anglican Church, as a mediating factor between the Christian extremes of Protestantism and Roman Catholicism. The Orthodox Church is a vital force towards ecumenism since joining the World Council of Churches in 1937. Paul Tillich says that the Orthodox provide something lost to western Christianity centuries ago, namely, a spiritualization of all reality. Modern theology, like modern science, is non-dualistic. Just as matter and energy are convertible forms of one substance, so are the spiritual and the material unified aspects of God's creation. Since the Orthodox Church never made the mistake of assuming that all matter is evil, it can play a crucial role in helping give a theological foundation to the global village, the modern version of the coming of the kingdom of God.

References

[1] Heinrich Zimmer, *Philosophies of India* (Meridian Books, 1960), p. 349. Zimmer was Professor of Religion at Columbia University.
[2] Campbell, *Oriental Mythology*, pp. 339-40.
[3] Quoted in Vergilius Ferm, ed., *Living Schools of Religion* (Littlefield, Adams & Co., 1956), p. 13. Hindu scholar Nikhilananda translated the Upanishads.
[4] A.C. Bhaktivedanta, *Bhagavad Gita As It Is,* abridged edition (Bhaktivedanta Book Trust, 1975), pp. 144, 195. Bhaktivedanta founded the International Society for Krishna Consciousness.
[5] Schuon, p. 425.
[6] Zimmer, pp. 366-67.
[7] Ibid., p. 368.
[8] Louis Renou, ed., *Hinduism* (Braziller, 1962), pp. 171-72.
[9] Quoted in Rousseau, p. 33.
[10] Nikhilananda, in Ferm, p. 12.
[11] John B. Noss, *Man's Religions,* 3rd ed. (Macmillan, 1963), p. 148. Noss was Professor of Religion at Franklin and Marshall College.
[12] Campbell, *Oriental Mythology,* p. 342.
[13] Geoffrey Parrinder, *Mysticism in the World's Religions* (Oxford University Press, 1976), p. 104.
[14] Radhakrishnan, p. 331.
[15] W.C. Smith, *Faith and Belief,* pp. 53-56, 61-63, 68.
[16] Thomas J.J. Altizer, *Oriental Mysticism and Biblical Eschatology* (Westminster, 1961), pp. 120-22, 146.
[17] Christmas Humphreys, *Buddhism* (Penguin, 1954), pp. 18-19. Humphreys founded the Buddhist Society in London.
[18] Noss, p. 212.
[19] Richard A. Gard, ed., *Buddhism* (Braziller, 1962), pp. 19- 20.
[20] Clarence H. Hamilton, *Encyclopedia Britannica*, 1971, vol. 4, p. 359.
[21] Watts, p. 170.
[22] Humphreys, p. 186.
[23] Ibid.
[24] Hamilton, p. 359.
[25] Watts, p. 145.
[26] Radhakrishnan, p. 158.

[27] Radhakrishnan, pp. 185-86.
[28] Ninian Smart, *Beyond Ideology: Religion and the Future of Western Civilization* (Harper & Row, 1981), p. 171.
[29] Gard, pp. 213-14.
[30] Quoted in Campbell, *Oriental Mythology*, p. 428.
[31] William L. Newell, *Struggle and Submission: R.C. Zaehner on Mysticism* (University Press of America, 1981), pp. 17-18.
[32] Jack Finegan, *The Archeology of World Religions* (Princeton University Press, 1952), p. 386.
[33] Quoted in Huston Smith, *The Religions of Man* (Harper & Row, 1958), p. 174. Smith was Professor of Religious History at the Univ. of Calif., Berkeley.
[34] Will Durant, *Our Oriental Heritage* (Simon & Schuster, 1954), p. 702.
[35] Quoted in Arnold Toynbee, ed., *Half the World* (Holt, Rinehart & Winston, 1973), p. 130.
[36] Das, pp. 71-72.
[37] Finegan, p. 458.
[38] "Shinto," *Encyclopedia Britannica,* 1971, vol. 20, p. 397.
[39] Ibid., p. 396.
[40] Noss, p. 438.
[41] Albright, p. 238.
[42] Adrio König, *Here Am I* (Eerdmans, 1982), p. 16.
[43] Campbell, *Occidental Mythology,* pp. 108-10.
[44] Quoted in Arthur Hertzberg, *Judaism* (Braziller, 1962), p. 38.
[45] Ibid., pp. 190-91.
[46] Albright, p. 280.
[47] Ibid., p. 308.
[48] E.W. Heaton, *The Hebrew Kingdoms* (Oxford University Press, 1968), pp. 266, 268, 274.
[49] Ghirshman, p. 133.
[50] Max I. Dimont, *Jews, God, and History* (New American Library, 1964), pp. 89-90.
[51] Hertzberg, p. 34.
[52] Edward Gibbon, *The Decline and Fall of the Roman Empire* (Harcourt Brace, 1960), p. 193.
[53] Quoted in Dimont, p. 153.

[54] Dimont, p. 177.
[55] Gershom G. Scholem, *Major Trends in Jewish Mysticism,* rev. ed., (Schocken, 1946), p. 96.
[56] Dimont, p. 267.
[57] Alexander Altman, *Encyclopedia Britannica,* 1971, vol. 4, p. 537.
[58] Ibid., p. 538.
[59] Scholem, p. 111.
[60] Scholem, p. 284.
[61] Edward Hoffman, *The Way of Splendor* (Shambhala, 1981), p. 57.
[62] Scholem, p. 284.
[63] Hertzberg, pp. 109, 111.
[64] Rufus M. Jones, *Spiritual Reformers in the 16th and 17th Centuries* (Beacon, 1959), p. 127.
[65] Will Durant, *The Age of Louis XIV* (Simon & Schuster, 1963), pp. 629, 634.
[66] Campbell, *Occidental Mythology*, p. 334.
[67] Angus, p. 310.
[68] George Brantl, ed., *Catholicism* (Braziller, 1962), pp. 178-179. Brantl was Professor of Religion at Rutgers University.
[69] Brantl, pp. 74., 77.
[70] Quoted in Brantl, pp. 79-80.
[71] Roland H. Bainton, *The Medieval Church* (Van Nostrand, 1962), p. 106.
[72] Schuon, p. 248.
[73] Bainton, p. 65.
[74] Bainton, pp. 179-80.
[75] Ibid., pp. 178-79.
[76] Ibid., pp. 182-83.
[77] Will & Ariel Durant, *The Age of Reason Begins* (Simon & Schuster, 1961), p. 363.
[78] Brantl, p. 176.

Chapter 4

Religious Ritual: Humanizing or Inhumane?

Sir James Frazer, author of *The Golden Bough,* describes religious ritual at its divisive worst: "The Polynesians seem regularly to have killed two-thirds of their children. The Jagas, a conquering tribe in Angola, are reported to have put to death all their children. They recruited their numbers by adopting boys and girls of 13 or 14, whose parents they had killed and eaten. Among the Mbaya Indians of South America the women used to murder all their children except the last."[1] Fortunately, few religious rituals ever get this inhumane.

In the Enga tribe of Papua New Guinea when one warrior on either side is killed or even seriously wounded, the battle ends. Thus, religious ritual can be used to somewhat humanize even such dreadful activity as warfare. The Judaic law of *lex talionis* ("an eye for an eye") sounds somewhat cruel, but can be preferred to limitless revenge which one group might seek against a rival group.

In the 20th century individuals as diverse as Mahatma Gandhi and Adolf Hitler have employed rituals. Like religion, rituals have been used as high points, good and bad, of human endeavors.

Theology professor Tom Driver feels that ritual is needed to help us handle life's passages: into birth, puberty, marriage, child bearing, divorce, illness, and death. Cultures with rituals for puberty help teenagers appreciate what it means to be sexually mature. Cultures lacking such rituals have teenagers who are sexually active without being sexually mature. In Driver's view rituals need not be idolatrous or shackling, but can be a liberating force, promoting peace, justice, and inter-cultural respect.

Religious Ritual: Humanizing or Inhumane? 103

What functions do religious rituals serve? They provide order, morality, community, and social cement, and can at their best transform a society in the direction of liberty and justice. How do rituals provide order? They help denote seasons, as well as the stages in one's life cycle. They also provide a structure for social and economic events. The Maring people in New Guinea, for example, limit fighting to non-agricultural times, provide economic trade during good weather, and through regulating pig exchange assure their people of high quality protein when they most need it.

Biologist Julian Huxley said that ritualization was the means by which society imposes the kind of order necessary for the creation of shared worlds. Sometimes when a society has a serious breach of custom (such as one brought about by a murder or some serious crime), the society needs to reorder itself through the ritualization process. Some of the rituals used are healing rites, exorcisms, or prayer ceremonies. The extensive television coverage of the burial rites for President John Kennedy helped our nation bear a heavy tragic burden. When the Oklahoma City bombing in 1995 provided a national trauma, President Clinton and other leaders were involved in rituals to bring national healing.

Religious rituals help show the pathway for national morality to follow. Often the ritual marks the boundary at which moral anomie stops. For example, since 1945 the nuclear arms race has held the entire human race hostage. If one can support the construction of a bomb to kill a million innocent people, one loses all moral restraint concerning lesser crimes, like robbery or assault. Since the modern world is morally adrift, humanity's ritualizing impulse, "laid down for us in structures older than consciousness," says Driver, comes into play. Tension results when our historic rituals prove inadequate to handle such current problems as the split atom, space travel, and the hole in the ozone layer.

Rituals help humans to build a bridge to God. "Without ritual," says Driver, "the divine-human relationship is broken, and everything that can be truly identified as either divine or human perishes."[2] A ritual can be either a symbol or a sign, Ken Wilber feels. When it acts as a symbol, the self is dissolved in God consciousness. But when it is merely a sign, the self is sustained as a substitute for God. "Every great world religion has both exoteric and esoteric aspects," Wilber says.[3] The exoteric rituals serve the masses and the esoteric serve the more spiritually advanced persons.

Rituals unite people by reinforcing their feeling of community, their sense of belonging. One function of ritual is to redirect aggressive instincts so as to keep aggression under control. Rituals can act as a safety valve on the emotions, controlling them to prevent rash action, but encouraging them when necessary, as in expressions of grief.

Rituals motivate humans to action. "There comes a time when people need, for the sake of moral development, to assume responsibility for their rituals, and this brings them to the confessional mode of performance," says Driver.[4] Although Yahweh in the Old Testament first requires rituals, He later despises them when He sees them as a substitute for righteous conduct.

Confession, we are told, is good for one's soul. In Alcoholics Anonymous the individual begins by confessing addiction, but then also confesses belief in a higher power who will help one overcome addiction. "Confession always changes the relation between the self and the world," Driver says.[5] In the civil rights movement of the 1960s two phrases were powerful: "black is beautiful" and "we shall overcome," for they blended faith and determination. These phrases were more effective, at first, at the spiritual than at the political level.

The ethical mode of performance is the ultimate goal of all religious ritual. Here society is directly impelled towards improvement, not just through prayer but through political action. This is the goal Driver seeks for ritual to attain—a society whose people live in dignity and justice.

Ritual can lead to desirable social change. Rituals "are more like washing machines than books," says Driver.[6] "A book may be *about* washing, but the machine takes in dirty clothes and, if all goes well, transforms them into cleaner ones."

Some rituals bring about transformation, as in marriage, ordination, inauguration, and puberty rites. There are also rituals of healing, and of moral and spiritual cleansing. When a ritual loses its trans-human significance, as in many Protestant communion rites, that which once transformed now becomes largely show.

Prayer is usually thought of as a request for the deity to grant a petition. But also "prayer may establish or reestablish relationships—between the people who pray, the deity to whom they pray, and the people or circumstances for which they pray. Hence, prayer may transform isolation into community, emptiness into fullness, and despair into hope."[7]

Religious rituals are often open to multiple interpretations. For example, Christian baptism is seen variously: one person says that it is necessary to save a soul from damnation; another views it as a death to sin and a rebirth into a new life; still another calls it a dedication of one's life to God. Thus symbols may have equally valid interpretations. Like symbols, rituals have not only denotation but also connotation.

Modern rituals often seem to be ineffective. Some are boring or vacuous, says Driver, and many are not understood. When rituals no longer work, the society may have lost its way. We need to reform our religious ritual life, Driver feels, "so that our longing for ritual and our longing for freedom may come together. It is a tragedy they were ever split."[8]

All rituals need to have prescribed limits. Sacredness lies in the relationship between the individual and the deity. When limits are transgressed, ritual moves from being unitive to becoming divisive. Driver believes that "there is something terrifying, because motiveless, in ritual sacrifice." A rabbit or a lamb substitutes for a human who might be killed to propitiate a god.

Driver says that human sacrifice has been used in religious rituals for three reasons:

1. Our species has developed ritualization to a very elaborate level.
2. We lack a genetically coded proscription against killing our own species
3. Approved ritual killings lead to senseless killings in human society through what René Girard calls "mimetic desire." A player in a computer game, after "killing" perhaps 100 "enemies" has a mimetic urge to drive 100 miles per hour on a highway, or even take part in a drive-by shooting.

Old Testament prophets warned against rituals which transcend limits. In this century fascist and communist governments have used rituals effectively to get their people to slaughter innocent victims. "To be sure," said Driver, "rituals have made us human, but part of what it means to be human is to lose by what you gain."[9]

Rituals in Primitive Religions

Every purposeful activity in primitive society was a ritual, for all life was considered sacred. All early dance and drama were religious in nature. As desacralization occurred, what once was sacred became profane. Empty rituals are boring and dangerous. Primitive rites, said Frazer, are "magical rather than propitiatory. In other words, the desired objects are attained not by propitiating the favor of divine beings through prayer or praise but by ceremonies which have a physical resemblance between the rite and the desired effect."[10]

Divisive ritual is found among primitive tribes. The initiation rites at puberty in the Wonghi tribe of New South Wales involve knocking out the youth's tooth, to show that he is now a man. The Niska Indians of British Columbia isolate a young man at puberty. A mock funeral ceremony is held for him, and he is sent away from his family for a year. In puberty rites on the Lower Congo River, priests fall into a trance, pretending they cannot walk or feed themselves. If their wishes are not granted, they may beat or kill tribal members with impunity, since it is assumed that they are dwelling in the spirit world.

All primitive tribes have creation myths. In Mesopotamian tradition humans were formed at the earth's navel. Early temples were conceived of as the center of the spiritual universe. "Through the paradox of rite," said Mircea Eliade, an authority on comparative religion, "every consecrated space coincides with the center of the world."[11]

For primitives, human rituals are modeled on what the gods did at the beginning. Australian aborigines and Pawnee Indians in North America allege that their rituals came from God at creation. Construction rituals, blessing a house, church, or bridge, are also done with the divine prototype of creation in mind. Many herbal cures used in rituals allegedly had divine forerunners. Some rituals used to bolster civil laws are believed to paraphrase God's divine laws. Among Navajo Indians and Fiji Islanders curing rituals involve a symbolic return to the pristine world that existed at creation. By way of contrast, many tribes have sexual orgies at springtime to encourage abundant harvests. Some Polynesian divorce rituals employ chants describing the separation of earth and heaven.

Ancient Egyptian priests imitated their primordial god Thoth. Also some animals were considered to be sacred by Egyptians. Thus they would sometimes eat human flesh to keep from starving, rather than eat the animal totem of their tribe.

In many tribes the medicine man or shaman recounts the various stages in God's creative activity. Sometimes the curative ceremony recalls the demonic origin of the disease, and tribute is paid to the god who exorcised the demon and nullified the disease.

The Avestan code in ancient Persia had numerous ceremonies for cleansing body and soul. There were severe penalties for those who spread contagious diseases. Sodomy was strictly banned. The family was considered the holiest of all institutions. Dogs were to be treated with kindness.

Hindu Divisive Rituals

In early India the religious ceremonies were performed by chieftains or kings, with the Brahmins or priests as mere assistants. In the epic *Ramayana* a warrior objects to a woman of his caste marrying a "prating priest and Brahmin!"[12] Warriors have high status in early societies, but workers are considered expendable. In early Vedic practice if a Sudra worker "chances to overhear the recitation of a Vedic hymn, he is to be punished by having his ears filled with molten lead."[13]

In one way or another, Hindu castes are mutually untouchable. Each caste is supposed to wear its distinctive dress, and obey its particular dharma (laws). One's caste determines one's conduct, one's vocation, and one's outlook on life. Each trade has its own overseeing god.

"Thug" is the Sanskrit word for "conceal." The Thugs were a secret Hindu society in 18th and 19th century India who committed thousands of atrocious murders to placate Bhavani, a form of Kali. Before strangling their carefully selected victims they would rob them, and soon the term "thug" came to stand for any gangster or robber. Because this was supposed to be a religious ritual, and because some Indian people confused divisive religion with true religion (love of God and humans), no witnesses could be found to testify against the thugs as criminals.

Hindu Unitive Rituals

In early Vedic India a religious sacrifice was considered to be a repetition of the act of creation. When a new territory was added, it was consecrated in God's name, bringing order out of chaos. Early marriage rites paralleled the original union of earth and heaven.

The great Hindu sage Shankara said he could not believe in a God who denied the existence of His rivals. To serve his followers better, Shankara reestablished six different religious sects. In a further effort at unity, King Harsha ordered the erection of statues of Buddha, Siva, and the sun god.

True to the principle of unitive religion, a Hindu can worship in any church, mosque, synagogue, or temple. The monks of the Ramakrishna order celebrate the birthdays of Buddha, Christ, and Krishna. Over the home of the family of Rabindranath Tagore is the inscription: "In this place no one's faith is to be despised." Mahatma Gandhi stated, "I believe in the Bible as I believe in the Gita. I regard all the great faiths of the world as equally true with my own."[14] True religion, says A.C. Bhaktivedanta, is to serve God and humans: "If one be Hindu, Moslem, or Christian, one is always a servant. The particular faith is not the religion; service is the religion."

Arthur Avalon shows intriguing parallels between Hindu rituals and those of Catholic Christianity. He amends the Roman Catholic creed as expressed at the Council of Trent with Hindu counterparts: "The Catholic Church, rich with the experience of the ages, has introduced mystic benediction *(mantra),* incense *(dhupa),* water *(acamana),* lights *(dipa),* bells *(ghanta),* and flowers *(puspa),* to excite the spirit to the contemplation of the profound mysteries which they reveal. As are its faithful, the Church is composed of both body *(deha)* and soul *(atman).* It therefore renders to the Lord (Isvara), a double worship, exterior *(vahya-puja)* and interior *(manasa-puja),* the latter being the prayer *(vadana)* of the faithful, and the former the outward motions of the liturgy."[15]

Buddhist Rituals

Gautama Buddha had little use for ritual. He considered it dreadful to kill innocent animals for a so-called religious sacrifice. To a follower trying to purify himself by bathing in a river, Gautama asked, "If you do not kill, lie, steal, or boast—are you not already purified?"

Within 100 years after Gautama's death, however, monks in the Bihar province were warned about ten heretical practices to avoid. The dissident monks founded their own order, and a civil war ensued. Literalists wanted strict observance of laws and rituals; liberals said that more important than law or ritual was to enable each person to discover and nourish his potential Buddhahood. There were 227 rules for monks to obey, leaving little time for meditating on achieving Buddhahood. There was also a tendency for the monks to look down on the common people as being too stupid to engage in advanced spiritual exercises.

Taoists encountering Buddhism liked the Buddhist medicine and breathing exercises. In the Pure Conversation movement of the 4th century A.D., Taoists, Buddhists, and Confucianists engaged in friendly witty conversations. Renowned scholar Hui-Yüan said that monks, being "other worldly" need not bow down to earthly sovereigns. This established a precedent of separation of religious personnel from political authority.

Religious Rites in China and Japan

In China, every human union has its model in the cosmic union of the elements. Music is highly prized. The Chinese *Book of Rites* states that "music makes for common union. Rites make for difference. Music comes from within; rites act from without. Music produces serenity of mind. Rites produce elegance of manner. Let music achieve its full results, and there will be no resentments. Let rites achieve their full results, and there will be no contentions."[16]

The twelve terrestrial branches of the Chinese zodiac are represented by symbolic animals: rat, ox, tiger, hare, dragon, serpent, horse, goat, monkey, cock, dog, and bear. It is assumed that each animal exercises an astrological influence every two hours of each day. Also, each presides over a year, every twelfth year.

Kuan Yin, the Buddhist goddess of mercy, is perhaps China's most revered deity. Legend states that she turned back from immortality at the gate of the Western Paradise when she heard a cry of anguish from the earth and returned to earth to aid the distressed. In her iconography she bears a striking resemblance to medieval depictions of the Queen of Heaven, the Virgin Mary.

Unlike in the West, in China the dragon figure symbolizes a deity. In building a home, many Chinese consult a Feng-shui geomancer to see if the location suits friendly dragon spirits. Within the home a niche is preserved as a shrine to the protective dragon, who is installed with a sacred rite when the home is dedicated.

Ancestor worship provides a means of immortality to Chinese believers. The family unit, considered to be the keystone of Chinese culture, is preserved intact through rites recognizing the spiritual authority of deceased forbears. Respect for the dead grants them continued life in the spirit world. One has the assurance that some day one's progeny will endow oneself with similar immortality.

The Tibetan Book of the Dead is an 8th century description of the plane of consciousness between earthly incarnations. Bardo is the Tibetan name of this meta-consciousness, which lasts for a symbolic 49 days, from blissful envelopment in "Clear Light" to confrontation with one's mirror of karma. We are told that the Bardo dweller produces his own surroundings from the contents of his mind.

In the discarnate state one experiences the harmony of the universe. Knowledge of Bardo intensifies human responsibility, for Bardo explains why we are on earth and what we are expected to do while here. A person selects his or her soul mate, in order to repeat a past pleasant experience, or to make amends for a previous error. The "soul mate" refers to a person "with whom one has purposefully reincarnated many times in the cause of mutual growth."[17]

In Japan, polluted persons needed to be cleaned by the Great Purification ritual. Their pollution might have come from incest, murder, stealing, or from having had contact with blood or death. This last taboo may have been responsible for the Japanese abandonment of their using human sacrifices as part of a rite to placate the gods. This happened in the early medieval period, much earlier than in China and India.

The modern visitor to Tokyo finds a cosmopolitan synthesis. "Here there meet and mingle the twenty-six civilizations of Toynbee, the eighteen religions of Turchi, the five *kalpas* (Buddhist cosmic eras), von Eickstedt's thirty-eight races and subraces of mankind, and the fifty-six ways of making love of the Kama-sutra."[18] In the Temple of Philosophy one finds an altar with statues of Confucius, Buddha, Socrates, and Kant.

Buddhist monks and laymen go down the river Sumida to say prayers for the drowned, and to apologize to the fish for having taken their lives. Zen Buddhism flourishes in Japan. One Zen scholar says that trying to perceive God with one's intellect is like trying to catch a catfish with a gourd. A Zen goal is *wabi,* poverty of the spirit in which one shuns material wealth in order to attain spiritual strength.

Advice to a painter is as follows: "Draw bamboos for ten years, become a bamboo, and then forget all about bamboos when you are drawing." Love of nature is an integral part of Japanese religion. In the words of one scholar, "Every old tree of any sort inspires a beholder with a mystic feeling which leads him to a faraway world of timeless eternity."[19]

Divisive Rituals in Judaism

Belief in being God's chosen people leads to rituals which tend to reinforce separateness. The explanation that Jews gave for their getting Canaan as their promised land was that previous occupants had defiled it through sinful living. But for centuries their own prophets reminded them of their sinful occupation of the promised land.

As Rabbi Hertzberg says, "The life of obedience to the inherited Law requires of the Jew a considerable conscious apartness."[20] Samson Raphael Hirsch grants this to be true, but says that without its sense of peculiar mission, Judaism would long ago have ceased to exist. The detailed food rituals performed by Orthodox Jews are seen as not only dietary recommendations but also a reminder of their special designation as a chosen people.

Unitive Rituals in Judaism

The Jewish Shema is one of the world's great prayers: "Hear, O Israel: The Lord our God, the Lord is One. Praised be His glorious sovereignty for ever and ever." But the Old Testament prophets point out that when ritual loses its sacred content, it is meaningless and dangerous.

"What to me is the multitude of your sacrifice?" asks the Lord. "I do not delight in the blood of bulls, or lambs, or he-goats. Cease to do evil. Seek justice, correct oppression, defend the fatherless, plead for the widow" (Isaiah 1:11,17). Isaiah predicts a coming day when the Lord will say, "Blessed be Egypt my people, and Assyria the work of my hands, and Israel my heritage" (19:25). It will be a golden age, when "swords are beaten into plowshares, and no nation draws a sword against another."

Isaiah says that God used King Cyrus of Persia to restore Israel to Palestine, not just to save the Jews. It is "too light a thing that the energies of Israel should be expended solely on restoring Israel to Palestine. I will also give thee for a light to the Gentiles that thou mayest be My salvation unto the end of the earth" (49:6). God is revealed not as a lord of battle but as one of lovingkindness and tender mercy.

Isaiah warns against a mechanical reliance on ritual and law. Instead of a temple in Jerusalem, God wants humility, contrition, reverence, and obedience. "Heaven is My throne, and earth is My footstool," says the Lord. "What is this house which you would build for Me?" (66:1).

Jeremiah narrowly escaped death for saying that the temple was not needed for the worship of God, and that God did not want sacrifices to Him. It was superstitious to expect magical safety from enemy conquest within the temple, he said. "If you truly execute justice, if you do not oppress the alien, the fatherless, or the widow, or shed innocent blood in this place, then I will let you dwell in this land," said the Lord (Jeremiah 7:5-7).

Jeremiah's great contribution was that there was a new covenant, this one between God and individuals who would be true to Him (not just with the Jews as a people). Even if Babylon carries off Jews into captivity, He will still be with those who love Him and keep His commandments. Religion now becomes an individual rather than a group matter. The individual, as a moral integer, is responsible directly to God for his behavior.

In fact, Nebuchadnezzar of Babylon was Yahweh's servant, said Jeremiah, for the captivity would help Israel return to true religion. Thus, because of a prophet's fearless sermon, one of Israel's darkest hours politically became one of its real triumphs spiritually. Jeremiah scolded Shallum, son of King Josiah, who was reigning in place of his father: "Woe to him who builds his house by unrighteousness, who makes his neighbor serve him for nothing! Did not your father do justice? Is this not to know me?" says the Lord (22:13-16).

The essential rule of Jewish conduct is imitation of God. Thus, since God rested after six days of creation, the sabbath should also be a day of rest for humans. Repentance in Hebrew is *teshuvah* (returning), a person's turning back to one's original pure nature. But even on Yom Kippur, the Day of Atonement, one can atone only for sins toward God; sins toward humans must be pardoned by the offended one, after restitution.

Critics have said that the use of the phylacteries, or prayer box, are merely superstition, but even the rational Maimonides said that "great is their holiness, for as long as they are on the arm and head of man, he is humble and God-fearing."[21] Rabbi Hirsch gives a new interpretation of how the Jews are a chosen people. It is not that Judaism has a monopoly on God's love but that on the contrary, God has a monopoly on Israel's devotion and service. Judaism's most cherished ideal, says Hirsch, is the universal brotherhood of mankind.

Religious Ritual in Classical Greece and Rome

Frazer points out that at Byblus, Phoenicians required women to shave their heads in a ritual mourning the death of Adonis. Reluctant women were forced to give themselves up to a stranger, and donate the income to the worship of Astarte.

Romans used a charm to dispel evil influences. The god in charge of the specific activity needed to be addressed. Votive offerings showed gratitude to the gods for wishes granted. Festivals were light-hearted and happy occasions, with parades and pageantry. On Lupercalia, priests struck women with thongs from sacrificed animals, to purify the women and cause them to be fertile. At Saturnalia gifts were exchanged, and slaves were waited upon by their masters. Religion and family loyalty helped weld the iron character that allowed Rome to rule the Mediterranean world for centuries.

The Mystery Religions

An authority on the topic, Professor Angus feels that the mystery religions of classical Greece and Rome are a good example of an effort to use elaborate ritual when the supporting doctrine was inadequate. If ever rites alone could have saved a religion, it would have happened here, Angus said. Among rites used were: startling use of blazing lights and dense darkness; ceremonial mass purifications in pools; baths in bull's blood; nude religious parades; priests gashing their flesh with knives; and the babbling of unintelligible gibberish as prayers.

"The Mysteries seem to corroborate the unpleasant truism that where ritual abounds the spiritual vision is oftener marred than quickened," said Angus.[22] As the Mysteries lost their substance, they proved to be no match for the rise of Christianity. A religion of universal love, founded upon a historical person who practiced what he preached, filled a spiritual vacuum that existed in the Mediterranean world as classical religion waned. Beneath Christian ritual lay a doctrine of substance, practicality, and idealism that gave the world one of its great religions.

Divisive Rituals in Christianity

Christian rituals intended to be unitive have often proved to be divisive. The holy eucharist or communion, for example, intended to unite persons with God, throughout history has separated many Christian believers from their fellow Christians. Baptism has suffered a similar fate, when worshippers get lost in outward forms and forget about the underlying substance of the sacrament. The sign of the cross can be an observance of great significance, "ritually connecting heaven and the earth, and then its west and death to its orient and dawn, imparting a ritual order to chaos when facing something momentous."[23] But believers often used the sign of the cross as magic, and began to worship the images of saints, despite Augustine's attack on such practices. "In such matters it was not the priests who corrupted the people," said Will Durant, "but the people who persuaded the priests."

When the Christian Church split in 1054, rituals that differed further widened the breach between Roman and Eastern Christianity. More recently, at an ordination mass of seven priests in Haiti, Tom Driver observed the strict division between the choir, made up of men in luxurious vestments, and the nave, containing mostly women in ordinary garb. Here the ritual reinforced division rather than unity.

Unitive Rituals in Christianity

In the early Christian church, the agape, or love feast, promoted friendship among worshippers, male and female. By the close of the second century the Christian mass took form. By raising marriage to a sacrament, the church elevated the marriage contract from a civil ceremony to a religious ritual. Christianity now offered itself to all persons, of whatever nation, sex, or financial condition. By the year 200 Tertullian could say that "every age, condition, and rank is coming over to us."

Baptism can be unitive as well as divisive. John the Baptist preached immersion, "an ancient rite," says Joseph Campbell, "coming down from the old Sumerian temple city Eridu, of the water god Ea." The Roman Catholic Church recommends baptism, following Christ's admonition to Nicodemus: "Except a man be born of water and the Spirit, he cannot enter the kingdom of God" (John 3:5). But there can be symbolic baptism. For example, those who died for Christ, though not formally baptized, are considered to have a baptism of blood. Also, a person who lives a godly life is considered to have baptism of desire, that is, he would have been baptized had he been aware of the necessity. Many Christians believe that baptism cleanses the soul of original sin, and infuses the theological virtues of faith, hope, and love, and the cardinal virtues of fortitude, justice, prudence, and temperance.

The medieval Christian church presented many types of unity. For example, some of the great church hymns, because of their melodiousness, grace, and tenderness of thought, rank them among the best literary devotional lyrics. Also, the construction of the great Gothic cathedrals not only provided employment for many types of craftsmen, but also helped preserve a focus upon God as the center of one's life and activity.

In the 20th century the ecumenical movement, particularly as aided by the support of Pope John XXIII, has helped Christianity to move from divisiveness towards a unitive perspective.

Divisive Rituals in Islam

Women are restricted in their status as individuals in Islam. For example, during their menstrual cycle women are forbidden not only from reading the Koran but even from touching it. Menstrual taboo is frequently found in primitive religions, but rarely in more modern faiths.

All Moslems are required to participate in five daily prayers. "When a Muslim abstains from saying his prayers from negligence, one should ask him three times to repent. If he refuses, it is lawful to put him to death," says Ubada b. al-Samit.[24]

It is difficult to regard the *jihad,* or holy war, as anything but divisive. To kill others, and then say you do it in the name of the God of Love, may be sacrilegious. Religion loses respect when it condones what civil society recognizes as at best an anachronism and at worst a crime against humanity.

Unitive Rituals in Islam

The daily prayers in Islam are recited in the prostrate position, showing one's total submission to the will of God. In daily ablutions, one says "In the name of God!" at first, and then at the end "There is no god but God." Most Western people lack the spiritual depth to keep God as a constant part of every aspect of daily life.

The Koran asks Moslems to regard the People of the Book (Jews and Christians, since the Book is the Bible), with special care and tenderness. What a travesty that fundamentalist Moslems ignore those parts of their own scripture! For example, Moslems are taught that in the ritual of purification, it is acceptable to use utensils of People of the Book. Also, unlike other non-Moslems, the People of the Book use garments considered to be pure, unless otherwise known to be contaminated. It is true, however, that Buddhists and Hindus might find little consolation in the toleration permitted Jews and Christians.

The Need for Ritual in Modern Life

Modern civilization, says Tom Driver, by desacralizing the cosmos, threatens us first with wide-scale environmental pollution and second with extermination by the hydrogen bomb. Human desires most in need of ritual constraint today are food, sex, violence, and the power to dominate, Driver feels. When rituals are discarded in favor of so-called rational technology, humane values are jeopardized, because the self-regulating process of ritual is lost. Ritual boredom and ritual misunderstanding signify to Driver a time of dehumanization. "The world becomes an impersonal thing, defined by numbers and not by ceremonial actions. Of this development, the atom bomb may serve as our preeminent symbol."[25]

Driver sees rituals as a type of playful work. "Play done workfully risks becoming empty, while work done playfully becomes charged with energies and meanings. As work done playfully, ritual remains in touch with what is 'other.' Ritual is about relation to not-self. In Christian perspective, work done playfully is a sign of grace. That is, it cannot be accounted for rationally, for it is transformative."[26]

Ritual as Transformation

Ritual, like prayer, can be magical, in Driver's opinion. Magic achieves results without rational explanation. "The aim of religion," to Driver, "is not simply intellectual understanding; it is primarily transformative action, for which the principal technique is 'ceremonies, rites, and services.' Ritual-making is religion's most essential word."[27]

Driver sees the genius of religion in this: "Change in the self and change in the outer world bound in an intimate connection. Religion is not about the elimination of desire but its *transformation* from lower to higher forms—the transformation of the suffering world into one more compassionate, loving, and just."[28]

To Driver the priest is not God's sole mediator. After the congregation has listened to the priest, he should listen to the congregation—in songs, prayers, plays, dance, and sermon response.

How can rituals again become an integral part of modern life, furnishing not only comfort but also solutions? Driver responds that "since the message of the gospel is liberation, and since a sacrament celebrating that gospel is the performance of a freedom, a Christian sacrament tends to break through any particular form." Driver defines a Christian sacrament as "an action of God together with the people of God, ritually performed to celebrate freedom and to hasten the liberation of the whole world. A ritual in which deity is not active is no sacrament. The end toward which Christian sacramental action turns is the health and harmony of all creation. The ultimate aim is the overcoming of evil (oppression) and the transformation of the whole earth into the commonwealth of God."[29]

References

[1] James G. Frazer, *The Golden Bough* (Macmillan, 1951), p. 341.
[2] Tom F. Driver, *The Magic of Ritual* (HarperSanFrancisco, 1991), p. 98. Driver is Professor of Theology at Union Theological Seminary.
[3] Wilber, *Up From Eden*, p. 66.
[4] Driver, p. 112.
[5] Ibid., p. 116.
[6] Ibid., p. 93.
[7] Ibid., p. 96.
[8] Ibid., p. 4.
[9] Ibid., p. 106.
[10] Frazer, p. 477.
[11] Mircea Eliade, *The Myth of the Eternal Return* (Princeton University Press, 1971), p. 20.
[12] Durant, *Our Oriental Heritage*, p. 398.
[13] Zimmer, p. 59.
[14] Radhakrishnan, p. 313.
[15] Quoted in Zimmer, p. 586.
[16] Joseph Campbell & Charles Musès, eds., *In All Her Names* (HarperSanFrancisco, 1991), p. 73.
[17] Joe Fisher & Joel L. Whitton, *Life Between Life* (Warner Books, 1988), p. 44.
[18] Fosco Maraini, *Meeting with Japan* (Viking, 1960), p. 39.
[19] Daisetz T. Suzuki, *Zen and Japanese Culture* (Pantheon Books, 1959), p. 370.
[20] Hertzberg, p. 17.
[21] Ibid., p. 83.
[22] Angus, p. 249.
[23] Elémire Zolla, in Ibish, p. 109.
[24] Quoted in John A. Williams, ed., *Islam* (Braziller, 1962), p. 99.
[25] Driver, p. 47.
[26] Ibid., p. 99.
[27] Ibid., p. 169.
[28] Ibid., pp. 171-72.
[29] Ibid., pp. 202, 207.

Chapter 5

The Status of Women in Religion

It is probably true that the human species has worshipped chief feminine deities much longer than we have worshipped masculine deities. Numerous sculptures of women, some dating back to about 25,000 B.C., have been found in the Gravettian-Aurignacian cultures of the Upper Paleolithic Age. The sites seem to span a period of at least ten thousand years.

The Great Mother — Unitive

A female triad figure from about 13,000 B.C. has been found at Vienne in Europe. Professor Ken Wilber states that "as far back as the Paleolithic caves, the chief object of sculpture is the female figure. These figures were apparently the first objects of worship of the species Homo sapiens."[1]

Archeologist James Mellaart says that human art made its first appearance about 9000 B.C. in the form of animal carvings and statuettes of the Mother Goddess, the supreme deity. The Hindu scholar Ananda Coomaraswamy said that it cannot be doubted "that a cult of the One Madonna existed already in the Paleolithic Age."[2]

Archeologist Marija Gimbutas reports that the many early statues of the Creator Goddess show her with a pregnant belly, large vulva, and exaggerated breasts and buttocks. These distortions stress Her role in life giving, life sustaining, life taking, and regeneration. Wilber says that some early art depicts Her as a cow-goddess, since the period that produced Her was an agricultural era. She is seen as the mother and nourisher of life.

The Gaia hypothesis, proposed by biologists James Lovelock and Lynne Margulis, states that the Earth is a unified living system designed to give and sustain life. Gaia is the ancient

Greek name for the Mother Goddess, the Creatrix. Other names are Nammu in the Fertile Crescent, Nut in Egypt, Nana Buluka in Africa, and Goddess of the Serpent Skirt in the Americas. Joseph Campbell believes that an infant moves from considering the mother as universe to regarding the universe as mother. Modern ecology warns us that we have only one ecosystem, and thus that we should treat mother earth with tender loving care. Sometimes we treat her so roughly that we seem to be at war with our own mother. We must protect her and care for her in our own self interest!

The Great Mother was worshipped in Europe from 7000 B.C. to 500 A.D., a much longer period than the current masculine deities have reigned. During this era many important human customs and institutions developed, such as agriculture, architecture, ceramics, government, law, medicine, metallurgy, textiles, wheeled vehicles, and written language.

"Most Near East and Middle East feminine deities were called Queen of Heaven. The Celtic Cerridwen was the Goddess of Knowledge, the priestesses of the Goddess Gaia provided the wisdom of divine revelation at pre-Greek sanctuaries, while the Greek Demeter and the Egyptian Isis were both involved as lawgivers and sage dispensers of justice."[3]

From early Jericho clay figures of the Great Mother have been found. Such statues are common in many Neolithic sites. Karnak, Chartres, and Mont-St. Michel have also revealed similar carvings.

In this agricultural era a kinship was felt between mother (mater) and matter (materia). Durant lists Ishtar and Cybele, Demeter and Ceres, Aphrodite, Venus, and Freya as "comparatively late forms of the ancient goddesses of the earth."[4] Their fertility guaranteed an abundant harvest to believers. Their birth, marriage, child rearing, and death symbolized the annual rotation of the seasons.

Most evidence indicates that this was a peaceful period in human history. Hesiod, the classical Greek poet, called it a Golden Age, before mankind learned the art of collective warfare. In many of the early societies, such as Crete, Sumer, and Egypt, women served as priestesses, a role difficult for them to achieve in many modern churches.

The Great Mother — Divisive

In about 7500 B.C. it seems that humans did not understand that sexual intercourse produced new human life. Since pregnant women did not menstruate, these people felt that the retained blood produced the new baby. Thus, the Great Mother needed new blood to produce a child. At first humans, and later animals, were sacrificed to give the Great Mother the needed blood.

Wilber explains that when the Great Goddess succeeded the Great Mother (about 3500 B.C.), the sacrifice could be merely symbolic rather than literal, since the Great Goddess required consciousness instead of blood. Wilber states that fundamentalists in a religion take beliefs literally rather than symbolically. Such believers in Christianity and Islam perpetuate the Great Mother (rather than the Great Goddess) approach, and murder, in blood sacrifice, those who disagree with them. "Holy war is nothing but thinly rationalized Great Mother worship, and the exoteric Christians and Muslims have killed more people in the name of a 'divinity' than any other peoples in history."[5]

Early kings were considered sacred, thus consorts of the Great Mother, and thus suffered ritual regicide, often at their own hands. "What we call civilization, and what we call human sacrifice, came into being together," says Wilber.[6] Why did the king have to die? First, to expiate guilt for incestuous wish to have sex with the Great Mother. Next, it was felt that the rite would magically insure fertility of crops and humans. Finally, this was a way for the king to achieve immortality, for to die in the body is to live in the spirit.

The Great Goddess

There were important differences between the Great Mother and the Great Goddess. Whereas the Mother was material, natural, and biological (with cosmic overtones), the Goddess was transcendent, spiritual, and immortal. The Great Goddess opposed every type of evil, not only the external form such as war, but also the internal form, such as anger and desire.

Instead of sacrificing someone else (as the Great Mother demanded), the Great Goddess wanted self-sacrifice, not in a literal manner, but inwardly and symbolically. As in Hinduism, the motto was to die to self in order to live to Self (the Holy

Spirit within oneself). Even today in India the Great Goddess is widely worshipped in non-Aryan regions.

Riane Eisler has pointed out that just as patriarchy is wrong, so is matriarchy, since both are dominator societies. What is needed in both deity and in life is a partnership concept. Wilber explains that "there is One Ground or Archetypal Deity which underlies all manifestation. Historically the transcendent or esoteric Great Goddess myths were the first to reflect this subtle-level oneness or archetypal ground."[7] The Ground is neither feminine nor masculine, but Being.

Women in Primitive Society

Passage to patriarchy was deadly to primitive women. Now she was bought with a dowry, like a slave. When her husband died, she was bequeathed as property. In countries like New Guinea, Fiji, and India, she was killed and buried with her dead husband, or expected to commit suicide so that she could wait on him in the next world. Now the double standard of sexual morality arose. In old Russia the father struck the bride gently with a whip, and then gave the whip to the groom! Mothers sometimes destroyed their female children to keep them from misery. In Fiji, dogs, but not women, were allowed in some temples!

The favorite primitive taboos involved women. For countless reasons a woman was considered to be "unclean." Menstruation was a time of special "uncleanliness." Many women felt ashamed during their periods. Menstrual blood is considered taboo by many tribes. The Encounter Bay tribe of South Australia say that if a boy sees menstrual blood his strength will fail prematurely. The Dieri of Central Australia say that if a menstruating woman bathes in a river, the fish will die and the water will dry up. In Muralug, an island in the Torres Straits, such a woman cannot eat any sort of fish, lest it cause the fisheries to fail. Many North American Indian tribes secluded menstruating women as unclean.

In some tribes childbirth was an unclean state for the mother, and she had to purify herself through laborious religious rites. In Northern Papua a man should not be seen associating with a woman, even his wife. Sexes are often segregated in primitive society, and males often form secret societies which serve as a refuge from women. In Madagascar women had to dance night and day while husbands engaged in warfare. In Mexico a young girl was sacrificed as a personification of the Maize Goddess. She was beheaded and skinned, and a priest danced in her bloody skin to assure a good maize harvest.

Among the Sea Dyaks of Banting in Sarawak women must observe strict rules while their husbands are hunting. They must arise at earliest light so that husbands, who are away, will not oversleep. They may not oil their hair, lest their husbands slip on the hunt. Daytime naps are taboo, for their husbands might get drowsy while hunting. At each meal some rice is left in a pot, so that the husband will not go hungry. Wives cannot sew with a needle, lest their husbands cut themselves on sharp sticks. At the Norse rites for the worship of Baldur, a man who had sexual intercourse with a woman was considered to have defiled himself.

Divisive religion was the rule once men established their dominance in primitive society. But unitive religion was found in rare instances. For example, in Africa among the Gallas a woman who tires of housekeeping has a way out. If she raves and acts peculiarly, her husband assumes she is possessed of the holy spirit Callo, so she is freed of her housework and called "Lord" by her husband.

Ancient Germans believed that there was something holy in women. Sacred women were used as oracles, and some were worshipped as a goddess. For instance, in the reign of Vespasian a woman named Veleda, of the Bructeri tribe, was considered to be a deity. She was regarded as so holy that men were not allowed to be in her presence.

Women in Ancient Egypt

Women's status was relatively high in ancient Egypt. Men married their sisters partly to enjoy the family inheritance, which passed from the mother to the daughter. James Frazer found Isis to be the stronger half of the combination deity with her brother/husband Osiris. Herodotus wrote that in Egypt women transacted the business while their husbands stayed at home and wove. Dr. Margaret Murray studied Egyptian royalty, and determined that in most periods Egyptian culture was matrilinear. Charles Musès, in a tirade against modern warfare, says that "we hypocritically condemn ritual killers like 'the Manson family,' while condoning the same monstrous behavior politically on a mass scale. We had better recall the ancient teaching, especially in Egypt, of the sacredness of individual life."[8]

Women in Mesopotamia

Both unitive and divisive religion are found in the status of Mesopotamian women. James Hastings, in his *Dictionary of the Bible,* says that Ashtoreth (Astarte) as goddess was "the chief divinity of the Semites in their primitive matriarchal stage of organization."[9] The Babylonian goddess Inanna, later called Ishtar, is also identified with the ancient Germanic Oster (which became our word Easter), and the Greek Astarte. The Code of Hammurabi showed that Babylonian women had the right to hold and manage their own estates.

On the other hand, in ancient Sumeria young girls were considered honored to serve as temple concubines. Adultery was a forgivable whim in men, but a fatal offense in women. Girl infants were not desired in ancient Persia, since they would be reared for some other man's profit. The Persians said that "men do not pray for daughters, and angels do not reckon them among their gifts to mankind."[10]

Manicheanism, begun by Mani in Persia in A.D. 242, taught that woman is Satan's masterpiece, the chief temptress of man into sin. Magian clergy ultimately succeeded in getting Mani crucified.

Women in Classical Greece and Rome

In Homeric Greece many of the deities were goddesses, with centers for Hera at Argos, Athena at Athens, and Demeter and Persephone at Eleusis. There were many female trinities: Fates, Furies, Graces, Hours, and the judges of Paris (Aphrodite, Athena, and Hera). Women prophets were recognized in both Greek and Roman religions. In the early period women mingled freely in public with men, and had serious discussions with them.

Later, Spartan women were given strenuous physical games, and were encouraged to parade nude in public, to stimulate them to take good care of their bodies. Strictly controlled by the state, Spartan women were given no mental education. In Athens the *hetaira* was common—a woman who lived with a man in an unlicensed union, with admission to men's circles. Aspasia, companion to the ruler Pericles, ran a school of rhetoric and philosophy, open to men and women alike.

Most Athenian women, however, although they could take part in religious observances, were excluded from most contact with men. Euripides, the famous playwright, said that intellect handicaps a woman, and Aristotle, perhaps the greatest mind of antiquity, said that slaves and women were inferior beings! In *Lysistrata* Aristophanes says that women should go on a sexual moratorium until men give up their stupid war making. Greek drama has some of the greatest women characters in all of world literature: Alcestis, Antigone, Cassandra, Electra, Hecuba, Iphigenia, and Medea.

In 205 B.C. Romans believed that if the Great Mother (Magna Mater) were to be brought to Rome, Hannibal (the Carthaginian general) would leave Italy. So a black stone, believed to be an incarnation of the Great Mother, was paraded through Rome, and self-emasculated priests served her. No Roman was emasculated—foreign converts served the purpose. Every April the Feast of the Great Goddess was held in Rome, first with wild sorrow and then with profound rejoicing.

Rome's goddess was Roma. Great games were held in connection with her annual festivals. Emperor Claudius urged Romans to worship the Great Goddess at her festival at the spring equinox. Other Romans worshipped Isis, the Egyptian goddess of motherhood.

The goddess Ma was worshipped by fanatic priests (*fanatici* meant belonging to the *fanum* or temple), who slashed themselves with knives and spread their blood on the statue of the goddess. The priests of the goddess Cybele emasculated themselves, and cut their arms and drank their own blood, out of mourning for the death of Attis, Cybele's son.

The Roman family had a family hearth honoring the goddess Vesta, goddess of the family. The Vestal Virgins protected the city's sacred fire. Other Roman goddesses included Terra Mater (Mother Earth) and Bona Dea (the Good Goddess), who provided fertility to women and fields.

There were, of course, disparaging views of women, too. Pliny said that the mere touch of a menstruous woman turned wine to vinegar, blighted crops, killed bees, blunted razors, and caused mares to miscarry.

The Role of Women in Judaism

Both divisive and unitive roles are found in Jewish religion. The Talmud permitted polygamy, but adultery was a rarely enforced capital crime. A man could divorce his loud-mouthed wife! Desertion by a husband was not ground for a wife's divorce. Talmudic law blamed woman for Eve's sinful acts. One rabbi ruled that the testimony of 100 women constituted only one witness! Women's earning and estate belonged to their husbands. A husband could beat his wife "within reason." Women were restricted to a secluded spot of worship in the synagogue, and were not given the advantage of an education. In the Mishnah rabbis declare that women who try to be church leaders are immodest, since they are trying to play men's roles. Women were not allowed to read the Torah aloud in a public place. The Talmud says that if a woman at the beginning of her period passes between two men, one of the two men automatically dies.

On the other hand, in Proverbs 8:22-32 the Great Goddess as Wisdom reveals that She was with Yahweh at the creation of the universe. In the older Jewish synagogues women held such exalted roles as elder, priest, ruler of the synagogue, and mother of the synagogue.[11] Women attended religious feasts with men (I Samuel 1:1), took part in sacrifices (Judges 13:20), and even joined in the Temple choir (Ezra 2:65).

Although in general women were in subjection to men, some wives are seen as their husbands' true helpmates, as in Sarah, Rebecca, and Rachel. Women could be prophets, like Huldah, or leaders like Esther, Miriam, and Deborah. Motherhood was exalted, since the Jews wanted more population. They made marriage compulsory after the age of 20, even in priests, and made abortion and infanticide heathenish customs abominable to the Lord.

The Status of Women in Christianity

Jesus Christ changed the whole idea of women's subjection to men. His teachings on marriage, adultery, and divorce were revolutionary, and His personal treatment of women showed unprecedented tenderness, understanding, and love.

The Apostle Paul's treatment of women is paradoxical. Everyone knows that he said that women should be quiet in church and be subjected to their husbands. But his behavior shows other feelings. When he first came to Philippi, Paul stayed with Lydia, the founder of the Christian church there. His letter to the Philippians is addressed to three women there. Phoebe, Christian minister of the church at Cenchreae, carried Paul's letter to the Romans. Paul called Phoebe his patron. Of the 28 Roman Christians thanked by Paul, 10 were women. Paul called Junia, in Rome, "foremost among the apostles" (Rom. 16:7). Paul also said that in Christ "there is no male or female" (Gal. 3:28).

Other New Testament sources also spoke highly of women. Acts 2: 17-18 indicates that women, blessed by the Holy Spirit, could prophesy. Both Elizabeth and Mary prophesied (Luke, chapter 1). Luke says that four daughters of Philip were prophets (Acts 21: 8-9). An epitaph on the Greek island of Thera shows Epiktas, a woman, as a priest. A Roman basilica has a mosaic lettered Bishop Theodora. In A.D. 312 Lucilla, head of the Christian clergy in Carthage and Numidia, got a bishop deposed for opposing veneration of Christian martyrs.

But women had to swim against the tide. Many Church Fathers, like Origen, Tertullian, and Chrysostom, said that women should confine themselves to domestic affairs. These leaders avowed that women's virtues were chastity, silence, and obedience. One argument used against women church leaders was that, since they challenged men's natural superiority, they were undoubtedly unchaste and untrustworthy persons. As long as church services were held in homes, women could serve as leaders, since the home was their territory. But in the fourth century, when most services were held in public places, women rarely served in positions of authority in the church. An ascetic woman was sometimes considered to be good enough to be regarded as "an honorary man!"

St. Augustine had trouble with Genesis 1:27, which stated that God created humans in His image, male and female. True, said Augustine, both sexes had a rational soul capable of contemplating God, but with this difference: the masculine element concentrated on knowing God, but the feminine element focused on perpetuating the species, and thus on sex. Augustine concluded that therefore the male body reflected God's image in a way that the female body could not!

The modern Vatican declares that "the incarnation of the Word took place according to the male sex." A medieval abbot refused responsibility for supervising a nunnery, saying, "We, and our whole community of canons, recognizing that the wickedness of women is greater than all other wickedness of the world, have unanimously decreed for the safety of our souls, that we will on no account receive any more sisters, but will avoid them like poisonous animals."[12] Although Martin Luther favored marriage for priests, he agreed that "woman was not the equal of man in glory and prestige."[13]

An exception in this general downgrading of women was always made for the Virgin Mary. In A.D. 431 Archbishop Cyril of Alexandria applied to her many of the terms formerly used at Ephesus for the Great Goddess Artemis-Diana. That year the Council of Ephesus granted Mary the title of "Mother of God." Gradually Mary assimilated the better features of Astarte, Cybele, Diana, and Isis. The Feast of the Assumption of Mary was later dated on August 13, the date of the ancient festivals of Artemis and Isis. It was not so much the Church as the people that encouraged Mariolatry. The pity of the mother of Christ assuaged the stern warnings of sinners facing hellfire and damnation. Mary, being human, understood temptation and sin and could more readily forgive it than could a perfect deity, it was felt. By medieval times many Christians believed that Mary had reversed the original sinfulness of Eve, and Eva became Ave. as in Hail, Mary (Ave Maria).

In medieval Europe a feudal master who seduced his female serf against her will paid a fine of three shillings. The church did not condone divorce, but permitted separation for adultery, apostasy, or extreme cruelty. The usually kind St. Thomas Aquinas said that woman was subject to man because of her weak body and mind! His view was that "Man is the beginning of woman and her end. Children ought to love their father more than their mother."[14]

After many centuries in which priests were allowed to marry, the Lateran Council in A.D. 1123 forbade the marriage of priests. Whether priests should be allowed to marry is at present an extremely divisive issue in the Roman Catholic Church.

Men are nine times as holy as women, according to figures compiled by Sister Martha Ann Kirk.[15] Of all entries in the

Dictionary of Catholic Biography, fewer than eight per cent refer to women, Kirk found. She also reported that men saints outnumber women saints by the ratio of four to one. But some female saints have been outstanding. Monica, the mother of Augustine, and Helena, the mother of Emperor Constantine, are early leaders who did much for the Christian church. St. Catherine of Siena confronted the pope in Avignon, and told him to forget about French luxury and get back to the business of spiritual leadership in Rome. St. Catherine of Genoa became a hospital administrator (a rarity for a woman in 1492), and she also developed the doctrine of purgatory that became standard in the Roman Catholic Church in later years. St. Teresa of Avila not only steered St. John of the Cross into effective ministry but also founded 17 reformed convents for women and 15 monasteries for reformed monks. In our time Mother Teresa is respected as one of the greatest persons of the 20th century.

The Status of Women in Islam

Huston Smith, an authority on comparative religion, points out that viewed in a historical perspective, Mohammed vastly improved women's rights. The Koran forbids infanticide, and grants daughters rights to inheritance. The rights to education, suffrage, and vocation are open to women, and are being increasingly made available to them. Marriage rites were tightened. Marriage was sanctified by making it the sole lawful focus of the sexual act. A woman must give her free consent in marriage, even to a sultan. Divorce regulations were clarified, and women were to be granted alimony if the marriage failed. Four witnesses were required to prove adultery in a wife. Every effort must be made to keep a marriage from dissolution.[16]

A recent meeting of Moslem women, however, indicates that many ideals for equal treatment are not being realized. The Sisterhood Is Global Institute, an organization to promote women's rights founded in 1984, organized a conference in May 1996 to try to further their cause. Moslem women from many countries protested that they still lack access to education and to political action, and often are restricted in their right to travel. Some of the women are asking to argue their request for equality within the code of the Sharia, the Islamic legal code. Elizabeth Mayer, a professor who has studied Moslem women's conditions, admits there is much ground to be covered before Islamic women have the rights afforded Western women. But she sees more improvement coming, for the Moslem women are "actually better organized than American feminists these days. The United States is the only country in the Western world," says Mayer, "except for a few Roman Catholic states, that has not ratified the United Nations convention on discrimination against women."[17]

The Role of Women in Oriental Religion

In Vedic India (2000-1000 B.C.) women had relatively high status. They appeared at public games and feasts, and took part in religious ceremonies. Because of their customs, "marriage by consent was considered slightly disreputable; women thought it to be more honorable to be bought and paid for, and a great compliment to be stolen."[18] But in the Heroic Age (1000-500 B.C.) *purdah*, the seclusion of women, began, and the practice of *suttee* (widow immolation), little known in Vedic times, increased.

Hindu legend says that Twashtri, the Divine Artificer, exhausted most of his materials in making man, and so he had to use nature's odds and ends to create woman: "the curves of creepers, the trembling of grass, the bloom of flowers, the glances of deer, the gaiety of sunbeams, and the fickleness of winds."[19]

The Code of Manu, of Brahmin origin, says, "The source of strife is woman; therefore avoid women." A woman was expected to walk behind her husband in public, and address him as "master." She ate what was left after all the male family members were finished eating. If a woman reads the sacred texts, it is a sign of confusion in the realm. Brahmins often kept their wives illiterate, fearing that if they learned to read they would try to escape subjection. A woman could not hold property or divorce her husband.

Suttee (a wife dying on her husband's funeral pyre) came from the Scythians and the Thracians. Some widows seem to have wanted to die with their husbands. Other widows lived celibate lives in honor of their dead husbands. Sexual propriety was very high in ancient India, and prostitution relatively rare.

In the Padma Purana one reads "There is no other god on earth for a woman than her husband." If she remarries, she disgraces herself, she is told, and in the next incarnation will enter the womb of a jackal.

In early China women could not divorce their husbands, but could return to their parents. The Chinese word for "wife" meant "equal." The wife preserved her own name after marriage. In the third century A.D. women held high administrative posts in Chinese government.

Tantrism, as found in Tibet, is unique in escaping the male chauvinism found in most early religions. Since all human beings are perceived to be members of the mystical family of God, there can be no racial or sexual discrimination. Thus there are no castes in Tantrism, and women are eligible to receive the highest initiation rites, and can even become gurus. One achieves nirvana not by denying nature but by enjoying it. The body is *devata,* the visible form of Brahma. A person can be one with the divine not only through meditation but in every daily act. When one drinks wine, it is "the Savior Herself in liquid form."[20] Sexual intercourse becomes a symbolic act; in sexual union one forgets one's own ego and thinks of oneself as Siva, engaged in divine ecstasy.

As in China, women held a higher position in early Japan than later, when feudalism made women something like serfs. There were six empresses in the imperial age. But the father always ruled the family. "He could kill a child convicted of unchastity or a serious crime. He could sell his children into slavery or prostitution, and he could divorce his wife with a word."[21] Despite all this, filial piety continued to be the highest order of manners in Japan.

The Witch Hunt — Divisive Religion at Its Worst

Witches have always been a thorn in the side of religion, but the witch hunt in Europe from 1484 to 1760 plumbed new depths. In 1484 Pope Innocent VIII issued a bull declaring the absolute reality of witches, and the Bible said that witches should be put to death. In 1485 141 women were burned to death as witches in Italy. Two Dominican inquisitors, Jakob Sprenger and Heinrich Kramer wrote *The Witches' Hammer,* purporting to describe how witches behaved. "All witchcraft comes from carnal lust, which in women is insatiable," they declared.[22] Witches were alleged to cast spells, cause disease, and eat children. Any eccentric or individualistic woman was suspected of witchcraft. Victims would be tortured until they confessed, and then they were killed.

The expulsion of the last Jews from Europe in the 1490s left Christianity with the need for convenient scapegoats. Germany, where the witch hunt was most virulent, was used to persecution, having practiced vicious anti-Semitism during the Middle Ages. Inhuman practices against the Jews were justified because the Jews were considered to be less than human. The same line of crazy reasoning led to persecuting women as witches. In fact, Jews and women were considered to have similar undesirable traits: both practiced magic, both had devil's marks on their bodies, both travestied the Christian rite of communion, both caused storms and plagues, and both had rituals with demons. Satan was depicted as having Jewish features. Witches were depicted as ugly crones with hooked noses. In Hungary, for a first offense a witch had to stand all day in the public square wearing a Jew's hat.

The Protestant Reformation was a further contributor to the witch craze. John Calvin condoned the burning of witches. "The violent breakup of the unity of Christendom led not only to creative religious ferment within both Protestant and Catholic churches but to massive confusion, anxiety, and suspicion as well. Part of this was defused through witch hunting."[23]

In about 1560 Europe experienced convulsive problems: the Reformation, population increases, religious wars, food shortages, and runaway inflation. Probably three-fourths of all executions for witchcraft occurred in the Holy Roman Empire, centered in Germany. Of these three-fourths took place in the Catholic section of Germany. A total of over 200,000 persons were accused of witchcraft during the craze, and of these 100,000 were killed. Of the accused 80% were women, and of those killed 85% were female.

Kangaroo court procedures were used in witchcraft trials. Often the court held secret sessions, denied the use of defense lawyers and cross-examination, presumed guilt, and employed prejudiced witnesses. The belief was that the church needed to protect itself from heretics at all costs. The families of the accused often had to pay for bizarre entertainments and banquets for the judges and priests who conducted the trials.

In 1583 in Vienna a 16-year old girl suffering from stomach cramps was exorcised by Jesuit priests for eight weeks. The priests alleged that they had expelled 12,652 demons from her, demons which her grandmother had kept as houseflies. After torture, the grandmother confessed she was a witch and had had sex with Satan. Naturally she was burned at the stake.

A midwife, Walpurga Hausmänin of Dilligen in Germany, was killed as a witch in 1587. The court of the Bishop of Augsburg had these things done to her: her breasts and arms were branded five times with hot iron; her right hand was cut off; her body was burned at the stake, and her ashes thrown into a river. Her estate went into the bishop's treasury.

Midwives and folk healers were watched for signs of witchcraft. It was said of them, "If they can cure, they can kill." If their cures did not work, they were also guilty, accused of practicing black magic.

In Trier, from 1587-1593, 368 witches were burned under the direction of the Jesuit priest Peter Binsfeld. At Quedlinburg 133 persons were executed in one day in 1589, and at Eichstätt 274 were burned at the stake in the year 1629. Sometimes a prominent man, when accused of witchcraft, would permit his wife to be persecuted in his stead.

In Luxembourg women convicted of infanticide were buried alive, but men convicted of the same offense were fined or let go free. At Wurzburg 41 young children were executed as witches. Anna Pappenheimer, a Lutheran in Catholic Munich in 1600, was tortured until she confessed to being a witch. Then, before being burned at the stake, her breasts were cut off. This "dewomanized her, saying that the most dangerous thing about this evil woman was her sexuality, that her only hope of salvation lay in not becoming a woman."[24]

At the same time at witchcraft trials in Lorraine the chief judge Nicolas Remy "boasted that he had sent eight or nine hundred to their deaths and tortured as many more, and sentenced the children of convicted witches to be beaten with rods as they watched their parents being burned alive, and then wondered if he had been too lenient!" Remy said that "owing to its feebleness of understanding, the female sex is least able to resist the wiles of the Devil."[25]

During that period in Franche-Comtè witchcraft judge Henri Boguet said that women witches passed their craft down to their daughters. Women became witches because of their inordinate love of carnal pleasure, Boguet stated, and they permitted Satan to speak through the women's "shameful parts." To his crazed mind all werewolves were female.

Where demonological beliefs were weaker than in Germany and France, there was less persecution for witchcraft. Also, where there was no church inquisition, there was less cruelty and violence. So in Britain, Russia, Scandinavia, and Islamic countries the witch hunt was relatively subdued. English law forbade torture, and so few witches were found to be guilty in England and Wales.

Scotland, however, was an exception to this trend. It seemed that from 1590 until 1700 the Scottish church and the government competed to see which was "the most godly," that is, the most cruel. When the courts would restrain the hunt, the Presbyterian national church would redouble its intensity. Then, when the church relaxed, the Privy Council would declare an emergency concerning witches. Calvinist tenets backfired as a boon to women. Calvinism declared women adults as fully responsible for their souls, but then blamed them because so many chose to serve Satan as witches In Scotland a woman was burned at the stake after being convicted of having turned her daughter into a pony!

In the New England trials for witchcraft, women who were inheritors were unusually liable to accusations. Financial independence was something many Puritan men denied to women. The church reinforced the idea that a woman belonged in the kitchen.

New England's witchcraft trials were far fewer than those going on in Europe at that time. Also, there were no executions for witchcraft in French or Spanish America. This is remarkable, in view of the fact that magic was widely believed in by the native Americans, the African Americans and the European Americans. There were, of course, religious persecutions by the Inquisitional courts in Central and South America. The final legal execution of a witch occurred in Switzerland in 1782.

What were the results of the witch craze? Women learned to be quiet, for almost anything could be turned against them.

Fewer rapes were reported. Women feared to make any sort of overt protest. During the slave-taking period, women and slaves had much in common: "Neither had control over what they produced, and their labor could be coerced. Both were seen by the law as children. Both could legally be beaten, debased, and humiliated. Under certain conditions defined by their masters/husbands, both could be put to death for being what they were—female, or black."[26]

Modern Feminism

After reviewing the lowly status in which religion kept women through most of recent history, it is no wonder that modern feminism has demanded equal treatment with men. In 1792 Mary Wollstonecraft wrote *A Vindication of the Rights of Women,* in which she said that it dishonored God to assume that God created women as inferior beings. The Scottish feminist Frances Wright came to the United States in 1819, and immediately crusaded for equal educational opportunities for women. As the Grimké sisters, Angelina and Sarah, spoke against their own slave-holding family and were rebuked, they were reminded of how many other rights were being denied American women at this time.

America's first great spokesperson for women was Ralph Emerson's friend Margaret Fuller. In 1845 she published *Woman in the 19th Century,* based upon the assumption that God created men and women in His image, to be equal partners as stewards of God's creation. She noted the many inequities in women's status: They could not vote or hold public office. In the eyes of the law they were considered to be minors. They could not hold property in their own names. Wife beating was legal in almost all states. Unfortunately she drowned, with her husband and child, in a storm in 1850.

In 1848 at Seneca Falls in New York a Women's Declaration of Independence was adopted, protesting, among other items, the subordinate role permitted women in the church. Recent books by women have sought to construct a feminist theology. Rosemary Radford Ruether, a theology professor, has attempted to use the prophetic principles of the Bible to denounce all oppressive ideologies, such as masculine chauvinism, in the name of a liberating God. Elisabeth Schüssler, a professor at Notre Dame

University, calls for a return to early Christianity, when women were active leaders in the church. Sherry Ruth Anderson and Patricia Hopkins, in *The Feminine Face of God,* invoke the spirit of the Great Goddess to show how the divine feminine can provide the modern world with much needed insight and love.

In the United States today one out of two women is a victim of domestic violence or sexual assault in her lifetime. In 1989 a man massacred 14 female students, meanwhile screaming that he hated women. An English archbishop in 1968 opposed ordination of Anglican women, explaining that "if the church be thrown open to women, it will be the death knell of the appeal of the church for men."[27] An Episcopal bishop in San Francisco in 1971 said that Christ's sexuality as masculine was not accidental, but by divine choice. Even today Jewish men pray daily, "Blessed art Thou, O Lord, who has not made me a woman." Islamic women cringe to hear the words of Mohammed: "When Eve was created, Satan rejoiced."

Slowly, all too slowly, churches are learning what an affront it is to God to assume that God plays favorites. Some churches now ordain women. "The bird of the spirit of humanity cannot fly with only one wing," wisely commented the Hindu scholar Vivekananda. "Women," says Hans Küng, "should have at least that dignity, freedom, and responsibility in the Church which they are guaranteed in modern society: equal rights in canon law, in church decision making, and in opportunities to study theology and be ordained."[28]

References

1. Wilber, *Up From Eden*, p. 120.
2. Campbell, *In All Her Names*, p. 53.
3. Merlin Stone, *When God Was A Woman* (Dorset Press, 1976), p. 4.
4. Durant, *Our Oriental Heritage*, p. 60.
5. Wilber, *Up From Eden*, p. 137.
6. Ibid., p. 127.
7. Ibid., p. 140.
8. Campbell, *In All Her Names*, p. 49.
9. Stone, p. 165.
10. Durant, *Our Oriental Heritage*, p. 375.
11. Karen Jo Torjesen, *When Women Were Priests* (HarperSanFrancisco, 1995), p. 2.
12. Ibid., pp. 226-27.
13. Ibid., p. 240.
14. Durant, *The Age of Faith*, p. 825.
15. Martha Ann Kirk, *St. Anthony's Messenger,* November 1982, p. 19.
16. Huston Smith, *The World's Religions* (HarperSanFrancisco, 1991), pp. 251-53.
17. *New York Times*, 12 May 1996, p. 3.
18. Durant, *Our Oriental Heritage,* p. 401.
19. Ibid., p. 492.
20. Zimmer, p. 577.
21. Durant, *Our Oriental Heritage,* p. 860.
22. James A. Haught, *Holy Horrors* (Prometheus Books, 1990), p. 74.
23. Anne Llewellyn Barstow, *Witchcraze* (Harper Collins, 1995), p. 60.
24. Ibid., p. 150.
25. Ibid., p. 65.
26. Ibid., pp. 159-60.
27. Stone, p. 238.
28. Hans Küng, *On Being A Christian* (Doubleday, 1976), pp. 526-27.

CHAPTER 6

UNITIVE RELIGION: A SOLUTION TO JEWISH-MOSLEM DISCORD

This age of survival has forced all religious groups to undergo a reconception of their goals and practices, eliminating divisive tendencies as much as possible and stressing unitive traits instead. As Judaism and Islam face up to reconception, they can find historic foundations of oneness between these two great faiths. This chapter will delineate these areas of common unitive religion in Judaism and Islam.

Both the origin and the solution of the Jewish-Moslem conflict are scriptural. Descendants of the half-brothers, Ishmael and Isaac, are quarreling over their patrimony. The Jews were told in the Old Testament that they are to inherit Canaan as God's preferred people. The Moslems were told in the Koran that followers of Ishmael are God's preferred people, and that the Canaanites were forerunners of the Moslems. Each faith feels it has a holy sanction to its claims.

The solution, however, is also found in scriptures. From Judah the prophet Amos visited Israel in the north and warned the people that God had no greater regard for Israel than for other nations. He was a God for all peoples, with a universal morality. If the Israelites ignored this teaching, great calamity would befall them. In their day, the calamity was capture by the Assyrians. In Amos 9:7 we read: "'Are ye not as children of the Ethiopians unto me, O children of Israel?' saith the Lord. 'Have not I brought up Israel out of the land of Egypt? And the Philistines from Caphtor, and the Syrians from Kir?'" Isaiah said that the God of Israel was the God of Egypt and Assyria: "In that day there shall be a highway out of Egypt to Assyria. In that day Israel shall be the third with Egypt and Assyria, whom the Lord of hosts shall bless, saying, 'Blessed be Egypt my people, and

Assyria the work of my hands, and Israel mine inheritance'" (Isaiah 19:23-25).

In the Koran, God tells Mohammed how He saved the children of Israel and told them to dwell in the Holy Land (xvii, 104-09). The Koran brings out Islam's alliance with Judaism: "Children of Israel, remember My blessing and that I have preferred you above all beings" (ii, 40). "And We gave to Moses the Book and the Salvation" (ii, 53). The Koran also states that God gave to Christ the gospel, "wherein is guidance and light, and confirming the Torah before it, as a guidance and an admonition unto the god fearing" (v, 50-53).

Judaism

The doctrine of universal salvation is found in Judaism. God is quoted as asking, "Have I any pleasure at all that the wicked should die, and not that he should return from his ways and live?" (Ezekiel 18:23). Arthur Hertzberg cites the *Seder Eliahu Rabbah*: "The spirit of holiness rests upon each person according to the deed that each does, whether that person be non-Jew or Jew, man or woman, manservant or maidservant." He also quotes from the *Exodus Rabbah*: "The Holy One does not disqualify any creature. He accepts everyone. The gates are always open, and who wants to enter may enter."[1]

Salvation open to all is likewise the view expressed in a letter by Moses Maimonides: "Our sages say 'The pious men among the Gentiles have a share in the world to come,' namely, if they have acquired what can be acquired of the knowledge of God, and if they ennoble their souls with worthy qualities. There is no doubt that every man who ennobles his soul with excellent morals and wisdom based on faith in God certainly belongs to the men of the world to come."[2]

The Old Testament admonishes us to be worthy members of the human family. "Have we all not one Father? Hath not one God created us? Why do we deal treacherously every man against his brother, profaning the covenant of our fathers?" (Malachi 2:10).

Judaism envisions the unity of the human race. At creation the entire species begins with one man and one woman. God's covenant with Noah involved the entire human race and the animal kingdom. Although Edomites were bitter enemies, the

Jews were told, 'You shall not abhor an Edomite, for he is your brother" (Deuteronomy 23:7). Ruth, from whose lineage came both David and Jesus, was from the hated Moabites. In the Talmud, when the ministering angels want to sing for joy over the Egyptians dying in the Red Sea, God replies, "My handiwork is drowning in the sea; would you utter song before me?"[3] This spirit of compassion and humanity is needed at the present time in the Middle East.

Erich Fromm called the Old Testament a revolutionary book, for it depicted mankind's liberation from submission to idols, from slavery, and from incestuous ties to blood and soil, to freedom for the individual, the nation, and all of humankind. Fromm noted the evolution from the concept of a limited god to a religion with faith in a nameless God, a Father who wants His family unified in love. Fromm points out that in His covenant God promises to respect all life, not merely that of the Jewish nation.

In later times, driven out of Christian lands, many Jews fled to Arabia. They almost equaled the number of Arabs in Medina, and their presence prepared the Arab mind for the Judaism of the Koran.

The Koran

Mohammed believed that from man's beginning, God had revealed the same faith to mankind through a succession of prophets, of whom he himself was the last. He stated that Abraham, Moses, David, and Jesus taught the same religion. This meant that the Pentateuch, the Psalms, and the Gospel are identical in substance with the Koran.

Mohammed had a Christlike love of children. When a Bedouin admitted that he never kissed children, Mohammed rebuked him, saying, "What shall I do to give back to you the mercy God has taken from your heart?" Imagine Mohammed's reaction to current Moslem terrorism that kills children indiscriminately along with adults.

A steady vein of altruism permeates unitive Islam. Mohammed describes a meeting he had with God, who told him: "As for the virtues, they consist of feeding the hungry, spreading peace, and performing the *Tahajjud* prayer at night." Mohammed further said that "God has no mercy on those who do not have mercy," and "No one has tasted the sweetness of faith who does not love his fellow man."[4] Consider how widely modern divisive Islam has fallen away from the intent of its founder!

Mohammed had part of the mosque set aside in which Christians could perform their rites. I wonder if those who bombed the U.S. marine barracks in Beirut were familiar with the fundamentals of their faith.

"One is struck," says John Alden Williams, "by the essential similarity of Mohammed to the prophets of the Old Testament. There is his tenderness for his people, his personal mildness where his own affairs were concerned, and his relentless zeal where he considered that the affairs of God were concerned."[5]

The Koran can be quoted several ways on the topic of salvation. In Sura 2 we read that "no one that follows any other religion than Islam will be accepted by God or saved from perishing in the life to come." But in Sura 3 we find the statement that "all such as believe in Allah and in the last day, who do that which is right, whether they are Jews, Christians, Sabeans, or Moslems, shall have their reward from Allah, who will take away from them all fear and grief." Faced with a choice, persons interested in human survival are urged to follow the unitive rather than the divisive teaching.

To Jews, Christians, and other People of the Book, the Koran says: "We have faith in that which has been revealed to us and in that which has been revealed unto you. Our God and your God are one, and unto Him we are resigned" (xxix, 46). Would that this tolerance characterized present-day religionists in the Holy Land!

Unitive parts of the Koran stress ecumenism and good works. For example, we read that "in religion there is no compulsion. Rectitude has become clear from error."[6] The Koran states that true piety is not to turn your face to the East or the West but "to believe in God, and the Last Day, the angels, the Book, and the prophets; to give of one's substance, however cherished, to kinsmen, orphans, the needy, the traveler, beggars; and to ransom the slave" (ii, 174-5) Be not deceived, warns the Koran, by everyone who says, "I believe in God and the Last Day," for many such are "workers of corruption." Rather, "give good tidings to those who believe and do deeds of righteousness; for them await gardens underneath which rivers flow" (ii, 1-23).

Moslem Syncretism

Organized at Basra about A.D. 983, the Brethren of Sincerity tried for a reform of Islam based on Greek philosophy, Christian ethics, Sufi mysticism, Shia politics, and Moslem law. They taught that every soul is restless until it rejoins the World Soul. In seeking purity, they said, we should model ourselves on the intellect of Socrates, the love of Christ, and the modest nobility of Ali. The educated person should interpret symbolically the Koran, whose crude expressions were fit for uncivilized desert people. This group was very influential on Jews and Moslems alike. Among the Jews influenced by the Brethren were Ibn Gabirol and Judah Halevi. Moslems who were influenced include al-Ghazzali, al-Ma'arri, and Avicenna, who in turn influenced Averroës of Islam, Moses Maimonides of Judaism, and Thomas Aquinas of Christianity.

Sufism

The most important Moslem mystics are the Sufis, that is, those who wear the *suf,* a simple woolen robe. The basic tenet of Sufism is the mutual love of God and man. To the Sufi love, or God, is what the world comprises. Who shows love shows God. Who shows hate shows Satan. The hatred underlying terrorism in the present Middle East would be something very far from God.

We should not fall in love, Sufis say, but rather rise in love. The worship of the Sufis bears very practical results: In loving another person, one is loving God. Helping someone else means helping God. To serve your neighbor is to serve God.

The Moslem mystic Jamal ad-Din al-Qasimi pointed out God's immanence and transcendence: "Not an atom's weight of anything exists apart from His knowledge," yet "space does not encompass Him, nor do the earths and the heavens contain Him. He is many stages beyond the earth and the watery abyss, yet in spite of this He is near to every existing thing. The Koran, the Torah, the Evangel, and the Psalter are Scriptures of His which He sent down to His messengers. He also spoke to Moses."[7]

The Sufis have been the Moslems who most stressed both mysticism and missionary work. The scholar Louis Massignon believes that it is its mysticism that has made Islam an international and a universal religion.

In the ninth and tenth centuries some Sufis became extreme ecstatics. Either they fell into ecstatic trances or else they became preoccupied with contemplating Divine Perfection until they experienced the unitive state attested by the mystics of all religions.

One ecstatic Sufi, Husayn ibn Mansur al-Hallaj, chose Jesus as his model, and following John 14:6, proclaimed, "I am the Truth." Since the Truth is one of the Moslem names for God, Hallaj was accused of claiming divinity. Hallaj had asserted that his mystical search had brought him into a temporary oneness with God. He was publicly scourged and crucified. He became a martyr to many Sufis. Before his crucifixion, Hallaj pronounced a benediction of Christlike forgiveness: "And these thy servants, who are gathered together to slay me in zeal for Thy religion, seeking Thy favor, forgive them. For if Thou hadst revealed to them that which Thou hast revealed to me, they would not have done that which they have done."[8]

Sufi mysticism demonstrates the basic similarity of all mystical religious search. Abu Sa'id ibn Abi Khayr was a Khurasani Sufi who wrote Persian quatrains mingling sacred and divine love. He wrote that "if men wish to draw near to God, they must seek Him in the hearts of men. They should speak well of all men, and like the sun, show the same face to all. To bring joy to a single heart is better than to build many shrines for worship. Thy praise, whatever tongue doth give it Thee, is fair."[9] Shunning ritual, Khayr sought good works. Modern divisive religionists in the Middle East would do well to learn to speak well of all persons, as he requested.

Jalal al-Din Rumi is called the theologian of Persian poetry. Achieving the supreme identity, he expressed it as follows:

> What is to be done, O Moslems? For I do not recognize myself.
> I am neither Christian nor Jew nor Gabr nor Moslem.
> I am not of the East, the West, the land, or the sea.
> My place is the Placeless.
> 'Tis neither body nor soul; for I belong to the soul of the Beloved.
> I have put duality away, I have seen that the two worlds are one.
> One I seek, One I know; He is the first, He is the last.[10]

Sufi doctrine has a message for international relations. It teaches that intense personal penitence can bring society into penitence, and thus generate the humility needed to bring down the pride of headstrong nations, which through arrogance like to act as if they are God's sole spokesmen. "The true way to hurt the enemy," it is said, "is to be occupied with the love of the Friend. On the other hand, if you engage in war with the enemy, he will have obtained what he wanted from you and at the same time you will have lost the opportunity of loving the Friend."[11]

Sufis teach that if someone is hostile towards you, you should do what God commands. If you do not defend yourself, God will defend you. If you defend yourself, God will leave your defense to you.

The Moslem mystic Ibn 'Arabi, who died in A.D. 1240, underlined the difference between the finite God of divisive religion and the infinite God of mysticism. He said that the narrow believer is self-centered and thus praises his God as if He were none other's. But "if he understood the saying of Junayd, 'The color of the water is the color of the vessel containing it,' he would not interfere with the beliefs of others, but would perceive God in every form and in every belief. The God of religious belief is subject to limitations, for He is the God who is contained in the heart of His servant. But the Absolute God is not contained by any thing."[12]

A fellow Moslem mystic, Farid ud-din, also asserted the oneness of God. He believed that "the One God is adored in every form of worship—by Moslems, Christians, Jews, Zoroastrians; even those who go astray from Him are none the less seeking Him."[13] Farid's advice to mystics was to shun asceticism in favor of unselfish conduct, humility, poverty, and repentance.

As with other mystics, Sufis believe that we must lose our selves in order to find our true Self. The true mosque, they say, is built within the lonely confines of the human heart, and that is where humans should worship God.

The Sufi Hazrat Inayat Khan describes the stages involved in God-realization: First we know God as our Friend. Then He becomes our Lover. Then we see the Beloved in all: friends, strangers, enemies. Finally, we lose our selves in His Self. In this final stage, outwardly we are smaller than a drop of water, but inwardly we are wider than the largest ocean, for the true Self in us is in all other persons too. Thus, self-realization becomes God-realization, and one understands that all the different dogmas and roads to God arrive ultimately at the same destination. Mysticism culminates in a universal brotherhood of all of God's peoples.

Raising the consciousness of mankind results in identifying with all of God's creation. Those who are satisfied with mere self consciousness are too shallow to be mystics, and they shall never experience religious enlightenment.

Sufis make use of mantras, sacred words and phrases that further spiritual development. The Rasul, like the *ishtadeva,* is one who represents God's perfection overcoming human limitations. Religious seekers tend to follow the Rasul familiar to them, but at the higher levels all Rasuls merge in their approach to the Godhead.

Abu Hamid al-Ghazzali was the great unifier of Islam who combined the teachings of the Sufis and the ulama. All five types of love, he taught, unite in the love of God:

1. Love of oneself—to know oneself deeply is to realize that existence is from God and for God.
2. Love of one's benefactor—the benefactor's gift comes from God.
3. Love of one's friends—their goodness comes from God.
4. Love of beauty—the author of all beauty is God.
5. Love of kindness and mercy—these attributes of love come from the absolute in love, namely, God.

Jewish Mysticism

Talmudic tradition reveals that esoteric teachings, strongly tinged with Gnosticism, existed among leading rabbis since Old Testament times. The purpose of this ecstatic mysticism seems to have been a search more for the divine throne of God's glory than for a vision of God Himself. By merging Gnostic ideas with Neoplatonism, early Kabalists in Spain evolved the doctrine of the Godhead as a dynamic complex of *Sefirot* ("potencies") emanating from the inaccessible God.

The Kabala was the mystical teaching in which Jewish scriptures were interpreted symbolically as guideposts to daily living. Many of the Kabalists expressed views similar to those of Tibetan Buddhism. Some early writers refer to a future resurrection for all of mankind. Others saw life as a balance between male and female, between assertive and submissive, very similar to the Oriental balance of Yin and Yang that captures the rhythm of the universe. There was even a bodhisattva figure: the Kabala states that the most spiritually advanced individuals, although free from the cosmic wheel of rebirth, voluntarily return to this world in order to help others.

In the eleventh century Bachya ben Joseph ibn Paquada wrote *Duties of the Heart,* a work very much like the Sufi writings of the period. The "Jewish Yoga," Abraham ben Samuel Abulafia (1240-1292) was on friendly terms with Christian and Islamic mystics. He developed techniques for using musical chants and intonation to enhance mystical contemplation, resembling Hindu and Sufi practices. The Jewish esoteric stress on a female deity echoes similar views found in Hinduism and Shintoism, and echoes the Mariolatry of the Roman Catholic Church.

Modern science seems to be rediscovering Kabalist truths. Physicist David Bohm's implicate order was prefigured in *Sefer Bahir* ("Book of Brilliance") in Provence about 1175, which says there is a vast unseen order beyond what we normally experience in everyday life. The *Zohar* ("Book of Splendor") by Moses de Leon (1250-1305) describes a seamless web of cosmic forces, now a fundamental tenet of quantum physics.

There are further likenesses between recent science and medieval Kabalist thought: matter is both continuous and discontinuous; particles are destructible and indestructible; space-time is a relative dimension; the universe achieves a balance of opposite but reciprocal forces. Some scientists now state that each of the four universes described in the Kabala may really exist: energy, force, pattern, and substance.

The Kabala teaches that the divine energy of the *Sefirot* flows in all of us, and that Abraham's greatness stemmed from his heightened awareness of the divine presence in everyday life. Isaac Luria (1534-1572) taught that humans harbored this divine spark. Because the seven lowest energy states in man were too weak to hold the awesome light of creation, Luria said, they shattered and scattered. Mankind's chief task is to restore the holy shards to their original Source. This is done through meditative prayers and good deeds. The Hebrew term for cleaving to the Divine is *devekuth*: it involves an inner ecstatic state of oneness with God and man.

If God is all-just and all-powerful, why did He permit the torture and slaughter of Jews in the Inquisition? Reincarnation became a key part of Jewish esoteric teaching during the sixteenth century. Martyred Jews were seen as being returned to this world enhanced and rewarded for their faithfulness.

The Kabala taught that dying was but one stage in the soul's evolution, a gateway to other realms of awareness. For Jewish mystics, *Gehinnom* or Purgatory is a state of consciousness in which the soul is purged of all defilement.

Joseph Karo, a Safed mystic of the sixteenth century, spoke in tongues, as described by Paul in I Corinthians, Chapter 14. Many Christian scholars studied the Kabala for spiritual insight in this era.

Jews in Islam

Jews, like Christians, were regarded by Moslems as the *Dhimmi* or People of the Book, and were therefore given better treatment than other non-Moslems. Jews living in Moslem countries were accorded more rights than Jews living in Christian Europe. In the early Middle Ages there was a Jewish-Moslem symbiosis, built upon basic affinities between the two cultures— a creative pluralistic interfaith coexistence. Outside invaders, whether Mongols or Christian Crusaders, tended to make Islam more monolithic and less tolerant of divergent faiths such as Judaism.

Even in the sixteenth century, however, when Jews were undergoing severe persecution in Europe, they could thrive in Moslem countries, where they could hold high financial positions and attend to their affairs with little hindrance. Later that century all Palestinians, including Jews, began to have trouble with the Ottoman government as it experienced a wave of Moslem nationalism.

Hasidism

Around the year 1740 a Jewish lime digger, Israel ben Eliezer, began attracting crowds in Moldavia by his comforting sermons and his mystical interpretations of scripture. Miraculous cures were attributed to him. People started calling him the Ba'al Shem

Tov (for short, Besht), meaning "the master of the good name." He taught that an awareness of the presence of God in everything leads to true communion with Him. His followers, called the Hasidim, or pious ones, were given to emotional exuberance, such as dances. Like the spiritual search of the Moslem whirling dervish, these Jews expressed their devotion to God in a spontaneous dance supposed to culminate in unity with Him.

Religious ecstasy marks the Hasidic expression. Singing and dancing are considered to be key pathways to knowledge of the Divine. Each person, it is believed, has a unique song as a gateway to a higher state of consciousness. Every individual comprises a song of existence, the one by which his innermost Self was created and is defined. Music is not only a healing force but a source of spiritual unity.

Synchronicity was preached by Besht, who said that in God's well planned universe there are no meaningless coincidences. Twentieth-century persons who held similar views are Einstein, Jung, and Nobel Prize winner Isaac Bashevis Singer. Jung would also like the view of Hasidic mystics that we view hostile thoughts as part of ourselves, not as outside objects to be fought as something foreign.

In Hasidic thought, the ultimate manifestation of the Divine through the human is the Messiah. When one's spiritual life ripens, say the Hasidim, he feels the Messiah nature moving within him. The enlightened rabbi or *tzaddik* carries on the mystical function of the Messiah, regathering the sparks of Divine Nature that were scattered from creation and remain latent at the unconscious level.

The Hasidim recognize something like the Holy Spirit. Elie Wiesel in *Souls on Fire* says that "in every man there is something of the Messiah. The Cabala says it, the mystics repeat it. To free mankind, one must gather the sparks and integrate them into a sacred flame. The Messiah nature is secretly irradiating all beings, ready to manifest itself to individuals the moment they open in holy ecstasy."[14]

Erich Fromm liked to quote Genesis 3:5, where God told Adam and Eve that "ye shall be as gods." He also often cited Psalm 82:6, "You are gods, and all of you are children of the Most High."

Judaism is firmly rooted in the soil of human dignity. Rabbi Isaac of Worka said that "in every man there is a spark of the Divine Soul. The power of evil in man darkens this flame and almost puts it out. Brotherly love among men rekindles the soul and brings it closer to its source."[15]

Arthur Hertzberg states that "the rights of individuals are absolute, for every man is created in the divine image. The essential rule of conduct is the imitation of God." Since God practices mercy and justice, so must man. "To be like God in the Jewish view means to be His partner in carrying forward the work of making a just order in the world. Man's task is to hallow life, to raise the workaday world to its highest estate, so that his every act reflects the divine unity of all being."[16]

Rabbi Samuel Laniado from Aleppo explained the passage from Leviticus 19:18, "You shall love your neighbor as yourself; I am the Lord." Since the soul of one man and the soul of his neighbor are both carved out of the same throne of Splendor," said Laniado, "the love of your neighbor will be considered as if God received it."

This constant stress on the sacredness of all human life is violated by Israeli terrorist attacks upon modern Palestinians. Unitive religion insists on love as the proper response, even to those who have different religious and political views.

Rabbi Nachman of Bratslav (1772-1810) met with Sufis while studying the Kabala in Safed. He gave a personal account of mystical unity: "Man must forget himself completely in order to partake of Divine Unity. By withdrawing into intimate dialogue with God, man can attain the complete abandonment of his passions and evil habits. When man attains this level, his soul ascends from the realm of the possible to that of the eternal. Once he himself has become eternal, he sees the whole world in the aspect of its eternity."[17]

Unconscious identity with fellow humans is the most vivid expression of Hasidic enlightenment. Elie Wiesel tells of Rebbe Wolfe at a circumcision party, who volunteers to watch the coachman's horses on a bitter cold night. Several hours later, when people find Wolfe jumping from foot to foot to keep from freezing, he cannot understand why people make a fuss over his sacrifice—he just naturally felt like helping the cold coachman.

"If a man has himself firmly in hand and stands solidly upon the earth," a Hasidic proverb states, "then his head reaches up to heaven." In this sense, says Ira Progoff, "man is the connecting link of the universe. In him heaven and earth come together. It is a union that is possible only because both the earthly and the spiritual are present in the nature of man."[18]

The joy, the optimism, and the humanitarian concern of Hasidic Judaism make it clear that rapprochement with Islam is possible, as long as unitive rather than divisive elements are stressed.

Modern Jewish-Moslem Discord

As recently as 1900 there was little animosity between these two great faiths. Moslems were slow to copy the anti-Semitism that European Christians had practiced for centuries.

The capture of the Holy Land from the Ottoman Empire by Arab and British forces in World War I led to the establishment of the British protectorate there. With good intentions, the British bungled into accepting Jewish Zionist demands for a homeland in Palestine (which means home of the Philistines). Throughout history the Jewish people have hardly ever dominated all of Palestine. They now control more land than they did through most of their history.

Under David and Solomon the kingdoms of southern Judea and northern Israel had been combined. But during most of their history the Jews shared Palestine with the Philistines, the Samaritans, and others, and often they had been exiled into captivity by surrounding nations.

As Zionism gathered force as a realistic movement, Moslems understandably united in opposition to having Jews moving in on what had been their land for centuries. Violence broke out between Jews and Moslems.

The great Jewish theologian Martin Buber rejected the more virulent forms of nationalistic Zionism. Worried over Moslem rights, he fostered Jewish-Moslem dialogue in an effort to seek a peaceable solution to the conflict. He stressed the unitive approach of Hasidism, which was under Nazi attack at the time.

Buber and Dr. Judah Magnes, U.S. Reform rabbi who became president of Hebrew University in Jerusalem, helped organize the *Ihud* (Union) Association. Buber and Magnes predicted continual violence unless a bi-national state, resembling Switzerland, were set up, with governmental guarantees of equal rights for Jews and Moslems.

In the Peel Report of 1937 David Ben-Gurion stated that it was not the Zionist goal to make Palestine a Jewish state. He and Dr. Chaim Weizmann said that Zionists would accept parity with the Moslems—that the legislative council would have an equal number of Jews and Moslems, even if the Jewish population outnumbered the Moslem people. Later, drawing upon his personal friendship with many Moslem leaders, Weizmann, as President of Israel, said that Jews and Moslems could live together in peace.

Dispossession of Palestinians from their homeland, fed by the fiery fury of divisive Islam, led to a conflagration of hatred, violence, terrorism, and war. During World War II the Mufti of Jerusalem, Haj Amin al-Husseini, collaborated with Hitler and spent several years in Berlin. Violence broke out after the state of Israel was established in 1948.

In 1964 the Palestine Liberation Organization was founded. After the Six Day War of 1967, some Palestinians were ready to accept a bi-national state, but the Israelis were no longer interested in it. In 1968 Yehia Hammouda, leader of the PLO, said it was ridiculous to expect Zionist Jews to leave Palestine. The best solution, he felt, would be a Moslem-Jewish Palestinian state with constitutional safeguards to equal rights for both groups.

Each use of violence and terrorism feeds the causes of divisive religion in both camps, with ensuing calls for vengeance, one of the tools of divisive religion. The voice of unitive religion, asking for peace and love based on the divine spark in all humanity, can scarcely be heard.

Yet on a personal basis, there is still a heartening humanity between individual Jews and Moslems in Palestine. There are also calls for the healing force of unitive religion to take over in the Holy Land.

The novels of Chaim Potok and the stories of Isaac Bashevis Singer exude the humanism of the Hasidic vision. Kaufman Kohler, a Reform rabbi, preaches that God reveals Himself in progressive revelation, and that religion can use conflict to purify its own insights into God and His will for man. Rabbi Albert Plotkin celebrates holy days by defining the steps involved in atonement: recognition of sin; recitation or confession to God; renunciation of any repetition of the sin; and reparation of any damage that one's sin has caused to others. Working behind the scenes, many rabbis and other spiritual leaders are striving to avoid further hatred and bloodshed.

In 1983 King Fahd of Saudi Arabia called for a Moslem *ijtahad* (literally "exertion"), the learned Moslems' intellectual struggle to interpret the Prophet's intent in matters of daily conduct, law, and religion. This effort could not only reduce civil fighting among Moslems but also provide the basis for better relations with other religious groups.

A contemporary Sufi, Bawa Muhaijaddeen, is striving to build communities founded on mankind's love for God and God's love for His children. As a ray of the divine light, each person can best practice reverence for God by showing love for his fellow creatures, Bawa teaches. Bernard Lewis, a leading American scholar on the Middle East, has shown a cautious optimism that differences can be reconciled in a just and nonviolent manner.

The Jewish sense of justice, grounded in the belief in God's justice, will not permit Israel to indefinitely deny Moslems some more of their traditional homeland. Yitzhak Rabin admitted that "without Palestinians being part of the negotiations, there will be no lasting solution." Former Foreign Minister Abba Eban states that "the idea that we can rule over all the area between Jordan and the sea seems to me the most extraordinary fantasy to which any large number of Jews has been attached since the false messiah Shabbetai Zevi in the 17th century."

Yehezkel Landau, spokesman for the religious peace movement *Oz ve Shalom,* says, "We now have the anguish of power instead of the anguish of powerlessness. The occupation is untenable. The young Palestinians won't accept it, and there is no reason why they should. The prophets came to remind the kings that they lived under God, with a system of values. That was true in ancient times, and it is now."[19]

Religion itself is on trial in the Middle East. Will it feed the forces of terrorism and warfare, or will it be the so badly needed healing factor? Divisive religion has helped turn the Holy Land into one of the most unholy spots on the globe. However, the best teachings of Moses, Christ, and Mohammed are more than enough to lay the foundation of a just and loving society. The religions of the area are called upon to stress their unitive, rather than their divisive, tendencies, as the human race struggles to survive in this nuclear age.

References

1. Hertzberg, p. 34.
2. Ibid., p. 35.
3. Erich Fromm, *You Shall Be As Gods* (Holt, Rinehart & Winston, 1966), pp. 84-85. Fromm, German-American psychoanalyst, wrote many books in the field of religion.
4. John A. Williams, p. 87.
5. Ibid., p. 81.
6. Mircea Eliade, *From Primitives to Zen* (Harper & Row, 1967), p. 74.
7. Ibid., pp. 623-24.
8. John A. Williams, p. 149.
9. Ibid., pp. 150-52.
10. Ibid., p. 164.
11. Kenneth Cragg, *The Wisdom of the Sufis* (New Directions, 1976), p. 48. Cragg was Professor of Religion at the University of Sussex.
12. Reynold A. Nicholson, *Studies in Islamic Mysticism* (Cambridge University Press, 1967), p. 159.
13. Ibid., p. 198.
14. Les Hixon, *Coming Home* (Anchor Press, 1978), p. 136.
15. Hertzberg, p. 111.
16. Ibid., pp. 178, 183, 185.
17. Ibid., p. 182.
18. Ira Progoff, *Depth Psychology and Modern Man* (McGraw-Hill, 1973), p. 130. Progoff was Director of Research in Depth Psychology at Drew University.
19. *New York Times,* 24 January 1988, 4:2.

CHAPTER 7

MYSTICISM

Although orthodox religion is in disfavor in many areas, mysticism is the religion of the future. Why is this so? "If the churches are emptying today, the cellars are filling, with men and women engaged on the mystical understanding of their own natures and intent on communion and union with the Divine. The world becomes increasingly unified, religiously as well as commercially and politically, and this brings a shift away from exclusive organizations of former times. That mystical claims are made in many religions is taken both as proof of the universality of the inner life of the soul and as the real link between religions which may be divided by dogma but are really united in their quest for the universal One."[1]

Virtually all religious mysticism is unitive, since it involves a search for the union of the individual with God, an action that can occur only if the individual achieves a simultaneous union with his neighbor.

"The measure of the mystic's real progress," said Evelyn Underhill, an authority on mysticism, "must always be his progress in love. Mystics are indifferent to all else save the supreme claims of love." Mysticism, she stated, "is the expression of the innate tendency of the human spirit towards complete harmony with the transcendental order, whatever the theological formula under which that order is understood."[2]

Mysticism is a union of total life functions. It is a spiritual means of achieving practical physical results. If there is no real-life outcome that is positive, the mystical search is a mask and a fraud. Mysticism involves recasting one's life at a higher level, as one spirals progressively upwards towards union with the One. Mysticism is never self-seeking, but always has the passion for perfection for Love's sake. Those who are selfish in this pursuit are "spiritual gluttons," said St. John of the Cross. Serving without hope of reward, the mystic obtains satisfaction because he does not seek it. The Sufi Rumi said:

While the thought of the Beloved fills our hearts
All our work is to do Him service and spend life for Him.

It is not mysticism simply to encounter the Other. "There must be a unifying vision, a sense that somehow all things are one and share a single divine life, or that one's individual being merges into a Universal Self."[3] God is seen as both immanent (within oneself) and transcendent (infinitely beyond all other life). The Greek Deus (or Zeus) comes from the word for "daylight," showing God's infinity. The Latin Theos means "inward love," demonstrating God's immanence. Mysticism unifies both concepts of God in its synthesis.

"According to true mysticism, each individual life represents a distinct value, a unique purpose, which will be retained so long as the cosmic process lasts. The ends and values, though striven for in time, have their source and consummation in eternity."[4]

The central characteristic of mysticism is "the apprehension of an ultimate non-sensuous unity in all things, a oneness or a One to which neither the senses nor the reason can penetrate." The Mandukya Upanishad says that this unity is "beyond the senses, beyond the understanding. It is the pure unitary consciousness, wherein multiplicity is completely obliterated. It is ineffable peace. It is the Supreme Good. It is the One without a second. It is the Self."[5]

Mircea Eliade points out that myths, on which much mysticism is based, arise from hierophanies which are genuine religious experiences, and thus are paradigms for human behavior. Myths occur not in secular but in sacred time, and thus have universal significance. The archetypal symbols in myths, which arise out of the transconscious, are universal. Mysticism is not a theory about the Divine, but a direct experience of the One.

Most mystics accept three levels of awareness: the sensory world, the inner world (including memory, imagination, and abstract thought), and the world of spiritual and divine Reality, as one opens the "third eye," or the eye of the soul. Through images of ascension, entering, or journeying, the mystic engages in an interiorization which is a transformation, resulting in penetrating beyond ordinary levels of consciousness to radically new levels.

S.N. Dasgupta says there are four chief types of Indian mysticism: bhakti, Buddhist, Upanishadic, and yogic. Bhakti, meaning "devotion," suggests a close personal relationship between the worshipper and God, in which the worshipper is an infinitesimal part of an infinite Whole. Bhakti is the form closest to types of Christian and Moslem mysticism.

The Confucian mystic Chang Tsai (1022-1077) said that "since Heaven is my father, all people are my brothers and sisters, and all things are my companions." Both Mencius (380-289 B.C.) and Gregory of Nyssa (337-400) believed in human perfectibility, based upon the awareness of a divine presence within each person. Both felt that a person must discipline his passions in order to permit the innate virtues to govern his conduct.

The first appearance of the concept of divine union in Europe occurred in the Orphic mysteries in Greece and southern Italy in the sixth century B.C. St. Paul, Augustine, and many of the Church Fathers employed mysticism regularly. The Christian mystic Jan van Ruysbroeck (1293-1381) said that "the essential union of our spirit with God does not exist in itself, but flows forth from God, and returns to Him. Were our naked nature to be separated from God, it would fall into pure nothingness."[6] Thus it is not a question of our seeking God, but of our opening ourselves to His constant pursuit of us. The mystical experience has two poles: God's outflowing love and our human response.

The mystic is unified in three ways: within one's self, towards one's neighbor, and towards God. The inner integration of the personality reflects the outer integration with the world. But the basic process is an undifferentiated unity. Each religion can interpret this unity according to its own beliefs. Buddhism calls it nirvana, Plotinus sees it as the One, and the Dominican Meister Eckhart experiences it as the birth of the Eternal Word in the soul. Many Christians call it "the peace that passes human understanding."

Although humans never do become God, various attributes of ours partake of a divine nature because of this encounter. St. John of the Cross says that after such a unifying experience, the understanding is guided by God's divine light, and the will is changed into "the life of divine love." Along with this comes a weakening in one's self-centeredness. The Sufi poet Jami (1414-

1492) exclaimed "I am the Truth," meaning that "the Truth of God is speaking through me."

Mystical Convergence

"The great mystics of every religion," said Trappist monk Thomas Merton, "live together at the summit of their own Olympus, far above the mists of religious doctrine, priesthood, liturgy, church discipline, and all the other tiresome things which separate the common run of men into religious groups."[7] It is a religious law, said Joseph Campbell, "proven time and time again, that where the orthodoxies of the world go apart, the mystic way unites. Orthodoxy generally tries to protect a privileged social order. But the mystic way, on the other hand, plunges within to those nerve centers that are in all humans alike."[8] All mystics are ultimately monists, since everything is a manifestation of God. There is thus no outsider to a mystic—no one to discriminate against, and no one to whom one must feel superior. To say that one is a Moslem mystic, or a Jewish mystic, or a Christian one is superfluous, since all mystics are alike in the important inner dimension.

It is natural for a mystic to perceive Divine Union in the trappings of his own religious tradition. Yet underlying the accidental fingerprints is the essential heart of Divine Love, which is the same substance in all religious traditions. Thus, Dionysius the Areopagite speaks of ascending hierarchies of angels to the God enthroned beyond time and space. St. Teresa describes exploring the Interior Castle for the indwelling God. The Kabala leads from the material world of Malkuth, via Beauty, Justice, and Mercy to the Supernal Crown. Each religious Way gives its characteristic flavor to the essentially same spiritual pilgrimage.

The philosopher W.T. Stace found that mystics agreed on seven basic matters: The One can be perceived in a unifying vision, in which "All is One." The One is perceived as an inner life, in an ineffable experience. The experience is paradoxical, true reality, blissful, and sacred. Stace thus found a universal core at the heart of all mysticism.

Mystics do not so much discard traditional religion as transcend it. "They realize that the true content of faith in an Ultimate can neither be identified with a piece of reality, as sacramental faith desires, nor be expressed in terms of a rational system." But "there is a place where the Ultimate is present within the finite world, namely, the depth of the human soul. To go into it, man must empty himself of all the finite contents of his ordinary life. He must transcend even the deepest division, that between subject and object. To reach the Ultimate he must overcome this division in himself by meditation, contemplation, and ecstasy."[9]

Mystical religion is both more and less conservative than traditional religion. It is more conservative in that it hopes to de-emphasize nonessentials in order to focus on the core of the religion. It is less conservative in that it assumes that rituals and creeds can frequently obscure this quintessential core.

Paul Tillich finds mystical religion more unitive than prophetic religion. "The advantage of classical mysticism," he says, "is that it does not take the concrete expression of one's ultimate concern seriously, and therefore can trespass the set of concrete symbols. The exclusive monotheism of the prophets, the struggle against the limited gods of paganism, the message of universal justice in the Old Testament and of universal grace in the New Testament—all this made Judaism, Islam, and Christianity intolerant of any kind of idolatry. These religions of justice, history, and the expectation of the end could not accept the mystical tolerance of India They are intolerant and can become fanatical and idolatrous. This is the difference between the exclusive monotheism of the prophets and the transcendent monotheism of the mystics."[10]

Feeling a oneness with nature, what R.C. Zaehner called nature mysticism, is a low form of religious experience, he said. But William L. Newell pointed out the positive value of nature mysticism: "This expansion seems to free the contents of a very deep level of man's psyche, which contents manifest a commonality with those of other men. They seem, in fact, to be transpersonal, or beyond personality. Here we are in contact with something both deep and communal. Since mysticism is, by definition, a unitive experience, what we have here is a unity of man with all things, not just with himself. In fact, the unity is with things beyond man." Sometimes it is "psychological healing, or integration of man's powers within himself, or of ego with the transcendental Self."[11] So even though nature mysticism may not be religious in origin, it can be very fruitful and unitive.

Theistic vs. Monistic Mysticism

Unlike most students of mysticism, R.C. Zaehner says there are two distinct types, the theistic and the monistic. The Oriental approach tends to be monistic, he feels. The Hindu uses the monistic or identity approach, saying "Thou art That" or that Atman (the individual soul) equates with Brahman (the World Soul). The Theistic, or communion, approach is typical of theistic religions such as Judaism, Christianity, and Islam, and by monotheistic Hindus such as Ramanuja and the author of the Bhagavad Gita. Some Christian mystics, like Eckhart and Angelus Silenius, were at times monists but as a rule Christian mystics prefer a dualistic approach. Ramakrishna, said Zaehner, although ostensibly a monist, shows dualism when worshipping God as Mother (as Juliana of Norwich had done). In this instance Ramakrishna, whose whole attitude towards life was one of love, shows that the God of Love can break through any religious philosophy.

Anne Fremantle finds a dichotomy between the East and the West in the way life is approached. In the Orient, she says, man is social before he is individual, but in the West he is individual before he is social. In the West salvation means separation from the world but in the Orient it implies union with the cosmic design. In the Orient the universe is subjective, but in the West it is objective. In the West man is a stranger in the universe but in the Orient man is everywhere at home. At the mystical level, however, all of these distinctions vanish, in Fremantle's opinion.

Rudolf Otto shows how, in the depth of mysticism, the two approaches intertwine. Otto quotes the psalmist: "Deep calls unto deep." Otto found many mystics using the inward approach to union with God: Eckhart, Hallaj, Plotinus, and Shankara. Even Aristotle said that "the soul is itself all." By withdrawing from the outward world, one retreats into the Ground of one's own soul. This leads to self-knowledge, and ultimately to union with God.

In the other approach, the mystic looks to the outer world, but with a unifying vision. The search is not so much for Brahman as it is for Unity. Successfully resisting every effort at division, the soul eventually finds liberation and blessedness. The commonness of separate things is perceived as a unity. Everything is seen in the light of eternity, and hence as a oneness. The One is seen in the many, and the many in the One. Finally one realizes that in terms of permanence, there is only the One. Great mystics like Eckhart and Shankara have both of the mystical methods converging in their respective approaches.

The Mystical Way

Many mystics identify three stages in the mystical way of life: the purgative life, the illuminative life, and the unitive life. Each stage can be broken down into its fundamental processes.

The purgative life begins with soul searching, as one tries to define one's self, God, and one's relationship to God. An honest identification of oneself as a being results in the humble acknowledgment that, in the balance tins of eternity, no one individual counts for much. Self-abnegation seems to be in order. A similarly honest inquiry into the nature of God reveals that He is All—without Him there would be nothing. But since God created the individual, presumably out of love, each human being has a value, a preciousness, as a child of God. We who seem to be relatively valueless according to mankind's standards acquire a dear significance when viewed from God's standpoint. This requires, out of honest gratitude, a continual striving to achieve a oneness with God.

In preparation for union with God, one's self must be purged of all that stands between it and the goodness of God. Disappointed after perceiving the vast chasm between oneself and God, one endeavors to escape one's sinful nature, what Evelyn Underhill called "the prison of I-hood." Dying to self means living to God. As the selfish self departs, the Holy Spirit takes over.

The mystical way is easy and difficult—easy because all one has to do is constantly focus on God, but difficult because it is human to keep forgetting about God. This world is full of separation, caused by manmade barriers. But if one overcomes the main alienation, that from God, there is no longer any significant separation. "To the angels," says Schuon, "our formal, or separating, world presents itself as a pile of debris. What is in reality united is separated in form and by form."[12] The soul, craving unity, roots itself in the world, which is diversity. Until the soul roots itself in God, the tree of life has no substantial or permanent roots.

Paradoxically, human birth is the beginning of separateness. Human death is the end of separateness in an ultimate reunion with the Creator. Christ said that unless a person die, he cannot live. One must die to his selfish self in order to live to his real Self, that is, to the Holy Spirit. Christ further said that he was the way, and that no one came to the Father except through his way, which is a complete surrender of his will to the Father's will, a total absorption of the individual self into the Universal Self. The certainty of death is full of sweetness when one sees life's true meaning as a search for oneness with God. But one need not wait for physical death for this to occur. As one eradicates one's selfish self in this world, one's true divine self emerges. As we put aside the kingdoms of this world, the Kingdom of God emerges in our hearts.

What elements are involved in self purgation? To be ready for union with God, one must divest oneself of the selfish ego, of inordinate self-love and self-concern, of the worship of worldly possessions, of passionate sexual lust, and of the stubborn promptings of the individual will. The classical monastic vows of poverty, chastity, and obedience show that one must prepare one's thoughts, words, and deeds for spiritual union with the One.

The root of the word "mystic" means "to close." By closing the outward gate of physical desires and sensations one opens the inner spiritual gate leading to God's garden of love. One has made progress along the mystical path when one realizes that the process is not one of search but of being sought. One's reaction is more passive than active, an opening of oneself to permit God to reach one's soul, for God is ever seeking us with a loving concern.

The initiate into mysticism now encounters another paradox. The closer he grows to God, the wider the gap seems to be between him and his Maker. The reason for this is that, in getting more spiritually honest, one's self diminishes to its true insignificant size, and God's goodness, love, and glory appear in something like their infinite proportions. The more honest one is, the easier it is to perform the necessary self-abasement. The earlier one is freed from the impediments of selfhood, the sooner one can realize the importance of one's true Self.

Purged of self-love and self-desire, the soul is ready to progress towards union with the Divine. Almost inevitably one can benefit at this stage from assistance from one's *ishtadeva*. The *ishtadeva* is that form of the deity that has been revealed to you. For Christians the two *ishtadevas* are Christ and the Holy Spirit. In Hinduism the *ishtadevas* might be any of the avatars of the savior God Vishnu. Both human and divine, the *ishtadeva* is superbly equipped to act as a spiritual guide into the presence of the One. The *ishtadeva* might prescribe creeds, rituals, laws, or methods of mental and spiritual discipline. A sure sign of the authenticity of the regimen is whether it is grounded in agape, or divine love.

Another sign of the veracity of the *ishtadeva* is subservience to God. A divine modesty motivates each *ishtadeva* to interpret himself as a vehicle towards a greater union. At their lofty level, all *ishtadevas* merge, so that it is meaningless to ask whether Vishnu is greater than Christ, or Krishna than Gautama Buddha. In geometrical language, things equal to the same thing are equal to one another.

Description of the ultimate union with God cannot be achieved in words. Mystics discuss the melting away of one's individuality into the Infinite as entering a condition beyond time and space, a condition of ineffable peace, love, and joy. Since this state seems to be ultimate, it is, of course, non-sectarian.

Realizing the infinity of his inner depths, the mystic is finally in the presence of Beauty, Goodness, and Truth. Contemplation of God is wordless because it is Word-full. In the mystical encounter God finds God within us, and all is at one again. The Lover and the Loved are once again one. There is no more divisiveness, no separation, no partiality, discrimination or hatred. The unitive unselfishness of agape has replaced the divisive strains of selfish possessive lust, greed, and desire.

Some mystics describe the ineffable union as a spiritual marriage with God, in which the uniate condition is something of which the mystic is constantly aware, even in everyday activities. One can wash dishes to the glory of God. This group of mystics includes Gregory of Nyssa, Origen, Jan van Ruysbroeck, St. John of the Cross, and St. Teresa of Avila.

Mystics in the uniate state are aware of the image of God within them. Dante, Gregory of Nyssa, and Origen conceived of the image as a blinding mirror of light. The Kabala and Meister Eckhart speak of the reunion of the divine sparks into the holy fire of God. Johann Arndt, Jacob Boehme, and Johannes Tauler experienced this condition as a realization of the soul's Ground. All mystics assume that the light of God shines constantly, like the sun, but that it is bedimmed or clouded over by the smog of sin, pride, and self-concern.

Mysticism and Good Works

Most mystics do not consider the achievement of the uniate condition as an end in itself, for this would be very selfish. Eckhart said that if a person were in mystical ecstasy and knew of a poor person who needed his help, he should desert his ecstasy in order to serve the poor person. Christian mystics stress that spiritual ecstasy must lead to a deeper love of one's neighbor, as shown by deeds of charity, mercy, and self-sacrifice. Many mystics feel that the mystical consciousness is the secret source of all love, which is the foundation of morality. In the mystical consciousness all distinctions between "thou" and "me" disappear. Your neighbor's suffering is yours, as is his joy. Because of the mystical cord connecting all of mankind, it can truly be said that "no man is an island unto himself."

Mysticism and ethics are complementary. The mystical can serve as a foundation for the ethical, and vice versa. Each is enhanced by their interrelationship. God is a God of thought as well as of love, and hence neither type of experience is at its best without the other. The lives of the saints show how inextricably intertwined are these two facets.

"No genuinely religious person," said Zaehner, "is likely to be impressed by one who claims to be in direct communion with God, if his conduct is, in fact, sub-human. So far as he is united with God, the mystic will be absolutely free from sin."[13] To the extent that he sins, to that extent he is apart from God. The mystical goal is to be ever closer to God and ever farther from sin.

Mysticism culminates in brotherhood. Since this brotherhood is founded in God, it is stronger than the ties of family, race, religion, or nation. By calling God "Father," Christ united mankind in a divinely ordained family. Mystics know that God is the God of their enemies as well as of their friends, and that by loving God, the Father of all, enemies can be converted into friends. A beginning mystic finds God at the center of his true Self. A more mature mystic discovers God at the center of his neighbor's true Self. When the God within oneself unites with the God within one's neighbor, the union is complete, and there can never again be discord between the neighbors.

Love which is not fruitful of good works is heretical, not mystical, said Evelyn Underhill. Properly followed, the mystical way of life is a growth in love, and the only proper end of love is union. St. Teresa said that "good works are the best proof that the favors we receive have come from God. To give our Lord a perfect hospitality, Mary and Martha must combine."[14]

Mystics can never be so busy contemplating God that they forget that the best result of their contemplation is to show love for God's creation. As a result of his mystical love of Christ, Paul single-handedly organized the Christian church. St. Francis exhibited superhuman energy in finding ways to help the needy. The aged and ill St. Teresa left her convent for the purpose of reforming a large religious order. Joan of Arc, a simple peasant girl, led the French army to victory over the English. St. Catherine of Siena, illiterate and poor, rose to become a dominant power in Italian politics. Her namesake, St. Catherine of Genoa, became one of the world's first capable hospital administrators. Ignatius Loyola, as a result of his mystical encounters, was able to pour great strength and energy into reviving a flagging church. The mystical way, founded in love, can reach its natural fruition only in works of love.

A continual joy in the Holy Spirit pervades the mystic's outlook on life. Francis of Assisi would take two sticks, pretend he was playing a viol, and sing songs in French to the Lord Jesus. St. John of the Cross wrote love songs to God. St. Rose of Lima sang duets with birds. St. Teresa wrote hymns in Old Castile for her fellow nuns to sing. St. Catherine of Genoa was so full of peace that she joyously repeated simple poems all day long.

Joseph Campbell lists several traits of authentic mysticism. One is a distrust of such extraordinary experiences as visions; instead there is a reliance on simple everyday piety and love of God. Another test is silence concerning the nature of the ecstatic union. Still others are love of and service to one's neighbor, as a form of worshipping God. Mysticism at its best is highly unitive.

As a result of a mystical experience, the individual is filled with agape, and feels joy, peace, and gratitude. He is overcome with an emotion of self-giving. When a society has a critical number of such persons, it is inevitably less militaristic, less aggressive, and more caring. Then, as Jesus would say, the Kingdom of God is at hand.

Jewish Mysticism

Discussion of the Kabala and some elements of Jewish mysticism took place in Chapter 3. It remains to delineate the comparison of the Jewish form with other types of mysticism. Especially in times of great distress, the Kabala seemed to be more important than the Torah or the Talmud in giving the Jewish people comfort, consolation, and direction.

There are many parallels between Hindu and Jewish mysticism. The *Sefer Bahir* (Book of Brilliance) tells how to attain higher spiritual awareness by channeling the body's life energy, in a manner similar to kundalini yoga. Like a yogi master, Abulafia recommended body postures, forms of breathing, and contemplation as pathways to the divine. Others who taught spiritual disciplines similar to yoga include Joseph Karo, Isaac Luria, Rabbi Dov Baer of Mezritch, and Rabbi Nachman of Bratslav. Like the Hindus, Hasidic masters advocated the use of wordless songs to focus concentration, and they cautioned against the development of paranormal abilities as a part of the spiritual ascent towards God.

As in Hindu and Buddhist writings, the Kabala stresses that one's state of mind as he enters death helps determine the state of being he enters after death. Thus, "bodily death is a key event in the transition of our consciousness."[15] As in Hinduism, the Kabala speaks of reincarnation.

The concept is found in both the *Sefer Bahir* and the *Zohar*. After their expulsion from Spain and Portugal, the Jewish people found comfort in the idea of a rebirth into better times. In sixteenth century Safed there was a great deal of interest in reincarnation. Luria and others even tried to identify the souls who had been reborn into their colleagues. Marriage and family life were seen as opportunities for one's soul to grow, to fulfill itself and its mission, so as to finally escape reincarnation. The early Kabala had stressed a resurrection for humanity, when the perfected soul re-enters the perfected body. Later Kabalists, however, tended to reject this concept.

There are also similarities between Buddhist and Jewish mysticism. In The Act of the Divine Chariot, the Jewish meditator descends deeply into the recesses of his mind to find the ethereal chariot of Ezekiel's vision, which gives the contemplator Ezekiel's heavenly vision. So too in Tibetan Buddhism, meditators experience visions of deities as reflections of spiritual processes in this life.

The Sefirot, or flow of divine energy, is similar to concepts found in Tibetan Buddhism. Other parallels are the control of the body when exposed to extreme temperatures, the chanting of sacred mantras, and the assumption that each daily act tunes us either into, or out of, divine harmony. Hasidic masters, the Zaddikim, like Buddhist gurus warn that miracles they perform are really done by God rather than by them. The Kabala resembles Buddhist texts in seeing death as a gateway to a higher realm of awareness. The highest part of the Self, the Neshamah, never dies.

In both religious views, reincarnation involves having the soul reborn in order to fulfill its unmet commandments. The Kabala states that the most spiritually advanced persons, who could be free of the cosmic wheel *(gilgulim),* return out of compassion to help others. They are thus bodhisattvas.

There are also likenesses between Taoism and Jewish mysticism. The *Zohar* echoes the words of Lao-Tse that "a journey of 1000 miles starts beneath one's feet." Isaac Luria devised special techniques for focusing people's thoughts during meditative prayer, in a manner similar to Taoist practices. Sounding like the Taoist concept of yin/yang, the Kabala states the world consists ultimately of the union of apparent opposites: male/female, light/dark, and active/passive.

There is not much apparent influence of Christian thought on Jewish mysticism, although Kabalists like Abraham Abulafia had friends who were Christian mystics. By 1500 many educated Christians read the Kabala. In 1587 *Artis Cabalisticae Scriptores* appeared, containing "a variety of articles by Christian scholars on Kabalistic works. It sought to prove that the *Zohar* actually affirmed the divinity of Jesus of Nazareth."[16]

There are some parallels between Sufi writings and the works of Jewish mystics. "The classic 11th century Jewish work by Bachya ben Joseph ibn Paquada, *Duties of the Heart,* is highly similar to Sufi writings of the time." Abulafia and Rabbi Nachman also have ideas not unlike those found in Sufi works. "During the Jewish 'Golden Age' in the Iberian world, which was then under Islamic influence, Kabalistic and Sufi paths frequently crossed." Sufis, for example, had long studied the effects of music on our bodies. "Abulafia devised special techniques, resembling those of Islamic and Hindu disciplines, for using sound to catapult us into paranormal mental states."[17]

Israel ben Eliezer (also known as the Ba'al Shem Tov), founder of the Hasidic movement, describes a heavenly vision he had: In the vision he ascended to the place of the Messiah. Eliezer asked when the Messiah would return and was told, When your teaching will be so widespread that all readers will be capable of "performing unifications and having soul ascents as you do. Then all evil will be consumed, and it will be a time of grace and salvation." The unifications referred to various combinations of the names for God. "By studying the Torah in complete devotion and by having these names in mind," Louis Jacobs says, "the Ba'al Shem Tov brought all things together so that the unity of God became established throughout all creation."[18]

As described by the Ba'al Shem Tov, the Hasid, or godly person, is one who believes in universal love and humility. He loves his enemies as much as his friends, in order to help reunite the scattered light (which are the divine sparks in people). The Hasid is taught, "Let no one think himself better than his neighbor, for all serve God, each according to the measure of understanding which God has given him." One must humble oneself so as not to feel superior to the person of lesser understanding. Evil is "but a lower grade of good, owing to the diminution of the Divine Light illuminating it." In this view, there is no limit to the possibility of God's forgiveness.

As can be seen, Hasidism is very unitive. As one finds and fans one's divine sparks within oneself, he discovers the interconnects with the divine sparks of others, and ultimately there is the unity of the whole human race. In the process, each individual achieves a healthy inner wholeness.

The Ba'al Shem Tov was not a pantheist but a panentheist, one who sees all things in God. For him there was no place empty of God. "The Zaddik, 'righteous,' seek constantly to please the Unique One by apprehending the divine unity and the unification of all in Him."[19] The Zaddikim were popular with the common believers, being neither ascetic nor autocratic. They built a bridge of understanding between the esoteric religious beliefs and the everyday faith of the common people. They tried to avoid clashes with rabbinical Judaism, but instead endeavored to reform it from within. Unlike many reformers, they were able to keep the tension between themselves and the rabbis at a constructive and a creative level.

Rabbi Moses Hayyim Luzzatto (1707-1746) was so profound a religious genius that his works were quoted by both the Hasidim and their opponents. He taught that the world is governed by the commingling of three Sefirot lights: Hesed, or naked love; Din, or judgment; and Rahamim, the harmonizing principle of compassion.

Zechariah Mendel of Jaroslav in 1800 wrote to his uncle in defense of the Zaddikim: "Their company is exceedingly pleasant to God and man. Complete unity prevails among them. It all stems from their great longing to do the will of God. They assist one another to serve God in truth. Each one of them is inferior in his own eyes and his friend is superior to him." The Midrash states that "the Zaddikim cause the quality of judgment to be converted into the quality of mercy."[20]

Roman Catholic Mysticism

Paul Tillich said that every religion is built on a mystical base. When Christianity loses that base, he continued, it becomes merely intellectualized faith and moralized love, and it then loses its force. Mysticism, he felt, was the mother of rationalism. By merely a slight shift the inner light is converted into the autonomous reason. All of the medieval Christian scholastics were mystics, since each had experienced a personal encounter with God.

"What is primary in Christianity," says William L. Newell, "is mysticism, not visions and ecstasies, but the stuff of mysticism, which is a loving relationship with Christ. Mysticism in the

Catholic sense is the experience of God in which one is loved, feels he is loved, and wishes only to love in return."[21]

Jesus said, "Inasmuch as you have done it unto one of the least of these my brethren, you have done it unto me." He mystically identified with all who suffered, were needy, or lacked love. For him the supreme law was the love which makes us at one with God and with our fellow humans. In his final instructions to his followers, Jesus described this mystical unity: "That they may all be one, as Thou, Father, in me and I in Thee; that they may also be one in Us; that they may be one, as We also are one—I in them and Thou in me; that they may be perfect in one" (John 17:21-23).

In the view of Ken Wilber, "Christ clearly left an esoteric circle of gnostic disciples, who eventually would include John, Mary Magdalene, Theudas, Marcion, and the great Valentinus."[22] In addition to John, Peter and Paul expressed mystical sentiments. Peter promises that we may "become partners of the divine nature" and "share in the very being of God" (II Peter 1:4). Albert Schweitzer wrote a book summarizing Paul's mysticism. Paul speaks of Christ dwelling in him, and he in Christ. He says there is only one Holy Spirit and one God and Father of mankind.

The chief mystical influences on Christianity were Jewish mysticism, the Essenes, Philo, the Greek mystery religions, and Neoplatonism. Augustine and Pope Gregory the Great both spoke of the mystical union with God in terms of illumination. John Scotus Erigena said that "every visible and invisible creature is a theophany or an appearance of God." Bernard of Clairvaux said that the only way to experience Christ is mystically. He recommended three steps:

1. Consideration — one uses reason to evaluate the world externally.
2. Contemplation — by exploring inner resources, one enters the holy temple.
3. Rapture — without losing steps #1 and #2, one goes outside oneself into God.

The *Theologica Germanica* calls God "the Perfect Nothing," a phrase reminiscent of the Taoist negation and the Buddhist

Void. The negative statement (God is not this, not that) ends up by asserting God's cosmic and all-inclusive Greatness.

Jan van Ruysbroeck said that those who tell you that one can love God but not God's creation, human beings, are false mystics. Shun them, he says, as you would "the fiend of hell, for they are all the forerunners of Antichrist." Ruysbroeck stated that "when we are caught up and transformed by God's Spirit, then we are led into fruition. And the Spirit of God Himself breathes us out from Himself that we may love, and may do good works. He dwells in God, and yet he goes out towards all creatures, in a spirit of love towards all things, in virtue and in works of righteousness. And this is the supreme summit of the inner life."[23]

Ruysbroeck felt that a person's true essence is his soul. Louis Dupré summarizes Ruysbroeck's position: "Before its creation the soul is present in God as a pure image; this divine image remains its super-essence after its actual creation. The mystical conversion consists in regaining one's uncreated image. Through the mystical transformation the soul surpasses its createdness and participates actively in God's uncreated life. To Ruysbroeck the soul is from all eternity an archetype within God. To the extent that its actual existence in time is connected with this archetypal image, it 'dwells in God, flows forth from God, depends upon God, and returns to God.' In the mystical state the mind comes to live 'above nature in the essential unity of God's own being, at the summit of His Spirit.'"[24]

Johannes Tauler (1300-1361) expressed the unitiveness of mysticism in saying that "mercy is the attribute that God shows forth in all His works; therefore a merciful person is a truly Godlike one. For mercy is brought forth by love and kindness. Therefore the true friends of God are much more merciful and compassionate than those who are not loving."[25]

Henry Suso (1295-1366) describes a state in which both the subject "I" and the object "the world" are temporarily excluded from consciousness, as the soul is completely absorbed in the Holy Spirit. Richard Rolle said that "charity is truly the noblest and most excellent of virtues. It makes the creature most like to the Maker." Mechthild of Magdeburg reported that God told her that "whoso knows and loves the nobleness of My freedom cannot bear to love Me alone; he must also love Me in my creatures." Margery Kempe said that if a man beat a horse, she thought she saw Christ being beaten. The author of *The Cloud of Unknowing* declared that although the human understanding cannot penetrate the mystery of God's Presence, love, especially agape, can do it.

St. Catherine of Siena (1347-1380) was at once a great mystic and a great activist. As a teacher, politician, and contemplative, she achieved a perfect balance between the inner and outer life. She has been called "the mother of thousands of souls," for her *Divine Dialogue* inspired countless Christians into a more dedicated and charitable life.

Ken Wilber feels that some Christian mystics have, on occasion, soared to the level of the *ishtadeva*. Among these Wilber includes Meister Eckhart, Jacob Boehme, Dame Juliana of Norwich, and St. Catherine of Genoa.

Like many of her contemporaries, Dame Juliana experienced God as love. The very act of seeking God is as good as seeing Him, she said, for to seek Him sincerely, one must purge oneself of anger, greed, lust, pride, and selfishness; thus one is constantly reforming oneself in God's image. The love of God makes mankind one family, she declared. "The charity of God makes in us such a unity that, when it is truly seen, no man can separate himself from any other." To Juliana, salvation was a condition of peace and love. "We may not be blissfully saved," she said, "until we are truly in peace and love, for that is our salvation. We are not safe in our possession of endless joy until we are entirely in peace and love, that is, completely pleased with God, His works and His judgments, and loving and peaceable with ourselves, with fellow Christians, and with everything God loves. The soul is suddenly made one with God when it is truly at peace in itself, for in Him no wrath is found."[26]

St. Catherine of Genoa (1447-1510) said, "My me is God, nor do I know myself save in Him." For twenty-two years she lived in the nearly unbroken consciousness of the Divine Presence. Serving the sick poor, she founded Genoa's first hospital. An original teacher, she was very influential on subsequent religious thinkers.

A Roman Catholic cardinal, Nicholas of Cusa taught that God is at once the center and the periphery of each of His creatures. Nicholas believed in the coincidence of opposites, the union of the finite with the infinite. He said that in heaven it is recognized that the Logos, the divine word, is present in every religion, as Paul himself testified, that the world religions were diverse rays of one eternal light, the light of truth. As a mystic, Nicholas kept abreast of the latest science. As a church official he made many reforms, raising the standards of religious education and priestly morality. The learned abbot Trithemius said that Nicholas appeared in Germany as "an angel of light and peace amid darkness and confusion. He restored the unity of the Church." Nicholas influenced such moderns as Ernst Cassirer and Paul Tillich.

St. John of the Cross (1542-1591) was a short shy Carmelite whom St Teresa persuaded to remain in the order so that he could help reform it. After a stormy convent election he was imprisoned in Toledo for nine months and treated badly there. In one sense, said John, God is united with all of His creation. But this is as nothing compared to the conscious and willful experience of union by one who is in love with God. John taught, "That thou mayest have pleasure in everything, seek pleasure in nothing. Coveting nothing, the spirit finds repose, for nothing wearies it by elation, and nothing oppresses it by dejection."[27] If we divide the world into "mine" and "not mine," John said, unreal standards are set up, and craving begins to fret the mind. We become slaves of our property, which becomes not a treasure but a chain. If, however, we accept poverty and demolish ownership, we at once own the cosmos, for we merge into the greater life of the All.

St. John of the Cross declared that "God dwells in every soul, even in the soul of the greatest sinner. By this union He sustains their being." But each individual must strive to also achieve a union of likeness, by copying God's love. The soul, being purged of things repugnant to God, is conformed to His will. Just as a dirty window bars sunlight from entering, so our souls, unless purged clean of sin, prevent the light of God from penetrating therein.

Speaking of John, Thomas Merton stated that "his only purpose is to bring the whole man, body and soul, under the guidance of the Spirit of God. He was relentlessly opposed to the formalism and inhumanity of those whom he compared to 'spiritual blacksmiths,' violently hammering the souls of their victims to make them fit some conventional model of ascetic perfection. He well knew that this kind of asceticism was often a manifestation of incorrigible spiritual pride. He is by far the greatest of all mystical theologians," Merton judged, because of his clarity, logic, and knowledge of God.[28]

St. Teresa of Avila had, according to Evelyn Underhill, rare powers of unification. St. Teresa felt that the most important phase of the mystical quest was the return to everyday life in order to witness in a uniate faith. She played a vigorous role in the reform of the Spanish Carmelites, including the founding of eighteen convents. Her visionary insight made it possible for her to merge the God of the Bible, found through transcendence, with the God of the Neoplatonic Dionysius, found through the inner search for immanence. The result was an affirmation of the Trinity:

1. The Father, the Creator, was the One of Neoplatonism.
2. Christ, the Logos, was the Bridegroom of every soul.
3. The indwelling Holy Spirit was God seeking God in man.

Louis of Blois summarized the goal and the rewards of the mystic's search for divine union. He stated that "it is an exceedingly great thing to be joined to God by a mystical union. This takes place where a pure and humble soul, burning with ardent love, is carried above itself by the grace of God, and through the brilliancy of the divine light on the mind, it melts away into God. God is then its peace and fullness."[29]

Meister Eckhart

The Dominican friar Johannes Eckhart (1260-1328) is known to us as Meister Eckhart because of his authority in the field of Christian mysticism. Because of his important role as a mystic, he deserves special mention.

Eckhart says that our birth into God is a continual process, for our birthing takes place every day. And still the soul is as young as the day when it was born. If a person thinks of God constantly, "he becomes one with God in every thought." The pure in heart see God because they are in unity with Him. Rid of dualism and separateness, they do not think of God as "out there" in the heavens. Two as a duality do not produce love, Eckhart said, but two as a unity do. If we emerge completely from ourselves for God's sake, He will emerge completely from Himself for our sake. What results is a unity of love in which the Holy Spirit flowers.

The mystical man must become feminine, Eckhart believed. To receive God, the soul must be passive, must be the bride to God's groom. "If man remained always a virgin," Eckhart taught, "no fruit would proceed from him. If he is to become fruitful, he must necessarily become a woman. 'Woman' is the most noble word one can apply to the soul, more noble than 'virgin'."[30] The Christian Henry Suso and the Moslem al-Ghazzali would agree with this position.

Eckhart is full of shocking but apt paradox. The highest exaltation of the mystic, he says, results in his highest humility. When one loses oneself in God, one is utterly lost, but since God is found, the death is worth it. We each possess the divine spark which, nourished, becomes a bonfire of blessing. This spark is the light of the Holy Spirit desiring to achieve full consummation. When our spark unites with others', in the unity of our origin in God, all barriers and superficial distinctions break down. Were one to fan the spark assiduously, there could be no separation from God. In Eckhart's words, "There is something in the soul so closely akin to God that it is already at one with Him and need never to be united to Him. If one were wholly this, he would be both uncreated and unlike any creature."[31]

Let go and let God, says Eckhart. Let go of your selfish self and let God take over your life. Let go of what separates you from God and from your neighbor. The more you abandon, the easier it is to let go. By letting go and letting be, you let God be God in you.

Sin is surrender to the selfishness of the ego, which demands that we worship it in place of God. Divided, if we can surrender our will to God's we shall have an undivided will, ours being absorbed in His. Sin is a betrayal of the divine image within us. It postulates a false dualism, posing the ego as if it were eternal. Separateness is a journey into death. Christ and the Torah are a journey into life.

Christ, the Word of God, should be our model; then we become the byword of God, Eckhart said. In what ways should one follow Christ? The answer is given by Christ's life. He surrendered his will to God's. Full of compassion and justice, he gave of himself unselfishly for others. He overcame the dualism of humanity versus divinity in a unique oneness.

The Holy Spirit Eckhart called the Transformer, since he transforms the commonplace into the divine. All holiness comes from the Holy Spirit, which is Christ's first gift to us. Whenever God gives us a gift, Eckhart says, it is with a higher purpose in mind: He wants to give us Himself. It is because we are God's children that we can know the Holy Spirit, which takes us on a journey into purity, into oneness, a return to our pristine origin. A fiery love, the Holy Spirit melts the ice that people erect between themselves and others by their egotistic self-centeredness.

To Eckhart, compassion was the highest art. Being Godlike, we find that compassion leads us to God. In compassion, all otherness vanishes. Compassion turns enemies into friends, builds interpersonal relationships upon the principle of justice, clothes us in our proper divine image, and bestows heavenly blessings on all of us, thus helping inaugurate the Kingdom of God.

Good works are more important than contemplation, this mystic said. "In contemplation you serve only yourself, but in good works you serve many people." If you were in a state of rapture like Paul on the Damascus road, and a sick person wanted a cup of soup, leave the rapture and serve the sick person, and Christ will commend your choice, Eckhart said. The phrase "our daily bread" means that we should share it with our neighbors. When we fail to oppose injustice, we are basically stealing our neighbor's bread.

Eckhart, like Christ, deplored the "merchant mentality" which always tries to make money out of one's neighbors. Since our souls are God's temple, we should aspire towards Christ-likeness rather than towards money making. We should love God for Himself, not for what we can get out of Him. After all, we do not own any property—everything we have is a gift from God. A good steward makes sure that the Lord's property is used for the benefit of all the Lord's people.

What is it to be human, Eckhart asked. Humans are earthly, grounded in the soil, the humus. Made of dust by the grace of God, humans should have humility and be humble ("on the ground") before their Creator.

Rudolf Otto pointed out countless similarities in the teachings of Eckhart and of the Hindu sage Shankara. Both postulate a suprapersonal Godhead above the personal God. Both are concerned with salvation: "That the soul is eternally one with the Eternal is the fact upon which the salvation of the soul depends."[32] Both shun such traditional paranormal paths as visions, trances, magic, and rituals. Both employ the style of hyperbole, using astonishing boldness in enunciating spiritual truths. Yet both are theists, having theological bases for their positions.

Eckhart and Shankara perceive of human life as divine rays split from God, and never at peace until at one with Him. Life is thus a constant process of birth, death, and rebirth. The Godhead beyond God is the Ground out of which all things come, including God. God ultimately vanishes into the Godhead. Paul too says that Christ's time will come when he will go, and God will be All in All (the Godhead) (I Corinthians 15:28).

The Hindu Chhandogya says that "when one perceives no other, hears no other, recognizes no other, there is fullness." Complete happiness is attained through oneness with the Absolute. Eckhart's words are similar: "So long as the soul still beholds a divided world, all is not well with it. Only when all that is formed is cast off from the soul, and she sees the Eternal One alone, then she is blessed."[33] Rudolf Otto also listed the differences between Eckhart and Shankara. Eckhart has more stress on happiness, righteousness, and justification by grace. Shankara puts less emphasis on good works and more on the value of asceticism.

D.T. Suzuki found similarities between Eckhart and Zen Buddhism. Both see nature's beauty, as in the epiphany of a flower, as an expression of God's love. Both perceive the "eternal now," that each moment is a part of eternity. Zen Buddhists understand Eckhart's paradoxical statement about a person being "ignorant with knowing, loveless with loving, dark with light."[34] Eckhart said that the love that God has for Christ, and Christ for God, is the Holy Spirit. Mortals, by receiving the influx of the Holy Spirit, participate in the divine love. In Zen terminology, this is one mirror reflecting another with no shadow between them.

Eckhart's theology has counterparts in Buddhism, Hinduism, the Celtic faith, and in Eastern Orthodox Christianity. All of these religions stress the creation, joy, nature, and women. Moderns influenced by Eckhart include Saul Bellow, Rufus

Jones, Carl Jung, Thomas Merton, Ira Progoff, Josiah Royce, and Alan Watts.

Eckhart's doctrine fed democracy. Every person, he says, is an aristocrat, being a child of God the King. Instead of pulling down aristocrats, Eckhart raises every peasant to their level. The soul is sacred, and therefore its possessor, who is everybody, should be treated as a dignitary. A person who feels in close personal communion with the Lord of Lords is a poor prospect to remain as a serf.

The equality of mysticism produces peace. Since one is equal to, but not superior to, all of creation, one should identify with and love all of creation. The only authentic peace comes from this cosmic consciousness and love. We should love as God does, that is, holistically. In a daring phrase, Eckhart says that like Mary, we too can give birth to God, for His seed lies within us. A sure sign of agape is that God is more eager to give it than we are to receive it.

Protestant Mysticism

Protestant mysticism is united with Roman Catholic mysticism in the essentials of its doctrine and experience. The central feature of Protestant mysticism is the divine spark, sometimes called the divine light, within all people. Hans Denck spoke of the witness of the divine light in Jews and heathens. Sebastian Frank found it in the writings of Plato, Cicero, Seneca, and Plotinus. Describing the views of Plotinus, Joseph Marechal said that "God the One, casts out His rays like a single sun to the very confines of non-being." But the rays, "divine fragments scattered in the infinite, bear within them each in its own degree a homesickness for Being, a desire for the return to unity with absolute Good."[35]

Jacob Boehme (1574-1624), like most mystics, had an ecumenical outlook. Like Isaac Luria, Boehme said that God had potential wrath within Him, and that separation of wrath from God's divine love resulted in evil. But the separation was due to man, not God. Like the Gnostics and the authors of the Kabala, Boehme believed that this separation took place in the multiple Fall—of Lucifer, of Adam, and of ourselves. To heal the breach, one must put aside one's will and replace it with God's, and then the unitive life will be restored.

Evil, to Boehme, was a possible good spoiled—Lucifer sought the light but found the darkness. Boehme differentiated desire from love. Desire is a universal individualizing tendency, but love is God's gravitational pull on us back to oneness. Sir Isaac Newton, an admirer of Boehme, may have been influenced by Boehme's theory of gravity.

The divine spark, said Boehme, makes everyone holy. When divine love takes over one's life, these are the signs:

1. There is no room for hatred or war in one's heart.
2. One feels God's constant Presence in one's life.
3. A radiant feeling of joy pervades one's being.
4. One clearly understands the relation of the soul to God.
5. There is a tremendous integration of one's powers into a unified personality.
6. One has a sharp perception of moral values, and a will to observe them.

The Cambridge Platonists, such as John Smith, agreed that the Holy Spirit is at work in all people. The mystical poet Thomas Traherne believed that "God is infinitely prone to love," and that holiness and happiness were the same quality. An angel, said Traherne, would be happy anywhere, while an evil spirit would be happy nowhere.

George Fox, who founded the Society of Friends, said that the Holy Spirit is God within us as a seed, ready to be nurtured. Fox cited the conscience of American Indians to show how universal was the Inner Light. Fox said that he was "ravished with the sense of the Love of God," but also "under great suffering in his spirit" because of human cruelty and inhumanity.[36] Valentine Weigel defined the universal church as all faithful souls, including Jews, Moslems, and pagans. Many Protestant mystics were critical of churches and sects which were very exclusive, especially when the grounds for exclusion were creeds and rituals which were definitely manmade.

William Law (1686-1762) rejoiced that "so many eminent spirits have appeared in so many parts of the heathen world. They were apostles of a Christ within." For Law, Christ was a universal principle, "the life and light and holiness of every creature that is holy." Salvation, he said, is everywhere the same: "the desire of the soul turned to God. The new birth in Christ is found in those who never heard of his name." The church is redefined as that place where love rules. All sin, said Law, is the kingdom of the self—self-love, self-esteem, and self-seeking—which denies the Kingdom of God. Although sin is real, it is not ineradicable, Law felt, but can be overcome by being possessed with the love of Christ.[37]

Charles Wesley included mystical concepts in many of his Methodist hymns. In a hymn to the Holy Spirit he speaks of being "plunged in the Godhead's deepest sea, and lost in Thine immensity."

William James said that mysticism has four distinguishing marks:

1. It is ineffable, like listening to great music or falling in love.
2. It is noetic, that is, it provides an authoritative insight of great worth.
3. It is transient, usually lasting no longer than two hours.
4. It is passive, giving the feeling of being grasped by a higher power.

In a mystical experience, James says, one's higher and nobler self absorbs one's lower self into its being. Out of the conflict of selves, almost as described by Hegel, comes a unity which is greater than the original self. James preferred mysticism to ordinary religious experience because of his great stress on three things: the importance of feeling, the primacy of direct experience, and the unmatched supremacy of the sovereign individual. "What most attracted James to mysticism," says John E. Smith, "becomes clear: it brings religion back again to the individual, and is a constant reminder to institutional religion that no individual should be subordinated to any system."[38] As a pragmatist, James saw mysticism culminating in good works. Contemplation of the divine, without the accompanying love of one's neighbor, was mere narcissism, falling in love with one's own mirror image, rather than allowing God's light to penetrate and overcome one's selfish tendencies.

James finds the city of God existing in every culture. He said that "in mystic states we both become one with the Absolute and we become aware of our oneness. In Hinduism, in Neoplatonism, in Sufis, in Christian mysticism, in Whitman, we find the same recurring note. There is about mystical utterance an eternal unanimity which ought to make a critic stop and think. The mystical classics have neither birthday nor native land."[39]

Modern Unitive Mysticism

For mystics in the tradition of Eastern Orthodox Christianity, the unitive life is not one of renunciation but one permeated with the positive power of love. Isaac the Syrian said that the God-possessed person has "a heart burning with charity for the whole of creation." Such a person prays even for evildoers and enemies of the truth. John of Cronstadt felt that when one unites with the Holy Spirit, one releases the power of the Holy Spirit within the objects of one's prayers. St. Maximus declared emphatically that "he who sees in his heart a trace of hatred towards another is a complete stranger to the love of God, which can in no way tolerate hatred of man."[40]

Moslem mysticism continues to find followers in Sufism. *Tawhid* ("to make one") is a central term in Sufism. Since God is the only reality, we non-real human beings can exist only in Him, Sufis teach. *Fana* ("annihilation") is the term describing the soul's absorption into God. Many modern Sufis regard Jesus as "the seal of the saints." Geoffrey Parrinder recalls the concept of the Persian poet Rumi: "Rumi said Jesus taught unity, a unicolority which was changed into diverse colors by his followers. The 72 sects will remain until the Resurrection; love alone can end their quarrel."[41] Rumi believed that even Pharaoh worshipped the truth, and that all devout persons will be saved.

Albert Schweitzer said that "rational thinking which is free from assumptions ends in mysticism." Jacques Maritain believed that "the love of the creature for the creature is a natural analogue of the most obvious sort for the supernatural mystical experience. Whenever there really exists a mystical experience by means of union with love, this experience is supernatural."[42] John Haynes Holmes also saw the mystical vision as love in action. Holmes averred that "religion is the mystic impulse working within us to make us greater than we are, and the world through us better than it is. Religion belongs to man not because he can build churches but rather because he can sense the whole of life, catch a vision of the ideal in things real, and is willing to give his life to fulfilling this vision."[43]

Ariel Bension describes the Sephardic mystics of Beth-El in Jerusalem, who did not follow the Hasidic tradition observed by the Ashkenazi Hasidim. "Practical Kabala was completely prohibited," said Bension. "In its place came the insistence on the living of a pure and holy life underlying which was a joy, sincere and silent, and a brotherly love. It was a community which agreed to live in unity and sanctity." A pure personal life is required, "based on a sense of personal responsibility for the discord in the universe. All Hasidim say that only through joy can man recognize the Infinite. But the Sephardi find that joy in silent meditation."[44]

Thomas Merton said that God is white light, but most of us perceive Him in only one of His composite colors. "God is never really known," Merton believed, "unless He is also loved. And we cannot love Him unless we do His will. Love is thus both the starting-point of contemplation and its fruition. Contemplation is that intensification of faith that transforms belief into vision."[45]

Marghanita Laski polled 63 persons, many of whom were avowedly agnostics, on whether they had ever had a mystical experience, a sensation of transcendent ecstasy. In the group 60 replied in the affirmative. Etienne Gilson explains that the mystical encounter is one of union of disparities with God rather than unity with Him, since that would presuppose being of the same substance as God. We can, says Gilson, be one with God but not One with Him. Our union with one another through the Holy Spirit does not mean that we become the Holy Spirit. "Since the soul is a likeness to God," Gilson states, "the more it conforms itself in will to God's will so much the more does it become its self. Man tends, by way of love, to make himself invisible," by permitting God to shine through his life.[46] What the mystic achieves is not deification but divinization. Deification, or apotheosis, is to become a god; divinization, or theosis, is to discover and reveal the spirit of God working within oneself.

Kenneth Wapnick distinguishes between mysticism and schizophrenia. Both processes involve a retreat from the outer world in order to pursue the inner life. But there are important differences:[47]

    1. The mystic consciously chooses the inner life.
    2. The mystic experiences divine unity, not chaotic diversity.
    3. The mystic is stronger upon his return to the "real" world.

4. The mystic enjoys reliving the spiritual encounter.
5. The mystic has freed himself from distracting encumbrances, but the schizophrenic is slave to them.

Ken Wilber presents a new version of the Great Chain of Being. The downward movement, or involution, on the ladder of existence was creation, which was a separation from the Creator. Salvation, or evolution, simply retraces what first was involuted. It is a rejoining of things parted, a remembrance of a simpler original Unity. "The union of science and religion," Wilber says, "is the union of evolution and involution." The final stage of evolution is spirit joining Spirit. All individuals possess enlightenment, but may not be conscious of it. Meditation and prayer help them identify their divine sparks. "Spirit is both the highest rung on the ladder and the ladder itself. Nothing less than that paradox will suffice in any discussion of Spirit."[48] In Christian terms, Christ is the highest rung on the ladder, and the Holy Spirit is the ladder itself.

William Ernest Hocking demonstrates how ritual needs the reinforcement of mysticism. Ritual's purpose is to "conserve moments of common feeling and elevation within a community." But it is so hard for ritual to achieve this purpose alone that "it requires for its success a parallel development of private mysticism." Highly ritualized churches from time to time have revivals of "personal religion." Also non-conformist and non-ritualistic churches often employ mysticism as their unifying principle. Mystical movements give Protestant churches three qualities, Hocking feels: seriousness, since each individual is responsible for his own salvation; sincerity, as one introspects to ensure that one's ethical code is consistent with one's high religious ideals; and dignity, for if each individual is a priest, he must carry himself with priestly mien, and be a minister to all persons.

Within Protestant mysticism has been a unifying force, Hocking feels, for when sectarians differ over externals, they can always return to religious fundamentals, which is mysticism's area of concern. Mysticism looks beyond externals to love, the heart of any valid religion. If God can be found within every person, then external scriptures and church hierarchies, which tend to separate people, are not very important. Protestants say, not that authority is unnecessary but that each individual, by his personal access to God, has the ability to distinguish true authority from false.[49]

References

[1] Parrinder, *Mysticism in the World's Religions,* pp. 4, 195.
[2] Evelyn Underhill, *Mysticism,* 16th ed. (Dutton, 1948), pp. xiv, 311, 326.
[3] Ronald Hepburn in Steven T. Katz, ed., *Mysticism and Religious Traditions* (Oxford University Press, 1983), p. 95.
[4] Radhakrishnan, p. 292.
[5] Walter T. Stace, *The Teachings of the Mystics* (New American Library, 1960), pp. 14, 20.
[6] Gerry C. Heard, *Mystical and Ethical Experience* (Mercer University Press, 1985), p. 35.
[7] Thomas Merton, *The Ascent to Truth* (Harcourt Brace Jovanovich, 1951), p. 243.
[8] Campbell, *Occidental Mythology,* pp. 448-49.
[9] Tillich, *Dynamics of Faith,* pp. 60-61.
[10] Ibid., p. 123.
[11] Newell, pp. 135-36
[12] Schuon, p. 451.
[13] Robert C. Zaehner, *Mysticism, Sacred and Profane* (Oxford University Press, 1961), pp. 200, 206.
[14] Underhill, p. 429.
[15] Hoffman, p. 192.
[16] Hoffman, p. 25.
[17] Ibid., pp. 11, 156.
[18] Louis Jacobs, *Jewish Mystical Testimonies* (Schocken, 1977), 150-51, 154.
[19] Parrinder, *Mysticism in the World's Religions,* p. 118.
[20] Jacobs, pp. 213-14.
[21] Newell, p. 292.
[22] Wilber, *Up From Eden,* p. 244.
[23] Underhill, pp. 435-36.
[24] Louis Dupré, in Woods, p. 462.
[25] Voss, p. 227.

26 Juliana of Norwich, *Reflections on Divine Love* (Doubleday, 1977), pp. 16-61, 202.
27 Underhill, p. 206.
28 Merton, p. 331.
29 Voss, p. 252.
30 Newell, p. 219.
31 Woods, p. 452.
32 Rudolf Otto, *Mysticism East and West* (Macmillan, 1932), p. 17. A German theologian, Otto wrote the influential *The Idea of the Holy*.
33 Ibid., pp. 57-59.
34 Anne Fremantle, *Pilgrimage to People* (David McKay, 1968), p. 59.
35 Joseph Marechal, *Studies in the Psychology of the Mystics* (Magi Books, 1964), p. 297. Marechal, a Catholic priest, has made a careful study of the Upanishads. Hans Denck (1495-1527) was a German humanist. Sebastian Frank (1533-1588) was a German mystic.
36 Sidney Spencer, *Mysticism in World Religion* (A.S. Barnes, 1963), p. 287. Valentine Weigel (1533-1588) was a German pacifist.
37 Ibid., pp. 287-88, 296.
38 John E. Smith, in Katz, p. 277.
39 Woods, p. 255.
40 Spencer, pp. 229-30.
41 Parrinder, *Mysticism in the World's Religions,* p. 136.
42 Woods, pp. 485, 495.
43 Voss, p. 113.
44 Jacobs, pp. 157-58.
45 Merton, pp. 10, 13, 116.
46 Woods, p. 506. Etienne Gilson, a French philosopher, was a leader in the Catholic Neo-Thomist movement.
47 Ibid., pp. 334-36.
48 Wilber, *Up From Eden,* p. 292.
49 Woods, pp. 198-202. Hocking was Professor of Philosophy at Harvard.

CHAPTER 8

INTERFAITH DIALOGUE, ECUMENISM, AND SYNCRETISM

Interfaith dialogue is an urgent necessity in a world where divisive religion produces terrorism and war, and where unitive religion can spread seeds of love, fellowship, and forgiveness. Fortunately there is much interfaith dialogue in the twentieth century.

Interfaith dialogue can lead to the unitive movements known as ecumenism and syncretism. Ecumenism is unitive because it involves an effort to secure widespread cooperation and/or unity among a number of individual churches. The motto of the 1954 Evanston meeting of the World Council of Churches was "Our oneness in Christ is more important than our differences as denominations." The ecumenical movement strives to ignore differences in creed and ritual in the effort to build a broader family of love. The movement has been fed by the harm done to Christianity by sectarian and partisan Christian witness by denominations engaging in missionary work.

"The ecumenical movements," says Wilfred Cantwell Smith, "have been in part the result of pressures from the mission field. Unless men can learn to understand and be loyal to each other across religious frontiers, unless we can build a world in which people of profoundly different faiths can live together, prospects for our planet's future are not bright. Constructing even that minimum degree of world fellowship necessary for man to survive is far too great to be accomplished on any other than a religious basis. From no other source can man master the energy, devotion, vision, and resolution necessary for this challenge. Cooperation among people of diverse religion is a moral imperative."[1]

By definition syncretism is unitive, since it is the merging of two or more religious faiths. For the merger to endure, each merged faith must be considered the spiritual equal of its companion. Ideally, thus, all discriminatory barriers are removed between what were once competing approaches to God. All religions are somewhat syncretistic, Smith feels. Since a religion often grows out of an antecedent faith, and frequently spawns one or more succeeding faiths, it would be rare to find a wholly independent religion. Strong religions learn openly from others, Smith judges, but weak ones recede into their shells, become isolated, and try to assert uniqueness. At its best, syncretism is a dynamic synthesis, with a dialectical transcending of conflicts through inner mediation.

John V. Taylor quotes the Bible to show that God's covenant is with all mankind, not just adherents of one or two religious confessions. God's promise to Noah following the flood included the entire human race. Taylor points out that Yahweh is the God of the Israelites, the Philistines, and the Syrians (Amos 9:7). In another context He declared Himself to be the God of Israel, Egypt, and Assyria (Isaiah 19:25). "From the rising of the sun to its setting," we read in Malachi 1:11, "in every place incense is offered in My name." Matthew (in 8:11) records Christ saying that "many from the East and the West will sit down with Abraham in the Kingdom of Heaven" (even though Abraham never confessed Christ as his savior). Justin Martyr said that since they lived according to the Logos, even alleged atheists like Socrates and Heraclitus are types of Christians. The elderly Augustine concurred when he said that "the reality which we now call the Christian religion was present among the early people."[2]

"The question for any ecumenically oriented religion," said Ileana Marculescu, "is how to prevent the political-ideological model from becoming its dominant form of expression, while maintaining intact its historic originality." Yusuf Ibish shows how al-Arabi's theory of the earthly journey is "a theosophical teaching which conveys the message of unity through the metaphor of a journey whose stations are each a stage in the religious consciousness of mankind."[3]

Comparative religion frequently studies the interface among faiths. Raymond Panikkar states that comparative religion is not just a comparison of faiths, but a study of universal problems, such as life, death, peace, freedom, and salvation, seen under the guidance of more than one religious tradition. Comparative religion does not necessarily solve social problems, but it does describe the inner attitudes that make possible the solutions.

The ecumene, or the house of the family of God, has been mankind's perennial search. "The thrust towards universalization," says Panikkar, "has undoubtedly been a feature of Western civilization since the Greeks. If something is not universal, it looms as not really valid."[4] The Oriental view of the One out of the many is found in Western civilization from Heraclitus and Pico della Mirandola to St. François de Sales and R.C. Zaehner. It was Einstein's dream to find the formula describing unified field theory, in which all of the fundamental physical forces would be seen as varieties of a single parent force.

Science, in its search for universals, can be said to be ecumenical and syncretistic. Modern science originated in theology, for the milieu of Francis Bacon, Robert Boyle, and Isaac Newton was "theologically secure." All believed in a divine creation, seen in the order of nature. All believed in a worshipful attitude towards the divine Author of nature's laws. Johan Baptist van Helmont (1577-1644) was the Flemish scientist who discovered carbon dioxide. Helmont's mysticism called for penetration into, rather than flight from, the world of nature. Since God, as Supreme Wisdom, was presupposed in all knowledge, science would be a handmaid of theology. "For Helmont, the Whole dwells abundantly in each part." Helmont saw that amoral science was a threat to man, and so he asked the scientist for humility before God and charity toward man, in a spiritual understanding which would unify all modes of knowledge in service to God and one's neighbor.[5] Given God's eternal unity, said Helmont, man, who was made in God's image, also had an immortal unity. Both medicine and theology should use the holistic approach, he advised.

Nature was assumed by Christian scientists to be orderly, precise, and predictable. Mathematics was the language to be used in describing nature. Galileo said that "the book of nature is a book written by the hand of God in the language of mathematics."

Robert Boyle stated that the scientist is a priest, whose function was to celebrate the glory of God and serve the cause of humanity. The first person to distinguish between a chemical element and a compound, Boyle praised the Bible for its variety:

"God, knowing that some persons must be wrought upon by reason, others allured by interest, some driven by terror, and others again brought in by invitation, hath by rare wisdom so varied the heavenly doctrines into reasonings, mysteries, promises, threats, and examples" that each person can find in the scriptures food to nourish his spiritual hunger.[6]

Isaac Newton thought that the world was in the "end times" predicted in the Bible by Daniel and John, and he therefore felt obligated to use his brain power as a part of the end-time increase in knowledge. In a letter he wrote that planetary motions "could not spring from any natural cause alone but were impressed by an intelligent agent." Speaking of gravitation, "he affirmed a similar divine regulation of bodies, much as a human will regulates its body." Newton said that "the entire universe was rightly designated a Temple of God."[7]

Like science, religion also strives for universality, often through interfaith dialogue. Two obstacles in interfaith dialogue are a false feeling of superiority, and the fear of surrendering a precious heritage. Roman Catholic Bishop J.K. Matthews addressed these issues: "An unseemly anxiety to preserve our heritage is to lose it and at the same time, to attempt to limit God. But a willingness to risk even the loss of our heritage in the service of God and man is to find it. When there is a readiness to risk all, God may be trusted to be faithful in giving all back again in a renewed and enlarged perspective."[8]

Leonard Swidler has drawn up a set of rules for interreligious dialogue:[9]

1. The primary purpose of the dialogue is to learn.
2. Required are mutual trust, and complete honesty and sincerity.
3. One's ideals cannot be compared with another's practice.
4. Each participant must be willing to compromise on some matters.

Gotthold Lessing's play *Nathan the Wise* describes an encounter between Judaism, Christianity, and Islam. After losing his wife and seven sons to Christian Crusaders, Nathan, a pious Jewish merchant, rears a Christian orphan girl, teaching her only those religious doctrines on which all three faiths agree. Here each religion's encounter with the others teaches it its own relativity. Lessing believed that all history is a divine revelation, and that each successive religion advances that revelation.

Syncretism in Christianity

"Christianity is one of the most obvious and generally successful syncretisms, between Hebrew and Greek," declares Geoffrey Parrinder. The Christian tradition comes from different strains, Parrinder states, "which were the price of its universal aims. Christian writers like Clement and Origen used terminology from the Greek mysteries. The persecutions forced Christians into secret meetings, and the inner mystical teachings enabled Christianity to enter into the heritage of the mysteries and expand them far and wide."[10]

For example, both Christmas and Easter were pagan holidays which were adapted by the Christians for their use. The spring resurrection of the savior god is an old religious archetype, as is the birth of the wonderful child.

Wilfred Cantwell Smith says that "if we take seriously the revelation of God in Christ, then two things follow. On the moral level, there follows an imperative towards reconciliation, unity, harmony, and brotherhood. At this level, we do not become truly Christian until we have turned mankind into one total community. At another level, the intellectual one, it is the business of theologians to construct doctrines. Traditional Christian doctrines tend to affirm Christian exclusivism, and have in fact encouraged Christians to approach other men immorally. Christ has taught us humility, but we have approached them with arrogance. Any position that alienates rather than reconciles is *ipso facto* un-Christian."[11] The God revealed by Christ is one of love, Smith says, and thus dutiful Buddhists, Hindus, Jews, and Moslems cannot possibly be condemned to eternal hellfire.

Are Christians disloyal when they admit the validity of other religions? No, says Leonard Swidler, "rather they would be disloyal to their Christian commitment if they did not seek to recognize the same truths and insights wherever they find them. In dialogue with non-Christians, they will learn that there are many valuable insights in their own Christian tradition that they had overlooked or suppressed or distorted."[12] They may also find in other traditions insights not found in Christianity but equally valid.

Eastern Orthodox Christianity has produced many ecumenical thinkers, including Vladimir Solovyov and Nicholas Berdyaev. Solovyov had a vast vision of a free theocracy and a united creative Christianity. In Gnosticism he discovered Sophia (Divine Wisdom) as the personal cosmological principle uniting the divine and the created worlds. Solovyov influenced many of the Russian symbolist writers. Berdyaev synthesized many strands: Marx, Boehme, Nietzsche, Tolstoy, and the Slavophile Alexei Khomyakov. Berdyaev's great stress is upon human dignity as proper to be shown to all of mankind as God's children.

Christian-Hindu Dialogue

R.C. Zaehner pointed out parallels between Roman Catholicism and the Hinduism of Ramanuja. Both say that although God is greater than the universe, He is at the deep center of the human heart. Also, both say that the universe, including mankind, is distinct from God but wholly dependent upon Him.

Frank Whaling states that in Hinduism God as Brahman (Ultimate Reality) is both with qualities *(saguna)* and without qualities *(nirguna)*. This in Christianity is like the unknowable Father, the impersonal Creator *(nirguna)* and the revealed Son, the personal Savior *(saguna)*.

John Moffitt describes further similarities. Hinduism's *jnana* (intuitive wisdom or thought) is found in Christianity's assumption that God lies deep in one's soul, as depicted by John, Paul, and many Christian mystics. The yoga discipline finds parallels in teachings by Paul, Loyola, John Wesley, and other Christian leaders. Hinduism's bhakti (devotional self-giving) finds remarkable examples in Christ's self-sacrifice, and in Christ's doctrine of love. Karma, the reward for works and service, has an analogue in Christ's picture of the judgment: "Inasmuch as you have done it unto the least of these, you have done it unto me."

The Indian Christian Pandipeddy Chenchiah spoke for many of his countrymen when he stated that "we do not see any reason why Aristotle, Plato, Kant, and Hegel should be regarded as safer guides for Christian theology than the Indian philosophers Shankara and Ramanuja." Jules Monchanin and Bede Griffiths both find in Advaita Hinduism "an almost wholly satisfying vehicle for expressing the heart of the Christian mystery: the unity between Father, Son, and Holy Spirit, and between God and the believer, can readily be stated in terms of *ekatvam,* oneness of essence."[13]

Raymond Panikkar, an Indian Christian, interprets the Christian cross as a crossing; thus, a Christian admires the positive features of other religions because he denotes there a veiled presence of the mystical spirit of Christ. Just as Aquinas incorporated Aristotle into Christianity, says Panikkar, so do modern Christians need to incorporate the Vedanta of Shankara.

Hans Küng, the Roman Catholic theologian, notes similarities between his faith and Hinduism. Both have many holy places, and both have henotheism: the worship of one God, but with quasi-divine veneration given to other figures. Many Hindus, says Küng, accept the eternal law of love as seen in Christ's Sermon on the Mount. Enculturation is a two-way process, in Küng's view. Thus, as many Hindus accept Christian teachings, Christians should be open to consider introducing such Hindu practices as meditation, music, and dances; the use of nature symbols (such as flowers, light, sunrise, and sunset) into Christian worship; and the liturgical use of appropriate texts from the Veda and other Hindu scriptures.

Only mutual love can overcome the egocentric position of an entrenched religion, says Panikkar. Thus, although Christ can be an excellent meeting ground for the two faiths, Christianity cannot so serve, for it has had so many bureaucratic growths and appendages that the essential love of Christ at the heart of the religion can scarcely be discerned. Only when one is completely empty of oneself will Christ dwell fully within him, Panikkar believes. At the same time, the individual is ready for the ultimate encounter with Brahman. With no dogmatic creeds, "Hinduism can take as many forms as the circumstances require." Hinduism would be willing to sacrifice its special characteristics in a unified world religion, but no other religion is ready to make such a sacrifice. But "Christ does not belong to Christianity," Panikkar avers, "He belongs only to God. Nobody knows how Christianity will look when the present Christian waters and the Hindu river merge into a bigger stream, where future peoples will quench their thirst for truth, for goodness, for salvation."[14]

In his book *The Trinity in World Religions* Panikkar states that trinity concepts are found in all of the world religions. In

Hinduism, in addition to the Trimurti, Panikkar relates karma spirituality to God the Father, bhakti spirituality to God the Son, and jnana spirituality to the Holy Spirit. In the words of Frank Whaling, "ritual worship of God, loving devotion to God, and inward realization of God are related aspects of an integral spirituality which finds concrete expression in service for God in the world."[15] Hinduism, Whaling observes, stresses the practical application of the Trinity doctrine more than speculation about its metaphysical explanation.

Classical Hindu thought conceived of the Absolute (Brahman) as Being, Intelligence, and Bliss, which could be thought of as the transcendent Father, the incarnate Logos, and the immanent Giver of Joy, or the Holy Spirit. St. Augustine said that the Holy Trinity was Being, Knowledge, and Love

Ram Mohan Roy (1775-1833) built a syncretism out of Hinduism and Christianity. Roy accepted Christ as a divine figure, and at the same time salvaged the eternal teachings of the Upanishads. Roy influenced a number of subsequent syncretists.

Vivekananda (1863-1902) said that although we cannot know the Absolute, God the Father, we can experience Him through one of His manifestations, such as Buddha, Krishna, Christ, or Ramakrishna. Recent scholars are finding many parallels between the Gospel of John and the Upanishads. Maharaj Charan Singh, a Sikh, has written a book on *St. John, the Great Mystic.*

An English Benedictine monk, Bede Griffiths, left his monastery to live as a Hindu ascetic. Another to do this was the French Benedictine monk Henri Le Saux, who acquired the Sanskrit name *Abhishiktananda,* meaning "bliss of the anointed one." These monks are building a bridge of understanding between the two faiths in a way understood by the Hindus, that of contemplative silence. Le Saux feels that "India restores the sense of the sacred to Westerners who have lost it or never experienced it, and this helps them to discover the true meaning of Christianity."[16]

Hinduism's *advaita* (or non-duality) states a Christian truth: God's being in our being. We cannot separate ourselves from God, at the level of the Spirit within us (John 14:17), a concept called *atman* in Hinduism. When Christ spoke of being in his Father, "and you in Me and I in you" (John 17:20), he spoke not a hope but a spiritual truth, says Anthony E. Gilles.

Recent books by Robin Boyd and M.M. Thomas explain how the Christian-Hindu syncretism is developing. The constantly used analogy is the one showing how the early Church Fathers created a synthesis out of Greek philosophy and Christianity. This movement, John A.T. Robinson feels, can help Christianity escape from "the Latin captivity of the Church. For India has a tradition of immersion in Being beyond the screen of appearances which is as rich and deep as anywhere in the world, and a culture where the relation between religion and philosophy has always been more vital than in either ancient Greece or modern Europe."[17] Brahmabandhav Upadhyaya has written a Sanskrit "Hymn to the Trinity" which expresses Christian concepts in Hindu forms.

The Englishman George Birdwood sees three great steps in spiritual evolution. The Jews discovered that there is but one God, the Christians that God is a loving Father, and the Hindus that mankind should be a universal brotherhood under that Heavenly Father. "India may be destined," Birdwood declared, "to prepare the way for the reconciliation of Christianity with the world, and hasten the period in the moral development of humanity when there will be no divisions of race or creed or class or nationality, for they will acknowledge their common brotherhood."[18] Primitive cultures are unified, Birdwood points out, so that religion permeates one's entire environment. To survive, mankind must regain this consistency of the religion of the God of love permeating all of our institutions.

A further sign of religious synthesis is the fact that in Madras, India, the Missouri Synod of the American Lutheran Church has a center where Christian dances are created, following the example of traditional Hindu temple dancing. When religions can sacrifice non-essentials to focus on essentials, there is hope that religion can indeed be a unitive rather than a divisive force in human affairs.

Christian-Buddhist Dialogue

Thomas Merton says that communion must precede communication. In religious terms communion means penetrating to the ground of one's beliefs. At that point both Christians and Buddhists find Absolute Being and Absolute Love. Contemplation of God is a universal language, usable in all faiths. "Instead of beginning with distinctions," says Paul F. Knitter, "we should start with the original unity between the Ultimate and the finite—a unity which is available, Buddhists tell us, in 'pure consciousness.' A true religious experience is the experience of God being subjective in us. God is not an Other," for "the Ultimate and the finite make up a non-dual Reality; both have their being in each other.

"Christianity seems to have taken its words and concepts, whether biblical or papal, much too seriously. This obsessive insistence on right words or doctrines (orthodoxy) blurs the fact that all religion originates from a deep personal experience and not from an affirmation of propositions. Orthodoxy provides a clear and distinct concept of God which too easily becomes Freud's transcendent crutch for our insecurity and anxiety. And the security of right knowing debilitates so readily the primacy of right acting."[19]

To worship the spirit of Christ within us is to truly imitate Christ, making the Christian a contemplative, says Joseph Campbell. Both Christ and Buddha, he adds, "have entered as archetypes into the Western and Eastern unconscious. Their historical lives had such power that they superimposed themselves on an already existing image in the unconscious."[20]

John B. Cobb, Jr., offers an additional refinement, saying that he concurs with Alfred North Whitehead's conviction that "Christianity and Buddhism represent the culmination of Western and Eastern religious developments, that both are in decline, and that neither can regain its vitality except as enriched through the other. Buddhism insists that whatever is, is relational through and through, interdependent with everything else. Christians must ask themselves whether they have been truly faithful to their own Scriptures and experience in depicting God as beyond all real relations or relativity. I believe we have not, and that the encounter with Buddhism can be an occasion for freeing our concept of God from the absolutist straightjacket."[21]

Speaking of Burmese Christianity, Khin Maung Din states that "no Christology, traditional or contemporary, has said the final word about God in Christ." Din quotes David Jenkins as saying that "the truth, the uniqueness, and the absoluteness of Christ are not exclusive but inclusive." Din feels that "God in Christ has spoken a human language for concrete humanity. It is in this common meeting, loving, caring, and struggling for and with their common neighbor that all religions and ideologies develop together toward their common destiny. The final test for religions is not their knowledge of God but their concrete love for man. So the most important problem facing Burmese Christian theology today is 'how to feed His lambs.'"

"Some of the traditional Christian terms," Din continues, "like 'atonement,' 'sacrifice,' and 'blood offering,' may have had supreme religious significance for Old Testament Jews, but these terms take on an anti-religious meaning for men of Oriental faiths. Human sacrifice in Burmese history belongs to the ancient pre-Buddhist period. Such primitive practices were abandoned after the arrival of Buddhism. If conventional Christianity insists on using these relative Jewish concepts in an absolute way, then it will be imposing an unnecessary stumbling block to the 'Gentiles' of the East. In other words, if the Gospel is meant to be universal, we must interpret it in terms of truly universal categories."

"The historical advent of Jesus," Din feels, "reveals the coming of God to man not only in that particular moment of history but even *before* that time, as well as in ages to come. In this sense we can better understand the Cross as the 'Center' of history. The preparation for the coming of Christ can also be discerned in the particular histories of other people. In our attempt to seek the living Christ we must also listen to what He has spoken, and keeps on speaking, in and through the living faiths and ideologies of other men. We shall seek the Word that has already come and dwelt among them."[22]

Paul Martinson finds an analogue to Christ's parable of the Prodigal Son. Buddhism has the story of the Burning House, in which a wealthy father saves his sons from their burning home by promising them a cart of toys. When they rush out, thereby saving their lives, they each get a bullock cart.

Hans Küng believes that a continuing dialogue between Christians and Buddhists is essential for world peace. Küng brings out the many similarities between the two faiths. Both Christ and Buddha pointed away from themselves and toward their teachings. Each had an allegedly divine birth, was tempted, performed miracles, was an itinerant preacher, and had a small band of devoted disciples. Their ethical teachings are very similar. Christ is the supreme example of com-passion (suffering with us); Buddha showed his followers how to master suffering. Already, said Küng, there are Zen Christians and Christian Buddhists. A Canadian Roman Catholic monk, J. Edgar Bruns, has recently written a book *The Christian Buddhism of St. John.*

Buddhism's influence on Christianity can be salutary, says Knitter. Under this influence, "God will be seen not so much as a Super-Being relating to finite beings but as the unitive Mystery which lives and moves and has its being within finite beings, as they have their being in It." Buddhism also encourages non-duality, Knitter reminds us. "A non-dualistic notion of God-world will lend coherence to the claims of liberation theologians, for if God is subjective in us, He cannot carry out His liberating action without us (nor we without Him) so that our actions are His, and the Kingdom we build here on earth is His reality."

Knitter goes on to say that man's Fall, according to Buddhism, was due not so much to sinfulness as to ignorance: "The pseudo-knowledge acquired from eating of the Tree of Knowledge leads us to think that we are individuals and that the purpose of existence is to maintain and augment that individuality." Buddhism is a corrective for Christian individualism, which can lead to selfish exclusion of concern for others. Thus both religions can prepare humankind for the "quantum leap" from "individuality to communality, from a world of divided, warring tribes to a global village." Humans must "profoundly realize that to be themselves they must be part of others—only then will they be able to form authentic community" and achieve world peace.[23]

Syncretism in India

Kabir (1440-1518) was an Indian weaver who, because of his religious tolerance, is now thought of as a saint. Born a Moslem, Kabir also practiced Hinduism. He was a follower of Ramananda, who led a Vishnu sect that opposed caste and food taboos. Kabir rejected outward religious forms, such as caste, ideology, and rituals, in favor of a simple love of God. A monotheist, he said that the love of God would free one from the law of karma. His approach synthesized the best elements of Hinduism and Islam. He performed many unusual deeds of kindness, including curing the Emperor Sikander Lodi of a great fever. Kabir taught that "the man who is kind and practices righteousness, who remains passive amidst the affairs of the world, who considers all creatures on earth as his own self, he attains the Immortal Being, the true God is ever with him."[24] As a mystic Kabir believed that "God is one. There is no second. He is everywhere. Search in thy heart; there is His abode. The soul that is joined with Him is indestructible."[25]

Kabir profoundly influenced Nanak (1469-1539), the founder of Sikhism. A Sikh ("disciple") is one who adheres to the best teachings of Islam and Hinduism. Nanak was taught by gurus in both faiths. At the age of thirty he had his first mystical experience. Presumed drowned, he emerged from the stream three days later, saying, "There is no Hindu, there is no Moslem." Criticized when he refused to face Mecca in prayer, he replied, "God is in all directions." He called God "the True Name," and said that He is known by many names but is eternally one. If a name is needed, Nanda felt that Hari (the Kindly) would be appropriate in delineating God's nature.

"Religion consists not in a yogi's staff," said Nanak, "or in ashes smeared over the body. He who looks on all men as equal is religious. Remain pure amid the impurities of the world; thus shall you find the way to religion."[26] Salvation, Nanak stated, comes from works performed for the love of God. One must learn to conquer one's five inner enemies: anger, false pride, greed, lust, and attachment to worldly things. Since all human nature is one to Sikhs, women are considered as men's equals. Many religions could accept Nanak's morning prayer, which begins as follows:

> There is one God. He is the Supreme Truth.
> He, the Creator, is without fear and without hate.
> He, the Omnipotent, pervades the universe.
> He is not born, nor does He die to be born again.
> By His grace shalt thou worship.[27]

Like many a noble religious dream, Sikhism, which was founded in love and peace, eventually came to condone violence. The fifth guru, Arjun, led the Sikhs from 1581 to 1606. When Emperor Akbar died, Arjun supported Akbar's son Khusran instead of Khusran's brother Jahangir. When Jahangir had Khusran tortured and killed, Arjun recommended that Sikhs arm themselves in self defense. Soon the Sikhs were sword bearers with a reputation as fierce fighters. Sikhs took the name "Singh" (meaning "lion") as a part of their name. In 1761 Ahmad Shah of Persia destroyed the Sikh temple at Amritsar, piling the heads of dead Sikhs in the ruins. For revenge, Rajah Ranjiy Singh in the early 1800s rebuilt the temple, using materials scavenged from various Moslem buildings.

Further syncretism occurred when a Hindu banker, Shiv Dayal (1818-1878) of Agra, founded the group Radha Soami Satsang, a compound of elements from Hinduism and Sikhism. Dayal described God as the union of Radha (soul) and Soami (creator). There are over two million modern adherents of this faith, including persons from the Christian, Hindu, Moslem, Parsi, and Sikh faiths.

Brahmo Samaj is a movement founded in Calcutta in 1828 by Ram Mohan Roy, a Brahmin willing to sacrifice parts of Hinduism in order to achieve a more universal religion. Roy found in all religions a similar spiritual core: the unity of God. He welcomed all witnesses to God's unity. The precepts of Jesus, he said, were the guide to peace and happiness. Although the movement split into several sects, all branches support a universal religion based on the Fatherhood of God and the brotherhood of man.

Ramakrishna Paramahansa (1836-1886) taught that all faiths, if followed sincerely, led to God. His saintly life reinforced his message. The chief tenets of his faith are:

1. To realize God is the goal of human life.
2. God is one, but He has various names and forms.
3. A person can choose his name or form of God, and can reach Him if he has genuine longing, devotion, and steadfastness.
4. Different religions are merely different paths to God.
5. Since the essentials of all religious are harmonious, there is no place for religious intolerance.
6. "God is manifest everywhere. See Him in all human beings and serve Him in them."[28]

Ramakrishna inspired his follower Vivekananda to establish the Ramakrishna Mission, whose twofold purpose is to serve

God and human beings, especially the poor, the sick, and the illiterate.

Syncretism in China and Japan

In the 1940s Fung Yu-lan developed the New Rationalism in China in an attempt to synthesize Confucian philosophy with Western science. "As the world feels more keenly the need of peace and democracy," says Chan Wing-tsit, "the Confucian sayings that 'All men are brothers' and 'There is no class distinction in education' are becoming familiar quotations. The basic Confucian concept that Heaven is rational, moral, purposive, and good, will continue to enlighten the Chinese."[29]

A modern Chinese secret religious group is very syncretistic. The I Kuan Tao (Way of Pervading Unity) accepts the teachings of all of the major world religions. It encourages abstinence from meat, tobacco, and alcohol, and stresses the reduction of desire through mental discipline. Although the Communist government has tried to suppress this group, it still had numerous adherents in 1960.

Douglas J. Elwood states that modern Christian missionary work in China involves permitting the Chinese to respond meaningfully to the Christian gospel within the framework of their own culture. Thus Confucianism, which has been called "the law and the prophets" (which Christ said he came not to abolish but to fulfill) might perhaps serve as a Chinese Old Testament, giving the necessary scriptural background for the gospel of Christ. China, says Elwood, can have Confucian Christians, just as the Western world has Aristotelian Christians, or Christian existentialists.

Syncretism comes naturally to the Japanese. The peasant sage Ninomiya Sontoku (1787-1856) founded the Hotoku ("repayment of blessings") Movement, which he said had two parts Shinto, one part Buddhism, and one part Confucianism. "Since the life of each generation is made possible only through the devotion and labors of its forbears," the movement teaches, "it is the duty of each generation to repay its blessings and pass them on, through hard work, frugality, and human kindness."[30]

In 1930 Taniguchi Masaharu began Seichno No Ie ("house of growth"). Its fundamental doctrine is that since all humans are God's children, they therefore share in divine perfection and happiness. This movement is a synthesis of Buddhism and Christianity. It states that sin and guilt are unreal, but can be experienced as if they are real.

Christian-Moslem Dialogue

Jesus has a special status in the Koran. He is called "a sign to all beings," the only person in history who did not die. His mother Mary was a virgin, "chosen above the worlds." Seen as a miracle worker, Jesus is called the Messiah eleven times in the Koran. Other titles ascribed to Jesus are Messenger, Prophet, Servant of God, Spirit of God, and the Word. "Jesus has been revered in the Islamic world as a model of sanctity and poverty," and in some Islamic sources is called "the Lord Christ." The Koran states that "there is no People of the Book but will surely believe in him before his death, and on the day of resurrection he will be a witness regarding them. Muslim tradition has long thought that Jesus will come again to restore all things and reign as a just king." Both the Bible and the Koran place emphasis upon "the universality of God, His unchanging goodness, and His unbounded grace towards all men in all ages."[31]

Pope John XXIII was well accepted in Moslem Algeria and Morocco. Eulogies of Pope John at his death in 1963 on Morocco's official state radio far surpassed those usually given to Moslem leaders. In 1964 Roman Catholic Cardinal Leon-Etienne Duval of Algiers suffered a number of plastic bomb attacks on his churches by his own parishioners because he wanted to show Christian brotherly love towards Moslems. To mark the beginning of Ramadan, the Moslem month of fasting, Duval donated blood to a Moslem hospital in Algiers. In its official expression of gratitude to Duval, the Algerian government pledged itself to welcome all faiths equally.

In 1987 the Presbyterian Church (U.S.A.) adopted a resolution stating that "in many instances Christian perceptions of the resurgence in Islam are distorted by ignorance and prejudice. We describe the Islamic renewal in our own terms, calling it Moslem fundamentalism and referring to its followers as fanatics, zealots, or radicals. Both Christians and Moslems are challenged to allow God to guide them into a future free of hatred, free of fear, and directed by hopeful love."[32]

Also in 1987 Mujahid Rashada, a Moslem, had a house built for his family by the Christian philanthropic society Habitat for Humanity. He exchanged a copy of the Koran for a copy of the Bible, and described the common Jewish, Christian, and Moslem heritage that goes back to Abraham. "He spoke with conviction about the better world that would be possible if all three groups would really live by the dictates of their faith. Habitat seeks the dissolution of all superficial divisions between people by following the simple commands of Christ to help all of our brothers and sisters in need. Could the elimination of poverty housing also aid the dismantling of needless barriers—misunderstanding, distrust, hate, fear—that are so harmful in our world?"[33]

Hans Küng has suggestions for furthering the dialogue between Christians and Moslems. Christians, Küng feels, should see Islam not as a heresy of Christianity but as a fruit-bearing branch of both Judaism and Christianity. The common Old Testament background of both religions should be stressed. Jesus has a message of lasting importance for Moslems, Küng avers, for he sets mankind free from legalisms and gives the human race a deeper concept of God's love. On the other hand, Christians should accept the fact that Mohammed could be God's prophet, "a prophetic corrective for Christians in the name of the one and only God." Küng quotes Moslem theologian Mahmoud M. Ayoub, who speaks of "an Islamic Christology. The free spirits of Islamic mysticism," said Ayoub, "found in the man Jesus not only the example of piety, love, and asceticism, which they sought to emulate, but also the Christ, who exemplifies fulfilled humanity, a humanity illumined by the light of God. This reflection of the divine light in the human heart and soul is known as *tajalli,* the manifestation of divine beauty and majesty in and through man. In this concept of divine manifestation, the Christian and Muslim images of Jesus converge at many points."[34]

Modern Moslem Syncretism

In the late 19th century Mirza Ghulam Ahmad proclaimed himself as at once the long-sought Mahdi, an avatar of Krishna, and Christ in the Second Coming. His goal was to unite all world religions into a broadened Islam. Since he stated that the holy war can be carried on solely through words, his followers tend to be pacifists.

The spiritual father of modern Pakistan, Sir Muhammad Iqbal (1876-1938) wrote poetry in Persian and Urdu, and philosophy in English. He proposed a synthesis, along Sufi lines, of Islam, modern science, and the best of Hindu and Christian thought. He believed that the Koran made all men brothers. Atrocity, even by his adherents, horrified him. He said, "Is this really supposed to be progress—that people destroy one another in mutual hatred and make man's stay on earth impossible? Man can have his position on earth only by honoring mankind. Modern man has ceased to live soulfully. He finds himself incapable of controlling his careless egoism and his infinite appetite for gold. Medieval mysticism, by means of which religious life in its highest manifestations developed in both the West and the Orient, is now gone awry. Only by rising to a new vision of his source and his future can man triumph over inhuman competition."[35]

Shaykh Muhammad Ashraf in 1948 began publication of a monthly journal called *The Islamic Literature.* In the journal Ashraf asked for a reconception of Islam which would cut out the accumulated dross and reassert the eternal truths. This kind of Moslem reevaluation has been going on throughout the Moslem world.

A Turkish educator expressed the need for Moslem reform. "The Muslim world is waiting for a purified true Islam," he said. "We need a new interpretation, and it must be based on values. A religion that does not base itself on love and goodness is nothing. It is imperative that we find that inner nature of religion, unencumbered by the formal accoutrements of a bygone day, and the divisive particularities of the diverse creeds. Man needs this, or all is lost. This is the moral and spiritual crisis of mankind today, and if we do not solve it, we are finished. The new mysticism must use science. But the thing we are looking for is beyond science. And it will bring in all mankind."[36]

Musa Sadr, a Lebanese Shi'ite leader, was a humanitarian and social reformer who worked assiduously for cooperation among religions. The only Moslem at the installation of Pope John XXIII, he was also the first imam to preach in a Christian church. When a surprised priest found him saying his prayers in Strasbourg cathedral, he asked, "Are we not in the house of the

Lord?" Violent Moslems resented his efforts on behalf of religious peace, and so in 1978 he vanished, presumably kidnapped or killed.

In Iraq the ruling party, the Baath, aim at an Islamic renaissance, uniting the best of Moslem and of Western culture. Elias Farah, a high Baathi official in Baghdad, is a Christian Arab. He says that the Baath is trying to erase distinctions between Sunnis and Shi'ites in Iraq, and to emphasize respect for all religions. "What we cannot accept," Farah declared, "is the abuse of religion for political ends."[37]

Seyyed Hossein Nasr believes that Frithjof Schuon's enlightened version of Islam is an antidote to the chaos and nihilism growing out of the collapse of traditional religion in today's world. "Schuon's works," Nasr believes, "demonstrate in a unique fashion not only the unity of the Divine Principle but also the unity within the diversity of the Principle in the form of religions and cultures which the manifestations of that Principle have brought into being."[38]

Changes are occurring in Islam. Moslem women can now secure a divorce, for reasons ranging from mistreatment to lack of support. The Verse of the Sword in the Koran (sure 9:5): "Slay polytheists wherever you find them" is seen to differ with 124 other Koranic verses advocating patience and toleration. Thus many modern ulama interpret the passage as justifying the use of violence only in self defense. Principle 154 of the Iran Constitution states: "The Islamic Republic of Iran regards the happiness of people in the entire human community as its ideal, and recognizes independence, freedom, and the rule of law and of justice as a right of every person in the world. Although it refrains from any intervention in the internal matters of other nations, it supports the just battle of the oppressed against the aggressors all over the world."[39] The final statement sounds just like those made by representatives of the United States, Russia, and other modern powers.

A modern Sufi, Hazrat Inayat Khan, has evolved a syncretism sympathetic to all religions. Since there was only one creation, says Khan, there is only one religion, the religion of the Creator. All religious teachings lead to one goal: self-realization. A sure sign of it is the recognition that other persons have different but equally effective paths to that goal. Truth, Khan feels, can be found both in Roman Catholic symbols and in the Protestant lack of those symbols. We should not fall in love, he says, but we should rise in love. Follow Jesus, he recommends. Do not be a slave to your base nature, but rise above it and let the divine personality shine through.

Each faith has its own Rasul, or *ishtadeva,* Khan believes. The Rasul represents God's perfection as seen through human limitations. When people argue that their Rasul is better than someone else's, it is like an artist saying that his portrait of a subject is better than that of another artist. The mystic uses the Rasul familiar to him, but respects other Rasuls, since he understands the spiritual process. Were he to deprecate another's Rasul, it would mean that he did not understand his own. It is natural for us to express our appreciation through our Rasul, Khan says, because he is the one who brings us closer to God.

The Baha'i faith, which grew out of a branch of Shi'ite Islam, is one of the most all-inclusive of all world religions. The founder Baha-u-llah (1817-1892) felt that the founders of world religions were one in purpose, taught virtually identical values, and illumined separate pathways toward one goal, God. All mankind should worship their common Creator. "They deem us," said Baha-u-llah, "a stirrer up of strife worthy of banishment because we believe that all nations should become one in faith and all men as brothers; that the bonds of affection and unity between people should be strengthened; that diversity of religion should cease, and differences of race be annulled. Yet we see your rulers lavishing their treasures more freely on means for the destruction of the human race than on the happiness of mankind. This bloodshed and discord must cease, and all men be as one kindred and one family. Let not a man glory in this, that he loves his country; let him rather glory in this, that he loves his kind."[40]

The chief Baha'i teachings are as follows:

1. All mankind consists of one family.
2. There is only one religion—the religion of God.
3. Since truth is one, science and religion are in agreement.
4. If your religion does not bring you closer to your neighbor, discard it.
5. As God's children, women are equal in importance to men.

6. There should be no discrimination based on race, religion, or nationality.
7. There should be universal disarmament among nations.
8. Free public education should be available to all persons.
9. There should be an international language that all learn to speak.
10. There should be an international parliament and court under a world federation of sovereign nations.

Some of the most interesting forms of syncretistic Islam are found in modern Africa. African culture has no separation into the sacred and the profane. African art depicts priests alongside dancing girls. Always there is a celebration of the natural world, a life-affirming philosophy. In Ibo culture it is assumed that a person will define himself as a part of the group. "The many brotherhoods and saint cults of the Islamic area permit variations within a general uniformity." Great religious tolerance is practiced. "In the same family in the tropics it is possible to find Christians, Muslims, and pagans."[41] To survive, the many Christian denominations have learned to live together in harmony.

The Songhay observe Islamic ceremonies on Friday, and then on Sunday they worship traditional river spirits in ecstatic dances. Some Moslem traders sell magical charms to the Songhay. Islamic shrines in some areas are thinly disguised holy places of traditional African religion, with sacred trees, wells, and rocks. Yoruba ethics resemble those of Islam and Christianity, praising love and aid to others, and outlawing lying, stealing, and treachery.

Recent Ecumenism and Syncretism

When the London Missionary Society was established in 1795 as a nondenominational organization, one speaker announced, "Here are Methodists, Presbyterians, Episcopalians, and Independents all united in one society. Behold us here assembled with one accord to attend the funeral of bigotry." Many interdenominational activities sprang up, such as Bible societies and Sunday School unions. In 1809 Thomas Campbell condemned Christian divisiveness, and called for a simple unity of New Testament Christianity. Unfortunately his Disciples of Christ soon became yet another denomination, and was itself torn by divisions through the years. In 1839 S.S. Schmucker, a German

Lutheran, published an ambitious plan for Christian unity, based upon fundamentals accepted by most Christian groups. The plan called for federation, with each church keeping its identity. Although it was never implemented, the plan was influential among Protestant church leaders.

Modern theosophy, founded by Helena Petrovna Blavatsky and Colonel H.S. Olcott in New York in 1875, strives for a universal brotherhood of mankind, built upon ancient esoteric wisdom. Comparative religion is studied in an effort to find synthesizing spiritual concepts. Under the guidance of spiritual masters, it is believed, humankind will some day drink from one Fountain of Wisdom from which all religions have so far drawn their partial truths.

Ecumenicity has been the outstanding feature of 20th century Christianity. In 1908 Presbyterians and Congregationalists merged in India to form the South India United Church. Also that year the Federal Council of the Churches of Christ in America was organized. The first World Missionary Conference at Edinburgh in 1910 determined that denominationalism was ruining the Christian missionary movement in the Orient. John R. Mott, an American Methodist who was chairman of the conference, did much to further the cause of Christian unity. The International Missionary Council was set up in 1921 to help coordinate Christian missionary activities throughout the world. This Council in 1928 declared in Jerusalem that "we would repudiate any religious imperialism that would desire to impose beliefs and practices on others in order to manage their souls in their supposed interests. We obey a God who respects our wills and we desire to respect those of others." The American Commission of Laymen said that "the relations between religions must take increasingly hereafter the form of a common search for truth."[42]

At Lausanne in 1927 400 delegates from 108 churches gathered for a World Conference on Faith and Order. Their unanimous finding was that "doctrine divides; service unites." They immediately embarked on a search for more areas for united witness through service. Additional conferences on faith and order were held in Edinburgh in 1937, in Lund in 1952, and in Montreal in 1963. Eastern Orthodox Catholics, but not Roman Catholics, have been attending these sessions.

In 1937 two ecumenical conferences—one on faith and order and one on life and work—elected a joint committee to formulate plans for a world-wide Christian council. In 1948 at Amsterdam the World Council of Churches of Christ was organized, proclaiming "the essential oneness of the church of Christ and to keep prominently before the Council and the churches the obligation to manifest that unity." Assemblies of the World Council have been held at Evanston in 1954, at New Delhi in 1961, and at Uppsala in 1968. At the New Delhi assembly the Orthodox Churches of Bulgaria, Poland, Rumania, and Russia joined the Council, and the Roman Catholic church sent observers. Also in 1961 the Council was united with the International Missionary Council.

At Nairobi in 1975 the Fifth Assembly of the World Council took as its theme "Jesus Christ Frees and Unites," feeling that Christ frees one from sin and selfishness, and unites one with God and one's fellow humans. An additional dimension was added: "The Gospel of Christ leads us to become ever more active in identifying and rectifying violations of human rights in our societies."

The World Council is not a superchurch—it can give no orders to any member church, which retains its full autonomy. The Council's two main objectives are the unity and the renewal of Christianity. The leading Christian churches still not members of the Council are the Roman Catholic, the Southern Baptist, and some Lutheran jurisdictions.

Mergers between churches have become increasingly frequent in recent years, as Christianity searches for greater unity. Denominations having important mergers include Baptist, Lutheran, Methodist, and Presbyterian. In 1961 the Congregational Church merged with the Evangelical and Reformed Church to constitute the United Church of Christ. In Canada the United Church of Canada is the product of a confluence of Congregational, Methodist, and Presbyterian churches.

John B. Noss explains why ecumenism is in the air this century. First is the realization that a divided Christianity is a weak Christianity—efforts spent battling each other could be used better in spreading Christ's gospel of love. Secularism and scientism have tended to drive religious adherents closer together. As the world grows more interdependent, religious differences seem less significant. Religious cooperation has proved fruitful in missionary work, summer camps and conferences, common hymnals and instructional materials, city ministerial alliances, and in interdenominational boards and agencies, such as the American Bible Society and the Gideons. In the growing dialogue between Roman Catholic and Protestant Christianity, both the Anglican and the Orthodox Churches have served as mediators and as common ground.

The goals of inter-religious dialogue are not one world religion, says Leonard Swidler, but rather "to know oneself ever more profoundly, to know the other ever more authentically, and to live ever more fully accordingly."[43] As one expands in depth and breadth, one discovers one's truest self in terms of interconnectedness.

This dialogue will strangely restore old faith through the process of evolutionary renewal. Paul Knitter says that "if Christians, trusting God and respecting the faith of others, engage in this new encounter with other traditions, they can expect to witness a growth or evolution such as Christianity has not experienced since its first centuries. This growth will paradoxically both preserve the identity of Christianity and at the same time transform it. Such paradox is no mystery. We are acquainted with it in our own personal lives as well as in nature."[44]

References

1. Quoted in John Hick & Brian Hebblethwaite, eds., *Christianity and Other Religions* (Fortress Press, 1981), pp. 90, 95.
2. Ibid., pp. 219-20. John V. Taylor was Bishop of Winchester.
3. Ibish, pp. 260, 267.
4. Swidler, pp. 120-21.
5. Eugene M. Klaaren, *Religious Origins of Modern Science* (Eerdmans, 1977), pp. 61, 74.
6. Ibid., p. 108.
7. Ibid., pp. 158, 174.
8. Hick & Hebblethwaite, p. 163.
9. Swidler, pp. 14-15.
10. Parrinder, *Mysticism in the World's Religions*, pp. 146-47.
11. Hick & Hebblethwaite, pp. 97-98.
12. Swidler, p. 45.
13. John A.T. Robinson, *Truth is Two-Eyed* (Westminster, 1979), p. 13. Robinson was Dean of Trinity College at Cambridge University.
14. Raymond Pannikar, *The Unknown Christ of Hinduism* (Darton, Longman, & Todd, 1964), pp. 19, 20, 23. Pannikar is Professor of Religion at the University of California at Santa Barbara.
15. Quoted in Rousseau, p. 49.
16. Anthony E. Gilles, *St. Anthony Messenger* (May 1988) 95:8.
17. Robinson, p. 138. Boyd studies the Christian-Hindu dialogue. Thomas is a Protestant theologian in India.
18. Radhakrishnan, pp. 74-75.
19. Quoted in Rousseau, pp. 95-97.
20. Joseph Campbell, ed., *Spiritual Disciplines* (Princeton University Press, 1960), pp. 23-24.
21. Rousseau, pp. 56, 58.
22. Ibid., pp. 84-86, 89.
23. Ibid., pp. 99-101.
24. P.L. Basu, in Keith Crim, ed., *Abingdon Dictionary of Living Religions* (Abingdon Press, 1981), pp. 395-96.
25. Finegan, p. 547.
26. Voss, p. xxvii.
27. Khushwant Singh, in Crim, p. 376.

[28] Swami Satprakashananda, in Ferm, p. 401.
[29] Wing-tsit Chan, in Ferm, p. 110.
[30] H.N. McFarland, in Crim, p. 329.
[31] Geoffrey Parrinder, *Jesus in the Qur'an* (Barnes & Noble, 1965), pp. 30, 34, 40, 118, 123, 173.
[32] *New York Times*, 21 June 1987, 4:7.
[33] Tom Hall, *Habitat World* (March 1988) 5:3.
[34] Küng, *Christianity and the World Religions*, pp. 127-30.
[35] Wilhelm Dietl, *Holy War* (Macmillan, 1984), pp. 29-30.
[36] Wilfred Cantwell Smith, *Islam in Modern History* (New American Library, 1959), pp. 182, 202-03.
[37] Milton Viorst, *The New Yorker* (12 October 1987) 63:109.
[38] Schuon, pp. 2-3. Nasr is an Iranian university administrator.
[39] Dietl, p. 284.
[40] Voss, p. 269.
[41] Geoffrey Parrinder, *Religion in Africa* (Praeger, 1969), p. 235.
[42] Radhakrishnan, pp. 345-46.
[43] Swidler, p. 26.
[44] Ibid., p. 50.

CHAPTER 9

VIOLENCE IN RELIGION

"Kill them, Jesus!" is the prayer of two Christian groups in Ireland, each trying to exterminate its rival Christian church. Christian Croatians and Christian Serbians in Bosnia keep trying to kill one another. In 1994 gunmen entered a Baha'i church in South Africa and killed the white church members; they said their faith did not permit the intermingling of races.

Human hatred and killing are not genetic components of human beings, but are learned reactions. Mass murder was unheard of around 10,000 B.C., before religion got organized on a large scale. It is ironic that religion, which is supposed to be based on love, has fed many conflagrations of hate.

Primitive Religion

As explained above, when the Great Mother mistakenly was thought to need blood in order to become pregnant, human sacrifices began to occur. Then the killing of human beings to placate gods became widespread. In ancient Phoenicia, boys were burned as a sacrifice to Adonis. In Carthage, nobles sacrificed slaves' children in place of their own children. In Tibet shamans performed ritual killings. In Africa the Ashanti killed 100 persons each September to assure a good yam harvest. The Mayans in Central America and the Incas in Peru killed humans in their worship services. In Egypt around 3000 B.C. men were sacrificed to the god Osiris.

The Celts practiced human sacrifice by fire. Every five years they burned their criminals as a tribute to their gods. They believed that the greater the number of victims, the better the harvest would be. At Ibadan in Lagos the dead king's heart is eaten by his successor, to provide for a transfer of royal power. The Shilluk tribe of the White Nile River regularly killed their kings, saying that they wanted to preserve them for immortality before they suffered physical and mental decline. The Witoto Indians of South America practiced cannibalism, eating their prisoners as a part of a religious ritual.

In Assyria, Ashurbanipal boasted, "These warriors who had sinned against Ashur and had plotted evil against me, from their hostile mouths I have torn their tongues, and I have decreed their destruction. Those who remained alive I offered as a funerary sacrifice—their lacerated members I have given to the dogs. Thus have I rejoiced the heart of the gods."[1]

Hinduism

The ideals of Hinduism are so high that they would seem to outlaw violence. Swami Nikhilananda said that everyone's soul is divine, and thus each person should be treated with respect. "Violence, hatred, and malice toward others ultimately injure oneself. Those who desire religious harmony must never use malicious words against any faith."[2] But other advice also appears in Hindu scriptures. The god Indra, speaking as the Absolute, boasts of the violent actions attributed to him by the Rig-Veda: "With one who knows me, his world is injured by no deed whatsoever, not by the murder of his father or mother, not by theft, not by the slaughter of an embryo. Whatever evil he does, he does not blanch."[3]

Human sacrifice existed for centuries in India, especially among the followers of Kali, the consort of Siva. In the 16th century a king of Cooch Behar immolated 150 persons at Kali's altar. In the temple of Tanjore "a male child was beheaded before the altar of the goddess every Friday. In the Jaintia hills of Assam it was the custom of a royal house to offer one human victim at the autumn festival Durja Puja every year."[4] When widow sacrifice was banned by the British in India in the 1800s, the Brahmins protested a violation of their custom. Gov. Charles Napier replied, "We also have a custom to observe. When men burn women alive, we hang them!"[5]

The partition between Hindu India and Moslem Pakistan in 1947 cost approximately one million lives, as convoys of each faith passed through territory held by followers of the other faith. In 1984 Sikhs, attempting to set up an independent theocracy, barricaded themselves in their holiest shrine, the Golden Temple at Amritsar. Prime Minister Indira Gandhi sent troops to vacate the temple, and 1000 persons were killed. Then Indira was assassinated by Sikhs, and 5000 more Sikhs were killed. Sikhs retaliated with terrorist bombings, killing 1200 Hindus in 1988.

Buddhism

As one who practiced unitive religion, Gautama Buddha had little use for violence. He tested a disciple who wished to convert some wild jungle people. "What if they hit you?" he asked. "I shall consider them kind not to kill me," replied the disciple. "And what if they kill you?" asked Gautama. "I shall consider them kind to free me from this vile body," was the reply. "Well said," stated Gautama. "Go, Punna, yourself saved, save others."[6]

If a person were struck by a poisoned arrow, would we withhold treatment until we knew the doctor's religious background, asked Gautama. So to cure suffering, do not examine religious pedigrees, he said, but find specific causes and specific remedies. He told his followers to bear no ill will towards those who criticized him or his teachings. As a matter of fact, Buddhist monks wear ochre-colored garments, the color of criminals sentenced to death, because Buddhists were considered to be dead in the Hindu social hierarchy.

King Asoka Maurya (264-227 B.C.) converted Buddhism into a universal world religion. After a series of bloody battles, he became a Buddhist and expressed sorrow for the slaughter. His edict of tolerance said that "a man must not do reverence to his own sect by disparaging that of another. The sects of other people deserve reverence."[7] Asoka gave lavishly to Jains and Brahmins, feeling that respecting other religions was the best way to honor one's own faith. Here was unitive religion in its purest form.

History saw the most aggressive warriors of Asia, the Mongols, switch from divisive religion to unitive religion. Their contacts with Tibetans taught the Mongols the principles of universal compassion and non-aggression. Shortly after their conversion to a Tibetan form of Buddhism, the Mongols relinquished their wars of conquest and ceased being predators.

Judaism

On the whole, Judaism's moral code was more humane than that of its rivals. "Vicious religious customs," said archeologist William F. Albright, "such as child sacrifice, necromancy, and sodomy (which formed part of certain religious ceremonies in the ancient Near East) are forbidden. Work on the sabbath, which endangered the physical and mental health of the workers, was prohibited."[8]

The prophet Elisha showed great kindness towards his enemies. He treated with generosity Syrian troops sent to capture him. He also cured the Syrian general Naaman of leprosy. One wonders whether kindness would bear any good fruit if used today in the Jewish-Syrian dialogue.

On the other hand, despite the commandment, "Thou shalt not kill," the Old Testament teems with records of slaughter. In an effort to destroy Baal worshippers, King Jehu annihilated the royal house and all Baal followers in such a bloody slaughter that 100 years later Hosea, who loved Yahweh, denounced it. Ishmael, the son of Nethaniah, ruthlessly killed seventy innocent pilgrims at the Temple, to cover up a murder he had committed. King Manasseh misled his own subjects, through worship of idols, use of fertility cults, and the sacrifice of his own son to the fires of the child-devouring deity Molech (II Kings 21).

Ezekiel 9:6 says "slay old men outright, young men and maidens, little children and women," unless they wear a mark showing that they have complained against idol worship in the Temple. Captured cities were ravaged and war prisoners slain, allegedly in compliance with Yahweh's order. But there must have been some exaggeration in the record, as for example, "the children of Israel slew of the Syrians one hundred thousand footmen in one day" (I Kings 20:29).

The Roman Empire

The Romans combined political and religious reasons for persecuting Christians. They felt that the Christians undermined their political goals, and that Christian pacifism would weaken the nation. Pliny the Younger, governor of Bithynia in A.D. 112, reported to Emperor Trajan that he gave Christians three chances to renounce their religion. If they refused, they were killed. Trajan called the policy proper.

The persecution was multiform. Bound to crosses, Christians were eaten by starved animals. Some had molten lead poured down their throats. Some were beheaded, crucified, or beaten to death with clubs. In eight years of rule under Diocletian 1500 Christians were killed. Under Emperor Decius, Theodora, a beautiful young lady of Antioch, was condemned to a brothel for refusing to worship Roman idols. Didymus, a Christian, disguised himself as a Roman soldier and freed Theodora. But the plot was discovered, and the two Christians were beheaded and their bodies were burned. Emperor Julian, called the Apostate, tried to get Bishop Basil to renounce Christ. When Basil refused, "Julian commanded that the body of Basil should be torn every day in seven different parts, until his skin and flesh were entirely mangled."[9]

Violence in Early Christianity

The doctrine of the Holy Trinity has been one of the most divisive factors in Christendom. How are the three facets of God similar, how different, and how do they interrelate? Perhaps it is unfortunate that the Bible has so little to say on this subject.

Is Christ of the same nature as God, or a similar nature? Fighting over this distinction led to the deaths of tens of thousands of Christians. "Probably more Christians were slaughtered by Christians in these two years, 342-343, than by all the persecutions of Christians by pagans in the history of Rome."[10]

Even contemporaries were shocked at the civil war among Christians over dogma. Hilary (315-367), bishop of Poitiers, said that "every moon we make new creeds to describe invisible mysteries. We condemn either the doctrine of others in ourselves, or our own in that of others. Tearing one another to pieces, we have been the cause of each other's ruin."[11]

Ammianus, a pagan historian, said that the enmity of Christians towards one another exceeded the fury of savage beasts. Bishop Gregory Nazianzen stated that discord was transforming the kingdom of heaven into hell itself. He described "venerable bishops who put their personal squabbles before questions of faith." John Chrysostom (345-407), bishop of Constantinople, decried church division, saying that "nothing will divide the

Church so much as the love of authority. Nothing so provokes God's anger as the division of the Church."

Frequently Christian intolerance backfired. The Montanists and Novatians were Christian sects which alleged that the Holy Spirit had revealed to them than an apostate Christian could never again be redeemed, even by a change of heart. Strict against heretics, both movements ended up by being considered heretics themselves. By the year 384 Epiphanius listed the existence of 80 separate sects, each alleging that it was superior to the others. In 382 Emperor Theodosius published an edict against the Manichaeans, saying that they should be killed and their property confiscated. He then appointed inquisitors and spies to carry out the edict.

Converted Germanic tribes often made poor Christians. As Arians, the Vandals conducted a reign of terror in north Africa. Many Manichaeans were burned alive. Non-Arian Christians fared little better. Bishops were forced to till the land, naked. Choir boys and priests of Carthage were beaten. Refugees trying to flee had their tongues cut out. Persons were suspended naked and burned in the most tender places with red-hot irons.

Gibbon reports a cruel Christian foray. "Vitalian, with an army of Huns and Bulgars, declared himself the champion of the Catholic faith. In this pious rebellion he depopulated Thrace, besieged Constantinople, and exterminated 65,000 of his fellow Christians, till he obtained the establishment of the Council of Chalcedon. Such was the first of the religious wars waged in the name of and by the disciples of the God of Peace."[12]

The Samaritans in Palestine were considered outcasts by all: to pagans they were Jews, to Jews they were schismatic, and to Christians they were idolaters. Emperor Justinian decided that they must either convert or die. Since the killing of unbelievers did not count as murder, "Justinian piously labored to establish with fire and sword the unity of the Christian faith," Gibbon reported. As a result, 20,000 Samaritans were killed and a similar number were sold as slaves.

Christian Anti-Semitism

Tertullian had said that "the blood of the martyrs is the seed of the church." Seeming to thrive on adversity, the Christians won many converts by their bravery, deep faith, and excellent personal morality.

So it almost seemed that they were determined to persecute the Jews as they themselves had been persecuted by the Romans. For whatever reason, their conduct was shameful. It would be hard to find a better example of divisive religion than the Christian persecution of the Jews in medieval times. The teachings of he who said, "Love your enemies," and "Father, forgive them" were utterly lost sight of by narrow-minded zealots who blamed the Jews for killing Christ, and who could tolerate no faith other than their own.

It is a close race between the Crusades and the Inquisition as to which was the most heinous example of divisive and perverted religion. When the First Crusade was announced in 1095, Godfrey of Bouillon proclaimed that he would first kill all Jews in Europe and then all Moslems in the Holy Land. Some Christian leaders bravely but vainly tried to stem the Crusaders' violence. Archbishop Ruthard at Mainz hid 1300 Jews in his cellars, but Crusaders broke in and killed 1014 Jews in 1096. Bishop Hermann at Cologne endangered his life secretly aiding Jews to safe country homes. At Worms Bishop Allebranches hid 800 Jews in his palace, but Crusaders found them and killed them. Bernard of Clairvaux worked hard to protect Jews during the Second Crusade.

When Henry II of England levied a Crusade tax in 1187 it was one-tenth of the property of all Christians, but one-fourth of the property of Jews. At that time Jews, who constituted 1/4 of 1% of the British population, paid 8% of the national taxes. They paid for one-fourth of the British cost of the Third Crusade. During this crusade anti-Semitism increased. Many Jews were murdered in London in 1189. Other towns having persecution included Dunstable, Lynn, Norwich, and Stamford. In the castle in York, rather than be massacred the Jews committed mass suicide. "Led by their rabbi, all the heads of families killed their wives and children, and then fell on one another."[13] In 1210 King John ordered all Jews in England imprisoned and confiscated their property.

The Council of Avignon in 1209 forbade "Jews and harlots" from touching bread or fruit in the marketplace, and said that Jews were to be avoided "as a source of pollution." Pope Innocent III convened the Fourth Lateran Council in 1215. This inaugurated a new era of hostility against the Jewish community. The Talmud was burned publicly, and Jews were forced to wear an identity badge. They could not hold an office in which they could impose penalties upon Christians. They were ordered to stay indoors during Holy Week, partly for their own protection. Christians were not allowed to marry Jews, and were punished if they did.

Many Christian nations forbade Jews to serve Christians as bakers, carpenters, doctors, millers, shoemakers, smiths, or tailors. Jews were not allowed to sell butter, flour, oil, or wine in the marketplace, or to live anywhere but in the Jewish quarter. Thus restricted, Jews entered the fields of banking and international commerce, and soon gained a reputation as expert merchants. Sometimes Christian kings would declare all interest, and occasionally the principle, of debts owed by Christians to Jews to be forfeited.

English mystics like Margery Kempe and Juliana of Norwich, while ostensibly "filled with love for all of God's creatures," nevertheless agreed that Jews were "accursed and condemned without end" for having Jesus put to death. "England was the first nation in Europe to adopt the infamous Jew Badge, in 1218. The English clergy was the first to fabricate the ritual-murder accusations against the Jews, and the first in Europe to spread the myth of 'The Wandering Jew.'"[14]

In 1236 Christian Crusaders ordered all Jews to accept Christianity. When 3000 Jews refused to convert they were trampled to death beneath the hooves of the Crusaders' horses. All Jews in Belitz, near Berlin, were burned alive in 1243 on the charge that some had defiled a consecrated wafer.

When Henry III of England borrowed 500 marks from the Earl of Cornwall, he pledged to Cornwall all the Jews of England as security. When the persecuted Jews asked permission to leave England, it was denied. During a civil war in England from 1257 to 1267, pogroms almost wiped out Jewish communities in London and six other cities. Finally, in 1290 Edward I ordered all 16,000 Jews to leave England, and he confiscated their property.

When they got to France, the Jews were told they had to leave the country before Lent. Officially, Philip the Fair (so-called) in

1306 expelled 100,000 Jews from France and seized their property. He gave his coachman a synagogue as a gift!

In 1285 180 Jews were burned to death in Munich, falsely accused of a ritual murder. All Jews in Röttingen were burned to death in 1298 on the charge of desecrating a holy wafer. In half a year 140 Jewish congregations were abolished in Germany. Many Jews emigrated to live under the more tolerant Moslems in the Holy Land, or under Orthodox Christians in Slavic Eastern Europe.

To get national unity, nations wanted homogeneity, and thus nationalism begat anti-Semitism. The Council of Vienne in 1311 outlawed all social relations between Christians and Jews. The Council of Zamora in 1313 ordered that Jews must be kept in strict servitude. At Toulouse in 1320 500 Jews were killed for refusing to accept Christianity. For the same reason the Jews of 120 communities in southern France and northern Spain were killed. In 1321 120 Jews were burned to death, charged with poisoning wells. A German fanatic in 1336 announced that God had told him to avenge Christ's death by killing Jews. His mob of 5,000 peasants tortured and killed thousands of Jews.

In 1348 Christians accused Jews of spreading the Black Death. They tortured Jews until some "confessed" to poisoning some wells. Pogroms broke out in France, Germany, and Spain. "All Jews in Savoy, all Jews around Lake Leman and in Bern, Fribourg, Basel, Nuremberg, and Brussels were burned. All in all some 510 Jewish communities were exterminated."[15] To escape murder, Jews committed mass suicide in Frankfurt, Krems, Oppenheim, Vienna, and Worms. Cecil Roth called it "the most terrible series of massacres ever known in the long history of Jewish martyrdom."

Most Jews who escaped fled eastward into Poland and Russia. Some escaped into Italy, "where, because of the tolerant example of the Holy See, conditions were better. Rome is almost the only city of Europe to preserve its Jewish community undisturbed from remote antiquity down to the present day."[16] Popes often criticized bishops for their anti-Semitism. A Jewish historian, S.W. Baron, said that "had it not been for the Catholic Church, the Jews would not have survived the Middle Ages in Christian Europe."

Pope Clement VI made Avignon a merciful haven for Jews fleeing French persecution. Martin V in 1419 proclaimed that "whereas Jews are made in the image of God, and a remnant will one day be saved, we command that they not be molested in their synagogues; that their laws and customs not be assailed; that they not be baptized by force, constrained to observe Christian festivals, nor to wear badges, and that they not be hindered in their business relations with Christians."[17]

In 1391, however, a mob had broken into the Jewish area in Seville and killed thousands of Jews. Now the only secure havens for Jews seemed to be Moslem Granada and Portugal, where the king had stopped the slaughter. All told, over 70,000 Jews were killed at this time, all in the name of Christ.

In 1411 antipope Benedict XIII staged a mock debate between representatives of Christianity and Judaism. The outcome was prearranged: Benedict published a bull forbidding the reading of the Talmud and requiring Jews to attend at least three conversion sermons each year. Eventually hundreds of thousands of Jews became Marranos, that is, Jews who outwardly professed Christianity but secretly adhered to Judaism. Marranos were able to progress rapidly up the social ladder. Their duplicity, however, destroyed the unity of Jewish feeling and thinking.

During the fifteenth century, for various reasons the Jews were expelled from Augsburg, Cologne, Erfurt, Mainz, Nuremberg, Speyer, Strasbourg, Ulm, and Wurzburg. On the basis of tortured confessions 40 Jews were burned at the stake in Breslau in 1453. "The remaining Jews were banished, but their children were taken from them and baptized by force."[18] In 1463 Albrecht III, Margrave of Brandenburg, said that each new German king, "may, according to old usage, either burn all the Jews, or show them his mercy and, to save their lives, take one-third of their property."[19] When a three-year old boy was found dead in Trent in 1475, the Jews were falsely accused of murder, and all of them in the city were burned to death.

Since much of Spain was under Moslem rule, Jews were treated better there than in Christian Europe. After Spain captured Granada from the Moors, however, Ferdinand V of Aragon and his queen Isabella of Castile saw no reason to further conciliate the Jews. In 1492 they gave Jews three choices: leave Spain, convert to Christianity, or suffer death. Nearly 30,000 Jews were tortured and killed, and 180,000 left Spain and Sardinia, a Spanish possession. Jews were expelled from Portugal in 1497.

In the words of Will Durant, "the supreme crime of those centuries was the deliberate degradation of an entire people, the merciless murder of the soul."[20] When Christian Constantinople fell to the Moslem Turks in 1453 most Jews rejoiced, for they knew that they would be treated better. In 1492 Sultan Bajazet of Turkey said, "Call ye this Ferdinand 'wise'? He who depopulates his own dominions in order to enrich mine?"[21] Bajazet encouraged Jewish immigration, and soon Turkey had many skilled artisans, merchants, and scholars. Jews will always remember with gratitude that when scarcely anyone else would have them, Moslem Turkey gave them a warm reception.

By 1550, when Jews were expelled from Genoa, there were only a few left in western Europe. By some strange logic, the Roman Catholic Church began to blame the Jews for the Reformation protest. In 1555 Pope Paul IV had 25 Jews burned at the stake. He then issued a bull restricting Jews to their ghettos, preventing them from owning real estate, and forcing them to wear yellow hats. There were also compulsory conversion sermons, censorship of Jewish books, and constant fear that Jewish children would be kidnapped and baptized as Christians.

In Portugal hundreds of Jews were burned at the stake. During the Carnival season in Rome, especially fatted Jews were forced to run, nearly naked, in races before Christian crowds. When the races were abolished in 1668, Jews had to pay special taxes in lieu of the races.

Anti-Semitism flourished in Christian Orthodox Russia. Ivan the Terrible in 1565 ordered all Jews in Polotsk to be either converted or drowned. In 1648 Ukrainian Cossacks massacred Jews on a scale not seen since the Black Death. A Russian historian, S.M. Dubnow, said that "thousands of Jewish infants were thrown into wells, or buried alive." Cecil Roth estimates that between 1648 and 1658 there were 100,000 Jews killed in Russia.

Catherine the Great enforced an expulsion order against Jews, but three partitions of Poland (in 1772, 1793, and 1795) put 900,000 Jews back into Russian territory. So they were confined to the Pale of Settlement, the strip of land along Russia's western border. Here at least there were given a measure of self-government.

Konstantin Pobedonostzev, procurator of the holy synod of the Russian Orthodox Church, chose the Jews as scapegoats for all Russian ills. His persecution of the Jews served as diversion for the ignorant masses of the people. His announced program to handle Russia's five million Jews, the largest Jewish community in the world, was one-third converts, one-third expelled, and one-third starved to death. In the years from 1903 to 1907 50,000 Jews were massacred in 284 Russian towns.

A summary to this section was written in 1818 by Thomas Jefferson in a letter to a Jewish diplomat, Mordecai Noah: "Your sect, by its suffering, has furnished a remarkable proof of the universal spirit of religious intolerance, disclaimed by all while feeble, and practiced by all when in power. Our laws have applied the only antidote to this vice, protecting our religious as they do our civil rights by putting all on an equal footing. But more remains to be done."[22]

The Crusades

The immediate cause of the Crusades was the Turkish Moslem interruption of Christian pilgrimages to Jerusalem. Desiring to return Jerusalem (by now a city sacred to three faiths) to Christian control, a group of European Christians met in 1095 to organize a crusade. The fighting between Christians and Moslems was vicious. During sieges at Antioch, Nicea, and Tyre, Crusaders catapulted Moslem heads back into the encircled cities as a warning to the defenders. At Antioch the Moslems responded by sending Christian heads back into the Crusader ranks.

One wonders how Christ would have reacted to the treatment of Moslems, as described by Raymond of Agiles when Jerusalem was captured in 1099: "Some of our men (and this was most merciful) cut off the heads of their enemies; others tortured them longer by casting them into the flames. Piles of heads, hands, and feet were seen in the city streets. At the temple of Solomon, men rode in blood up to their knees. Indeed, it was a just and splendid judgment of God."[23]

Will Durant says that women were stabbed to death, and babies dashed against posts. A total of 70,000 Moslems were slaughtered. All of the remaining Jews were rounded up and burned alive in a synagogue. Thus had the cause of Christ returned to the Holy Land.

Taking time out from quarrels among themselves, leaders of the Third Crusade ordered a wholesale slaughter of Moslem prisoners. The historian Ambroise wrote, "They were slaughtered every one. For this be the Creator blessed!"[24]

By the Fourth Crusade the ardent Christians were ready to kill fellow Christians. "In 1183 Byzantine Orthodox Greeks had killed all Italians in the realm, and in 1204 Italians in the Fourth Crusade took their revenge with a carnage almost unparalleled in history. The bestiality of the Crusaders shocked pope, prince, and people, but their horror in no way stopped the slaughter."[25]

The Albigensians, also called the Cathari, of southern France were considered heretics for believing that Satan, the creator of all evil, was the ruler of the world, as Christ had said in John 12:31. When a papal legate was killed in Cathari territory, Pope Innocent III called for a crusade against them. "Hordes from northern France poured into the Midi ravaging, pillaging, and burning heretics with great delight. The abbot of Citeaux was asked how the Cathari were to be distinguished from the Catholics. 'Kill them all,' he answered. 'God will know His own.'"[26]

Pope Gregory IX established the Inquisition to deal with the remnants of the Cathari and the Waldenses, both of whom were charged with heresy. Since the Church wished to avoid the shedding of blood, heretics were burned at the stake. "The Church turned the condemned over to the secular arm with a plea for mercy (and, if granted, punished the official with excommunication). Such severity was deemed entirely consonant with love, for if the heretic recanted out of fear, his soul was saved. If he were obdurate, half an hour at the stake was only a foretaste of eternity, and by his ordeal multitudes might be deterred and saved. Many devices were used to extort confessions."[27]

Max Dimont says that "historians estimate that over one million Frenchmen suspected of being Albigensians were slain in thirty years by the Crusaders. The highest estimated number of Jews killed during the 200 years of the Crusades is 100,000."[28]

The Inquisition

The background of the Inquisition was scriptural. Exodus 22:18 says, "You will not permit a witch to live." Deuteronomy 13:6-9 states that "if your brother, son, daughter, or wife says, 'Let us serve other gods,' you shall kill him or her." Heretics should be stoned to death, we read in Deuteronomy 17:5. Roman judges, when no accuser denounced an offender, could hold an *inquisitio* or inquiry into the case. The Church put Dominican clergy in charge of formal inquiries into whether a person was a heretic, or was in some way offensive to the cause of the Church.

Franciscans, resenting the secularization of their order, called for a return to the strict rule of St. Francis. Pope John XXII called them heretics in 1323, and "a century after the death of Francis his most loyal followers were burned at the stake by the Inquisition," Durant reports.

This is how the Spanish Inquisition operated. The pope would appoint a priest or a monk as the inquisitor, who would preach in church, announcing that all who voluntarily confessed heresy would be granted absolution for a slight fee. Churchgoers were encouraged to report suspected heretics, and were paid bonuses to inform against their neighbors. This is a wonderfully divisive technique. Suspected heretics denounced by other people got severe treatment. The denounced was presumed to be guilty unless he could prove his innocence. The accused was not given the details of the charges against him, or the names of the informers. City magistrates who refused to enforce all laws against heretics were excommunicated.

Inquisitorial illogic ran rampant. Persons accused of civil crimes were inquisitioned, since their crimes might have grown out of a false concept of sin and God. Religious dissenters were considered to be likely heretics. Anyone sheltering a heretic was suspect, as well as lawyers and witnesses testifying on behalf of heretics. Jews and Moors who tried to convert Christians were considered heretics. The bones of dead heretics were dug up and burned.

The Inquisition spread to the Spanish Netherlands, where an ordinance in 1529 declared that "all laymen who discussed questions about faith should pay with their lives." Of the 877 Protestants put to death by Charles V and his son Philip II, 717 were

Anabaptists. When Protestants complained about his strict enforcement of the decrees of the Inquisition, Philip said he would sacrifice 100,000 lives rather than change his policy.

Once again the fury of divisive religion was seen as Christians destroyed Christians. In 1566 Protestants wrecked many Roman Catholic churches, smashing windows and breaking statues. They drank the sacramental wine, and fed consecrated wafers to parrots. In Flanders alone 400 churches had valuable religious art destroyed. Philip appointed the Duke of Alva to get revenge. Thousands of Protestants were arrested, and fifty at a time were put to death. Almost every family in Flanders had a member killed or jailed. A group of wild Calvinists, called the Beggars, tried to outdo the Catholics in barbarity. Some of them even killed their own Catholic brothers. Again Alva's forces retaliated, laying waste to Dutch towns, butchering the men and raping the women.

In 1576 Spanish troops gave Antwerp the worst pillage in Dutch history. Over 7000 Protestants were slain, 1000 buildings were burned, and many Protestants were tortured to reveal hidden gold and jewelry.

Back in Spain, royal birthdays were celebrated by the burning of heretics. In Toledo in 1560 several persons were burned to death to please Elizabeth, the new 13-year old queen. In 1680, to celebrate the marriage of Charles II to Maria Louisa de Bourbon, nineteen persons were burned to death. A book of 308 pages described "the splendid spectacle."

The New World was not spared the scourge of this monument to divisive religion. In 1565 the Spanish leader Pedro Menendez de Aviles had his soldiers knife to death 200 French Protestants on the beach south of St. Augustine. Only those who professed being Catholic were saved.

The Inquisition was formally introduced into Mexico City and Peru in 1570. Now even the revered image of St. Francis availed little. A Franciscan friar accompanying the conquistadores ordered the hands cut off of the King of Peru, and then informed the king, "Be baptized and you will go to heaven." "No," replied the king, "for if I went to heaven I might meet a second Christian like you."

In 1609 the Duke of Lerma issued an edict expelling the Moriscos (Christianized Moors) from Spain. Like the Jews, they left most of their property behind. Within two years 400,000 of Spain's most productive citizens were banished. Lerma received 250,000 ducats from the forfeited property, and his children a like amount.

From 1720 to 1727 the Inquisitors condemned 868 people, of whom 75 were burned to death, and the rest either scourged or sent to the galleys. During the reign of King Philip V of Spain (1700-1746), a total of 14,066 persons were punished by the Inquisition.

The Spanish Inquisition was abolished by Napoleon in 1808. A historian of the Inquisition says that of the 341,000 persons found guilty, a total of nearly 32,000 people were burned to death, with the rest receiving sentences ranging from light penance to life imprisonment.

"If Christ had returned to Europe in the Middle Ages," said Radhakrishnan, "he would certainly have been burnt alive for denying the dogmas about his own nature." There is no doubt that the Inquisition is one of the clearest examples of how vicious divisive religion can be. But despite its bloody record, we should be able to understand it, Will Durant feels, for we live in "an age which has killed more people in war and snuffed out more innocent lives without due process of law than all the wars and persecutions between Caesar and Napoleon."[29]

Christian Violence Since the Renaissance

The Council of Trent in 1560 did much to correct the Church's many evils, but it defined Roman Catholic dogma in such a way as to exclude the principles upon which the nascent Protestant movement was based. In France Catherine de Medicis, disturbed by rumors of a Huguenot coup, got her son Charles IX to agree to a religious purge. Early on St. Bartholomew's Day (August 24) in 1572, armed Catholics entered the homes of sleeping Huguenots and slaughtered 10,000 of them. "Embryos were torn from dead mothers and smashed," Durant reports. The Catholic Swiss guards of the king killed "for the pure joy of slaughter." Catholic children played games with Huguenot corpses. The head of the Huguenot leader Admiral Coligny was sent to the pope, who had a medal struck to commemorate the event and commissioned the artist Vasari to paint scenes of the massacre. In addition to those killed in Paris, another 10,000 Huguenots were slain when the rioting spread to the provinces.

In 1685 Louis XIV revoked the Edict of Nantes, closing all Huguenot churches and schools. Huguenot clergy were given two weeks to leave France, on penalty of a life sentence to the galleys. Many Huguenots were tortured, and Huguenot women were forced to stand naked in the streets. Over 400,000 "converts" were required to attend Catholic mass. All children born in France were henceforth to be baptized as Roman Catholics. Jean Pierre Espinas spent 23 years as a galley slave for the crime of giving lodging to a Protestant minister for one night.

In England, King Henry VIII was a theological conservative. In 1539 he had Parliament pass the so-called "Bloody Statute," which declared transubstantiation (the belief that Christ's actual body appears in the Eucharist) to be the faith of the Church of England, with denial of it punishment by burning at the stake and confiscation of property. It also forbade the marriage of priests, and banned private masses. Witchcraft was declared to be a felony punishable by death.

In 1543 three men were burned to death for denying the Real Presence of Christ in the communion ritual. Then the perjured witnesses against them were put to death when their lies were discovered. Then, in an abrupt change, Archbishop Thomas Cranmer in 1550 listed belief in the Real Presence as a heresy punishable by death. As the pendulum swung, Cranmer himself was burned at the stake in 1556, with one of the charges being his denial of the Real Presence.

In Queen Mary's short reign, 300 persons were burned to death, most of them for religious reasons. Queen Elizabeth I's long reign saw the execution of 123 priests and 60 lay people because of their religious beliefs.

John Knox (1505-1572), the founder of Scottish Presbyterianism, bravely opposed rulers on the grounds of religious conscience. But his bigotry made him a constant divisive force. All who provoke idolatry, such as Roman Catholics in the mass and in the use of religious statues, should be killed, he preached. Heretics, including Bloody Queen Mary, deserved death as described in Deuteronomy 13. Cities which were predominantly heretical should be razed, including all people and even the cattle. Asked whether it was cruel to kill infants in a heretical town, Knox retorted, "What impudence is it to prefer corrupt nature and blind reason to God's Scriptures?"[30]

English colonialism in Ireland was strongly tinged with Protestant-Catholic hatred. In 1641 the Irish rebelled against decades of English oppression and killed 4500 Englishmen in what came to be called the Great Massacre. Violence bred violence, and in 1649 Cromwell's army killed the entire garrisons of Irishmen at Drogheda and Wexford.

Religious differences accounted for a large part of the Puritan revolution. Placing great stress upon the Bible as the Word of God, Puritans felt that anyone who did not accept their interpretation of the Bible was opposing the will of God. In 1648 the Presbyterians argued in Parliament that all who denied the Trinity should receive the death penalty, and that life imprisonment was the proper sentence for all who taught Baptist, Catholic, or Quaker doctrine. The Calvinist view prevailed, that most people were foreordained by God to eternal hellfire, but that the Puritans were among the elect few who would be saved.

In America, the Puritans who came to Massachusetts desired religious freedom, something they refused to grant to those who had religious views that differed from their own. Although 20 persons were put to death for witchcraft at Salem, that was a tiny fraction of those being killed in Europe as witches at the same time.

Many of the writers of the American Constitution were deists. When many clergymen refused to let the crusading evangelist George Whitefield appear in their pulpits, Benjamin Franklin helped build a building "expressly for the use of any preacher of any religious persuasion," to be open even to Moslem missionaries. Franklin contributed to the erection of many church buildings, even Jewish ones. But he seldom attended church, for he felt that the preacher "tried to make us good Presbyterians rather than good citizens. Vital religion has always suffered," he said, "when orthodoxy is more regarded than virtue. At the last day our recommendation will not be that we said, 'Lord! Lord!' but that we did good to our fellow creatures. See Matthew 25."[31]

It pained George Washington to see the intolerant clashes between Protestants and Catholics in Ireland for, as he said, "Religious controversies are always productive of more acrimony and irreconcilable hatreds than those which spring from any other cause."[32] His solution was for persons to approach religion with a liberal and tolerant attitude.

Thomas Jefferson said that "the moral branch is the same in all religions, while in dogma, all have a different set. Millions of innocent people since the introduction of Christianity have been burnt, tortured, fined, imprisoned; yet we have not advanced one inch toward uniformity." Coercion makes "one half the world fools and the other half hypocrites. To love God with all thy heart and thy neighbor as thyself is the sum of religion."[33]

Despite the American views, Europe continued its divisive way. The Gordon Riots in London between Protestants and Catholics in 1780 led to destruction of Catholic property and 450 people killed or wounded. The Orange Order, founded in Ireland in 1796, had 1600 separate lodges by 1836. It is still active in England, Ireland, Scotland, and throughout the British Commonwealth. In 1828 the Grand Orange Lodge of Ireland opposed the Catholic Emancipation Bill then before Parliament. It said that "our religion is menaced by the attacks of popery. No man unless his creed be Protestant can associate with us."[34] The following year the bill was passed, giving Catholics the vote and eligibility to be members of Parliament, but barring Jesuits from entering England. The bill said it was "expedient to make provision for the gradual suppression and final prohibition of Jesuits and all other monastic orders of the Church of Rome."

In 1978 the Reverend James Jones persuaded 914 of his followers to commit mass suicide in Guyana. His church, the Peoples Temple, had $10 million deposited in various banks. Two defectors from his movement, Al and Jeannie Mills, were killed a year later in their California home, along with their 15-year old daughter.

Religious warfare continues in many places, among them Bosnia, Sri Lanka, the Holy Land, and Ireland. The Reverend Ian Paisley created the Free Presbyterian church in Ireland in an effort to combat the Catholic Church. Paisley insists that Catholics are not Christians; he calls the Roman Catholic Church "a blasphemy and a deceit." The Irish Republican Army responds with the bombing of civilians in London and other English cities.

Islam

Like all religions, Islam has high ideals for human dignity but has an imperfect record living up to those ideals. The Mogul conquest of India was accomplished through much bloodshed. In 1024 the Moslems led by Mahmud captured the sacred city of Somnath, and killed 50,000 Hindus. Later, in 1199, Moslems captured the university of Nalanda in Bihar and killed 6,000 Buddhist monks there, in what was one of the last Buddhist strongholds in India. Divisive religion was practiced by the Mogul ruler Aurangzeb, who in 1680 had many Hindu temples destroyed: 66 in Amber, 63 in Chitor, and 123 in Udaipur. In addition to forbidding Hindu worship he also destroyed many Christian churches. His excesses led to the fall of the Mogul empire.

Lebanon has long been a battle ground for divisive religionists. For example, in 1860 Druzes and Metualis massacred 20,000 Christians in Lebanese villages, and more would have been killed had not the exiled Abd al-Kadir intervened on behalf of the victims. In battles between Ottoman Turks and Armenian Christians from 1895 to 1920, hundreds of thousands of people on each side died.

A "holy war" in the Sudan from 1955 to 1972 led to a half a million deaths. The fighting was between ruling Moslems in the north, and Christians and animists in the south. Strict Moslems restored the shari'a teaching that thieves have their hands chopped off. In 1981 The Moslem assassin of Prime Minister Anwar Sadat of Egypt said that he was at "the peak of joy, because the cause of religion was at stake," and he knew he would soon be with God as a reward for his pious deed.

After the Muslim Brotherhood, a Sunni fundamentalist group, began an uprising in Hama in 1982, President Hafez Assad (an Alawite Moslem) of Syria sent in tanks that killed 20,000 rebels.

When 241 U.S. marines died as a result of a terrorist bombing of their barracks in Beirut in 1983, the military leader of the Amal Shi'ite militia said, "None of us is afraid. God is with us and gives us strength. We race to see who can die first and thus get to see God."[35] The following year the Ayatollah Khomeini told his followers in Iran: "War is a blessing for the world. It is God who incites men to fight and kill. Our young people are putting God's commandments into action. They know that to kill the unbelievers is one of man's greatest missions."[36]

In 1988 the Santa Barbara Peace Resource Center in California reported that of the 32 wars currently in progress, 25 had a "significant ethnic, racial, or religious dimension." Examples cited included the invasion of the Catholic island of East Timor in 1975 by Moslem Indonesia, resulting in hundreds of thousands of deaths over the next decade. Author Amos Elon also reported that in Jerusalem, religion and nationalism are virtually synonymous, where "one hates one's fellow man to the greater glory of God."[37]

Moslem fundamentalists who want to make Algeria a theocracy shoot teenage girls in the face for not wearing veils, and cut professors' throats for teaching male and female students in the same classroom. Moslem suicide bombers kill busloads of Jews in Israel, and other Moslem terrorists kill tourists in Egypt to show their love of God!

Sheik Omar Abdel Rahman is serving a life sentence for conspiring to blow up the World Trade Center in New York City, where six persons died, a thousand were wounded, and $500 million in damage was done. The terrorists said they were simply trying to destroy "the Great Satan," the United States.

In May 1996 the FBI warned Jewish organizations to be on guard against a threat from Moslem terrorists to kill 1200 Jewish executives and doctors in the United States, unless Israel withdraws its military forces from Lebanon and pays $12 billion in compensation for Lebanese killed in fighting Jews.

Moslem fundamentalism is now often called "the green menace," since it replaces the former communist red menace as a threat to world peace and order. Divisive religion is very much alive and well as we close the 20th century.

Conclusion

The most immoral act a human being can commit is to take a fellow human being's life. Yet this chapter shows graphically that this immorality is practiced widespread in most major religions. To make matters worse, a double crime is committed when the person blames God for giving the immoral orders. This is an attempt, overt or covert, to make God a criminal—sacrilegious behavior at its worst! What can be done to divert divisive religion into unitive religion?

One example of what can be done is shown in the statue called "St. Francis of the Guns" created by San Francisco sculptor Beniamino Bufano. He took some of the guns turned in after the assassination of Senator Robert Kennedy, and molded them into a huge statue of St. Francis. He decorated the statue with a colored mosaic depicting Senator Kennedy, his brother President John Kennedy, Martin Luther King, Jr., and Abraham Lincoln. At the base of the cross-shaped statue, Bufano placed a chorus consisting of the poor children of the world, rejoicing at the demise of the guns.

Mahatma Gandhi said, "I would not like to live in this world if it is not to be one world." When we were isolated, we had the luxury of improper behavior. But in the global town, our interrelations are too personal and too frequent to permit us such a luxury.

Ken Wilber says that "wherever there is a boundary there is a potential war. The aim of the mystics is to deliver men and women from their battles by delivering them from their boundaries. The discovery of the ultimate Whole is the only cure for unfreedom."[38]

After a look at the damage being done by contemporary divisive religion, the remainder of this book will concentrate on what we, as the human family, can do to make religion a part of humanity's solution rather than a part of humanity's problem.

References

1. Durant, *Our Oriental Heritage*, pp. 275-76.
2. Quoted in Ferm, p. 13.
3. Quoted in Zaehner, p. 187.
4. Campbell, *Oriental Mythology*, p. 5.
5. Haught, p. 34.
6. Noss, p. 193.
7. Zimmer, p. 497.
8. Albright, p. 269.
9. William B. Forbush, ed., *Fox's Book of Martyrs* (Universal Book & Bible House, 1926), p. 35.
10. Durant, *The Age of Faith*, p. 8.
11. Gibbon, p. 315.
12. Ibid., p. 615.
13. Cecil Roth, *A History of the Jews* (Schocken, 1961), p. 183.
14. Bernard Glassman, *Anti-Semitic Stereotypes Without Jews* (Wayne State University Press, 1975), pp. 16-17.
15. Will Durant, *The Reformation* (Simon & Schuster, 1957), p. 730.
16. *Encyclopedia Britannica*, 1971, vol. 12, pp. 1068-69.
17. Durant, *The Reformation*, p. 738.
18. Ibid., p. 731.
19. Durant, *The Age of Faith*, pp. 374-75.
20. Durant, *The Reformation*, p. 738.
21. Roth, p. 252.
22. *New York Times*, 2 November 1986, 4:9.
23. Bainton, p. 119.
24. Haught, p. 26.
25. Dimont, p. 217.
26. Bainton, p. 52.
27. Ibid., p. 53.
28. Dimont, p. 220.
29. Durant, *The Age of Faith*, p. 784.
30. Durant, *The Reformation*, p. 614.
31. Carl Van Doren, *Benjamin Franklin* (Viking, 1938), pp. 137-38.
32. Norman Cousins, *In God We Trust* (Harper, 1958), p. 67.

[33] Ibid., pp. 147, 160.
[34] E.R. Norman, *Anti-Catholicism in Victorian England* (Allen & Unwin, 1968), p. 130.
[35] Haught, p. 196.
[36] Ibid., p. 203.
[37] Ibid., p. 224.
[38] Wilber, *Up From Eden*, p. 334.

CHAPTER 10

CONTEMPORARY DIVISIVENESS: RELIGION AS BANE

Earlier chapters have cited numerous examples of how divisive religion can work against mankind's best interests. It is unfortunate how ubiquitous divisive religion continues to be right down to the present hour.

Frithjof Schuon points out the tragic consequences of the Industrial Revolution, which robbed people of two of the things they need most: faith in God, and meaningful work. The Industrial Revolution was based on scientism, which tends to deny the existence of a personal God. The chief component of the Revolution, the factory system, took away the creativity, as well as the expression of the worker's personality, in the person's craft or work. When both the church and the workplace became sterile institutions. modern life lost its meaning to many people.

R.H. Tawney emphasized the important role that religion played in the rise of capitalism. Somewhat misquoting John Calvin, Tawney argued that Calvin's influence was not only to justify profits for Christians, but also nearly to demand profits. Capitalism, a recently discovered economic system, came to be considered synonymous with Christianity in the minds of many businessmen. Making a large profit from one's neighbors was seen as wholly compatible with Christ's teachings about loving one's neighbor and helping the poor. Private greed was enshrined as public weal.

Max Weber added an explanation of how the Protestant ethic was anything but a protest against the status quo in economic and political life. Hard work, sobriety, punctuality, dependability, and obedience to orders were seen as the necessary qualities in a Christian worker. When John Wesley started to protest against the evils of the factory system, Anglican conservatives felt that he was being very un-Christian.

In a recent book *The Manufacture of Evil,* anthropologist Lionel Tiger describes how the corrosion of ethics took place. Tiger feels that religion codifies the natural morality with which the human species is endowed, perhaps being carried by genetic determiners. "Our inbred touchstone of right and wrong is loyalty to the other members of the community." When a community was small, the ethical system worked well. But when the community grew very large, possessive individualism took over, Tiger avers. We now each own ourselves. "The human essence no longer resides in being part of a family or other social whole, but in the freedom of the self from dependence on the will of others."[1] This ethic fits in well with a large-scale market economy, but the integrity of small-group ethical behavior has been compromised. Tiger's solution to this dilemma is to keep persons responsible within small-group situations, so the ethical code can operate. The small groups need to relate to ever larger groups, in such a way that loyalty to one does not vitiate loyalty to another. In case of conflict, the controlling value must always be mankind's natural morality, as reinforced by religious institutions which are unitive rather than divisive.

Religious groups themselves continue to be a major source of modern divisiveness. Tamils battle Buddhists in Sri Lanka; Jews and Moslems clash in Palestine; Protestants and Catholics continue to kill each other in Ireland. Despite some promising unitive trends to be discussed in the next chapter, religion continues to be a major source of humankind's prejudice, hatred, discrimination, and warfare. Sometimes it seems as if religion is more a part of the problem than a part of the solution.

"Even within their own ranks," Paul Davies opines, "religious organizations often sanction prejudice, whether against women, racial minorities, homosexuals or whoever their leaders decree to be inferior. The status of women in Catholicism and Islam, or blacks in the South African Church," are particularly offensive. "Bigotry seems inevitably to result once religious organizations become institutionalized." New religious movements, which stress "the importance of mysticism and quiet inner exploration, as opposed to evangelical fervor, attract those people who are critical of the social and political impact of established religions."²

Modern Anti-Semitism

Despite the incredible suffering of Jews throughout history, anti-Semitism reached new levels of barbarism in modern times.

Riots against Jews took place in 167 Russian towns in 1881. The property of Jews was confiscated. Comprehensive anti-Semitic legislation was passed in 1882 in Russia and Rumania. As a proponent of Orthodox Christianity, Czar Nicholas II spent personal funds to support anti-Semitic publications.

By 1900 there was an unorganized conspiracy against Jews in the United States, fed by the hate of fundamentalist Christians. Jews found it hard to rent hotel rooms. Country clubs and civic organizations refused to admit Jews as members. Jews could not buy property in certain areas. Law firms would not hire Jews. Universities set quotas in admitting Jews, and college fraternities barred them.

Lothrop Stoddard and Madison Grant wrote books on Nordic racial supremacy, alleging Jews to be an inferior people. The spurious *Protocols of the Learned Elders of Zion* purported to be the minutes of a council of rabbis who secretly run the world. Appearing in Paris around 1900, the *Protocols* said that a conspiracy of Jews and Freemasons was going to overthrow Christianity and rule the world. Translated into many languages, the *Protocols* became very popular among ignorant people. In the United States they were believed to be true by the Ku Klux Klan, the Aryan Nations Church, and similar groups. In 1921 the *Protocols* were proved to be a forgery, the work of the czar's secret police. Nevertheless, in the Soviet Union an organization called Pamyat considers the *Protocols* to be authentic, saying that there is a conspiracy of Jews, Freemasons, Russian dissidents, and Amnesty International which schemed to overthrow the Soviet government.

In 1915 a 13-year old white girl was raped and killed in an Atlanta pencil factory. One of the owners, Leo Frank, was convicted of the crime. Important "evidence" used in the trial was the "fact" that Jews are lascivious, that Frank was a pervert because he looked like one, that he had killed a previous wife, and that he had had numerous illegitimate children. Although all of these allegations were untrue, a jury found Frank to be guilty. While serving a life sentence, he was taken from prison and lynched by a mob.

World War I marked the break-up of two empires, those of czarist Russia and of Austria-Hungary. Both empires had many Jews, so Jews once again played their historic role as scapegoats in Christian nations that were in trouble. Disgruntled Christian mobs attacked Jewish ghettos. In Russia wherever the White armies were in the ascendancy, a wave of violence against Jews took place. Since a few Russian Communist leaders were Jewish, a hate slogan of "Jewish bolshevism" developed.

In *Mein Kampf* Adolf Hitler said: "The greatness of every mighty organization embodying an idea in this world lies in the religious fanaticism and intolerance with which, fanatically convinced of its own right, it intolerantly imposes its will against others." He also said that "the blessing of the Lord is with Germany and not with her enemies."[3]

Hitler made it abundantly clear that he considered the Jews to be the chief enemies of Germany. Shortly after Hitler came to power in 1933 German Jews lost their jobs in all levels of government, in the universities, and in the professions. Jewish businesses were boycotted. When a 17-year old half-demented Jew shot a German secretary of the Paris embassy in 1938, retaliation included gutting almost all of the 600 Jewish synagogues and sacking many Jewish businesses. One billion marks of Jewish property was destroyed, and another billion marks was levied as a fine upon German Jews. All Jewish property was transferred into "Aryan" hands.

Elie Wiesel describes some of the Nazi inhumanity. In 1942 during Purim in Poland, the Nazis hanged ten Polish Jews to avenge the death of Haman, as described in the biblical book of Esther. "The head of the Judenrat was forced to give a speech justifying the executioners' work." If Jews refused to kiss a cross, the Nazis would beat them unconscious. Nazis would "transform the synagogue into a stable, a latrine, before burning it. They would tear out the beards of pious Jews, bent on ridiculing them before killing them. They forced the victims to lick the executioners' boots, to drink the executioners' spit, to blaspheme, to humiliate themselves. The Germans were waging a veritable war of religion against the Jewish soul, against Jewish memory."

Rabbi Shimon Huberband, author of a book on the Holocaust, mentions some charitable Christians "but not many, he encounters them so rarely." Even some Jews turned against their own people: the ghetto's Jewish police and the Jewish *nouveaux riches*. But many Jews performed the tragic duty of *Kiddush Hashem*—"they died sanctifying the name of the Lord."[4]

The virus of hatred spread. In Yugoslavia the Jews were nearly exterminated by the Croatian Fascists (the Ustachi) and the Bosnian Moslems. Crete, Rhodes, and Salonika killed almost all their Jews. In most European countries Jews were discriminated against, deported, or killed.

"The record of German atrocities in France filled 13 volumes. Perhaps six out of every seven European Jews found in the occupied areas were killed by the Nazis. Of the 3,300,000 Jews in Poland at the outbreak of the war, not more than ten percent were alive in 1944. It is estimated that from 18 to 26 million persons—prisoners of war, political prisoners, men, women, and children of all ages and all nationalities—were put to death by the Germans through hunger, cold, pestilence, torture, medical experimentation, and other means in all the camps of Germany and the occupied territories."[5]

Cecil Roth gives a partial account of Jewish persecution:[6]

World War II Decimation of Jews

	1940	1945
Poland	3,350,000	55,000
Rumania	1,000,000	320,000
Czechoslovakia	360,000	40,000
Holland	150,000	30,000
Greece	75,000	8,000
Yugoslavia	75,000	8,000
Salonika	56,000	2,000
Vilna	54,000	600
Europe Overall	9,000,000	4,000,000

Alois Brunner, the most notorious Nazi war criminal still at large, regrets nothing that he did in World War II and said he would do it all over again. An assistant to Adolf Eichmann, Brunner was held responsible for the deportation to death and slave-labor camps of at least 128,500 Jews. "All the Jews deserved to die because they were the devil's agents and human garbage," Brunner said recently in Syria, where he lives under governmental protection.[7]

There was a shocking difference between Nazi bestiality and Jewish humaneness, between divisive and unitive religion. Pierre Durand, a witness in the Klaus Barbie case, tells of the day that liberation came to the concentration camp at Buchenwald: "We, the inmates, took 220 German prisoners. But we locked them up and delivered them to the American army intact, and they were all assassins. That was the difference between them and us."[8]

Jewish Divisiveness

Perhaps it is understandable that after serving as a religious scapegoat for Christians and Moslems through most of history, modern Judaism finds it hard to practice consistently the religion of Abraham, Moses, and Isaiah. It is both ironic and tragic that the people who led the world to God now lead the world away from God by creating suffering for others.

The background of the Israeli-Palestinian land dispute provides some understanding of the problem. In World War I England had trouble getting wood, for wood alcohol, from the United States. Wood alcohol was used to manufacture the explosive cordite. Prime Minister Lloyd George asked Dr. Chaim Weizmann, professor of chemistry at Manchester University, to work on a source of wood alcohol. Weizmann found a way to transform the starch of cereals into a form of wood alcohol. Asked what he wanted as a reward, Weizmann replied that he wanted nothing for himself but he desired a homeland for his people. Since the British army had recently captured the Holy Land from the Turks, the Balfour Resolution was drawn up. It promised that Britain would help the Jews establish a national home in Palestine, "it being clearly understood that nothing shall be done which may prejudice the civil and religious rights of existing non-Jewish communities in Palestine."

With keen political insight, Albert Einstein favored a binational state of Jews and Palestinians in the Holy Land. Einstein feared that a separate Jewish state might lead to a narrow nationalism which would undermine the spirituality of Judaism. In 1938 he said, "My awareness of the essential nature of Judaism resists the idea of a Jewish state with borders, an army, and a measure of temporal power, no matter how modest."[9]

In setting up Israel in 1947, the United Nations at the same time adopted a resolution guaranteeing the rights of Moslem residents in Palestine. The Israeli government has adopted the UN resolution which legalized it, but conveniently ignored the companion UN resolution which granted similar rights to the Palestinians. The Israelis have thus abrogated both fundamental documents that created their state.

Modern Israel is much larger than ancient Israel. During most of the biblical period, the Jews shared Palestine with other nations, and for long periods had been vassals of larger empires. Modern Israel includes the land of the Philistines and the Samaritans, as well as territory that the Jews had not held since 700 B.C. Common sense, as well as common justice, requires the Israelis to give due consideration to the people who have occupied the land in the interim.

"Israel practices apartheid in the name of national security," says David J. Sadd. "Israel's law of return allows any Jews from anywhere to immigrate to it, but Palestinians may not return to the place of their birth. Israel sets for itself a double standard."[10]

Palestinians naturally resent their unjust treatment, and violence continues to grow in Palestine. From 1977 to 1982 there were about 500 violent demonstrations per year by Palestinians living under Israeli occupation. Since 1982, when Israel invaded Lebanon and forced the PLO out of Beirut, the number has risen to about 3,000 per year. Hardly a day goes by without the Jews killing a Palestinian demonstrator.

Judaism's own great prophetic tradition is a troubling conscience for modern Israel. Prophets like Amos, Isaiah, and Jeremiah warned Israel that her God would turn against her unless she practiced righteousness and justice. Through the hard lessons of history the Jews learned to understand the great paradox: when there is great suffering, God is revealing Himself. The indescribable suffering of the Jews in the Nazi Holocaust called attention to their unique role in history, as a people who can show the world the way to God through suffering. If the paradox holds true, then the suffering of the modern Palestinians (ironically at the hands of the Jews) shows the world that the Palestinians are now God's chosen people. When Jews or Palestinians create suffering, they reveal Satan's nature instead of God's, for the unitive God of love wants none of His creation to suffer. Modern divisiveness continues to alienate people from people, and people from God.

Enlightened self-interest, as well as to remain true to its religious and ethical principles, requires that Israel share some of its presently-held land with the Palestinians. Harry Siegman, executive director of the American Jewish Congress, feels that Israel must relinquish the West Bank and the Gaza Strip, but not just to accommodate the Palestinians. Siegman says that the non-Jewish population growth in these two areas will equal the Jewish population within twenty years. He states that "Israel cannot hold on to the Palestinians in the territories without losing its democratic character and Jewish essence. Remaining locked in permanent embrace with one and a half million angry Palestinians poses security risks for Israel that far exceed any conceivable danger Israel faces across its borders."[11]

The Jews must face up to justice regarding the Palestinians, says Albert Vorspan, senior vice-president of the Union of American Hebrew Congregations, which comprises 804 Reform synagogues. Seeing Jewish brutality daily on television makes a Jew "want to crawl into a hole," Vorspan says. "This is the price we pay for having made of Israel an icon—a surrogate faith, a surrogate God. Israel could not withstand our romantic idealization. Now Israel reveals itself, a nation like all the others." Israeli soldiers drag protectors out of their homes and deliberately break their bones, he reports. "'Palestinians with broken hands can't throw stones,' says an Israeli spokesman. If all this is true, Israel has lost its moral compass, has become a nation in panic. I'm one of the signers of the statement calling for reconciling Israel's security with Palestinian self-determination," Vorspan stated. This statement has been issued by the U.S. Interreligious Committee for Peace in the Middle East.[12]

A Jewish prayer thanks God for not creating church members as heathens or slaves. Then the man prays: "Blessed are You, our God, who has not created me as a woman."[13] Perhaps the framer of the prayer felt that God was ashamed at having created women. This type of nonsensical divisiveness continues to parade in the disguise of religion.

Modern Christian Divisiveness

Christianity has never solved the dilemma of how to reconcile the idea of religious liberty with the underlying concept of the Christian church as the unified body of Christ. The Roman Catholic Church floundered through fifteen centuries of schism and heresy, without satisfactorily resolving the issue. If anything, Protestantism made matters worse, by focusing on individual liberty to the exclusion of the recognition of the oneness of Christ. Contemporary events point up this continuing dilemma.

In Uganda Anglicans battled Roman Catholics. King Mwanga of Uganda persecuted Baganda Christians. One day in 1886 thirty-two young Christians were burned to death. Later Mwanga was deposed, and the number of Christians, especially Anglicans, rose. "But meanwhile rivalries with the French Roman Catholic missionaries led to a civil war, in which F.D. Lugard supplied arms to the Anglicans so that they defeated the numerically stronger Roman Catholics."[14] Since that time chieftainships and control of the land have been divided among the Anglican, Roman Catholic, and Moslem spheres of influence.

Quarrels among Christian missionaries confused Africans over which one was the "true" Christian church. As a result there are countless autonomous Christian churches in Africa today. Geoffrey Parrinder reports a total of 500 separate Christian church bodies in West Africa, 500 in Central Africa, 300 in East Africa, and over 3,000 in South Africa. Many of these independent churches permit the use of traditional African costumes, dances, musical instruments, and in some cases such customs as polygamy. The toleration of such pluralism can be unitive, but insofar as groups profess exclusive claims to Christian orthodoxy, the overall effect can be divisive

The Church of Jesus Christ of Latter-Day Saints provides an interesting example of a uniquely American blend of religious divisiveness and unitiveness. In the view of R. Laurence Moore, Mormon clannishness "destroyed the relations between Mormons and their neighbors." Joseph Smith "taught his followers all too well to regard themselves as superior to others. A fundamental contradiction pervaded Smith's career. He said that he founded the Mormon church to put an end to the theological bickering that divided religious denominations. His professed aim was to restore the universal church. Yet throughout his career he constantly searched for new ways to distinguish his church from every other church. He appears to have used secrecy as part of his effort to give his followers a sense of distinct identity."[15]

By declaring themselves to be outsiders, they were really moving into mainstream America, Moore felt, since the United States is basically a union of outsiders. "By the end of World War I, the Mormons were more American than most Americans. Patriotism, respect for the law, love of the Constitution, and obedience to political authority reigned as principles of the faith."[16]

Divisiveness can be insidious. Asked about their religious differences a chaplain in World War I told his colleague: "We are serving the same Master—you in your way, and I in His." Putting nationalism ahead of religion, Pope Pius XI blessed the Italian aggression in Ethiopia in 1935. The theologian Karl Barth proclaimed all non-Christian religions to be unbelief in God. Asked how he knew this to be true, especially since he had never met a Hindu, Barth replied, "A priori." On such a tenuous foundation religion will always be subject to divisiveness.

R. Laurence Moore says that the name "Apostles of Discord" was aptly applied to such fundamentalist Christian leaders as Carl McIntire, Gerald Winrod, and Billy James Hargis. They denounced every application of the social gospel as un-Christian. "They equated their religious behavior with American patriotism. Until Pearl Harbor, Winrod wrote appreciatively of Hitler's attacks on world Jewry and Russian bolshevism."[17]

"The gods of the contemporary West are not always good gods," wrote Ninian Smart. "James Jones took devotees to vulgar unnecessary death in Guyana."[18] In a movement he called the People's Temple, Jones persuaded 914 followers to commit mass suicide as an alleged religious act in 1978.

One by one many of America's leading television evangelists are being revealed as more interested in building personal empires than in serving the humble Jesus. Jim Bakker, Jimmy Swaggart, and Oral Roberts, after building huge financial networks, have been widely criticized in the American press for playing up to the gullibility of the American religious public. For some American believers faith crumbles when once-respected Christian leaders are revealed to have feet of clay and thus forfeit the claim to national trust and respect.

Church ritual is always a rich source of possible divisiveness. As Jaroslav Jan Pelikan observes, "It is one of the supreme ironies of Christian history, evident already in the New Testament, that the Eucharist, intended as a means of fostering the unity of the church, has been a source of disunity and contention as well. Most Christian traditions teach that Jesus Christ is present in the Eucharist in some special way, disagree though they do about the mode, the locus, and the time of that presence. Both the unity of the church and the disunity of the churches continue to be symbolized by the Eucharist."[19]

Although Vatican II Council was conceived and largely executed in a spirit of Christian unity, some Roman Catholics have objected to the changes in church ritual and philosophy. Archbishop Marcel Lefebvre protested against the vernacular liturgy, changes in seminary training, and the decrees on religious liberty and ecumenism. "He has criticized Pope John Paul II for visiting the synagogue in Rome and for joining with other religious leaders in Assisi to pray for peace." Lefebvre then began to ordain bishops without approval from Rome. When he was excommunicated, he led a group of priests out of the Church. Why should Roman Catholics care about this break, asks Norman Perry. "We should care," Perry replies, "because every schism is a kind of dismembering of the Mystical Body of Christ. It destroys the unity of His followers for which Christ prayed. It obscures the sign value of unity to others. Schism is destructive of charity and faith and is damaging to evangelization."[20]

Sources of division in the current Roman Catholic Church include whether priests should be permitted to marry, and whether women should be allowed to be ordained as priests. In 1988 Pope John Paul II issued a letter "On the Dignity of Women," which received a mixed response. Some liked the Pope's emphasis on motherhood and virginity as reflected in the Virgin Mary, and others applauded his rejection of Paul's chauvinistic statements about women being subordinate to men. More severe critics, however, stressed that as long as women are denied the priesthood, they will have the status of second-class citizens in Roman Catholicism.

Divisiveness which is purely theological in the United States can become overtly cruel and harmful overseas. For example, in 1982 Lebanese military forces, under the command of a young Roman Catholic Maronite officer named Elie Hobeika, entered the Palestinian refugee camps of Sabra and Shatila to search for Palestine Liberation Organization troops. In the process, more than 1000 men, women, and children were massacred. In retaliation the Moslem Druze in 1983 killed 1000 Christians and left many more thousands homeless. By 1985 "the level of violence was rising, with not only Christians and Muslims shooting at each other but Muslims shooting at Muslims and Christians at Christians."[21]

In Ireland "the Ulster Volunteer Force is a shadowy paramilitary group that has periodically abducted and killed Catholics in a sectarian campaign of assassination driven by four hundred years of pure hate." The Irish Republican Army does similar things against Northern Ireland Protestants, for similar reasons. Four-year old children on both sides are taught to hate fellow Christians. Slightly older children are proud when they are allowed to throw fire bombs at the opposition. A 14-year old boy cheered when a British soldier was killed. When he found the dead man's teeth, he put them in a bottle and proudly displayed them as a trophy to family and friends.[22]

Edward Norman has decried the divisive effect of the politicization of Christianity, explaining that since politics divides people, religion which is political raises further barriers among people. As in Ireland, religious values are then lost sight of and are replaced by political goals. "In their death agonies," says Norman, "the western churches are distributing the causes of their own sickness—the politicization of religion—to their healthy offspring in the developing world."[23]

Modern Moslem Divisiveness

The chief victims of recent Moslem divisiveness have been fellow Moslems. In most Middle Eastern countries Moslem believers have been killed or injured by narrow Islamic fanatics. As long ago as the fourteenth century the Arab historian Ibn Khaldun said that life is hard in the desert, where people are held together by *asabiyya,* loyalty to one's clan and a willingness to fight to one's death against other clans. A modern wealthy Shi'ite businessman believes in an old Arab proverb: "Myself against my brother, my brother and I against my cousin, my cousin, my brother, and I against the foreigner."

In Sudan religious differences have led to political rivalries. The Mahdi, Muhammad Ahmad, died there in 1885. His son Sayyid Abd al-Rahman organized the Ansar, a group of Mahdists who were non-Sufi and non-mystical. Rahman's rival was Sayyid Ali al-Mirghani, leader of the Khatmiyya brotherhood, which advocated cooperation with Egypt and Britain after these nations conquered Sudan in 1898. The Mahdists used the slogan: Sudan for the Sudanese. Beginning to fear Egypt's rising power, the Mahdists began working with the British more closely than with Egypt. The Khatmiyya automatically became the pro-Egypt group. What had started as religious divisiveness ended up as political factionalism.

In Jerusalem Moslem hatred harmed Moslems. In 1933 Haj Amin, Mufti of Jerusalem, called for a holy war against non-Moslems, especially the British and the Jews. Although this was popular with the Moslem masses, it led to increased violence by the Jews, and thus ultimately harmed many of those who were supposed to be helped.

In 1934 a drunken Jewish soldier in the French army urinated against the wall of a mosque in Constantine, Algeria. The event triggered a series of anti-Jewish riots in which 27 persons were killed and 48 injured.

The Hamadsha are members of Moslem brotherhoods in Morocco. They practice a frenzy known as *jidba,* meaning "attraction." In this religious dance they hit their heads with axes, feeling that they have been ordered to do so by a camel-footed she-demon. They seem to feel no pain, and are surprised to see blood on their clothing when they come out of the trance.

The Ait Abdi, an illiterate tribe in the Atlas mountains of north Africa, tell this story on themselves: A man and his wife began fighting in a pasture, setting off a chain reaction of feuding and killing. The tribe knows the story but forbids telling it, fearing it might ignite another round of mayhem. They seem to abide by the adage: "We know that we ought not to be so quarrelsome, but we also know perfectly well that this is just how we are."[24]

The partition between India and Pakistan in 1947 scarcely began to bring religious peace to the area, although it was supposed to do precisely that. "Immediately after partition Pakistan Moslems massacred and raped and exiled Sikhs and Hindus by the millions." One Indian leader, Sardar Patel, in 1949 said, "We did not listen to Gandhi's appeal for unity, and when we got freedom, we know how the three communities, Hindus, Muslims, and Sikhs, behaved. It will always remain the blackest chapter in the history of India."[25] Countless Indians concur with this judgment.

A group of Pakistani Moslems accepted Mirza Ghulam Ahmad as a minor prophet, and set up their own mosques. Other Moslems considered the movement to be a heresy, a challenge to Mohammed's role as "the seal of the prophets." The Ahmadis were declared to be non-Moslems. When an Ahmadi, Zafrullah Khan, became foreign minister of Pakistan in 1952, he was openly opposed and religious riots ensued. The official governmental inquiry into the disturbances declared: "If there is one thing which has been conclusively demonstrated in this inquiry it is that, provided you can persuade the masses to believe something they are asked to do is religiously right, you can set them to any course of action, regardless of all considerations of discipline, loyalty, decency, morality, or civic sense."[26]

These Punjab riots were a vast heresy hunt. "Many thousands of citizens, with extremely wide popular support, rioted murderously, in almost pogrom-like fashion, against the dissident sect of Ahmadis and against the government for not declaring these to be religiously and politically outside the pale." The Ahmadis became the convenient scapegoat for a whole range of political failures. The form of protest was "religiously inept, ethically shocking, and practically disastrous." A portion of the official inquiry found the political leaders incompetent. No two of them agreed on the definition of a Moslem, yet they were "practically unanimous that all who disagreed should be put to death."[27]

Recent Moslem extremists include the Kashani party in Iran, the Daru-l-Islam movement in Indonesia, and the Khatm-i Nubuwat fanatics in Pakistan. These groups all show "at times a violent fury that almost rejoices in destruction, a bitter vehemence in opposition to the West, to local non-Muslims, to Muslims who disagree with them, and to all outsiders; and a telling combination of self-righteousness with lust and power-hungry ambition." Because of their violence, even their own Moslem governments have had to restrain them. In the words of W.C. Smith, "in striking respects they are sorry representatives of their faith."[28] These groups have trouble adjusting in the modern world. Their concept of their faith prevents them from reacting to change, and their ensuing frustration takes a violent form. This violence itself increases, rather than decreases, their frustration and maladjustment, and so they are locked into a divisive spiral of religious expression.

Lebanon strove valiantly to achieve a cooperative plan which would blend religious and political components in a popular-front government. In 1943 Lebanese leaders agreed to this compromise: Christians would be in charge of the presidency, the military, and 51% of the parliament. Sunnis would provide the prime minister, and Shi'ites would provide the president of the parliament. Other minorities would have control over certain governmental positions.

But in 1958 a civil war broke out, which was put down by U.S. marines. Another civil war started in 1975, and this time Syria occupied Lebanon. Between 1975 and 1982 65,000 persons were killed in the civil war. Israel then captured Beirut, and another 20,000 persons were killed. In the civil strife in 1983, peace-keeping forces from the United Nations were ignored. In October 1983 two Islamic terrorists exploded a kamikaze truck at a barracks in Beirut, and 241 U.S. marines and 58 French paratroopers were killed.

George Santayana said that a fanatic is one who redoubles his effort when he has lost sight of his goal. In 1988 Shi'ites spent the month of May killing each other. For several weeks "fundamentalist militiamen of the Party of God, which is financed and equipped by Iran, exchanged artillery shells and rockets with the mainstream Shi'ite militia, Amal, a group backed by Syria." Over 250 Shi'ites were killed and more than one thousand wounded. Shi'ite demonstrators chanted that the Party of God was "the party of Satan."[29]

Another indication of divisive Islam is the Muslim Brotherhood, which was founded in Egypt in 1928 by Hassan al-Banna and six other Moslems. Its goals include Moslem unity, anticolonialism, and a fundamentalist Islam. Quickly ten percent of Egypt's population joined the brotherhood. Banna's Confession of Faith said: "All things hark back to God. The flag of Islam should rule mankind. I vow to do everything I can to strengthen the brotherhood of all Muslims. I vow to adhere to these tenets, and if necessary to die in their service."[30] After a member of the brotherhood assassinated Egyptian Prime Minister Nukrashi in 1948, Banna was killed by government agents the following year.

Abdel Nasser outlawed the Muslim Brotherhood for opposing him. Omar el-Telmisani, the leader of the brotherhood in 1976, described his seventeen years in prison: "In 1954 I was hung up like a slaughtered cow. The young people who experienced such torture were unable to imagine that such deeds could be carried out by believers." Anwar el-Sadat released members of the brotherhood from prison. Nevertheless, Telmisani opposed Sadat and the Camp David peace accords. The brotherhood said that "the people of God must be prepared to rise up and throw themselves into the decisive battle whenever the suitable opportunity presents itself. The soil of Palestine is in its entirety usurped Islamic soil. For this reason the holy war is obligatory."[31]

The radical Islamic underground group Takfir wal Hejra also opposed the Camp David accords, saying that Sadat had "capitulated to the enemy." Members of this group assassinated Sadat on October 6, 1981.

The Muslim Brotherhood finds strong opposition in Syria. President Hafiz el-Assad of Syria is from the minority Alawites, a branch of the Shi'ites. Alawites comprise only 11% of Syria, whereas Sunnis account for 70% of the 10 million Syrians. The Muslim Brotherhood itself is 90% Sunni. In 1979 the brotherhood massacred 200 young cadets in Aleppo. Assad decreed that every member of the brotherhood should expect the death penalty. In 1980 government troops killed 300 rioting Sunnis and 550 prisoners, mostly members of the brotherhood, in a Palmyra prison. Later that year they killed another 180 members of the brotherhood in a helicopter raid in Palmyra. In 1981 Assad's forces viciously attacked the brotherhood, killing 30,000 Sunnis and completely destroying 95 Sunni mosques in the ancient city of Hamah.

In 1969 Muammar el-Qaddafi deposed King Idris and took over control of Libya. Qaddafi posed as an Islamic fundamentalist, closing Christian churches and banning alcohol, miniskirts, and prostitution. One of his targets has been the Muslim Brotherhood, and another the Islamic Liberation Party. He gets his money from oil, and from acting as an intermediary in shipments of weapons. Under his leadership Libya has become a sanctuary of international terrorism. Many of his opponents have been found dead.

The Koran demands non-violence during the hajj, the pilgrimage to Mecca. During this period pilgrims are urged to spare even flies, ants, and mosquitoes. But in 1986 violence broke out, when Saudi police caught Iranian pilgrims trying to smuggle in 330 pounds of plastic explosive. When the Iranians refused to disperse, Saudi soldiers fired tear gas into the mob, and later used automatic weapons. A total of 402 person were killed and 669 injured during this melee. In 1987 Iranian Shi'ites got a measure of revenge by beheading a Saudi policeman and carrying his head around on a stick.

The ulama, or religious leaders, have possessed unusual power in modern Iran. In countries like Egypt and the Ottoman Empire, where there were both a strong central bureaucracy and a modernized army, the power of the ulama dwindled. But in Iran the Qajar shahs of the 19th and early 20th centuries had no such strong governmental base, and so the ulama grew ever stronger as they stepped into the political vacuum.

The Shi'ites in Iran say that the only legitimate wielder of political power would be the imam, but since the occultation of the twelfth imam in 874, all present governments are usurpatory. Iranian Shi'ites eagerly await the coming of the Mahdi, but until then pledge themselves to oppose all autocratic governments (except perhaps their own). "All autocratic regimes are held to be similar to the Umayyads," they feel. For this reason many Shi'ites supported the constitutional reform that occurred in Iran from 1905 to 1911.

When Reza Shah created a strong Iranian army in the 1920s, he was fought by the ulama, who realized that they were losing power over the Iranian masses. The ulama increasingly became entrenched in opposition to the shah's government. Using the United States as a "demon nation," the Ayatollah Khomeini mounted a vigorous anti-shah campaign. He drew support from those opposed to the shah's land reform, the enfranchisement of women, and the westernizing, especially the close liaison between the army and the United States. Khomeini resented American support of Israel, and the fact that Americans living in Iran were granted special rights. Because of his opposition to the shah, he was exiled to Turkey in 1963. He moved to Iraq in 1965 and later to Paris. In 1970, when a consortium of American investors agreed to supply capital to Iran, Khomeini labeled it an example of "Yankee imperialism."

Partly because Shi'ites are an Islamic minority, and partly because other Moslem nations do not trust Iran's imperialistic aims, Khomeini failed to gain much Islamic support in his effort to oppose European and especially American influence. The Muslim Brotherhood, for example, has not backed Khomeini. One member said, "Our Koran states that one is not permitted to end one crime by committing another. Therefore we cannot blindly follow the Iranian model."[32]

Arab countries have been concerned that Khomeini's siren call to their people will find followers. "From their point of view, Islam is an awkward religion. It recognizes no distinction between religious and temporal power and it is hostile to nationalism. Moslems are supposed to belong to an *umma* (a single community of believers) united under the sacred law (the *shari'a*), not to separate national jurisdictions with a hodgepodge of secular laws. Most Arab governments have a long and bloody history of doing battle with Islamic extremists who want either to impose the full *shari'a* law or, better still, to replace their secular governments with an Islamic theocracy. These groups insist on their right to use violent means towards righteous ends."[33] But such extremists have generally been put down, usually by a strong show of force by Arab governments.

The disillusioned Khomeini had to realize by the summer of 1988 that the long war against neighboring Iraq had been lost. He had mistakenly expected to derive support from two sources: Shi'ites, and all dispossessed Moslems. Instead, Iraq received over $50 billion in support from Moslem countries. "It shows that most Arabs regarded the Iranian threat as much more menacing than the Israeli threat," said a Palestinian official. "All the Arab aid to Egypt, Syria, Jordan, and the Palestinians in forty years of war against Israel is a fraction of the aid they have given Iraq in only six years."[34]

Despite the fact that virtually all Palestinians consider Israel to be their common enemy, they are far from being united on how to demonstrate their opposition. Yasir Arafat heads the largest group, the Palestine Liberation Organization. Other resistance groups include the Popular Front for the Liberation of Palestine, led by George Habash; the Democratic Front for the Liberation of Palestine, headed by Nayef Hawatmeh; the Islamic Holy War; Hamas; and the Communist Party.

The Islamic Holy War and Hamas are two organizations which grew out of the now defunct Muslim Brotherhood. Hamas is an acronym for the Movement of the Islamic Resistance. While the PLO is speaking of working out a land agreement with Israel, Hamas takes a strident and divisive position. "The land of Palestine is an Islamic trust left to the generations of Moslems until the day of resurrection," Hamas declares. "It is forbidden for anyone to yield or concede part or all of it. The solution to the Palestinian problem will only take place by holy war. International conferences only waste time."[35]

Modern Asian Divisiveness

The lofty spiritual ideals of India have not kept that country free from religious hatred and violence. "When the Muslim state of Pakistan split off, millions of people killed each other in gruesome massacres. Since 1947, there have been reputedly more than 20,000 skirmishes in India."[36] Moslems have but meager representation in Indian social and political life, despite the fact that they comprise 136 million of the total 970 million people in India. Amnesty International has stated that Hindu policemen were directly involved in the killing or disappearance of dozens of unarmed Moslems in northern India in 1988. Hindu police are also charged with the mistreatment of other religious groups, such as the Sikhs in Punjab.

A current arena of religious discord is the island of Sri Lanka. Great Britain granted Sri Lanka independence in 1948. The Buddhist Sinhalese there feel that they, like the Jews, preserve a religious heritage important to the rest of the world. Citing the burning of Hindu priests and other atrocities, Tamil guerrillas, who carry suicide cyanide capsules on a neck string, advocate ruthlessness in vengeance against the Sinhalese.

In 1983 Velupillai Prabakaran led a Tamil attack on a Sinhalese governmental convoy in Jaffna, killing thirteen soldiers. Retaliation by Sinhalese youth and soldiers killed 1000 Tamils. In a reign of terror, Tamil homes and businesses were burned. Over 100,000 Tamils lost their homes. In the capital city of Colombo alone $300 million worth of damage was done. President Jayewardene of Sri Lanka admits that there has been discrimination against the Tamils, but feels that Tamil terrorism only makes the situation worse. Asked how long it would take to rebuild the damaged city, he replied, "It is impossible to measure. Physically we can rebuild. But minds, attitudes, friendships? I cannot speak of time."[37]

Thousands of frightened Tamil youths now undergo training in guerrilla camps, ready for revenge against the Sinhalese. In 1985 Sinhalese troops killed 150 Tamil civilians, in retribution for the death of a Sinhalese soldier whose jeep hit a land mine. A teacher's wife was breast feeding her baby when soldiers killed her, and then shot off her baby's toes in a test of marksmanship. On Good Friday in 1987 Tamil terrorists killed 128 unarmed Sinhalese soldiers, wives, and children returning from a Buddhist holiday. Five days later 113 civilians were killed by a Tamil bomb in Colombo.

"Saffron robes of Buddhist monks, traditionally an emblem of peace and tolerance, have become symbols of militancy and martyrdom," especially after 29 monks were killed by Tamil terrorists in 1987. On the other hand, Tamils are "regularly beaten, tortured, and sexually assaulted" in a Sri Lanka internment camp. After four years of civil war over religion, 7,000 Sri Lankans are dead and half a million have been forced from their homes. The Sri Lankan economy is in shambles. As in North Ireland and the Middle East, "every atrocity is justified as revenge for an earlier outrage. The cycle of revenge has no end because it seems to have no beginning." The country has been unable "to balance its assertion of ethnic and religious pride with the ideals of pluralism and secularism."[38] In an effort to keep the peace, India has signed an agreement with Sri Lanka to provide troops to stem any further religious violence.

Religion in China suffered under the communist rule of Mao Tse-tung. In 1952 the Chinese Buddhist Association was established, to help bring Buddhist doctrine into accordance with communist ideals. Leaders of the Association even attacked fundamental Buddhist concepts. In 1960 the president of the Association praised the majority of Chinese Buddhists for having discarded "their tolerant, transcendental attitude of rejecting the world, which has been handed down from the past," and having taken a new "positive attitude of entering the world."[39]

Japanese religions blend in readily with nationalistic goals. In the 1930s a prominent Japanese professor declared Shinto to be the religion of religions, saying that the first god mentioned in the *Kojiki* is the Lord of the Universe, the same deity to whom all religions pay homage. Hence, he concluded, all other religions are branches of Shinto, and that Lao-Tzu, Confucius, Buddha, and Christ were "unconscious" Shinto missionaries. One legend said that it was Christ's brother who died on the cross, and that Christ had died in Japan, his spiritual homeland.

Soka Gakkai (Japanese for "value creation society") is the lay organization of Nichiren Buddhism. Josei Toda, president of Soka Gakkai, "encouraged the destruction of Buddhist altars, Shinto god-shelves, Bibles, and family name-tablets in homes of members of other branches of Buddhism."[40] That Japanese Buddhism need not be divisive can be seen by the ecumenical outlook of another Nichiren sect, Rissho Koseikai.

Reasons for Modern Divisiveness

Various theories have been advanced to account for the large amount of divisiveness in the modern world. Psychiatrist R.D. Laing doubts that what the world needs is "a return to normalcy." "Normal men," says Laing, "have killed perhaps 100,000,000 of their fellow normal men in the last fifty years." Of course, he adds, "normal" people have always had "good" reasons for their behavior.

Anton Chekhov, the Russian writer, diagnosed the modern malaise a century ago: "Wherever you find boredom and degeneracy, you are certain to find sexual perversion, depravity, impotence, and disillusioned youth. In addition, a decline in art, hostility towards science, and injustice of every kind. A society that has lost its belief in God, yet still fears the devil—that kind of society has no right to claim it knows what justice is."[41]

Mircea Eliade describes the desacralization of modern humanity. Denying transcendence, modern man considers "the sacred the prime obstacle to his freedom" and feels "he will become himself only when he is totally demysticized. He will not be truly free until he has killed the last god."[42] Murder is no problem, because the human body has been desacralized. Pollution is not a problem either, for nature has become desacralized. Misuse of one's sexual partner is permissible, since nothing is sacred any more, including the human body. Rape and murder are particularly easy in a large city, where the process of desacralization is more advanced.

Ken Wilber sees the problem as one of eliminating unnecessary boundaries. We all begin in unity consciousness, Wilber says, but then we begin to build barriers, boundaries between ourselves and God, between ourselves and others, and even between different parts of ourselves. One's self-identity depends entirely upon where one draws the boundary lines. In the supreme identity, one expands his self-identity boundary to include the entire universe.

Wilber explains his position: "A boundary line, as any military expert will tell you, is also a potential battle line. The boundary line between the mind and the body is certainly a strange one, not at all present at birth. The boundary between the self and the not-self is the one we are most reluctant to surrender. Still, a boundary line not only separates but also unites what is on both sides of it. Growth fundamentally means an expanding of one's horizons," a pushing back of one's boundaries. It is a remapping and rezoning of the psyche, after first discovering and then mining the ever deeper levels of one's real self. "To realize the Whole is to escape the fate of a part, which is only suffering, pain, and death. Only parts suffer, not the Whole. God is the real self of all that is."[43] A person liberated from the illusion of seeming opposites is said to be enlightened, to have moksha, nirvana, salvation, or satori.

As the human ego developed, it separated what it considered to be a desirable picture of itself (persona) from an allegedly undesirable picture (shadow). Shirking responsibility, the individual tries to project the shadow outwardly on someone else, and Satan is always handy for the occasion. But then the ego is split, ill, and unreal. As Carl Jung pointed out, the solution is for the person to individuate, or unify the discordant aspects of the ego, and then the internal civil war will cease.

Gautama Buddha said that hatred and aggression arise wherever there is egoistical attachment. Mankind will never give up exploitation, murder, and war until humans rise to the transpersonal level, substituting Self for self. Sex and violence are the two popular topics on television, because the modern ego is dissociated. There is a separation of the mind from the body, and both from the soul. "Egoism and sex, which are normally developed and fulfilled within the life of the whole, are exposed as isolated tendencies seeking exhaustion in death, the substitute sacrifice," says L.L. Whyte.

Since we all fear death, we try to avoid it. This death fear projected outwardly produces murder and war. Living in the part instead of the whole, the misguided individual thinks that by robbing others of their lives, he can increase his own life span. Divisive religion breeds on this illusion that to harm or kill others somehow affirms one's own life force.

Warfare builds internal unity as it produces external division. Killing the enemy unites countrymen who might have been alienated from one another. But as the smaller fellowship is enhanced, the larger fellowship is destroyed, and the seeds of the next war are sown. As one sees one's dead adversary, one feels temporarily immortal. The conqueror feels godlike—he has survived the battle. War is a futile attempt to become God by the wrong means.

The psychiatrist Fritz Kunkel says that "characteristic of egocentricity is always the inexorableness of its demands. The ego acts like a monarch who tolerates no contradictions. Egocentricity without self-deception is not possible. Complete insight and egocentricity cannot exist side by side. The more egocentric a person is, the more cunningly does he arrange his self-deceit."[44]

The playwright Eugene Ionesco said that "as long as we are not assured of immortality, we shall go on hating each other in spite of our need for mutual love." The aim of all mystics, as well as of all those who practice unitive religion, is to deliver men and women from their battles by ridding them of artificially imposed boundaries. In Wilber's summary, "When the self sense dies, all that dissolves is not a real entity but a simple boundary, a boundary that was never real. To move from self-consciousness to super-consciousness is to make death obsolete."[45]

References

[1] Leo Marx, *New York Times Book Review*, 23 August 1987, p. 10. Tawney (1880-1962) was an English economic historian. Weber (1864-1920) was a German sociologist.

[2] Paul Davies, *God and the New Physics* (Simon & Schuster, 1983), p. 5. Davies is Professor of Theoretical Physics at the University of Newcastle-upon-Tyne.

[3] Radhakrishnan, p. 290.

[4] Elie Wiesel, *New York Times Book Review*, 17 January 1988, p. 11.

[5] *Encyclopedia Britannica*, 1971, vol. 2, p. 85.

[6] Roth, p. 407.

[7] *Arizona Republic*, 1 November 1987, p. 39.

[8] *New York Times Magazine*, 2 August 1987, p. 59.

[9] Lloyd L. Brown, *New York Times*, 10 April 1988, 4:30.

[10] David J. Sadd, ibid., 3 January 1988, 4:14. Sadd is Executive Director, National Association of Arab Americans.

[11] Harry Siegman, ibid., 10 April 1988, 4:30.

[12] Albert Vorspan, *New York Times Magazine*, 5 May 1988, pp. 40, 41, 51.

[13] Martin Marty, *The Pro and Con Book of Religious America* (Word Books, 1975) CON, p. 93.

[14] Parrinder, *Religion in Africa*, p. 131.

[15] R. Laurence Moore, *Religious Outsiders and the Making of Americans* (Oxford University Press, 1986), pp. 32, 33, 36, 37.

[16] Leonard Arrington & Davis Bitton, quoted in Moore, p. 43.

[17] Moore, pp. 156-57.

[18] Smart, p. 153.

[19] Jaroslav Jan Pelikan, *Encyclopedia Britannica*, 1971, vol. 8, pp. 807, 809. Pelikan was Professor of Church History at Yale University.

[20] Norman Parry, *St. Anthony Messenger* (September 1988) 96:56. Perry was editor of *St. Anthony Messenger*.

[21] Milton Viorst, *The New Yorker* (3 October 1988) 64:56.

[22] Ed Lion, *Arizona Republic*, 13 September 1987, p. 1.

[23] Edward Norman, *Christianity and the World Order* (Oxford University Press, 1979), p. 6.
[24] Ernest Gellner, in Nikki R. Keddie, ed., *Scholars, Saints, and Sufis* (University of California Press, 1972), pp. 319-20.
[25] W.C. Smith, *Islam in Modern History*, p. 269.
[26] Aziz Ahmad, in Keddie, p. 263.
[27] W.C. Smith, *Islam in Modern History*, pp. 232, 233, 235.
[28] Ibid., p. 96.
[29] Ihsan A. Hijazi, *New York Times*, 22 May 1988, p. 8.
[30] Dietl, pp. 33-34.
[31] Ibid., pp. 56-57.
[32] Ibid., p. 61.
[33] *The Economist* (London), reprinted in *World Press Review* (April 1988) 35:28.
[34] Youssef M. Ibrahim, *New York Times,* 24 July 1988, 4:1-2.
[35] John Kifner, ibid., 18 September 1988, p. 1.
[36] Dietl, p. 322.
[37] Mary Anne Weaver, *The New Yorker* (21 March 1988) 64:46.
[38] Steven R. Weisman, *New York Times Magazine*, 13 December 1987, pp. 34, 37.
[39] Donald P. Whitaker, ed., *Area Handbook for the People's Republic of China* (American University, 1972), p. 147.
[40] N.S. Brannen, in Crim, p. 697.
[41] John Tulloch, *Chekhov: A Structuralist Study* (Macmillan, 1980), p. 93.
[42] Eliade, *The Sacred and the Profane,* p. 203.
[43] Ken Wilber, *No Boundary* (Shambhala, 1981), pp. 6, 10, 13, 25, 46, 53, 74.
[44] Quoted in Dorothy P. Phillips et al., eds., *The Choice is Always Ours* (Re-Quest Books, 1982), p. 184.
[45] Wilber, *Up From Eden,* pp. 158, 159, 209, 283, 334, 337.

Chapter 11

World Law and Order

As if with prophetic vision, William James wrote in 1910 in *The Moral Equivalent of War:* "When whole nations are the armies, and the science of destruction vies in intellectual refinement with the sciences of production, I see that war becomes absurd and impossible from its own monstrosity." Refinements in the science of destruction since 1910 have more than justified the stand of James.

For the first time in history it has become necessary for us to develop a survival perspective. We have thus entered into the initial stages of world community.

A community is a group of persons having common problems. The persons need not agree on solutions to the problems—indeed, they characteristically disagree. Certain inescapable problems now confront the entire human race, and the smallest political unit which can address itself to these problems is the whole world. Most definitions of community mention geographical or spatial limitations. Modern technology has succeeded in eradicating these limitations. Global problems require global solutions. Only the world community can bear the responsibility for dealing with matters that refuse to be confined within national boundaries.

Saul Mendlovitz, Director of the World Order Models Project, believes that three revolutionary movements have propelled us toward world community: the revolutionary idea of equality; the scientific revolution; and the radical movement towards global economic interdependency. He further lists five specific global problems that have accelerated this trend: war, poverty, social injustice, ecology, and alienation, or the identity crisis.

The present world system no longer works, says Richard Falk. Falk states that "the intensification of conflict, the deepening awareness of deprivation, the proliferating technology of modern warfare, the crowding of the planet, the prospects of resource scarcity, and the alarming increase in global pollution present a cumulative profile of systematic decay."[1]

All citizens of planet earth agree that we must avoid nuclear war, and that we cannot live in a badly contaminated atmosphere. Consensus on problems reinforces community.

Nations, it is said, act upon self-interest. What greater self-interest can there be than survival? Nations have two main goals: perpetuate themselves, and nurture their citizens. Since the nuclear age threatens to destroy both goals, important changes must be made.

The modern state is not only incapable of protecting its citizens, says Norman Cousins, but worse still, by violating its citizens' rights it becomes worse than if it did not exist. The natural rights of man come ahead of the rights of the state, which exist only to reinforce those natural rights. Cousins lists the natural rights as the right to individual sanctity, the right to creative growth, the right to make life purposeful, and the right to keep our species from being debased and deformed.

Weapons Create Community

Weapons technology helps create world community. Our ability to manufacture power outruns our ability to control it. In the 1970s, each day five new nuclear weapons were added to the horrid stockpile of destruction.

Travel time for an intercontinental ballistic missile from Russia to America is less than ten minutes. In ten minutes General Washington's horse would have carried him about two miles.

In place of the atomic bomb which killed over 100,000 people at Hiroshima, we now have thousands of 20-megaton hydrogen bombs, each of which can kill a thousand times the number of people killed at Hiroshima. General John B. Medaris says that there is enough destructive nuclear power stockpiled in America to be the equivalent of 20,000 pounds of TNT for every human being on earth.

Representative Johnson of Colorado reported that there is enough lethal nerve gas stored in a depot in his state to kill all men, women, and children in the world. The ultimate weapon, the cobalt bomb, is now theoretically possible. If it is ever exploded, the first one will kill all living breathing things on planet earth.

Since the only defense is a stronger offense, striking power is now measured in overkill capacity. Do Americans feel secure to know that they can kill every Russian twenty times over? Even in an affluent society this must represent some type of wasteful surplus.

The pursuit of power means the pursuit of supreme power—coming out second is worthless. But only one nation can have superior power, and this can never be supreme power. Like the endless chore of Sisyphus, the mad pursuit continues towards the death embrace. By definition, national security (greater weapons) means international insecurity (inferior weapons). The more secure any nation becomes, the more insecure the rest of the world must be. General Douglas MacArthur said that in the next war there would be only losers. John Foster Dulles said that if there were another war, almost certainly totalitarianism would result all over the world. We are preparing for a war that we cannot win, and that will cost us our democracy even if we could win.

Control of fission by-products constitutes a global problem. Where can radioactive wastes be buried so as not to contaminate mankind? The atmosphere of our planet is a shifting one—who owns it? What nation has the moral right to contaminate the property of all mankind, present and future? There is, says Cousins, no way to wash the sky.

Hudson Hoagland, executive director of the Worcester Foundation for Experimental Biology, points out how nuclear war would do irreparable damage to all future generations. Our genetic material is a chemical code structured in molecules of DNA (deoxyribonucleic acid) located in the nuclei of our sperm and egg cells. All of the DNA in all of the germ cells in all of the world's people added together equals a small fraction of an ounce. There is one ten-trillionth of an ounce in a fertilized human egg. Nuclear war, says Hoagland, would cause mutations in our germ plasm; over 99% of all mutations are harmful, and all are inherited. It has taken us over two billion years to produce this precious store of coded material. We dare not damage it.

The Bishops' Letter

In the shadow of the atomic bomb, said Einstein, we must recognize that all men are brothers. If we accept this truth, we shall go on to ever higher achievements. If the angry passions of a nationalistic world engulf us further, we are doomed.

General MacArthur, in his book *Revitalizing a Nation,* wrote: "You cannot control war; you can only abolish it. Those who shrug this off as idealistic are the real enemies of peace—the real warmongers. Those who lack the enterprise, vision, and courage to try a new approach when no others have succeeded, fail completely the most simple test of leadership. Let us regain some of the courage and faith of the architects who chartered the course to our real greatness."

A Russian novelist, Daniel Granin, in 1967 wrote that only a planet-wide mobilization of brains and resources could deal satisfactorily with such problems as food and water supplies, weather control, radio astronomy, bacteria control, and other worldwide concerns. "The earth is gradually coming to be regarded as a unified organism," he said. "It is precisely the anxieties, disasters, and concerns for the future that further the unification of humanity."[2]

In 1983 the Roman Catholic bishops in the U.S. composed a policy statement on nuclear arms. Nuclear war is never justifiable, they said, but a policy of nuclear deterrence is permissible—only, however, as a step towards progressive disarmament. The only justification for any type of warfare, the bishops advised, was if the cause were just, if competent authority made the decision, and the resort to arms were a last resort. There can be no destruction of entire cities; hostilities must be against unjust aggressors and not against innocent civilians; and the damages and costs must be proportionate to the good to be achieved.

Longtime American diplomat George Kennan applauded the bishops' stand, particularly their statement that military values must never be treated as absolutes but are relative to the fundamental need of civilization for survival, observing "those elementary moral scruples beyond which horror becomes unlimited and hope impossible."

Kennan then listed his own recommendations, which included: halt in the arms race; deep bilateral military cuts; a comprehensive test ban treaty; removal of short-range nuclear weapons; and a reduction in conventional weapons. He quoted with approval the statement by Pope John Paul II that the scale of modern warfare, whether nuclear or not, makes it unacceptable as a means of settling differences between nations.

Professor William McNeill of the University of Chicago in his book *The Pursuit of Power* states that the only solution to the arms race is a "global sovereignty willing and able to enforce a monopoly of atomic weaponry," a universal society which would control population growth and put an end to the reckless rivalries that have characterized the past thousand years of human history.

A Smallish Globe

What other factors have created world community? I asked a student from Guam how long it took him to travel 6000 miles to the U.S. mainland. He replied, "I left Guam Thursday afternoon and arrived in San Francisco Thursday morning." Crossing the International Date Line by jet plane made a travesty of our time system. Dr. John Furbay of Trans-World Airlines describes his difficulty getting lunch. He has breakfast in New York, arrives in Chicago in time for breakfast, and deplanes in Los Angeles at breakfast time. A trans-Atlantic flight accomplishes the Pilgrims' seven-week journey in six hours. The incubation period of germs takes longer than a jet flight from India to America. Enlightened self-interest now requires that we help others as a way of helping ourselves. World citizenship means that we will not only be good neighbors, but we will also be true to our self-interest.

Marshall McLuhan's global village is a reality. "We are joined," says Marilyn Ferguson, "by satellite, supersonic travel, four thousand international meetings each year, tens of thousands of multinational companies, international organizations and newsletters and Journals, even an emergent pan-culture of music, movies, art, humor."[3]

Inis Claude of the University of Michigan sees the concept of one world as "a pressing reality, an actual condition of mankind," produced by recent change which has tied all the peoples of the world together in an unprecedented intimacy of contact, interdependence of welfare, and mutuality of vulnerability. Citing over a hundred public international organizations and many more private ones, he concludes that the world is engaged in the process of organizing.

Even grammar has been found to be a common denominator for mankind. Since language is rooted in non-verbal emotional experiences which can be a common ground for all humans, Noam Chomsky found commonalities in the grammar of all known languages. "Language," Erich Jantsch concludes, "apparently has to do with the structure of a genetically anchored neural apparatus."

Teilhard de Chardin found this planet a smallish globe. "We have come to constitute," he said, "an almost solid mass of hominized substance," with "human elements infiltrated more and more into each other, their minds mutually stimulated by proximity. Each individual finds himself henceforth simultaneously present in every corner of the earth."

We must broaden our scope of identity, Teilhard concluded. "We seek in vain to settle international disputes by adjustments of frontiers. As things are going now it will not be long before we run full tilt into one another. Something will explode if we persist in trying to squeeze into our old tumbledown huts the material and spiritual forces that are henceforward on the scale of a world."[4]

One Ecosphere

Philip Jessup, who has served as a Judge on the UN International Court of Justice, points to signs of the growing world community:

1. The International Postal Union oversees world mail delivery.
2. International quarantine regulations control disease.
3. Weather satellites and the International Iceberg Patrol exchange weather news among the nations.
4. Airplane flight patterns are controlled internationally.
5. Radio and TV wave-length frequencies are allocated amicably.

Ecological factors require that we have machinery for adjudicating conflicts involving the atmosphere, the oceans, and scarce resources. Weather modification can be, intentionally or not, a hazard to neighboring countries. We also need a global response to certain natural disasters such as volcanoes, tidal waves, hurricanes, and great floods.

No country is economically self-sufficient. The U.S., for example, needs to import bauxite from the Guianas, chromium from Africa, Asia, and Polynesia, graphite from Sri Lanka and Madagascar, manganese from Africa and Brazil, and tin from the Straits Settlement. Although the U.S. consumes 50% of the world's tungsten, all of North America produces only 14% of the world's supply.

The rise in income attributable to foreign investment, mainly in multinational corporations, is now the foremost generator of U.S. income. The larger multinationals are on a par with all but a few of the largest nations. The sales of General Motors, for example, exceed the gross national product of such countries as Argentina, Belgium or Switzerland.

Falk states that 71 of the largest American industries employ about one-third of their payroll overseas. He finds some good coming from the multinational corporations:[5]

1. They transfer technological and managerial know-how to lesser developed areas.
2. They tend to raise wage levels in underdeveloped countries.
3. They are a force for peace and order in the world community.
4. They tend to raise the social and economic life of the people in their area.

World Law

The Romans were great lawgivers. One of the secrets of their long reign in the Mediterranean was their ability to codify and enforce legal codes for both their citizens and the conquered.

In the days of Justinian it was accepted that all nations are governed partly by their own laws and partly by laws common to all mankind. Dante, writing *Of Monarchy,* argues for world government in order to enforce world peace. Since nations in contention cannot judge themselves, Dante says, a broader final authority is needed to avert war.

In *Six Books of the Commonwealth* in 1576, the French thinker Jean Bodin supported the need for absolute power in the sovereign, except that he must respect God's law, the law of nature, and the law of nations.

Restive under the government of Catholic Spain, the Protestant Netherlands found several legal spokesmen. Ulrlch Huber said that conflicts in laws between two nations should be resolved by adherence to the law in the nation where the transaction occurred. Hugo Grotius felt that rather than attempting to codify a body of international law, nations should evolve a legal system based upon the principles of the common law.

John Locke held that civil government originated as a contract between the people and their rulers, government being necessary to adjudicate differences among members of society. Civil society, he said, excludes war by providing legislatures as umpires to decide cases in question.

Immanuel Kant called for a "universal union of states analogous to that by which a nation becomes a state. It is only thus that a real state of peace could be established." Kant depicts the nations of the world, "after many devastations, overthrows, and even complete internal exhaustion of their powers," as being "driven forward to the goal which Reason might well have impressed upon them, even without so much sad experience. This is the advance of the lawless state of savages and the entering into a federation of nations. However visionary this idea may appear to be, it is nevertheless the inevitable issue of the necessity in which men involve one another."[6]

Many scholars find common agreement on the general principles of world law. Bin Cheng, in his *General Principles of Law as Applied by International Courts and Tribunals,* finds that the Permanent Court of International Justice, the International Court of Justice, and international arbitral tribunals have frequently applied such principles as an integral part of international law. "The general principles of law of civilized nations," says Kenneth Carlston, "provide the normative standard and source of rules to which state conduct must adhere if it is to possess validity."[7]

In his book *The Common Law of Mankind* Wilfred Jenks finds a surprising consensus among the major legal systems of the world—Civil Law, Common Law, African, Chinese, Hindu, Islamic, Japanese, Jewish, and Russian—on the basic legal principles relevant to world peace. These principles include the concept that the sovereign is under the law, disputes must be adjudicated by independent parties, self-defense is subject to certain defined limitations, and harm to others without justification is a legal wrong.

Charles Rhyne, former president of the American Bar Association, organized and then headed the World Peace Through Law Center. An international voluntary group of lawyers, it organizes workshops on how to resolve disputes amicably. It has worked in such areas as anti-hijacking, ecology, international aviation, and ocean law.

"The movement for peace through international law is on the march," Rhyne states. "The minds, the support, the faith, the enthusiasm, the confidence of mankind must be marshalled behind the law as the road to peace. The peoples of the world can do what is necessary to translate world order with justice into reality in our day."[8]

Adjudicating International Disputes

That great apostle of peace, Pope John XXIII, issued an encyclical on world peace, *Pacem in Terris,* which stated that relations between nations must be governed by the following factors:

Truth: Racism and ethnocentrism must go. Communication media must help people know other people better.
Justice: Disputes must be settled through neutral arbitration. Minorities and the poor must be given equitable treatment. Disarmament will not only reduce war potential but save money for humane expenditures.
Freedom: No country has the right to oppress another country or to meddle in its internal affairs.
Love: By loving others, one loves God, and even truly loves oneself.

Pope John XXIII declared that world community is now a technological and an historical fact. Changes should be made in a non-violent manner, he warned. He believed that the UN Universal Declaration of Human Rights was a good beginning toward stating safeguards to human dignity.

In his book *No More War* Nobel Prize winner Linus Pauling calls for a World Peace Research Organization to make a careful study of how past wars occurred, how they might have been avoided, and how certain perilous conditions were changed from warlike to peaceful through artful handling.

Kenneth Carlston suggests a principle for judging international disputes. When competing rules are presented by the disputants, he says, "that rule should be preferred which best promotes the viability of the international system."[9] This would provide an objective criterion so that fair-minded judges might rule against their own nations, just as an impartial official in an athletic contest must do. Muhammed Zafrullah Khan, a judge of the UN International Court of justice, says that the Koran (iv, 66) requires that a Moslem must accept the outcome of a judicial resolution of a dispute.

To assume that national self-determination automatically leads towards peace is to ignore history. As long as Latin-American countries were provinces of the Spanish colonial empire, they enjoyed relative peace. As soon as they gained their independence from Spain, they showed their national autonomy by declaring war on one another. A somewhat similar trend is apparent among the newly formed nations of Africa. The old *Pax Romana* was a reality because no one dared challenge the power of Rome.

In their book *Transnational Relations and World Politics,* Robert Keohane and Joseph Nye drew up a chart of 36 possible relationships among international bodies, including governments. Of these, only four were government-to-government relations. Examples of the other relationships were: governmental subunits reacting to international organizations; banks reacting to multinational corporations; and churches reacting to professional societies. Richard Falk cites the growth in specialized international institutions from 1 in 1815 to 192 in 1960. Very likely this figure would be over 600 in 2000.

Describing the American Constitutional Convention, Carl Van Doren called his book *The Great Rehearsal,* because he felt that the great American experiment in building a federal government over sovereign states would be a prelude for world organization later. In his book *Confronting War* Ronald J. Glossop showed the advantages of the American model:

1. Only one internal war in 200 years is a much better record than if there had been fifty separate war-making bodies.

2. The federal government provided for the peaceful westward expansion and the creation of new states.
3. Interstate disputes are settled by law, not by force.
4. Interstate tariffs, taxes, and other trade barriers do not exist.
5. Most state military expenditures are eliminated.

In addition, the American federation provides for some local autonomy and some variety in lifestyles and ethnic observances.

Americans who feel that there will be a loss of sovereignty under a limited world federation are mistaken. Right now the U.S.A. has no sovereignty to prevent a nuclear war, nor to control international terrorism, nor to curtail further radioactive contamination of the biosphere. We live in a condition of international anarchy. What is needed is a world of law and order. Under a limited international federation, we would gain some sovereignty, in areas of anarchy that are now a threat to world survival.

The chief lesson learned by the U.S.A. during the life of the League of Nations is that since this nation is going to be involved in wars even when it abstains from taking part in organizations designed to keep the peace, it had better join such organizations, first, to try to avoid war, and second, to try to align allies and help set the time and conditions if war should come. Ever since the League experience, effective isolation has been dead in America.

Intelligent conservatism, however, can play a valuable role in helping define values and spheres of authority as the concept of world community matures. Effective world citizenship must not break down desirable aspects of local and national citizenship. Robert Nisbet in *The Quest for Community* showed that such basic institutions as the family and the church have been somewhat disrupted by centralizing forces of the state power, often resulting in disintegration of values, social cohesion, and ethical certainty from the past. The good member of the world community begins by being an effective citizen in his other community memberships.

There is disorder in the international community. Whenever a community experiences disorder, law and order must be restored. This is a prime function of government. Government, however, is but an implement of law, and law, to endure, must be based upon principles of Justice. We need a new set of Founding

Fathers, with something like the wisdom and humanity of the original Americans, to help codify and declare what these principles of justice should be. These Founding Fathers must come from the world's universities.

Preserving Local Autonomy

Most people justly oppose the concept of a world state, fraught as it is with the potential for totalitarian controls of the worst sort. We are so opposed to this specter that we even risk the danger of nuclear terrorism that could culminate in a holocaust. Localisms must be preserved, except those that lead to international hatred, misunderstanding, and possible war.

William Hocking points out that, once the danger of nuclear conflict can be eliminated, localisms must flourish, for they save us from monotony and create precious solitude for fine art and creative thought. Self-reliant local communities are the goal of the future, but they must be insulated from any risk of outside oppression. Diversity within an embracing unity describes the world of the future.

Teilhard explains how unity produces diversity: "In any domain, whether it be the cells of a body, the members of a society, or the elements of a spiritual synthesis, union differentiates. In every organized whole, the parts perfect themselves and fulfill themselves. The only fashion in which we could correctly express the final state of a world undergoing psychical concentration would be as a system whose unity coincides with a paroxysm of harmonized complexity."[10]

World faiths also need to preserve localisms, Hocking reminds us: "In the civilization now coming, there is no more place for 'national religions' than for chosen people. Religions will always have two functions in reference to this national being: that of transcending all national limits, and of maintaining with loving piety the permanent values of domesticity in the interior groupings of mankind. A world civilization must be an organism, not an endless homogeneity. No more desolating prospect could confront mankind than that of undifferentiated identity. The quest for a world faith must retain, in its care for the whole, a continuing solicitude for its diverse members." We need "reverence for reverence, with the general insight that no soul through defects in the particulars of its faith stands apart from the mercy of God."[11]

Mankind's Political Staircase

WORLD STATE
WORLD GOVERNMENT
WORLD FEDERATION
LIMITED WORLD FEDERATION
COLLECTIVE SECURITY PACTS
UNITED NATIONS
LEAGUE OF NATIONS
BALANCE OF POWER
ISOLATIONISM
ANARCHY

Virtually no one would choose either end of this political staircase as a desirable way out of our nuclear dilemma. Anarchy, or no government, opens mankind to terrorism and the rule that might is right. A world state is over-government. Government is at least an inconvenience and at worst a threat to liberties. Nations should relinquish only that sovereignty to a limited world federation which they either have no power to enforce or may not be trusted to wield fairly.

Isolationism is untenable in the modern world for economic, political, and military reasons. Under the balance of power concept, nations constantly regroup, ganging up to keep a common enemy weak.

The League of Nations represented limited international cooperation, and the United Nations represents more extensive international cooperation. Despite great humanitarian gains being achieved by a number of UN subsidiary agencies, it is obvious that the UN has often failed to keep the peace among its warring members.

Collective security pacts constitute the present level of international organization to prevent war. The Monroe Doctrine, the Organization of American States, the North Atlantic Treaty Organization, and the former Warsaw Pact Alliance all represent the collective security apparatus that has helped prevent World War III from occurring.

Living on the brink of nuclear devastation, as we did during the Cuban missile crisis of 1962, takes a tremendous psychological toll out of the whole world, since nuclear radiation cannot be controlled. Now we must move up the next step of the staircase, into a limited world federation of sovereign nations which will unite to outlaw war and radioactive experimentation in the atmosphere. At each step up the ladder, it is prudent to err on the side of caution and not relinquish power and authority that needs to be retained locally.

By now, however, no sovereign nation has the power to protect its own citizens from cataclysmic destruction, nor the power to prevent a nuclear war. Thus no nation surrenders any of its sovereignty in abjuring war, for this is something beyond its present control. Moreover, the right to wage an aggressive war is something no nation should ever have, and in the past this so-called right was assumed, because of the absence of a world community. Now all good members of that community must see to it that law and order reigns in that community. To do this, we have to move into a limited world federation of sovereign nations, with the federation's powers being restricted to those necessary to ensure human survival.

If the social, economic, and political factors leading to war are seen to reside partly in the decisions of nations and even local communities, it may be necessary for the world to move into a more inclusive federation in future years.

It is difficult to foresee a time when the negative factors associated with world government would overpower the desirable factors, such as keeping the peace, but such a time may come. It seems to be in mankind's best interest to retard any super-governmental bureaucracies as long as possible. Our watchword should always be, "Let's make the current system work." Only as it clearly shows itself incapable of getting the job of survival done should we change it.

There is a way to resolve our dilemma of conflicting loyalties to the various groups of which we are members. The good citizen of the world community starts off by being a good citizen of his local community. He respects law and order at each level of his memberships. When he is caught up in a conflict of "law and order," he must fall back upon an ethos, a universal principle of right and wrong that will enable him to make choices that he can live with, choices that he will later be proud of having made. It is therefore important that he use an ethos that is not self-abasing (and is thus fair to himself), that embraces brotherly love (and thereby is fair to others), and is grounded in God (and thus is fair to his Creator).

Erikson's Synthesis of Self and Society

One such possible ethos is contained in Erik Erikson's concept of generative man, that is, a person who not only creates but sustains and nourishes through love. A widely read psychologist, Erikson has developed human relations training programs that have been effective in social work, psychiatry, nursing education, industrial relations, and secular and religious education and counseling.

"In his moral vision," says Don Browning, "there unfolds an arresting synthesis of a grand variety of present-day cultural fragments—evolutionary theory, religion (the cross, the Nativity, ahimsa), psychoanalysis, ethology, ecology, and nonviolence—all brought together to suggest a new world-image which would give controlled direction to an emerging technological world community."

Browning feels that Erikson's generative man achieves a oneness of self and society. Browning summarizes this unity: "Man's inmost private satisfaction and the outermost public relevance are found in one reality: the individual confirmation that rebound. to him from the affirmation of that which he has generated."

A generative person wishes to affirm not only his personal achievements and concerns but also those of his fellow humans. A person cannot be totally happy merely with self-achievement. Browning says that "generativity is also the ground for man's higher attempts to create a total environment ecologically supportive of the general health not only of family and tribe but of the entire human species."[12] Moreover, man quickly discovers that there is no way he can realize personal achievement without involving himself deeply in society's problems and achievements. Thus are his self and society inextricably intertwined.

The problem now is not to create world community—that community already exists. The problem is to recognize it, perfect it, and reinforce it. In a very real sense it is the community membership most vital to humans as they struggle to survive in the nuclear age.

References

1. Richard A. Falk, *A Study of Future Worlds* (Free Press, 1975), p. 281.
2. *New York Times*, 7 May 1967, p. 17.
3. Marilyn Ferguson, *The Aquarian Conspiracy* (Tarcher, 1980), p. 409.
4. Pierre Teilhard de Chardin, *The Phenomenon of Man*, 2nd ed. (Harper & Row, 1965), pp. 240, 253.
5. Falk, pp. 387, 396.
6. Mortimer J. Adler, ed. *The Great Ideas,* vol. 2 (Encyclopedia Britannica, 1952), p. 1018.
7. Kenneth S. Carlston, *Law and Organization in World Society* (University of Illinois Press, 1962), pp. 217, 219.
8. *The Rotarian,* April 1971, p. 18.
9. Carlston, pp. 154-55.
10. Teilhard, p. 262.
11. William E. Hocking, *The Coming World Civilization* (Harper, 1956), pp. 153-54.
12. Don S. Browning, *Generative Man: Psychoanalytic Perspectives* (Westminster, 1973), pp. 146, 149.

Chapter 12

Bill of Spiritual Rights

The Bill of Rights contained in the U.S. Constitution has been extended by legislation and judicial interpretation to cover social and economic rights, as well as political ones. The time has now come for the formulation of a Bill of Spiritual Rights.

The Bill of Spiritual Rights is founded on the doctrine of human dignity, the belief that every human being has a unique and sacred importance. Human dignity is based ultimately on the fact that all persons are God's children. He created each one of us out of His love, and thus each of us is important in His sight. This being so, each of us should be important in every other person's sight.

Recognition of our basic importance to God should keep down human brutality, terrorism, and war. Focusing on our superhuman origin can keep down subhuman behavior toward our fellow man.

Epictetus, the Greek slave turned philosopher, said, "Suppose Caesar were to adopt you, there would be no bearing your haughty looks. Will you not be elated on knowing yourself to be the son of God Himself?"[1]

"The world process reaches its consummation," says Sarvepalli Radhakrishnan, "when every man knows himself to be the immortal spirit, the son of God. The individual works in the cosmic process no longer as an obscure and limited ego, but as a center of the divine consciousness, transforming into harmony all individual manifestations."[2]

In the New Testament, Paul constantly reminds us of our regal inheritance: "Because you are sons, God has sent the Spirit of His Son into your hearts" (Galatians 4:6). "For as many as are led by the Spirit of God," said Paul, "they are the sons of God. And if children, then heirs—heirs of God, and joint-heirs with Christ" (Romans 8:14, 17).

Basing his view on the opening verses of John's gospel, Meister Eckhart proclaimed that "the seed of God is in us. Pear seeds grow into pear trees; nut seeds into nut trees; and God-seed into God!"[3]

Christianity establishes a new God-man relationship, said J.B. Phillips, since God Himself became a human being, exalting our kind forevermore. Jesus declared categorically that reconciliation with God is impossible apart from reconciliation with humankind.

Moreover, in his only parable about the final Judgment, Jesus used no test of creed or ritual but rather the way in which a person has treated his fellow humans. Because God has become man, all persons have a share in divinity. It is thus clearly a serious offense to injure or exploit other persons, because God has done man the incomprehensible honor of identifying Himself with our species. In other words, when an Irishman injures or kills another Irishman, he is really harming God Himself!

After World War II a group of Japanese leaders, studying American democracy, found it to be built upon the religious concept of human dignity under God. Edmund Sinnott, former Dean of Yale Graduate School, said that there can be no brotherhood of mankind apart from the Fatherhood of God. Situation ethics, ungrounded in the one Absolute, God, degenerates into mere convenience and rationalization.

The fact that God's Holy Spirit abides in humans leads to two important conclusions: we truly have an enhanced status, and we are equals in God's sight. Paul writes that "the love of God is shed abroad in our hearts by the Holy Spirit which is given unto us" (Romans 5:5). In the Bhagavad Gita we are told that the soul, enlightened by yoga, sees himself in all beings, and all beings in himself; all are equal in his sight.

The psychologist O. Hobart Mowrer says that modern therapy is confirming ancient religion. Instead of most mental breakdown coming from repressed sex and hostility, he says, it "comes rather from an outraged conscience and violated sense of human decency and responsibility. This radically revised perception of mental illness suggests an affinity with both classical and contemporary conceptions of the Holy Spirit, and points the way to a new synthesis of religion and contemporary psychological and social science."[4]

The Godlike in Man

Our divine origin demands that we live up to our high potential. In the *Theaetetus* Plato says that only by becoming Godlike can we know God. "Boldly," said Epictetus, "make a desperate push, man, for prosperity, for freedom, for magnanimity. Expel grief, fear, desire, envy, malevolence from your mind. But these can be expelled only by looking to God as your pattern."[5]

If you hate your neighbor, you hate God, declares the Bhagavad Gita. Given over to self-conceit, hunger for power, anger, and carnal lust, malevolent people hate God in the bodies of themselves and other persons. True religion, says Sri Aurobindo, regards every human society from the same standpoint, as sub-souls of a complex manifestation of the same Spirit, the Divine Reality.

Who are those who are like God? Eckhart answers that they are those who hold to an evenness of justice, who do not consider themselves to be superior to their neighbors, and who are as much concerned about their neighbor's welfare as they are for their own.

Human Dignity

The Tibetan Buddhist Gampopa said that "in whatever we do we are duty bound to be aware of being human beings, and our task must not be allowed to glide into a betrayal of human dignity but must be expressive of this dignity in benevolence and compassion."[6]

Harming others harms ourselves. John A. Sanford, an Episcopal priest who is a Jungian analyst, says that we cannot try to find happiness at someone else's expense without damaging our souls in the process. To the extent that I deprecate my neighbor or my enemy, to that extent I deprecate myself.

But the spiritually committed person can significantly reduce the amount of suffering in the world. A Schweitzer, a Mother Teresa, a Dr. Tom Dooley, will show us the upward limits of human excellence. The Hindu mystic Vivekananda said, "I worship and serve God in the form of the poor, the oppressed, the sick, and the ignorant."

The Nazi holocaust is perhaps history's best example of what happens when human dignity is not prized. If humans are not

God's creatures, then God's laws need not be observed with regard to them. Personal power and glory, national might and greed, become ruling factors in the absence of universal respect for the sacredness of human personality.

The Golden Rule reminds us that none of us like to be treated with less than human respect and dignity. It is unreasonable to expect dignified treatment unless we administer it to others.

Human Solidarity

A healthy-minded person cannot feel evil thoughts towards other people very long. Walt Whitman, for example, liked everyone he ever met, including those who attacked him. "He never spoke deprecatingly," said R.M. Bucke, "of any nationality or class of men, or against any occupations. He never spoke in anger; he never exhibited fear."[7]

Mankind, said Teilhard, is not the center of the universe, as we once thought, but rather something much more wonderful—the arrow pointing the way to the final unification of the living world. Encouraging signs all over the globe indicate a growing realization of the oneness of humanity and the sacredness of human life.

In 1972 a group of young people in Ommen, Holland, drew up this resolution: "The Group of Ommen, recognizing the oneness of the world and the interdependence of humankind, the need of a systematic analysis of the world's problems, the need to take account of long-term considerations, aware of the present conflict of humankind itself against itself and against nature; resolves to promotes values, policies, and actions at all levels to establish a just and equitable world society consistent with the dignity of the human person and the finite resources of earth."[8]

The human yearning for the ultimate is what Reinhold Niebuhr called the religious dimension of life. This yearning, he warned, can be creative or destructive. "It is creative," he said, "when an ultimate norm or value is set in judgment over historically relative achievements of man's existence. It is destructive and a source of evil if a simple identification is made between the ultimate norm and the norms and values which we cherish."[9] To insist that our local preference should be binding on all mankind is to play God, and no good comes from that.

The coming world order may not need America's brand of democracy but it does need the fundamental liberty and dignity of the person which American society has realized when unitive religion is employed as the basis of its value system. Freed from its divisive tendencies, the Judeo-Christian heritage can sponsor human dignity, see persons as ends rather than means, stress reason and brotherly love, and declare the supremacy of the spiritual over the material.

Augustine said that God Himself shows humility, and that man must copy the divine model: "Because it is pride that is the cause of all our sickness which the Son of God came to heal, He descended and was made humble. God teaches humility. Pride indeed does its own will; humility does the will of God."[10]

At bottom, our morality is based upon religion. Our constant prayer should be: "Help me, O God, to be utterly honest with You. For, once having been honest with You, I cannot then be false to any person created by You."

Purified Self-Love

Mystics in every religion teach us one overwhelming message: when we have eliminated the selfishness from our psyche, we are ready for the Holy Spirit to take over our lives. This purified self-love leads us to the realization of our true Self.

Loving our neighbor as ourself means a proper amount of self-respect. In the *Ethics* Aristotle advises us to choose magnanimity, the golden mean between self-glorification and self-deprecation. We can underrate ourselves as well as overrate ourselves, and the former is worse, Aristotle warns, because it leads to a person's shunning his responsibilities.

Excessive remorse can be harmful. Bishop Fénelon pointed out that "faults will turn to good, provided we use them to our own humiliation, without slackening in the effort to correct ourselves. Discouragement serves no possible purpose; it is simply the despair of wounded self-love."[11]

Nevertheless, we quite properly feel remorse over our sins. No doubt American remorse over the bombing of Hiroshima and Nagasaki is of far greater importance than the perfection of the A-bomb itself Also, America's willingness to lose its first war in history rather than employ nuclear weapons in Vietnam shows not only how great a nation can behave under extreme stress but also that the preservation of common humanity is now of greater importance than protecting national pride. There could hardly be a better demonstration of the spiritual progress being made in the modern world.

Preamble to a Bill of Spiritual Rights

Mankind cannot long survive in a world full of nuclear weapons and growing international ill will. World order is a prerequisite to survival. Underlying world order must be world law. Supporting world law there needs to be a consensus of public opinion regarding values and how to define and maintain them. Here, then, is a preamble of items of common concern that form the basis for a general bill of spiritual rights.

This bill of spiritual rights is built upon existing statements of political, social, and economic rights as contained in the U.S. Declaration of Independence, the U.S. Constitution, and court cases defining and extending rights, freedoms, and responsibilities.

"At this present time," says J.B. Phillips, "the Church is taken very seriously in atheistic-communist countries. Men with hard faces know intuitively that the Church is the implacable champion of human liberty, of the truly human values and the finest human aspirations. When the conflict becomes acute in a totalitarian society, it is the Church alone which can successfully stand up for human liberty and conscience."[12]

John Locke listed a number of reasons for religious toleration. He said that a resort to force might provoke retaliation upon the aggressor. Religious conflict is a public nuisance which can easily become a public danger. "Religions cannot be inculcated by force," he said. "Absolute Reality is a mystery to which there is more than one approach. Every church is orthodox to itself, to others heretical. The decision on that question belongs only to the Supreme Judge of all."[13]

It is shocking how religious controversy has led to such ungodly acts as terrorism and war. Divisive religion separates not only church from church but persons from persons and persons from God. It is amazing how patient mankind has been with divisive religion, seeing the heartache, brutality, and inhumanity it has fostered. Once again Eckhart has some practical wisdom to lead us out of the darkness: Let us each keep our own way, he advises, and absorb into it the good features of other ways so as to include in our way the merits of other ways.

Try not, said Paul, to offend others with the practice of your faith: "It is good neither to eat flesh nor to drink wine nor any thing whereby thy brother stumbleth or is offended or is made weak" (Romans 14:21). "The Kingdom of God," Paul declared, "is not meat and drink, but righteousness and peace and joy in the Holy Spirit" (Romans 14:17). God's Kingdom thus hinges on three unselfish conditions: righteousness, meaning giving to God and to others what is their due; peace, not just an absence of war but a right relationship with God and all of His people; and joy, meaning the gladness of heart that comes from bringing happiness to other people.

Let us now see what are the main components of a modern Bill of Spiritual Rights.

Bill of Spiritual Rights

RIGHT #1: Since you are a child of God. you are entitled to be free from physical, mental, and spiritual intimidation and violence.

Michael Polanyi defines a "morally inverted person" as one whose crusade for social justice, not rooted in faith in God, justifies the use of violence to achieve supposedly desirable goals. Lenin, in *State and Revolution,* says that in communist societies, it is possible to speak of freedom only when the state ceases to exist. Is not freedom important at all times? Is modern communism making progress towards a classless society?

To kill or torture human beings is to interfere with God's plan for their lives, and is thus a sacrilegious rebellion against the divine order. As governments curtail political and economic freedom, spiritual freedom is left as a bastion surrounding the individual. We dare not surrender this last safeguard to our liberties.

RIGHT #2: The relations between your soul and God are so sacred that no other person can be the ruler of your conscience; therefore you have the right to worship God in your own way.

Jeremy Taylor said that if we treat persons of another faith with kindness, they are favorably disposed toward our faith, but if we are hostile toward them, they will be hostile toward our faith.

Some people need a highly emotional religion, others a highly intellectual one. Some people need great stress upon ritual, others upon the social gospel. Some people need a very traditional faith, others a highly innovative one. Let us not all sing baritone—the heavenly chorus praising God consists of a rich harmony of diverse approaches.

Recently the U.S. Commission on Civil Rights has accused federal agencies and courts of failing to protect the rights of Americans to practice their religion. For example, despite the rights stated in the American Indian Religious Freedom Act of 1978, the Commission feels that such rights have been transgressed as the preservation of sacred land, access to religious sites, protection of ceremonial rites, and the return of religious artifacts.

RIGHT #3: You are entitled to the sanctity of your own personality. It is profane to fail to grant that sanctity to any of God's children.

One person cannot love another until he has given that person the right to his or her uniqueness. Albert Schweitzer says that all of us have a "modesty of the soul" which no one else has the right to invade.

Anyone who has studied human nature is aware of a wide range of individual differences in temperament, intelligence, values, and abilities. These differences must be honored. Strangely enough, self-determination (once a person achieves the Self of individuation) leads to overall harmony, for then one freely chooses to obey the highest law of one's being, which is the same as the highest law of all others' being.

RIGHT #4: You have the right to express your religious views in your own terms.

Our expression is the creation of our personality. Suppression of expression is a violation of personality. To deny a person the freedom of religious expression is to steal from him a guidepost towards spiritual illumination. This could well impair his ability to individuate and thus to find God.

RIGHT #5: The right to express religious opinions, hold religious offices, and secure religious respect will not be curtailed because of your sex, race, age, nationality, or the seeming oddness of your religious views.

Since most religious tradition has been organized by men, women are blithely ignored in many religious power structures. If God the Father loves all of His children alike, He cannot prefer His sons over His daughters.

It is still true that Sunday morning at 11 o'clock is the most segregated hour of the week. Religious organizations should try to emulate the entertainment world in practicing "color-blind" acceptance of persons.

Old people are not necessarily incompetent. Abraham was 99 when God made a covenant with him; Isaac was born a year later. Moses was 80 when God gave him the Ten Commandments on Mount Sinai.

No nation has a monopoly on spiritual insight. Hatred and animosity have turned the Holy Land into an unholy place. Perhaps if so many people there were not so ardently "religious," there would be more persons practicing the religion of love of God and of one's neighbor.

No doubt the itinerant Carpenter from Nazareth seemed an odd figure to orthodox believers in his day. Something strange is something odd, and may be something important!

RIGHT #6: Since there is a wide variety of human personality types and historical human cultures, there should be tolerance of a wide variety of religious expression and a recognition of the oneness of God behind all sincere religious search.

As Quintus Aurelius Symmachus told St. Ambrose, "'The heart of so great a mystery cannot ever be reached by following only one road.' However confident my conviction that my approach is the right one, I ought to be aware that my field of spiritual vision is so narrow that I cannot know that there is no virtue in other approaches."[14]

A believer has no right to try to limit God's way of doing His will. Why should not a Zimbabwe hunter be reached in a different way than a Manhattan stockbroker?

Christ said, "Judge not, that ye be not judged" (Matthew 7:1). In Chapter 14 of Romans, Paul says we should not make fun of those who believe in strict observance of rituals and religious laws. Such persons may be "weak in the faith," he says, thinking they will be saved by such works rather than by the grace of Christ. Things to avoid, Paul cautions, are irritation when someone differs from us, ridicule because others' beliefs seem ludicrous to us, and contempt growing out of lack of respect for our neighbor and his right to his beliefs.

Before our globe was so fully inhabited, religious parochialism was relatively harmless. Now that so many of our cultures interpenetrate one another, great harm comes from religious discrimination and assumptions of superiority and inferiority.

RIGHT #7: Because it is meaningless to say that you love God but hate your neighbor, other persons have the right to expect that your religion will work towards realization of a loving human family under God's divine Fatherhood.

Religious seekers should feel like spiritual brethren, pilgrims taking different roads toward the same glorious goal. If there must be competition, let it be competition for the greatest love. Toleration does not become perfect, said Toynbee, until it has been transfigured into love.

When the head of a major Protestant denomination said that "God does not hear the prayer of a Jew," Rabbi Albert Plotkin of Phoenix replied in the words of the psalmist, "'The Lord is near to all who call upon Him in truth.' It is the challenge of religion," Plotkin said, "to become inclusive rather than exclusive. Respect for each other's faith is more than a political or social imperative. It is born out of insight that God is greater than religion, that He hears the prayers of all of us, and that we are all precious in His sight.

"God loves all of us, and excludes no one. He hears the voices of all His children, whether they be Christian, Jew, Moslem, or Buddhist. No person said it better than Pope John XXIII in his encyclical *Peace on Earth*: 'Every human being has the right to freedom in searching for truth and in expressing his prayers and opinions. Every human being has the right to honor God according to the dictates of an upright conscience.'

"To quote from rabbinic literature: 'Pious men of all nations have a share in the world to come and are promised the rewards of eternal life. I call heaven and earth to witness that the Holy Spirit rests upon every person, Jew or Gentile, man or woman, white or black, in consonance with his deeds.'"[15]

RIGHT #8: Since the terror of nuclear destruction frightens and threatens the entire human family, all people have a right to expect that their governments will work to abolish this threat by achieving world peace and justice under God's law.

The most immoral act a person can commit is to take another person's life. What God bestows only God should take away. When the organized murder of warfare becomes so unspeakably heinous as to wipe out millions of people with one bomb, warfare becomes an instrument of Satan which all God-loving persons will vehemently oppose.

Food is basic to social justice. Without food, all other components of justice are meaningless.

We all instinctively resent the prospect of a world state, fraught as it is with the danger of totalitarian control over all aspects of our lives. But the world must become an orderly community if mankind is to survive in the nuclear age. A federation of sovereign nations, acting jointly in the interest of all citizens of our global village, must effectively outlaw both war and pollution of our atmosphere. We want to have a posterity, and we owe it a clean environment. Our stewardship of God's creation makes this the first order of business for every social group on planet earth.

RIGHT #9: Since no right exists without a corresponding responsibility, other persons have the right to expect that you will observe their spiritual and other rights as described herein.

I am really not concerned about rights and freedoms until I am concerned about my neighbor's. Granting freedom for someone to agree with me is scarcely a freedom at all. When I can adopt Voltaire's position, "I fully disagree with everything you say, but I will defend to my death your right to say it," then I am beginning to show love and respect for humankind which God Himself must applaud.

RIGHT #10: This being a preliminary statement in an important area of human conduct, you have the right to suggest improvements and modifications in it, and submit them to the conscience of the world community for ratification.

As is true with any statement of rights, the spirit of these laws is much more important than the phraseology. Any constitutional document needs to provide for its amendment. Time itself demands changes in our ways of thinking and acting.

But this is at least a step in the right direction. We cannot merely think our way out of the current human predicament. Thinking, feeling, loving, and praying can turn the current survival threat into the fruition of mankind's finest hour, bringing in the kingdom of love and peace that has been the goal of the human species throughout the ages.

References

[1] Alfred Harmsworth et al., eds., *The World's Greatest Books* (McKinley, Stone, & Mackenzie, 1912), p. 360.
[2] Renou, p. 240.
[3] Raymond B. Blakney, *Meister Eckhart: A Modern Translation* (Harper, 1941), p. 75.
[4] Frank Goble, *The Third Force* (Pocket Books, 1971), p. 131.
[5] Harmsworth, p. 362.
[6] Gard, p. 20.
[7] William James, *The Varieties of Religious Experience* (Modern Library, 1936), pp. 83, 84.
[8] Falk, p. 494.
[9] Reinhold Niebuhr, *The Structure of Nations and Empires* (Scribners, 1959), p. 291.
[10] Andrew Louth, *The Origins of the Christian Mystical Tradition* (Clarendon Press, 1981), pp. 155-56.
[11] Aldous Huxley, *The Perennial Philosophy* (Harper, 1945), p. 256.
[12] J.B. Phillips, *God Our Contemporary* (Hodder & Stoughton, 1960), p. 188.
[13] Arnold Toynbee, *An Historian's Approach to Religion,* 2nd ed. (Oxford University Press, 1979), pp. 253-57.
[14] Ibid., p. 251.
[15] Rabbi Albert Plotkin, *Arizona Republic*, 27 September 1980, p. E3.

CHAPTER 13

CONTEMPORARY UNITIVENESS: RELIGION AS BLESSING

It is encouraging to see the many examples of unitive religion in the modern world. For example, a television series called "The Long Search" presented the findings of comparative religion in 1979. Speaking of the series Conrad Hyers said that among all the major world religions "there is an intriguing consensus which finds a kind of religious unity, not in any common affirmation or attitude or even experience, but rather in the awareness of and response to an ultimate *mysterium,* which is beyond all picturability, and which no metaphors and myths can fully contain. Any claim to do so would stand in contradiction with both the ultimacy and the mystery with which we wrestle."[1]

Leonard Swidler feels that the deabsolutizing of truth in this century aids the process of interfaith dialogue. Given the relativity of historical truth, if Paul said that women should be silent in his church, they need not be silent in today's church. Since no language can describe the transcendent, language must be suspect as a bearer of God's word. Hermeneutics teaches us that "all knowledge of a text is also an interpretation of it. All knowledge is interpreted knowledge. The subject is part of the object."[2] Therefore our statements about other people's beliefs are, to a considerable extent, statements about our beliefs.

Speaking of world perspectives, Ruth Nanda Anshen states that "beyond the divisiveness among men there exists a primordial unitive power, since we are all bound together by a common humanity more fundamental than any unity of dogma. There is in mankind today a counterforce to the sterility and danger of a quantitative, anonymous mass culture—a new spiritual sense of convergence toward world unity on the basis of the sacredness of each human person and respect for the plurality of cultures."[3]

Martin Marty gives examples of unitive religion at work. If an older woman has a husband with a terminal illness and is a member of a caring church, "she probably does not have to turn to many professional services for chauffeuring, blood transfusions, meeting certain obligations, or finding counsel. She will be immediately surrounded by people who have come to know, care, and feel responsibility for her. In American colleges a Methodist coed studies with a Jewish young man in a class taught by a Catholic having to do with Buddhist or Hindu texts. These studies go on with less hostility than ever before. In a way the new awareness builds a sense of world community."[4]

Wilfred Cantwell Smith describes the large amount of interreligious penetration in process. The Jewish Martin Buber, the Hindu Radhakrishnan, and the Buddhist D.T. Suzuki all taught Christians much about Christianity. The Christian Paul Tillich similarly taught Buddhists much about their own faith. The old concept of unilateral missionaries has been replaced by a multilateral concept. "We have no right to send missionaries to any group from whom we are not ready to invite missionaries," in Smith's opinion. A part of each major religious heritage affirms that all humankind is a single community. The new missionary challenge, says Smith, is "to participate in each other's processes of moving towards God. We are the first generation of Christians to discern God's mission to mankind in the Buddhist movement, as well as in the Hindu, Islamic, Judaic, and Christian. Having discerned it, let us not fail to respond to it."[5]

Modern Jewish Unitiveness

Martin Buber (1878-1965) taught at Hebrew University in Jerusalem. A mystic, Buber recreated Hasidic legends, and helped broaden Hasidism into a great world mystical tradition. His doctoral thesis was on the Christian mystics, Nicholas of Cusa and Jacob Boehme. Later he edited the writings of Meister Eckhart. Along with Rabbi Judah Magnes, president of Hebrew University, Buber strongly advocated Jewish-Moslem concord in the Holy Land. Their group, called Ihud (Union), saw the only just solution there as a bi-national state with equal rights for Jews and Moslems. They accurately predicted that to repay violence with violence would only worsen conditions.

A follower of Buber, Abraham Joshua Heschel said, "How do we identify the divine? Divine is a message that discloses unity where we see diversity, that discloses peace when we are involved in discord. God is He who holds our fitful lives together, who reveals to us that what is empirically diverse—in color, creeds, races, classes, nations—is one in His eyes and one in essence. God means: No one is ever alone. God means: Togetherness of all beings in holy otherness."[6]

Rabbi Rudolph Grossman points out that heresy trials are unknown in Jewish history. Also, Jews have been notable throughout history for their charity. The American Jew Julius Rosenwald alone helped establish over 5300 schools for black students in the United States. Zionism is the organized Jewish reaction to centuries of world-wide anti-Semitic persecution.

In 1937 both Chaim Weizmann (later president of Israel) and David Ben Gurion (later prime minister of Israel) recommended a joint Jewish-Moslem state in Palestine. Zionists would accept parity, they said. They agreed that in the legislative council Jews and Moslems should have equal votes. "Ben Gurion stressed that it was not their goal to make Palestine a Jewish state."[7] President Weizmann in 1949 emphasized Israel's desire for peace with the Moslems. He drew upon his personal friendship with many Moslem leaders. He felt confident that in time Jews and Moslems would learn to live together in peace. Uri Avnery, a former Irgun terrorist, as a member of the Knesset became an outstanding advocate of Moslem-Israeli understanding in the 1950s.

In 1968 Yehia Hammouda became the leader of the Palestine Liberation Organization. He said that it was ridiculous to expect Jews who had come to Palestine since 1948 to return to their countries of origin. He asked Israel to return land taken since 1948, but said that the best solution in Palestine would be a joint Moslem-Jewish state with equal rights to both sides.

The aroused Jewish conscience has been critical of Israeli policy which denies Palestinian rights. American Jews critical of Israeli actions include Rabbi Elmer Berger, Alfred Lilienthal, and Moshe Menuhin. These people say that Jewish violence against Palestinians violates the Jewish spiritual heritage. Also, dissident Jewish groups in Palestine accuse the Israeli government of substituting hatred of the Moslems for love of God.

Even Yitzhak Rabin, the late prime minister, agreed that without Palestinian involvement, there can be no permanent solution to the complex problems of the Holy Land.

Max Dimont says that concord will help both parties. "For 700 years," Dimont states, "Arab and Jew lived side by side in peace and with mutual respect. It is up to Jewish leaders, in their own national self-interest, to convince Arab leaders that the Arab world can achieve its legitimate aims with the friendship of the Jews, as in days past. History has shown that Jew and Arab can live together without strife and with mutual profit."[8]

Jewish-Christian Concord

Many Christians heroically risked their lives to rescue Jews from Nazi cruelty. Even in Germany Jews were often hid in Christian homes in order to escape the Gestapo. In France thousands of Jewish children were saved by these means. "In Greece 600 priests were sent to concentration camps for refusing to preach anti-Jewish sermons and for urging their congregations to help the Jews. Thirty-four Budapest residents were sent to prison for sheltering Jews. The Protestant and Catholic churches of the Netherlands protested the persecution of Jews."[9]

Scandinavia was outstanding for its courageous stand against Nazism. Raoul Wallenberg of Sweden may have saved as many as 100,000 Jews from death in concentration camps. Many Swedes welcomed Jewish refugees. Bishop Eivind Berggraf of Norway led the Norwegian clergy in efforts opposing German cruelty. In Denmark eight bishops openly protested anti-Semitic policies. King Christian of Denmark flatly refused to carry out the anti-Semitic occupation laws of the Nazis. He said that he would wear the Badge of Shame himself if it were imposed on his Jewish subjects. As German troops moved in, the Danes ran a well organized evacuation of their Jews to Sweden.

The Altruistic Philosophy is a recent book by S.P. Oliner and P.M. Oliner, consisting of interviews with over 400 people involved in helping rescue Jewish people from Nazi cruelty. Father Ruffino Nicacci, for example, hid 300 Jews in the catacombs of Assisi, and then moved them through to Allied lines by the use of forged documents. His greatest help came from persons with tolerant religious attitudes, he said, since "more intense religiosity is frequently associated with greater prejudice."[10]

Rabbi Pinchas Lapide, in his book *The Sermon on the Mount,* calls the sermon the world's best blueprint for a peaceful and just world community. Dr. Ellis Rivkin, a professor of Jewish history, is a bridge of understanding between Christians and Jews. "For years," he says, "I was denied the richness of Christianity because I was unaware that Christianity might have something to say about God that Judaism hadn't already said." Christians, on the other hand, suffer "the loss of understanding the process by which the one God had come to be known to humanity through the Judeo-Christian tradition." Jesus modeled himself on prophets like Moses and Isaiah, Rivkin feels, adding that Christianity is "a treasure trove of spiritual insights into the nature and meaning of God." He makes clear that he is speaking of a Christianity which rejects as ungodly anything which tells its adherents "to be hurtful, hostile, or rejecting of any of God's creatures."[11]

Vatican II Council rejected the idea that the Jews killed Christ, and it firmly condemned anti-Semitism. "Rabbi A. James Rudin, director of inter-religious affairs at the American Jewish Committee, is fond of saying that more progress has been made in the last 25 years of Catholic-Jewish relations than in the preceding 1900."[12] Pope John Paul II has met with Jewish leaders to attempt to resolve tensions between the two faiths.

In 1988 the Episcopal Church joined the Roman Catholic Church, the Presbyterian Church, and the United Church of Christ in rejecting the doctrine of supersession, that Christianity supersedes Judaism. The early Christian church felt that it replaced Israel in having a special covenant with God. Now Judaism's covenant is accepted as valid. Rabbi Leon Klenicki of the Anti-Defamation League says this not only "requires Christians to rethink the Christian mission in the world" but also encourages Jews "to think about the meaning of Jesus and the mission of Christianity as a way of bringing all humanity to God. Perhaps what God is asking is a cooperative venture." The Presbyterian paper calls Christians and Jews "partners in waiting. Both wait with eager longing for the fulfillment of God's gracious reign upon the earth—the kingdom of righteousness and peace."[13]

A building in Ann Arbor has both a Christian cross and a Star of David on it, for it serves as both St. Clare of Assisi, a parish of the Episcopal diocese, and Temple Beth Emeth, a Reform Jewish congregation. After renting from the Episcopalians, the Jews learned to fellowship with them. "They held Passover seders together, organized pulpit exchanges, and prayed together for world peace." When the Jewish group had the money to build its own structure, neither side wanted to part, so they formed a corporation, with this statement of purpose: "Understanding that both congregations will maintain their separate identities, each believes that their actions herein will stand as a symbol of the power of reason and love to overcome distrust and the prejudices of our separate histories." One temple member said, "We like each other, we get along with one another, and we want our children to get along with one another. It works for us."[14]

Hans Küng believes that the original New Testament view of Jesus would be acceptable to both Judaism and Islam. The New Testament viewed sonship, says Küng, not as a relation of parentage, but as an appointment, in the Old Testament sense. Christ's role was "not a physical divine sonship, as Islam always rightly rejected (because it awakened associations of intercourse between a god and a mortal woman) but God's choosing Jesus and granting him full authority." This is a concept that both Jews and Moslems can accept, Küng feels. "Father" here implies not a mate for mother but a patriarchal symbol: a creator, one in authority, a protector with compassion. "Son" means not the product of a divine Father and a worldly mother but "an ambassador, Messiah, word of the eternal God in human form."[15]

Modern Roman Catholic Unitiveness

Pope Pius XI said, "Today we are all Protestants." By this he meant that modern persons choose their religion on a personal basis, with tradition being relatively unimportant.

His successor, Pius XII, announced the keynote of his pontificate in his first encyclical, "On the Unity of the Human Race." The spiritual unity of mankind, he said, outlawed all racial and religious discrimination. "The Church," said Charles A. Hart, "insists upon the inalienable rights of every human person simply because of his personality bestowed on him by God. The Catholic Church looks with the highest favor upon every effort of mankind to form a world society in view of its teaching upon the unity of the human race." The Roman Catholic Church has been a leading contributor to the formulation of world law, saying that no state can make itself independent of God's moral law. During the Middle Ages the Holy Roman Empire existed as an international Christian state. Unity was achieved through membership in the body of Christ. "The breakup of Christian unity has issued in the extreme nationalism that thwarts our present efforts for peace."[16]

According to Eugene Kennedy, Vatican II Council rediscovered "the essential unity of the human person and the universe. In the Ptolemaic world, the earth was the center and the heaven was 'out there.' Now, in the space-age, we are 'out there,' and that is where heaven is." Carl Jung detected the symbolism in the Roman Catholic dogma that Mary (the Blessed Mother) was physically assumed from the earth into heaven. This was a symbol of Mother Earth returning to heaven, re-experiencing the unity of the space age. The astronauts on the moon for the first time saw the earth for what it really is—a part of the heavens.

Vatican II Council speaks of a universal brotherhood. It said, "We cannot call on God, the Father of all men, if there are any men whom we refuse to treat as brothers, since all are created in God's image. Therefore the Church condemns all discrimination between men and all conflict of race, color, class, or creed, as being contrary to the mind of Christ. This Council appeals to believers in Christ to do their best to be at peace with all men, so that they may be true sons of the Father who is in heaven."[17]

The Council achieved a reconciliation of Jews and Christians. Referring to Ephesians 2:14-16, the Council stated that "the Church believes that Christ, who is our peace, has reconciled Jews and Gentiles through the Cross and has made us both one in himself. According to the Apostle Paul, the Jews still remain very dear to God. Given this great spiritual heritage common to Christians and Jews, it is the wish of this Council to foster a mutual knowledge and esteem, which will come from Biblical studies and brotherly discussions."[18] Taking responsibility for its own misconduct towards the Jews, the Church, through the Council, deplored all hatred and other anti-Semitism, "whatever the period and whoever was responsible."

Concord with Moslems was also enjoined by Vatican II: "The Church regards with esteem the Muslims who worship the one merciful and almighty God, the Creator of heaven and earth, who has spoken to man. If in the course of the centuries there has arisen not infrequent dissension and hostility between Christian and Muslim, this sacred Council now urges everyone to forget the past, to make sincere efforts at mutual understanding, and to work together in promoting for the benefit of all men social justice, good morals, peace, and freedom."[19] Perhaps now the bones of many Crusaders can rest in peace!

Theologian Karl Rahner states that Vatican II accepted as "anonymous Christians" those who live according to their consciences, since they are unconsciously accepting God as their highest value. Those who courageously accept themselves are automatically accepting their Creator, it is believed; the agnostic who lives in brave faithfulness to everyday life lives "life's mysticism," intuitively accepting life's mystical author, God.

Vatican II also stressed ecumenicity, declaring that "we must become familiar with the outlook of our separated brethren. Study should be pursued with a spirit of good will and on an equal footing." In 1970 the Vatican Secretariat for Christian Unity declared that "all Christians should be of an ecumenical mind. Those in authority in seminaries and universities should take pains to promote the ecumenical movement."[20] Vatican II said that "the unitive movement among Christians is inspired and fostered by the Holy Spirit, who is a certain body of unity among Christians, even though divided. This general doctrine was expressed independently by the World Council of Churches and is recognized as an incentive to further efforts towards complete unity."[21]

Long centuries of harsh persecution of dissenting views gave way to a much more tolerant attitude in Vatican II. From now on, "intercreedal relations were to be based on cooperation rather than on hostility. The alleged right of the church to use authority to suppress dissident religious views was abrogated. Recourse to anathemas and feudalist polemics was abandoned. Freedom of inquiry by theologians and other scholars was guaranteed. Untrammeled study of the scriptures was sanctioned. Ecumenical dialogue was fostered not only among Christians but between Christians and non-Christians."[22]

In 1964 Pope Paul VI stated that religious dialogue must be conducted with dignity. "Dialogue is demanded nowadays," he said, "by the dynamic course of action which is changing the face of modern society. It is demanded by the pluralism of society and by the maturity man has reached in this day and age."[23]

In 1983 the U.S. Catholic bishops issued a pastoral letter, "The Challenge of Peace," which stated that "in Jesus Christ God has reconciled the world, and manifested that His will is this reconciliation, this unity between God and all peoples, and among the people themselves. As children of God it is our task to seek ways to make the forgiveness, justice, mercy, and love of God visible in a world where violence and enmity are too often the norm.

Any act of war aimed indiscriminately at the destruction of extensive areas along with their population is a crime against God and man. It merits unequivocal condemnation. Total war today would be a monstrously disproportionate response to aggression. The arms race is to be condemned as a danger, an act of aggression against the poor, and a folly which does not provide the security it promises.

Mutual security and survival require a new vision of the world as one interdependent planet. We call for the establishment of some form of global authority adequate to the needs of the international common good."[24]

Pope John Paul II called October 27, 1986, the Day of Prayer for Peace at Assisi in Italy. "The Holy Father wanted to prove that peace is the desire of every man and woman of whatever faith; that peace is a gift of God even though its realization depends on humanity's response to that gift." The pope asked for guns to be silent that day, and for everyone, including heads of state, to pray for peace. Among those taking part were African tribal leaders, Buddhists, the chief rabbi of Rome, Native American leaders, Protestants, and Shintoists. Followers of St. Francis vowed to serve all mankind, not just their own church, in God's name. The audience was asked "to redouble our overall commitment to peace and justice, nonviolence, and the promotion of human development." Those in attendance vowed to become, like St. Francis, "an instrument of God's peace." Some ultraconservative Catholics denounced the pope as Satan's minion for fraternizing with persons of other faiths.[25]

The U.S. Catholic bishops stressed human dignity in a pastoral letter on economics which they issued in November 1986. The chief principles enunciated were these: Every individual, as a child of God, is entitled to a job. Human dignity requires the solidarity that comes from association with other persons. Christ calls his followers to show concern for the poor and the suffering. In a Christian economy, responsibility exists at all levels: Government should be a catalyst and a fair umpire of labor disputes. Management must involve workers in decisions affecting them. Labor unions must reeducate workers for new types of employment. The unemployed and the poor must ultimately take the responsibility for their own welfare.

Since Vatican II, the Roman Catholic Church has taken a holistic approach to missionary work. The missionary is seen as one to serve not only the spiritual needs of people, but also their physical, mental, and social needs. Thus the modern Church is inevitably concerned about such matters as education, health care, justice, and peace. Since Moslem countries forbid the making of Christian converts, missionaries there instead witness to Christ through acts of charity, kindness, and mercy, trusting that the cause of Christ will ultimately benefit from such witness.

Roman Catholic indigenization is going on in many places, especially in Latin America, Africa, and the Orient. This process involves validating the sincere religious expression of the native people, pointing out universals in their expression which are similar to the Lordship of Christ and the Fatherhood of God. Instead of destroying faith, it builds faith upon faith in a unitive manner.

Donald Pelotte, a native of Maine, has been appointed the first Roman Catholic Native American bishop. In welcoming Pope John Paul II to Phoenix in 1987 Pelotte said, "We deeply appreciate the many ways in which you have affirmed the gifts our Creator has given to the aboriginal peoples of Mother Earth. Your support of our basic human rights and dignity as aboriginal peoples of this land is welcome." The pope encouraged Indians "to preserve and keep alive your culture, your languages, the values and customs which have served you well in the past and which provide a solid foundation for the future. These things benefit not only yourselves but also the entire human family."[26]

A number of leading Roman Catholics emphasize the unitive role now being played by the Church. One of these is the popular musician Dave Brubeck, whose father was a Methodist cowboy who practiced Christian Science and then joined the Presbyterian Church. Dave's mother, a church organist, studied Oriental religions. In 1987 the New York premiere was given of Dave's "The

Voice of the Holy Spirit (Tongues of Fire)." He describes how this sacred jazz came to be written. In the trenches of World War II Dave had his first serious thoughts about how religion relates to war and peace. "The New Testament," he said, "tells us to love our enemies. I knew I had to write music that expressed concern over the fact that men know more about the destruction of the universe than about the Sermon on the Mount." Other sacred works Dave has written include a mass, a Christmas pageant, and an Easter cantata.[27]

Dom Bede Griffiths is a Benedictine monk who lives in an ashram in India. Griffiths welcomed the translation of the word "Logos" as "Tao" in the start of John's gospel, saying that this placed Chinese philosophy in the same relation to the gospel as John had done with his introduction of a term from Greek philosophy. Griffiths explained that "in the Hindu conception of the Atman and the Chinese conception of the Tao, we have perhaps the most profound of all insights into this mystery. I would like to see the spirit of ecumenism enlarged so that we can see the mystery of Christ, which we try very imperfectly to realize in our lives, is hidden in all ancient religions. It is the mystery of God who was present from the beginning. There has never been a time when God's grace, His Spirit, was not present in mankind, leading men toward the truth."[28]

The basic doctrine of theologian Karl Rahner might be described as "God in the world." For Rahner love of neighbor equates with love of God. Rahner's special skill seems to be to impart a Christlike concern for helping the needy. Dogma, says Rahner, must be constantly reinterpreted in order to remain alive. Christianity and Marxism can find common ground, he believes, in a united effort to prevent exploitation of the powerless in society.

Remi de Roo is the Roman Catholic Bishop of Victoria, British Columbia. His "Project Ploughshares" is a church-sponsored organization for conversion of war production to consumer production in Canada. "What we require," says De Roo, "is nothing less than the building of a new international economic and political order that is clearly based on the goals of justice and peace. This is not simply a moral imperative. It is now essential for the very survival of humanity. From both a religious and a humanistic standpoint, the fact that billions of dollars are spent every day on military weapons, while millions of people are suffering from poverty and starvation in the world, is a scandal of the highest proportions. We are confronted with profound moral disorder in priorities. The Christian conscience cries out against this evil."[29]

When theologian Hans Küng is called a revolutionary, he responds by describing himself as a follower of Christ the revolutionary. He delineates the radical message of Christ: "The entire moral teaching of Jesus aims at a new, true humanity, which manifests itself in solidarity with fellow humanity. It has a concrete program of action: It not only foregoes religious wars, persecutions, and Inquisitions but it practices religious tolerance and substitutes for its collective egoism a solidarity of love. Instead of calculating the history of guilt among the religions, it practices forgiveness. It does not simply eliminate religious institutions (often humanly divisive) but relativizes them for the welfare of humankind. Instead of overt or covert power struggles among religious systems, it strives for reconciliation—not a uniform religion for the entire world, but peace among the religions as a prerequisite for peace among the nations."[30]

Modern Protestant Unitiveness

In the 1920s seven Protestant denominations formed the Layman's Missionary Inquiry, to study Christian missions in the Orient. The study recommended that missions should be two-directional, that the East and the West should exchange missionaries.

The International Missionary Council in 1928 called for Christian unity, after finding that there were 120 separate Christian organizations in the mission field in China, 134 in Africa, and 158 in India. The natives were confused at the conflicting claims to uniqueness. Bishop Palmer said that "the disunited condition of the Church shocks those who are recapturing afresh the fellowship of the Spirit. They are indignant when they reflect that the divisions in which they find themselves imprisoned had their origins in the controversies of foreigners in distant lands, in which they had no part and have no interest."[31] The Council made sweeping suggestions for changes to avoid duplication of effort and overlap. Many of these changes were made.

Christianity has made many converts in Africa in the 20th century, and now it is assumed that there are about 100 million African Christians. Protestants have made the Bible available in over 500 African languages. Medical missionary work, such as that performed by Albert Schweitzer, has filled a crucial need. By 1938 half a million lepers had been discovered in Africa, and most of their treatment was in Christian clinics. Churches also attacked tuberculosis and other illnesses. Since traditional African beliefs see a close relationship between physical and spiritual ailments, Christian doctors try to respect this holistic attitude towards medical practice there.

Christian missionaries protested against racism in Africa. "In 1960 a conference of the World Council of Churches in Johannesburg rejected apartheid by 80% of the votes. Because of this, three Dutch Reformed churches withdrew from the Council in 1961. In 1964 the Methodists elected their first African president of the annual conference, and in 1964 the Anglicans elected their first African bishop. Within the Dutch Reformed churches there was some protest against racism."[32]

Christians were risking their lives in order to spread Christ's gospel. "In 1961 the American Methodist Board said that in Angola 17 pastors were dead, 30 in prison, 90 unaccounted for, and many churches and schools had been destroyed."[33] Christian missionaries were also killed in civil wars in the Congo. Sudan deported many Roman Catholic missionaries. At Juba in Sudan in 1965 hundreds of people were massacred in the Anglican cathedral.

In the early 20th century Walter Rauschenbusch and others developed the social gospel: that Christ's focus had been upon the coming of the Kingdom of God. Christ was thus seen, among other things, as a prophet of social justice whose teachings led to a more abundant life. "Here was a social gospel whose practice would solve modern man's problems; it could bring peace to the nations, justice among the peoples, and good will among the races."[34] Thus, said the unitive Christians, the church is once again relevant—in fact, it is indispensable for modern progress.

Christ was now being seen as the model of wholeness, the truly integrated personality, not as one who wills one thing and does another. "He is whole, therefore liberated, therefore transcending the fragmented, disintegrated, conflicting desires, ambitions, and motives which limit our lives. Salvation means health, wholeness, atonement—at-one-ment. Healing men's brokenness, within themselves, from each other and from God, is what Christ's life is all about. Caring for the broken and the despised ruined his reputation among the pious and the respectable. His flouting of professional religiosity and of political expediency brought him to his death so that we, and millions like us, might know the truth about God."[35]

Christ was being seen as being broader than Christianity. His Jewish origin gave him a deep feeling for the law and the prophets. "But *Christos,* the Christ figure, can stand also for the broader notion of the 'visibility of the invisible' (a phrase from Irenaeus), the mystery of *theos,* of the ultimate reality of God, or Brahman, made manifest, embodied in history. It is what the Greeks called the Logos; it is the avatara or descent of God in human form, or in Jungian terms, the God-image in us, the archetype of the Self. In the new interface both with Eastern mysticism and with Jungian psychology, there is greater hope for fresh light on Christology than at any time since the classical debates of the fourth and fifth centuries."[36]

The Indian Christian Raymond Panikkar explains the Christian significance of the Hindu concept of karma. "Karma is that unitary link which connects us with every speck of reality and makes us sense our unity with the whole universe." Everything is related to everything else in the universe, as modern science demonstrates. "Seen in this perspective, the nature of karma may help explain such fundamental Christian concepts as the connection of Adam's sin to all of mankind, as well as the relation of Christ's death and resurrection to the entire humanity. The *who* beneath the Buddhist's compassion or behind the Muslim's surrender is none other than the *who* of Christian agape."[37]

Some Christian leaders now admit that other religious figures, such as Mohammed, "may be carrying out, in very different ways, revelatory, salvific roles analogous to that of Jesus Christ. They have shifted from an inclusivist Christocentrism to a pluralist theocentrism, with God at the center. This includes Tom Driver, John Hick, Raymond Panikkar, Aloysius Pieris, Rosemary Ruether, Stanley Samartha, Arnold Toynbee, and Ernst Troeltsch."[38]

John Hick explains how a Christian can acknowledge the validity of other paths to God beside the Christian way. "The Incarnation," Hick feels, "is a mythological idea. It is a way of saying that Jesus is our living contact with the transcendent God. We believe that he is so truly God's servant that in living as his disciples we are living according to the divine purpose. When we see the Incarnation as a mythological idea, we no longer have to draw the negative conclusion that Jesus is man's only contact with God. We can commend the way of Christian faith without having to discommend other ways of faith. We can say that there is salvation in Christ without having to say that there is no salvation other than in Christ."[39]

Virtually every main Protestant denomination now contains important thrusts of unitive religion. In 1988 the Lambeth Conference of Anglicans came up with many unity statements, including efforts to discover increased oneness in doctrines and in forms of worship. There was endorsement of further interfaith dialogue with Roman Catholics, Lutherans, Eastern Orthodox, and numerous other branches of Christianity. In the United States Barbara C. Harris, a black priest, became the first woman bishop of the Episcopal Church.

The Society of Friends, or Quakers, has a long tradition of working for peace. Their founder, George Fox, said, "We utterly deny all outward wars and strife, for any pretense whatsoever." William Penn explained why Quakers are wary of creeds: "They judge that a curious inquiry into divine relations tends little to godliness and less to peace, which should be the chief aim of true Christians. Therefore speculative truths should never be made the measure of Christian communion." Robert Barclay added that the saved include "all, of whatsoever nation, though remote from those who profess Christ in words, as become obedient to the Holy Light, the testimony of God in their hearts."[40]

The American Quaker John Woolman believed that "to consider mankind otherwise than brethren, to think favors are peculiar to one nation and exclude others plainly supposes a darkness in the understanding. For, as God's love is universal, so where the mind is sufficiently influenced by it, it begets a likeness of itself, and the heart is enlarged towards all men."[41] Causes for which the Society of Friends has striven through the years include abolition of slavery, care of the insane, penal reform,

Contemporary Unitiveness: Religion as Blessing 305

temperance, and women's rights. Their service committees, noteworthy for providing assistance to the needy, in 1947 were awarded the Nobel Peace Prize.

In 1988 the general conference of the Methodist Church endorsed the concept of unity with diversity. One statement declared that for Methodism's founder, John Wesley, "there is no religion but social religion, no holiness but social holiness." The conference recalled that forty years previously *Life Magazine* had called Methodism America's "most characteristic church," being "short on theology, long on good works, highly organized, and incurably optimistic."[42]

The Baptist evangelist Billy Graham has done much to improve communication between the United States and Russia. He has also issued an important plea for an end to intolerance in religion. "The whole weight of Scripture," Graham believes, "is for treating all people with neighbor-love. We must dare to obey the commandment of love, and leave the consequences in God's hands. Teach love for other races in the home. Be careful not to pass on to your children the sins of prejudice."

A pioneer in ecumenicity, The United Church of Christ "is dedicated to the preservation of human dignity, the elimination of intolerance, the equality of men and women, ecumenical cooperation, and the responsibility of all to 'work and pray for the transformation of the world into the Kingdom of God.'"[43]

The Disciples of Christ has long been a church impelled by a passion for unity. This position was made clear in a book written recently by nine of the church leaders. The book states that the Incarnation, or the inhumanizing of God, means not only that Christ was the Word made flesh. In addition, "it declares that God entered fully into the totality of human experience, into the closest possible union with the whole of humanity. That union continues forever unbroken. God remains eternally enfleshed in our entire suffering humanity. Any action upon any person anywhere is therefore visited upon God.

The Holy Spirit clearly transcends the narrow confines of formal religion and of a particular people. Disciples have been particularly impressed by the explicit and implicit affirmation of unity in the New Testament, and have celebrated the unity of the church as a foretaste of the unity which God wills for all of creation.

The threat of war will continue to overshadow the planet until humanity is able to see that above all the nations is the human family, the sisterhood and brotherhood of all people, until we are able to see our wholeness and common destiny with more clarity than we see our divisions and differences. Part of the new vision will be the recognition that we are all 'members one of another' (Ephesians 4:25)."[44]

Jaime Wright, executive for the Brazil mission of the Presbyterian Church/U.S.A. and Paulo Evaristo Cardinal Arns, Roman Catholic Archbishop of São Paulo, recently published a book *Torture in Brazil,* which exposes the pervasive use of torture by Brazilian governments from 1964 to 1979. Philip Potter, general secretary of the World Council of Churches, provided funding to photocopy a million pages of records of sessions of the Supreme Military Court, which verified the use of torture. "Torture," said Potter, "destroys a person's dignity, emptying him of his humanity and turning him into a jellyfish."[45] Since in the past the Christian church had condoned torture, Potter, a Methodist minister, considers it important to show that the church has now completely reversed its stand.

Modern Orthodox Unitiveness

Although he disagreed so strenuously with the practices of the Russian Orthodox Church that he was eventually excommunicated, Leo Tolstoy can best be understood as a product of that faith. "Christ showed me," Tolstoy said, "that the unity of the son of man, the love of men for one another, is not merely an ideal, but that this unity, this love, is their natural condition, the condition in which all men would live if they were not drawn aside by error, illusions, and temptations. Christ clearly enumerated every one of the temptations that deprive men of this natural condition of unity, love, and goodness. Christ's commands give me the means of salvation from the temptations that have deprived me of happiness, and so I cannot help believing in these commands."[46] Tolstoy listed these temptations as anger, jingoism, lust, pride, vengeance, and lack of brotherhood.

Christ's message, Tolstoy thought, could be summed up in his one statement: "resist not evil," which means "never do anything contrary to the law of love." If someone harms you, you do not try to "get even" by resorting to violence and hatred. Instead, you try to "get better," by returning good for evil.

"I was driven from the Church," Tolstoy confessed, "by the strangeness of its dogmas, and the approval it gave to persecutions, the death penalty, wars, and the intolerance common to all sects. But my faith was chiefly shattered by the indifference of the Church to what seemed to me essential in the teachings of Jesus: love, humility, self-denial, and returning good for evil. The rules of the Church destroyed the desire for Christian truth. All human evil, the habit of judging private persons, nations, and other religions, and the wars and massacres that were the consequence of such judgments, all went on with the approval of the Church." The Church had missed Christ's main point, Tolstoy felt. It overlooked the messages contained in the Sermon on the Mount in order to find some obscure and unimportant phrase upon which "whole mountains of theology are based."[47]

The words that meant the most to him in the Church service, he said, were, "Let us love one another in unity." He added that "Jesus knew that his mission was to make clear to men, the children of one Father, their real unity, despite differences of religion. There shall come a time when all the temples will be ruined, with all the external God-worship; when all men will understand, and unite in love, to serve the one Father of life, by fulfilling His will."[48]

Tolstoy ultimately concluded that he would have no part in the war-making process, even to pay taxes which buy armaments. In a warlike society, he felt he had to do what Christ would do—speak up for peace. "I understand now that true welfare is possible for me," he explained, "only on condition that I recognize my unity with the whole world. I cannot recognize states or peoples. I can take no part in quarrels between peoples or states."[49]

The agnostic but Christlike Anton Chekhov said that religious faith is a spiritual faculty which only highly developed natures can possess. "Lord," he prayed, "do not allow me to condemn or to speak of what I do not know or do not understand."

The Russian philosopher Nicholas Berdyaev said that "for us Christians the Jewish problem does not consist in knowing whether the Jews are good or bad, but whether we are good or bad." He added that "nationalism is a terrible sin in relation to the image of God in man. He who does not see a brother in man, but another nationality, who, for example, refuses to see a brother in a Jew, such a one is not only not Christian, but is losing his own proper humanity. Christianity is a personalist and a universal religion but not a national or a racial religion."[50]

Despite all of its persecution by the Soviet regime, when the Russian Orthodox Church entered the World Council of Churches in 1961 it listed its membership at 40 million people, with 20,000 parishes, 30,000 priests, eight theological schools, and forty monasteries.

Joseph Campbell reported that a number of high state officials in the former Soviet Union belong to a secret society in which mystical union with God is sought through constant repetition, in Church Slavonic, of the phrase from Luke: "God, be merciful to me a sinner."[51]

In 1987 Orthodox Patriarch Dimitrios I and Pope John Paul II pledged to have their churches continue to work towards unity. They agreed to not proselytize each other's flock, and to work together for peace and justice. In 1988 Soviet leader Mikhail Gorbachev, in connection with the 1000th anniversary of Russia's conversion to Christianity, called on religious leaders to formulate a code of universal ethics, useful in adjudicating international disputes, similar to the religious and philosophical systems of medieval Christianity.

Modern Oriental Unitiveness

No country has shown more spiritual insight than has India. The modern period has seen important unitive contributions made by a number of Hindu spiritual masters. Aurobindo Ghose, a Bengali Brahmin, united East and West in a universal philosophy of love and peace. Through internal concentration a person can raise himself to a plane of close communion with God, Aurobindo taught.

Greatest of all modern unitive masters has been Mohandas Gandhi, called Mahatma (Great Soul) Gandhi (1869-1948). Although Gandhi was always tolerant of all religions, as a teenager he had little faith in God. But, he recalls, "a Gujarati didactic stanza gripped my mind and heart. Its precept—return good for evil—became my guiding principle:

For a bowl of water give a goodly meal.
For a simple penny pay thou back with gold.
The truly noble know all men as one,
And return with gladness good for evil done.[52]

Strong influences upon the young man were the Bhagavad Gita, Christ's teachings, and Leo Tolstoy's doctrine of non-resistance to evil. In 1921 Gandhi wrote: "I don't want my house to be walled on all sides. I want the cultures of all lands to be blown about my house as freely as possible. But I refuse to be blown off my feet by any."[53]

In order to validate his religion, Gandhi needed to validate the religion of others. Since there is only one God, there is, at base, only one religion. "We are turning away from God," he said, "from that religion which underlies all religions. Unless I accept the position that all religions are equal, and I have as much regard for other religions as I have for my own, I would not be able to live in the boiling war around me. I read the Gita, the Bible, and the Koran. I incorporate all that is good in other religions. The tree of Religion is the same. No branch is superior, none is inferior to the others.

There is no religion which is absolutely perfect. The many names of God do not indicate individuality but attributes. Living faith in God means acceptance of the brotherhood of mankind. Intolerance is a species of violence."[54]

Unitive religion was fully realized in this frail lawyer who said, "I have known no distinction between relatives and strangers, countrymen and foreigners, white and colored, Hindus and Moslems, Parsees, Christians, or Jews. My heart has been incapable of making any such distinctions."[55]

The duty of a human being, Gandhi taught, was to diminish hatred and promote love. "Jesus lived and died in vain," he said, "if He did not teach us to regulate the whole of life by the eternal law of love." Ahimsa, or non-violence, is the first step in the self-mastery by which the spiritually oriented person raises himself towards God. In Gandhi's words, "To see the universal and all-pervading Spirit of Truth face to face one must be able to love the meanest of creatures as oneself. Identification with everything that lives is impossible without self-purification."[56]

"Non-violence," he said, "is the law of our species as violence is the law of beasts. The dignity of man requires obedience to a higher law, that of the spirit. The Hindu holy men who discovered the law of non-violence in the midst of violence were greater geniuses than Newton. They were greater warriors than Wellington."[57] "When the practice of ahimsa becomes universal, God will reign on earth as He does in heaven. The first principle of non-violent action is non-cooperation with everything humiliating."

Thomas Merton summarized how the love unity of Gandhi worked. "The Indian mind that was awakening in Gandhi was inclusive, not exclusive. It was at once Indian and universal. It was not a mind of hate, of intolerance, of rejection, of division. It was a mind of love, understanding, and infinite capaciousness. The spirit which Gandhi was discovering in himself was reaching out to unity, love, and peace. It was a spirit strong enough to heal every division."[58]

Another unitive force was Sarvepalli Radhakrishnan (1888-1975), who was president of India from 1962 to 1967. His study of world religions led him to conclude that they had an underlying common core which could be perceived through mystical insight but not through reasoning and logic. Spiritual maturity meant a life of service and sacrifice, he stated. It also meant that a religious person, out of love, wished to cooperate with persons of other faiths.

A recent student of the Bhagavad Gita, A.C. Bhaktivedanta, lists the chief virtues, as revealed there, to be equanimity, humility, non-violence, pricelessness, self-control, tolerance, and unalloyed devotion to serving God. He summarized the mystical path to God as seen in the Gita: "One whose happiness is within is the perfect mystic. Ultimately he attains the Supreme. One who is always busy working for the welfare of all sentient beings, and who is free from all sins, achieves liberation in the Supreme. A true mystic observes Me in all beings; indeed, the self-realized person sees Me everywhere."[59]

A modern Japanese unitive sect is Rissho Koseiko, a branch of Nichiren Buddhism. Its founder and president, Nikkyo Niwano, told Pope Paul VI in 1965, "I clearly felt that there is little difference between God's love as taught by Christ or the love of humanity and the idea of compassion as advocated by Buddha." Niwano emphasizes the importance of dialogue among world religions as a foundation for world peace.

The profound reverence for nature in Shinto can make a signal contribution to a more ecologically pure environment. The pure heart, says Shinto, follows nature's forms. Pollution and contamination, seen from this religious perspective, are sinful violations of nature's simple beauty.

Modern Unitive Religion

After a lifetime assuming Christ's uniqueness, Professor R.C. Zaehner finally expanded his consciousness to see the spiritual validity in every sincere search for God. His study of comparative religion broadened his perception. Buddha and Zoroaster, he found, showed that the soul is immortal. The Gita and the New Testament indicate how a dying God can reveal His love for man. Thus, "all the major religions are the repositories of true revelations and therefore true mysticism. which seems to be working out of the revelations."[60] Zaehner employed the mysticism of Teilhard de Chardin to see how matter can become spiritualized, thus making possible rapprochement between Christianity and non-violent Marxism. To Zaehner, as to Teilhard, the Holy Spirit became one with matter in the creation, and Christ became one with matter in the Incarnation. Thus, "Marxism and Christianity are not necessarily inimical. Both describe a world on the move to convergence, but it is a convergence in love as well as justice."[61]

Zaehner nevertheless saw Christ as a unifying force in world religions "Jesus," he said, "fulfills the best hopes of India, Iran, Judaism, and China by being Incarnate God, Resurrected man, Compassionate One, Messiah, and Reconciler of human situations and the one to Tao."[62]

In his book *Spiritual Politics* Mark Silk has shown that for an exclusivist church to survive in the United States it must develop something in common with other churches, a process Silk calls "adhesion." The United States has by now engendered what sociologist Robert Bellah calls "civil religion," a common set of aspirations which is both "authentically religious and a good thing." In religion the converse of Gresham's law is finally beginning to operate: good (unitive) values drive out bad (divisive) values.

The Golden Rule, as a universal ethical principle, is already accepted by all of the major world religions. Thomas Merton reminded Christians that the Bible recognizes natural religion (in Acts 17:22-31 and Romans 2:14-15). "One of the marks of catholicity," said Merton, "is precisely that values which are everywhere natural to man are fulfilled on the highest level in the Law of the Spirit."[63]

John Hick is sure that God wishes for the salvation of all mankind. He says, "Does not the divine love for all mankind, and the divine lordship over all life, exclude the idea that salvation occurs in only one strand of human history? If God's love is universal in scope, He cannot thus have restricted His saving encounter with humanity. If God is the God of the whole world, we must presume that the whole religious life of mankind is part of a continuous human relationship to Him."[64]

At a peace conference in Kyoto, Japan, in 1970 221 representatives of the world's religions passed this resolution: "Resolved, the things which unite us are more important than the things which divide us. We possess in common a belief in:

1. the equality and dignity of all human beings.
2. the fundamental unity of the human family.
3. the inviolability of the individual and his conscience.
4. might does not make right.
5. love, compassion, selflessness, and the power of the spirit ultimately have greater strength than hate, enmity, and self-interest.
6. feeling for the oppressed against the oppressor."[65]

John Macquarrie, an Anglican theologian, suggests a worldwide Christian federation, with the pope serving as the presiding officer of a college of primates, each of whom would be the head of his individual church. The college would vote on common matters, and the pope would execute the wishes of the college. Such a pope as John XXIII would have no trouble in being accepted, Macquarrie feels. No church would surrender any of its existing autonomy, but collective action could be forthcoming in such problem areas as crime, discrimination, drug control, and war.

So much progress has recently been made in the area of unitive religion that the prayer of the Jewish Reconstructionist Foundation may someday soon be relevant: "We hope in Thee, O Lord our God, and in the coming of Thy kingdom, when Thy unity and supremacy will be realized throughout the world, and all men bound together to Thy law of righteousness. On that day people will be ashamed of exclusive and self-arrogant worship whereby nations, races, and churches profane Thy name. Then will people recognize in the soul of every nation, race, and religion a manifestation of Thy divine spirit, and will accord to every human society the equal right to serve Thee with whatever gifts Thou hast bestowed upon it. Men will not learn warfare any more, for the earth shall be filled with the knowledge of Thee."[66]

References

1. Rousseau, p. 6.
2. Swidler, pp. 8-9.
3. Werner Heisenberg, *Physics and Philosophy* (Harper, 1958), pp. ix, xiii-xiv.
4. Marty, PRO, pp. 37, 41.
5. W.C. Smith, *Religious Diversity,* pp. 131, 135, 137.
6. Voss, p. 211.
7. Richard Allen, *Imperialism and Nationalism in the Fertile Crescent* (Oxford University Press, 1974), p. 316.
8. Dimont, p. 205.
9. "Anti-Semitism," *Encyclopedia Britannica*, 1971, vol. 2, p. 86.
10. Thomas Keneally, *New York Times Book Review*, 4 September 1988, p. 18.
11. Judy Ball, *St. Anthony Messenger* (July 1987) 95:36-40.
12. Ari L. Goldman, *New York Times,* 6 September 1987, 4:7.
13. Peter Steinfels, ibid., 24 July 1988, 4:26.
14. Michael Ryan, *Parade Magazine,* 3 April 1988, p. 16.
15. Küng, *Christianity and the World Religions*, pp. 118, 120.
16. Ferm, pp. 135-36.
17. Hick & Hebblethwaite, pp. 85-86.
18. Ibid., pp. 83-85.
19. Ibid., pp. 82-83.
20. Swidler, pp. 25-26.
21. Bernard Leeming, "Holy Spirit," *Encyclopedia Britannica*, 1971, vol. 11, p. 618.
22. "Anti-Clericalism," ibid., vol. 2, p. 65.
23. Swidler, p. 7.
24. *St. Anthony Messenger* (October 1983) 91:14-16.
25. Ibid., January 1987, pp. 28-33.
26. Ibid., December 1987, p. 18.
27. Leslie Rubenstein, *New York Times*, 19 April 1987, 2:21-22.
28. Fremantle, p. 98.
29. *St. Anthony Messenger* (September 1988) 98:83-88.
30. Swidler, p. 248.
31. J. Leslie Dunstan, ed. *Protestantism* (Braziller, 1962), pp. 224-26.

[32] Parrinder, *Religion in Africa*, p. 147.
[33] Ibid., p. 148.
[34] Noss, p. 708.
[35] Hinchliff, p. 49.
[36] Robinson, pp. 42, 67.
[37] Ibish, pp. 93-97.
[38] Swidler, p. 229.
[39] Hick & Hebblethwaite, p. 186.
[40] Edward H. Milligan, *Encyclopedia Britannica*, 1971, vol. 9, pp. 941-42.
[41] Phillips, p. 414.
[42] Peter Steinfels, *New York Times*, 8 May 1988, 4:7.
[43] D.W. O'Connor, in Crim, p. 777.
[44] *Seeking God's Peace in a Nuclear Age* (CBP Press, 1985), pp. 51, 53-54, 85-86.
[45] Lawrence Weschler, *The New Yorker* (25 May 1987) 63:78.
[46] Leo Tolstoy, *My Confession: My Religion: The Gospel in Brief* (Scribners, 1929), p. 266.
[47] Ibid., pp. 79-81.
[48] Ibid., pp. 442-43.
[49] Ibid., pp. 273-74.
[50] Nicholas Berdyaev, *Slavery and Freedom* (Scribners, 1944), pp. 171-72.
[51] Campbell, *Spiritual Disciplines*, p. 266.
[52] Mohandas Gandhi, *An Autobiography* (Beacon, 1957), p. 51.
[53] Quoted in *Sketches of Gandhi* (Hindustan Times, 1953), p. 9.
[54] *Homage to Mahatma Gandhi* (Indian Ministry of Information, n.d.), p. 97.
[55] Gandhi, p. 276.
[56] Ibid., p. 504.
[57] Radhakrishnan, p. 56.
[58] *Gandhi on Non-Violence*, ed. by Thomas Merton (New Directions, 1965), pp. 5, 25, 28.
[59] Bhaktivedanta, pp. 100, 111.
[60] Newell, p. 23.
[61] Ibid., p. 40.
[62] Ibid.

[63] *Gandhi on Non-Violence*, p. 5.
[64] Hick, pp. 100-01.
[65] Swidler, pp. 29-30.
[66] Voss, pp. 272-73.

CHAPTER 14

THE UNITIVENESS OF MODERN SCIENCE

Once religion's chief adversary, science is now religion's greatest benefactor. In reading the findings of a modern particle physicist one wonders if perhaps he is perusing an ancient religious text.

Positivism, which was based on matter as the ultimate reality, died when Einstein demonstrated that matter is just another form of energy. The dialectical materialism of Marxism, which used a positivistic base, faded into the air along with the dissolution of matter. Karl Heim declared that "in a cubic yard of lead, the amount of rigid matter is less than a pin head."[1]

This century has witnessed the death of scientific absolutes. Einstein's theory of relativity dealt a fatal blow to previous notions of absolute space and absolute time. Werner Heisenberg's uncertainty principle, along with Gödel's theorem, laid aside notions of absolute causality, the idea that everything can be explained in terms of cause and effect, stimulus and response. Scientific objectivity has been redefined as researchers discovered that it is futile to speak of an absolute object apart from its relationship to a subjective observer. Heim paraphrases the First Commandment to have God saying, "I am the Absolute, and thou shalt have no absolutes besides me."

Heisenberg, Erwin Schrödinger, and other leading physicists have abandoned the traditional dualisms of space and time, matter and energy, and subject and object. Christ too rejected dualism—he never made the mistake of identifying himself with his body. In other words, he accepted no dualism, but was always at one with his Father.

Paul Tillich has shown why modern humans must be subjective. A person is a subject (sub-jectum), something standing upon itself. If a person becomes an object (something outside the self), he becomes a thing, is dehumanized, and is frequently treated inhumanely.

Michael Talbot describes the new scientific approach as "omnijective." "There is no strict division, Talbot says, "between subjective and objective reality. Consciousness and the physical universe are connected by some fundamental physical mechanism. This relationship between mind and reality is not subjective or objective but 'omnijective.'"[2]

This is by no means a new idea. Over two thousand years ago the Hindu Tantric tradition had a similar view, which stated that the chief human error is to perceive oneself as being separate from one's environment. Physicist Jack Sarfatti states that "the quantum principle involved *mind* in an essential way along the lines suggested by Parmenides, Bishop Berkeley, James Jeans, Alfred North Whitehead, and others." Another physicist, John A. Wheeler, declares that in scientific experiments we must replace the term "observer" with the term "participator."

As the distinction between subject and object vanishes, so does the dichotomy between science and religion. William Irwin Thompson summarizes current thinking on the topic: "If there is a structure to consciousness, and this can be expressed scientifically in mathematics; and if there is a structure to matter, and this can be expressed scientifically in the mathematics of the quantum theory, then the forms of one relate to the forms of the other through pure form, the structure of structures, the Logos."[3] Thus John 1:1 seems to be correct: "In the beginning was the Logos, and the Logos was God." So too the corollary (John 1:14): "And the Logos became flesh, and dwelt among us."

The interface between science and religion continues to bear fruit. Heisenberg said that his conversations with the Hindu poet Tagore helped him formulate his principles of physics. Niels Bohr acknowledged his indebtedness to Chinese religion in aiding in the development of the quantum theory. D.T. Suzuki said that Zen Buddhism avers that time and space are not separate but are interrelated, an assumption underlying Einstein's concept of the fourth dimension.

Modern biology, physics, and psychology tend to agree with two basic concepts of religious mysticism: the fundamental unity and interrelatedness of the universe, and the dynamic nature of the cosmos (known in mysticism as the many and the One). It is paradoxical that many traditional non-literate cultures have always seen the events of the universe as interconnected, and thus may be more modern than literate cultures which analyze and discriminate.

The change in the scientific paradigm involves a reinforcement of ancient religious teachings. It has been demonstrated that religious faith releases endorphins, brain substances which are not only transmitters but also pain killers. Nobel laureate Ilya Prigogine says that all open systems (such as a seed, a person, or a culture) are dissipative structures, that is, their parts can reorganize into a new whole, and the system can then escape upward into a higher order. Applied to religion, this means that closed systems, which demand conformity, are dying, but open systems, which invite newness and accommodation, are very much alive. To be alive means to be able to change. The brain may be a hologram, says Marilyn Ferguson, mathematically constructing reality by interpreting frequencies from a dimension beyond time and space. Neurologist Karl Pribram reports that modern knowledge of the operation of the brain validates experience reported from spiritual disciplines.

Modern physics now sees interrelationship between what were once thought to be contraries: rest and motion, wave and particle, structure and function, and mass and energy. "In ultimate reality," says Ken Wilber, "there are no boundaries." Nicholas of Cusa, the mystic, called God the reconciliation of opposites.

Alfred Kazin, reviewing physicist Spencer Weart's book *Nuclear Fear*, says Weart "finds some measure of hope in that reconciliation of opposites represented by the mandala, a mystical symbol of containment. Since Hitler convinced me of original sin," Kazin continues, "I am sympathetic to Weart's essentially religious belief that there is a fundamental unity to nature that must be recognized and realized in the human soul. All the leading physicists believe in that unity and their researches prove it. Weart believes, without saying so, that we must love, starting with ourselves, or die. But not everyone who talks about heaven is going there."[4]

Spiritual Views of Modern Scientists

Many modern scientists express views similar to or identical with concepts found in religion. Einstein said of physicist Max Planck (1858-1947): "The longing to behold harmony is the source of the inexhaustible patience and perseverance of Planck, a state of mind akin to that of the religious worshipper or the lover." Planck averred that modern scientists believe in miracles, in the power of mysterious agencies. This belief, he said, arises from the autarchy of the ego, but the ego can never consider itself driven by purely causal influences. "Those forms of religion which have a nihilist attitude to life," said Planck, "are out of harmony with the scientific outlook and contradictory to its principles. All denial of life's value for its own sake is a denial of science and religion. Over the gates of the temple of science are written the words: 'Ye must have faith.'"[5]

The astronomer James Jeans said that perhaps the mind is the creator and governing principle of matter. Maybe Bishop Berkeley was right, said Jeans—all objects exist in the mind of God. "The motions of electrons and atoms do not resemble those of the parts of a locomotive so much as those of the dancers in a cotillion. The universe shows evidence of a designing or controlling power that has something in common with our own individual minds. We are not so much strangers in the universe as we at first thought."[6]

Albert Einstein's empathy towards religion is well known. He said that "pure thought can grasp reality, as the ancients dreamed. The most beautiful and deepest experience a man can have is the sense of the mysterious. It is the underlying principle of religion as well as art and science. A human being is part of a whole, called by us 'Universe.' He experiences himself as something separated from the rest. This delusion is a kind of prison for us. Our task must be to free ourselves from this prison by widening the whole circle of compassion to embrace all living creatures. The striving for such achievement is a foundation for inner security."[7]

Science, said Einstein, can cure religion of superstition and fanaticism, and aid religion in its search for truth. "Civilized mankind is in grave danger," Einstein felt. "Nationalism and intolerance, as well as the oppression of individuals by economic means, threatens to choke these most precious traditions. There is no room for the divinization of a nation, class, or individual. Are we not all children of one Father?"[8]

In all of his theorizing, Einstein was more Kabalistic than logical. Religion, he believed, evolved. In early societies religion was based largely on fear, but in later times there was more stress on morality. The highest stage of religion is to experience a mystical cosmic feeling of oneness with the universe. This feeling, which motivated great scientists like Newton and Kepler, "is the strongest and noblest motive for scientific research," Einstein stated.

The astronomer Arthur Eddington wryly commented that the positivist, who thinks all things can be explained on material grounds, would have to admit that his wife would be "a rather elaborate differential equation!" "Physics is now formulated in such a way," said Eddington, "as to make it almost self-evident that it is a partial aspect of something wider." That something is, of course, the metaphysical. He continued: "The new physics gives strong grounds for an idealistic philosophy which is hospitable towards a spiritual religion. In short, the new conception of the physical universe puts me in a position to defend religion against the charge of being incompatible with physical science. I assert," he added, "that the nature of all reality is spiritual, not material nor a dualism of matter and spirit. The stuff of the world is mind-stuff. The mind-stuff is not spread in space and time; these are part of the cyclic scheme ultimately derived out of it." He added humorously that scientists like himself run around in circles, like a cat chasing its tail, never getting to the level of the mind-stuff at all.

Religion, he felt, gave persons a chance to experience the mind-stuff. "In the mystic experience, our minds are not apart from the world, and the feelings we have are not of ourselves alone, but are glimpses of a reality transcending the narrow limits of our own particular consciousness—that the harmony and beauty of the face of Nature is, at root, one with the gladness that transfigures the face of men. The idea of a universal Mind or Logos would be a fairly plausible inference from the present state of scientific inquiry; at least it is in harmony with it."[9]

Erwin Schrödinger (1887-1961) was another physicist who validated the mystical unity of mankind. "We know when God is experienced," he said "This is an event as real as an immediate sense perception or as one's own personality. It is not possible that this unity of knowledge, feeling, and choice which you call *your own* should have sprung into being from nothingness at a given moment not so long ago. Rather this knowledge, feeling, and choice are essentially eternal and unchangeable and numerically *one* in all men. You, and all other conscious beings as such, are all in all."[10] One wonders whether this is a physicist speaking or Plotinus!

Louis de Broglie was the physicist who discovered that moving electrons produce waves. His finding led to Schrödinger's wave equations, which are a basic part of quantum mechanics. De Broglie said that as we delve into particle physics, we find ourselves probing our most inward nature. Just beyond the grasp of the particle researchers, he felt, lay a metaphysical order which portrayed the harmony of the universe. Because our souls have not matured in proportion to physical knowledge, the Atomic Age, which could be an era of remarkable progress, might end up being a period of inexpiable strife, de Broglie feared.

Wolfgang Pauli, the Austrian Nobel Prize physicist, synthesized the rational with the mystical. He noted how Johan Kepler's concept of the Holy Trinity gave Kepler a symbol of the solar system. Pauli believed that modern science provides a Christian elaboration of Plato's mysticism in which, to quote Heisenberg, "the unitary ground of spirit and matter is sought in the primeval images, and in which understanding has found its place in its various degrees and kinds, even to knowledge of the word of God."

Pauli repeatedly sought "to break out of the accustomed grooves of thought in order to come closer, by new paths, to an understanding of the unitary structure of the world." Pauli said, "I consider the ambition of overcoming opposites, including also a synthesis embracing both rational understanding and the mystical experience of unity, to be the mythos of our present age."[11]

The uncertainty principle formulated by Werner Heisenberg states that it is impossible to determine both the position and the momentum of a particle at any one given time. A further application is the impossibility of knowing both the time an atomic event takes and the energy it involves. As a seminal thinker in modern physics, Heisenberg deserves attention also for his views on religion.

"In the final analysis," he said, "all the old religions try to express the same contents, and these all hinge around questions about values. We ought to make every effort to grasp their meaning, since it quite obviously refers to a crucial aspect of reality. Plato was much nearer the truth about the structure of matter than Democritus. For the smallest units of matter are not physical objects; they are forms, structures, or Ideas. Plato was right in believing that, at the heart of nature, among the smallest units of matter we find mathematical symmetries. If we wish to approach the 'one' in terms of precise scientific language, we must turn to Plato. Plato's images are probably connected with the unconscious mental patterns the psychologists speak of as archetypes, forms of strongly emotional character that, in some, way, reflect the internal structures of the world."[12]

Science and Religion

English physicist Paul Davies says that modern physics finds a closer accord with mysticism than with materialism. Science, asserts Davies, "offers a surer path to God than does religion." Religion, through myth and festival, arrives at the same point as does the particle physicist—the Big Bang, a given moment of creation. Davies proposes a set of modern scientific proofs for the existence of God:[13]

1. "The present arrangement of matter and energy, with matter spread thinly, would result only from a very special choice of initial conditions. Roger Penrose has computed the odds against the observed universe appearing by accident at $10^{10^{30}}$ to 1!
2. The large-scale structure and motion of the universe is equally remarkable." There is a delicate balance between gravity and expansion. "The matching was accurate to a staggering one part in 10^{60}. To give meaning to these numbers, suppose you wanted to fire a bullet at a one-inch target on the other side of the observable universe, twenty billion light years away. Your aim would have to be accurate to this same extent."

3. The universe is remarkably uniform, both in the distribution of matter and the rate of expansion. Although most explosions are chaotic, the Big Bang was very symmetrical. "It seems that the entire observable universe was immediately separated into at least 10^{80} causally disconnected regions. How is it possible to explain this cooperation without communication? Why are those regions that are causally disconnected so similar in structure and behavior?"
4. The universe has an extreme degree of cosmic isotrophy (uniformity with orientation). "Had the Big Bang been a random event, such exceptional uniformity would be almost impossibly unlikely. Channeling the explosive violence into such an organized pattern of motion seems like a miracle.
5. The seemingly miraculous concurrence of numerical values that nature has assigned to her fundamental constants must remain the most compelling evidence for an element of cosmic design." For example, the balance of forces within stars is so delicate that a change in gravitational force of one part in 10^{40} would destroy the necessary balance between blue giant and red dwarf stars.

Michael Talbot gives a scientific explanation of what are called gods in religion: "Our earth might exist in 'hyperspace' or in a space with four or more directions and 'hypertime' or a time which permits events and processes to occur in other than an irreversibly linear and unidirectional manner. On such a 'hyperhistorical' sphere, miraculous beings from our religion and folklore might become explicable intrusions rather than miraculous occurrences."[14]

Talbot then lists a series of modern scientific discoveries which help demonstrate the oneness of science and religion:[15]

1. The Hindu Satprem, biographer of Sri Aurobindo, says that "the realization of the Vedic holy men has become a collective realization: the Supermind has entered the earth-consciousness." As matter vanishes, spirit enters.
2. The physicist Robert Oppenheimer said that "discoveries in atomic physics are not wholly unfamiliar" but are a

"refinement of old wisdom" as seen in the Judeo-Christian tradition and in Buddhist and Hindu thought.
3. Mathematician Hermann Minkowski agrees with Hindu Advaita: In the beginning there was simply the Absolute, who revealed Himself to humans via the sensory modes of time, space, and causation.
4. Vivekananda said what the quantum theory confirmed: "There is no such thing as strict causality." The cause-effect theory impeded the discovery of the quantum theory. Instead, "mystical philosophies hold much more information to aid us in the startling world view of the new physics."
5. "The Hindu concepts of *nada* and *bindu* are identical to the concept of matter being both a wave and a particle. Nada means vibration; bindu means a point." Seen separately, matter seems to be a point. But seen in its interdependence (when everything collapses to one dimension), matter appears as a vibration.
6. In Hinduism, the primordial power Prakrti exhibits itself, in one mode, as a gross force, akasa. "Prakrti, or the universe of physical objects, is seen as being composed of vibration. In essence, the theory of the akasa is identical with physicist John A. Wheeler's quantum foam. Matter is vibrations in the akasa. Matter is undulations in the quantum foam." Here we find the non-Euclidean geometry of modern science confirming the mystical teachings of ancient Tantrism.

Talbot also provides a religious explanation of what astronomers call a black hole. At the end of their lives, stars as big as three times our sun collapse, and create a black hole in space. The gravitational field thereby created is so powerful that nothing, not even light, can escape it. "The entire universe could be swallowed up in a black hole and shrink to a point bindu or a point without dimension." Tantrism calls this the Siva bindu— "the universe is withdrawn into the Sakti which created it."[16]

American astronauts discovered that as they traveled through space, their consciousness expanded. A space perspective enabled them to conceive of the earth as a unit, and humankind as a unity. Edgar Mitchell did research into psychic healing. Rusty Schweikart investigated Maharishi's transcendental meditation.

James Irwin conducted an archeological expedition to search for evidence of the ark on Mt. Ararat.

Joseph Campbell agrees that an important discovery of the space age is the fact that the human species is a single unit, that Martin Buber is correct in saying that our relation to God is not I-It but rather Thou-I. Our divided schizophrenic world is now dead, Campbell says, and earth and heaven are one. "The exclusiveness of there being only one way in which we can be saved, the idea that there is a single religious group that is in sole possession of the truth, that is the world that must pass away. What is the kingdom? It lies in the realization of the divine presence in our neighbors, in our enemies, in all of us."[17]

Stephen Jay Gould, Harvard paleontologist, postulates a human brotherhood based on the earthly evidence. "We must realize," Gould says, "that all human beings, despite differences in external appearance, are really members of a single entity that's had a very recent origin in one place. There is a kind of biological brotherhood that's much more profound than we ever realized." Michigan paleontologist Milford Wolpoff believes that human history is somewhat longer than Gould assumes, but that "we have a long history of people mixing with one another and cooperating with one another and evolving into one great family."[18]

Another paleontologist, the Jesuit Teilhard de Chardin, concluded that "neither in its impetus nor in its achievements can science go to its limits without becoming tinged with mysticism or charged with faith." Physicist Andrew M. Sandorfi finds sermons in particles. "The basic building blocks of the human body," Sandorfi explains, "are protons and neutrons. Both of these bodies are made up of three entities (quarks), each of which is distinct, although they can never be separated. Michelangelo could not produce a better representation of a triune God."[19]

A pair of physicists agree that God is made manifest through physical forces. Mujaddid Izaz and Mansoor Ijaz said that "we believe that God as the ultimate unifying force is a solution as elegant as superstring theories and manmade universes. The evidence for our hypothesis is in the holy books. Whether we call the ultimate unification force God or something else is irrelevant. But incorporation of His attributes into our models and theories is an inevitability the physics community should not continue to ignore."[20]

The fact of creation now seems to be a unifying factor between the separate disciplines of science and religion. Paul Davies states "that there was some sort of creation seems, from the scientific point of view, compelling. The universe cannot have existed forever, otherwise it would have reached its equilibrium end state an infinite time ago. Conclusion: the universe did not always exist."[21] Not only matter but also space and time, Davies says, were created at the Big Bang.

The great astronomer William Herschel declared, "Let a man once know what sort of a being he is; how great the Being who brought him into existence; how utterly transitory is everything in the material world; and I maintain that then he is as happy as it is possible for him to be."[22]

Physicist Heinz Pagels marvels at the symmetry of the universe. "There is a complex interplay among all the objects we observe in the heavens," Pagels finds. "For example, the atoms of planets and the atoms in our bodies consist of many heavy chemical elements that were cooked up out of lighter elements in the nuclear furnaces of stars long ago. Life in the universe depends on a complex relation of parts to the whole. Remarkably, the largest things we see—galaxies and clusters of galaxies—may not only be structured by the smallest things we know—quantum particles—but actually owe their existence to them. A beautiful confirmation of the unity of the universe was William Huggins' development of visual stellar spectroscopy and Henry Draper's photographing the hydrogen-absorption spectrum of the star Vega in 1872." They established that a star is composed of the same atoms as those found on earth.[23]

The cosmological principle, Pagels says, states that "all places in the universe are alike." Thus, Nicholas of Cusa was correct when he said that "the fabric of the world has its center everywhere and its circumference nowhere." Pagels feels that "the isotropy of the universe is indeed amazing. The temperature of the microwave background radiation is nearly the same in every direction of the sky, in spite of the fact that this radiation originates from billion upon billions of regions of the universe that were causally disconnected in the Big Bang. How were all those distinct regions 'precisely instructed' to have the same temperature today? Likewise, what 'told' the galaxies and quasars to be distributed so uniformly?"[24]

Pagels believes that the spiritual is organic to human nature. Like sex, he observes, "the ubiquitous human need to find some ultimate foundation to existence seems to be organic or biological in origin. If this is so, then denying such spiritual impulses can only result in distortion of our humanity."[25]

Love as Healing Agent

Dr. Bernard Siegel, president of the American Holistic Medical Association, feels that "all disease is ultimately related to a lack of love, or to love that is only conditional. All healing is related to the ability to give and accept unconditional love. To me the true measure of holistic medicine is how the patient and doctor accept each other's belief system, even though their beliefs may differ."[26]

Siegel reports many cases in which love has served as a healing agent. Drs. Powell and Thoresen at Mount Zion Hospital in San Francisco, for example, have halved the infarction rate of post-coronary patients. Their therapy was to turn "raging impatience and hostility into consideration for and love for others." A San Francisco cardiologist did "a statistically valid double-blind study on the benefits of prayer in reducing post-myocardial infarction complications." Dr. Richard Selzer described a doctor's compassion: "Out of the resonance between the sick man and the one who tends him may spring that profound courtesy that the religious call Love."[27] Siegel states that when so-called "terminal" patients survive, most physicians consider such cases too "mystical" to report to a medical journal.

Siegel describes the characteristics of societies having low cancer rates. Aside from dietary factors, these traits include strong religious faith, respect for the aged, loving interpersonal relations, and a peaceful attitude towards neighbors.

Type A persons (those who are hard-driving and success-oriented) can drastically reduce the likelihood of heart attack through the use of meditation and exercise, Siegel believes. "Studies of people who meditate regularly have shown that their physiological age is much lower than their chronological age." Siegel reports the findings of Dr. Herbert Benson on the physical effects of meditation. "It tends to lower or normalize blood pressure, pulse rate, and the levels of stress hormones in the blood. Brain wave patterns show less excitability." Meditation lowers over-competitive behavior that may lead to a heart attack. It "raises the pain threshold and reduces one's biological age. In short, it reduces wear and tear on both body and mind, helping people live better and longer."[28]

Type B persons, as a rule, understand the cycle of love better than do Type A people. Type B persons would rather give than get, and have a greater need for cooperation than for power. Paradoxically, their altruism, although based on unconditional love rather than upon anticipated rewards, "reinforces a genuine self-esteem that enables people to care for themselves effectively. Both giver and receiver are rewarded by the act of love itself." Type B people are more resistant to illness than are Type A. Siegel points out that if he told a patient to increase his immune globulins or his killer-T cells, the patient could not respond. But if the patient is told to love himself and others more, the immune system can benefit if the patient follows the advice. "The only Hell," said Dostoevsky, " is the inability to love."[29]

Modern psychology also respects the healing power of love. Carl Jung, like a Buddhist monk, explained that as desire melts, evil dissolves. Individuation was Jung's solution to the problem of personal evil. Instead of projecting one's evil upon others, in a futile effort to escape responsibility for it, one should acknowledge one's dark side, understand it without acting upon its impulses, and thereby redirect its power into productive channels, achieving a wholesome and well balanced personality through the process.

Jung said that our archetypes are motivating forces buried in our collective unconscious. Many of them, such as the wondrous child, the risen savior, and the wise old man, have deep religious significance. But it is very possible for people to misuse their archetypes. Elémire Zolla says that people seek to serve their archetypes but "muddleheadedly. They still feel the spirit of their party or nation molding their ways; they still wave its flag, and also think it wholesome to offer up human sacrifices to it. And if one were to inquire about the meaning they attach to their party or class or nation, they would answer that it gives scope and shape to their lives, though their world of drab ghouls is not as rationally articulate as the spiritual world of the primitives."[30]

Jung found universal agreement on many of the religious archetypes. Michael Talbot explained this universality as due to what he termed retro-causality. If, said Talbot, there is a universal tachyonic background to the universe (tachyons are particles which, by traveling faster than light, exist outside of space-time), then Jung's archetypes might be explained by retro-causality (the effect *precedes* the cause). Jung encountered striking similarities in religious symbols across eons of time and space, so that they could not possibly have influenced one another. They seem thus to be inherently grounded in the nature of the universe.

Resolution of conflicts and drives through religious meditation can produce a wholeness in which illness and nervous tension are unlikely to occur. "According to Dr. Beatrice Bruteau, when the individual is in *samadhi* (or has the 'peak experience' that Abraham Maslow describes), the brain is at rest, in the sense that the alpha rhythm does not register. The entire mind, however, including all levels of the unconscious, is engaged in only one idea, so that all its usual functions are harmonized and integrated, and there is no internal conflict or blockage."[31]

Norman O. Brown defines the unconscious as "that immortal sea which brought us hither, intimations of which are given in moments of 'oceanic feeling'; a sea of energy embracing all mankind, without distinction of race, language, or culture, embracing all generations of Adam in one mystical body. It is the true psychic reality, the Holy Spirit."[32]

William Irwin Thompson envisions Doris Lessing as a medium of the collective unconscious of this age. The world depicted in her novels, Thompson says, is "a universe that is a paradigm of the new science and the new world view of our emerging planetary culture."

Biologist Edmund Sinnott sees the need for religion as the anchor of an ethical system. "The brotherhood of man will come," Sinnott feels, "only if the Fatherhood of God is recognized. Moral problems will never be solved unless they are treated as part of the structure of the universe."[33]

George Ritchie, in *Return From Tomorrow,* said that "God is busy building a race of men who know how to love. I believe that the fate of the earth depends upon on the progress we make—and that the time now is very short." Mahatma Gandhi cautioned that "we must not kill our enemies, but kill their desire to kill."[34] Gandhi reminded us that Sanskrit has no word for "exclusion."

Since modern science has effectively destroyed matter as the basis for ultimate reality, Mikhail Gorbachev has asked for a universal code of values, built on the type of religious base used by medieval philosophers. With matter no longer available as the basis of dialectical materialism, the way is open for a renewed spirituality in modern Russia.

Holistic philosophy emanates from modern physics. "The quantum theory demolishes some cherished commonsense concepts about the nature of reality. By blurring the distinction between subject and object, cause and effect, it introduces a strong holistic element into our world view."[35]

Process theology derives from the process philosophy of Alfred North Whitehead and Charles Hartshorne. It sees the whole of reality, and man in particular, as events in a single great process. Reality is a succession of events, rather than fixed entities such as molecules, trees, animals, and so forth. "God is seen as the God who guarantees the process."[36]

Wholeness is an outgrowth of modern scientific thought. In the words of the novelist John Brunner, "You shall know the truth and the truth shall make you you." Marilyn Ferguson says that "the separate self is an illusion. The self is a field within larger fields."[37] Brotherhood engulfs us. If we see a hungry child on television, we feel responsible. The world is process, and we identify ourselves as a part of the process. Wholes cannot be understood by dissection. General Systems Theory states that each variable in a system interacts with other variables so intimately that cause and effect cannot be separated. A variable is at once a cause and an effect. This theory asserts that the world is not a blind interplay of atoms but a marvelously unified organization. Nobel laureate Albert Szent-Gyorgi says that living matter possesses syntropy, a drive towards ever greater order. All of these concepts reinforce unitive rather than divisive religion.

The Seamless Web of the Universe

Modern field theory postulates the unity of the universe. Dr. Harold Saxton Burr says, "In the last analysis, the universe is a unit, all of its parts are related to the wholeness of the universe, and there is necessarily some interrelationship between its wholeness and the activities of its individual components. There is one unifying characteristic of the universe which we have ignored, and that is its field properties."[38]

Teilhard de Chardin states that the deeper we penetrate into matter, the more we discover the interdependence of its parts. Each particle is woven from all the others. There is no way to isolate a part without affecting the other parts, and the whole.

"The seamless coat of the universe" is what Whitehead called the unitary relationship existing among all things. In Buddhism *dharmadhatu* (meaning "universal realm") teaches that "between every thing and event in the universe there is no boundary." Like a string of highly polished pearls, each pearl contains the reflection of the rest of the string. "One is all and all is one," mystics say. Similarly a modern physicist says that each particle consists of all the other particles. Eastern mystics call this universal undifferentiated realm "Suchness" or ultimate reality. "When a Buddhist says reality is void, he means it is void of boundaries."[39]

Man-made boundaries are artificial, interfering with God's tendency to unite. A physicist and a mystic can unite in calling all life a product of a single force, call it what they will: energy, the mystical body of Christ, the universal field of Brahman, or the organic pattern of the Tao.

Physicist Geoffrey Chew has formulated the bootstrap theory, which avers that nature cannot be reduced to tiny fundamental entities, since it is a dynamic web of interrelated events. One unit consists of all the other units. John Donne said that "no man is an island unto himself." The principle of organization in the universe is simple but complex—simple in that it is natural, but complex in its intricate interrelationships.

Unity is the paradox of particle physics. The deeper we analyze the nature of physical structures, the more we find synthesis at the core. The closer we get to the basic building blocks of the universe, the more interdependence we discover. Of the four basic forces (gravitation, electromagnetism, radioactivity, and the nuclear force), the most powerful one is called the strong force, that which binds the nucleus of the atom together. In the light of modern physics, heaven itself no longer need be considered a fanciful delusion. In the words of Michael Talbot, "phenomena such as the quantum potential and the proposed existence of the tachyon suggest that at least portions of our universe (and if the bootstrap view of consciousness and reality is correct, portions of our consciousness) exist outside time. The existence of an 'elsewhere' region beyond space-time has long been suggested by mystics. Now it is being suggested by physicists."[40]

Much of Jewish mysticism is consonant with modern physics. The *Sefer Bahir* (Book of Brilliance) has as its central premise the idea that "there is a vast unseen order beyond what we typically experience in everyday life." The *Zohar* (Book of Splendor) of Moses de Leon postulates that "everything in the cosmos is in constant interplay, with an irreducible order underlying all." Rabbi Moses Chaim Luzzatto in the 18th century taught that everything in the universe was interconnected with every other thing. The Kabala speaks of four hidden universes. Some modern physicists believe that they may truly exist. Persons like Einstein and Bob Toben describe cosmic forces in virtually the same language as the Kabala, which states that "we cannot study persons as separate entities, apart from the rest of the universe."[41]

Ken Wilber believes that not only did Christ leave behind an esoteric circle of gnostic disciples (such as John and Mary Magdalene) but also that a number of later Christian mystics have, on occasion, soared to the causal level. Jacob Boehme, for example, found the Abyss or the Void, the seamless coat of the universe where all is one. St. Catherine of Genoa asserted "My *me* is God!" Dame Juliana of Norwich and Meister Eckhart are among the other mystics who have sensed this primal unity.

The Implicate Order

The German philosopher Gottfried Leibnitz (1646-1716) anticipated the findings of modern physics. He said that we mistakenly think of matter as being composed of ever smaller entities. But if we conceive of reality as energy, which has no extension, then perhaps the ultimate building blocks are energy units, which Leibnitz called monads. Each monad strives to sustain its self-existence, but total reality is a universe of coordinated powers, synthesized through God's laws. When the individual soul rises to the level of perceiving its interrelation with other souls, it becomes the mirror of God, the Prime Monad. Leibnitz found a pre-established harmony existing among all monads.

Drawing largely upon his knowledge of quantum mechanics, physicist David Bohm postulates the presence of an original implicate order, the forerunner of the explicate order that we sense in everyday life. Our selfish selves lead us into fragmented, atomistic thinking, Bohm declares, which blocks that tap into the non-manifest implicate order which is the universal consciousness of mankind. Self-centeredness induces self-deception, leading one into a hopeless round of competition, strife, and warfare—acts that take a person (and his group) ever farther from the implicate order, and thus away from union with humans and with God.

Humanity's fragmentation, Bohm believes, is based upon a faulty world-view: that totality consists of independent unrelated components. Since relativity and quantum theory imply an undivided wholeness of the universe, fragmentative analysis is a vain effort to divide the indivisible. Whenever men divide themselves from the whole of society and try to set up insulated groups, these groups inevitably develop internal strife and lose their identity. "True unity," says Bohm, "in the individual and between man and nature as well as between man and man, can arise only in action that does not attempt to fragment the whole of reality." The words "measure" and "maya" (illusion) come from the same Sanskrit roots. Thus, "when measure is identified with the very essence of reality, this is illusion. It is an inference from the quantum theory that events that are separated in space and that are without possibility of connection through interaction are correlated, in a way that can be shown to be incapable of a detailed causal explanation.

Particles no longer are considered as autonomous. Everything implicates everything in an order of undivided wholeness. Everything is enfolded into everything." There is a progression, Bohm states, "from explicate order to simple three-dimensional implicate order, then to multi-dimensional implicate order, then on to an extension of this to the immense 'sea' in what is sensed as empty space."[42] In other words, so-called empty space contains an immense reservoir of energy, and matter is like a speck in this ocean, a tiny ripple in a vast sea. Hindus use this same

The Unitiveness of Modern Science 335

figure to describe the relation between the individual soul and the Over-Soul.

Bohm further reminds us that "the Zuni religion says that every person is a brother because the Earth is his mother and the Sun his father. If people could understand the nature of ordinary experience better, they would see that mystical experience is really an intensification of something they participate in. The mystic says that the good can be explained: that it is wholeness, harmony. The trouble is that this unity does not communicate to ordinary experience." We need a new language, Bohm feels, whereby the mystic can communicate concerning the experience of the implicate order. Nicholas of Cusa said that "eternity both enfolds and unfolds succession."[43]

Jean Piaget showed that young children experience the implicate realm before they settle down to explicate everyday reality. Reneé Weber explains how a finite human being can communicate with the infinite being of God. The Infinite, being nondimensional, cannot be perceived by three-dimensional minds. But if one's consciousness expands, one can get direct access to the implicate order, where wholeness is holiness. One is converted from a contributor to mankind's suffering to a boundless channel of compassion. Mystics alleviate suffering by proclaiming the healing power of love. "God is love, and he who abides in love abides in God, and God abides in him" (I John 4:16).

Ken Wilber underlines the importance of being able to expand one's consciousness into an identification with not only all of creation but even with the Creator. Wilber holds that "altered states of consciousness (which reflect altered brain states) may be due to a literal attunement to the invisible matrix that generates 'concrete' reality. This may enable interaction with reality at a primary level." The pineal gland, whose secretion melatonin regulates the pituitary gland, may be the "third eye" referred to by mystics, Wilber thinks. "Synchronicity, meaningful coincidence, makes sense in a meaningful, holographic universe. Love, joy, confidence, and the creative process may reflect states of consciousness resonating with the holistic wave aspect of reality. Anxiety and anger represent fragmented states." Karl Pribram accounts for sensory reality "as a 'special case' constructed by the brain's mathematics but drawn from a domain beyond time and space, where only frequencies exist."[44]

Science and Unitive Religion

Persons who understand and accept the most recent findings in the fields of astronomy, biology, mathematics, and particle physics are unlikely to be adherents of divisive religion. The very lesson of nature and its laws is that the universe is indeed one unity, despite the fragmentations we try to force upon it, whether for convenience in studying it or as a distortion to try to force our narrow world-view upon those of a different persuasion.

Michael Talbot summarizes the lessons to be learned from the convergence of mysticism and unitive religion with the new physics. He says that the ultimate nature of reality transcends language. Are there modes of expression beyond language which can tap ultimate reality, as mystics say they can do? Yes, answer Robert Sohl and Audrey Carr, who add that "to confuse the indivisible nature of reality with the differentiations and conceptual pigeonholes of language is the basic ignorance from which Zen seeks to free us." The cerebral cortex gave us our ability to use language, Talbot concludes, "but to experience reality beyond our verbal training we must retreat to the body-knowing—those holographic portions of thought which literally lie beyond words."

John A. Wheeler's conception of superspace and Jack Sarfatti's Unified Field Theory suggest that the world is "omnijective," that is, at once objective and subjective. As Tantrists and all the great mystics say: there is no distinction between "I" and "Thou." "The convergence of mysticism and the new physics," says Talbot "has brought us to the gateway of our *humanness*. We travel through the worlds in search of something that forever lies within us."[45]

Radhakrishnan defines the type of unitive religion demanded by those familiar with the philosophical and religious implications of modern science. He says that "we require a religion which is both scientific and humanistic. We need a spiritual home, where we can live without surrendering the rights of reason or the needs of humanity. Reverence for truth is a moral value. We cannot rest the case of religion any more on dogmatic supernaturalism. Mysticism takes its stand on verifiable truth. It is not opposed to science and reason. If God is not found in each soul, He is unfindable. The code of ethics adopted by mysticism is noble and austere."

The elements common to all religions can serve to unify the human race, Radhakrishnan feels. "They are the common possessions of the great religions, though often embedded in superstitious accretions and irrelevances. The universality of the great facts of religious experience, their close resemblance under diverse conditions of race and time, attest to the persistent unity of the main Spirit."[46]

It must be emphasized that the kind of religion verified by modern science is that of a unitive kind. Moreover, it is universal religion, rather than the claims of any one church or sect, that is supported by experimenters on the frontiers of scientific knowledge.

Theologians as diverse as Ernst Troeltsch and Dean Inge agreed that, to save it from formalism and excessive institutionalism, Christianity must return to the mystical tradition for purification and revitalization. This same judgment could be applied with equal force to all of the world's great religions.

References

1. Karl Heim, *The Transformation of the Scientific World View* (Harper, 1953). p. 35. Heim was Professor of Theology at Tübingen University.
2. Michael Talbot, *Mysticism and the New Physics* (Bantam, 1981), p. 2.
3. William Irwin Thompson, *Passages About Earth* (Harper & Row, 1981), p. 92.
4. Alfred Kazin, *New York Times Book Review,* 1 May 1988, pp. 40-41.
5. Ken Wilber, ed., *Quantum Questions* (Shambhala, 1984), pp. 148-52.
6. Ibid., pp. 137, 144.
7. Quoted in Heinz Pagels, *Perfect Symmetry* (Bantam, 1986), pp. 1, 273, 381.
8. Wilber, *Quantum Questions,* pp. 106-07.
9. Ibid., pp. 10, 169, 180, 192, 206.
10. Ibid., pp. 89, 97.
11. Ibid., pp. 159, 162, 163.
12. Ibid., pp. 36, 46, 51, 52, 54.
13. Davies, pp. ix, 178-81, 189.
14. Talbot, p. 107.
15. Ibid., pp. 111, 113-15, 117-18.
16. Ibid., pp. 120-21.
17. Joseph Campbell, in Eugene Kennedy, *The Now and Future Church* (Doubleday, 1984), p. 78.
18. *Newsweek,* 11 January 1988, pp. 47, 51.
19. Andrew M. Sandorfi, *New York Times Magazine,* 18 January 1987, p. 78.
20. Mujaddid A. Izaz & M. Mansoor Ijaz, *Physics Today,* January 1988, p. 129.
21. Davies, pp. 10-11.
22. Quoted in Pagels, p. 3.
23. Pagels, pp. 7, 125, 159.
24. Ibid., pp. 143, 333.
25. Ibid., p. 384.
26. Bernard S. Siegel, *Love. Medicine. and Miracles* (Harper & Row, 1986), pp. 56, 180.

27 Ibid., pp. ix, x, 18.
28 Ibid., pp. 74, 150.
29 Ibid., pp. 151, 179.
30 Quoted in Ibish, p. 113.
31 Oliver L. Reiser, *Cosmic Humanism and World Unity* (Gordon & Breach, 1975), p. 48.
32 Quoted in Ken Wilber, *The Spectrum of Consciousness* (Theosophical Publishing House, 1977), p. 148.
33 Reiser, p. 105.
34 Siegel, p. 224.
35 Davies, p. 111.
36 König, p. 191.
37 Ferguson, pp. 57-58.
38 Talbot, pp. 57-58. Burr is a professor at the Yale Univ. Medical School.
39 Wilber, *No Boundary*, pp. 39-41.
40 Talbot, p. 97.
41 Hoffman, pp. 11, 16, 208.
42 David Bohm, *Wholeness and the Implicate Order* (Routledge & Kegan Paul, 1980), pp. 16, 23, 129, 155, 177, 193.
43 Ken Wilber, ed., *The Holographic Paradigm and Other Paradoxes* (Shambhala, 1982), pp. 194, 196, 199, 207.
44 Ibid., pp. 5, 7, 10, 11.
45 Talbot, pp. 122, 176, 177, 181-83.
46 Radhakrishnan, pp. 294-97.

CHAPTER 15

RELIGION: BANE INTO BLESSING

This chapter will focus on how to turn the bane of divisive religion into the blessing of unitive religion. After reviewing the inordinate suffering and misery caused by religion which divides, it is appropriate to point out ways that religion can return to its prime function of furthering the love of God and of humankind.

"We will never arrive at an authentic understanding of religion," said Thomas J. Altizer, "apart from a shattering of our own autonomy. Our time has witnessed the collapse of the traditional foundations of Western civilization, and by living this collapse within ourselves we can know authentically the dissolution of our own autonomy. Thereby we will be open to a deeper understanding of the highest expression of religious experience. Once we are liberated from an ultimate dependence upon the reality of the world, we can enter the experience of the religious seer, for in both mysticism and eschatology all awareness of the world is either suspended or dissolved as a means of making possible a total immersion in the religious Reality."[1]

A Baptist minister in New York City in 1910, J. Herman Randall, summarized religious development. Like everything else, Randall said, religion evolves. First there is the superstitious phase of nature gods, followed by a political phase, when religion is a handmaid to national ambition. The third phase is one of the growth of ethical and spiritual forces. In Christianity, Christ inaugurated the third phase by stressing two teachings: one should be perfect, even as God in heaven is perfect; and the kingdom of Heaven lies within us. Unfortunately, said Randall, within 200 years Christ's teachings were encrusted with "the gods of theology or ecclesiasticism." The modern world needs to return to Christ's main idea that "the only true worship of God is disinterested service to humanity."

This Baptist preacher saw not a very rosy future for organized Christianity, for he felt that it would probably maintain its petty sectarianism, and its preference for ritual as magic over service as ritual. But the world was on the threshold of a return to the religion of Christ, he believed, for the modern world wants love, unity, brotherhood, forgiveness, and sacrifice, the very things that Christ represents. "The religion of the future will be less theological," Randall predicted, "but profoundly more ethical and spiritual. It will care less about creeds and more about truth. It will require vastly less of ecclesiastical tests, and will demand only a life of sympathy and love and brotherliness."[2]

Catholic theologian Eugene Kennedy feels that the powerful biblical symbol of servanthood can reunite Christianity for service to mankind. In servanthood people can perceive their essential oneness with one another. It "implies a return to a feeling for our God-given unity and for the unity of God's creation. Servanthood is an invitation to take our existence seriously, not as slaves but as persons who realize fully the dignity of their calling and of their obedience to the needs of mankind."[3] Christ said, "He who is greatest among you will be your servant."

The Symphony of Religions

The modern world looks to religion for dialogue rather than debate. We need to communicate across our gaps rather than try to batter adversaries into defeat. Ananda Coomaraswamy said that the purpose of religious dialogue is not to convert the other person, but to persuade him that his religion is essentially the same as one's own. "In the beginning was relationship," said Martin Buber. Religious dialogue need not aim at syncretism nor absorption but rather at unitive pluralism. Each faith should keep its own creeds and rituals, provided they do not vitiate the divine love of agape which unites believers in a love of God and humanity.

Since people differ widely, their religious forms should be varied. But "we should not assume that these different apprehensions of God are mutually exclusive. God in His infinite reality may be both love and justice, both Thou and karma, both king and friend. Christ may be present in other religions, and their several awarenesses of God likewise present in Christianity."[4]

The enlightened modern person understands that salvation is available in various religious traditions, asserts Wilfred Cantwell Smith. "That Christian faith saves, but none other does, is the considered doctrine of no significant Christian theologian," Smith states. "Just as Christians have been saved by Christian faith, so have Moslems by Islamic, Buddhists by Buddhist, and Andaman Islanders by Andaman."[5] Being saved means being free from alienation, despair, and nihilism, Smith explains. Salvation gives one courage, dignity, and capacity to suffer without disintegrating and to succeed without gloating.

Religious unity is no mere modern fad, Smith avers, but a return to religion's original role. "The universalism that is beginning to become available to us, if we are wise, will be a recovery of a universalism that, it turns out, we lost only the other day." Religious pluralism has developed within each world religion. "It has presented itself as disruptive only because our first efforts to cope with it were uncouth and inadequate. The theology of comparative religion that we seek may legitimately be continuous with the highest formulations of classical Christian theology, and also continuous with the other great religious traditions." The mystics have felt world community all along, but up to now, only they have evolved a world theology of religions. But "throughout the world," says Smith, "all the various religious communities have begun the promising venture of becoming authentically aware of each other, and thereby of themselves, and of their several participation in the whole."[6]

Rabbi Rudolph Grossman showed the high stakes involved in the switch from divisive to unitive religion. He said that "when men and women in a spirit of respect and good-will follow the words of those whose faith differs widely from their own, a mighty step forward has been made in that true spirit of fair-mindedness and justice that will ultimately lead to the unification of the human race. Behind all the prejudice that has separated creed from creed, and deluged the earth with the blood of innocent victims, stands ignorance of the faith that is the subject of scorn and abuse."[7]

Alfred W. Martin speaks of a world-wide symphony of religions. All religions, he feels, have certain common elements. He lists them as similar moral teaching and spiritual sentiments, and an underlying search for a purer, diviner life. Johann Herder, the

German philosopher, said that each religion was like the string of a harp. Alone, the tone was thin, but sounded together, the harmonious blending was symphonic. Each faith had a distinctive contribution to make, Martin said. Hinduism provides toleration and stress on spirit above matter. Buddhism concentrates on self-control and self-purification. Confucianism stresses a beautiful order in all relationships. Judaism emphasizes righteousness and obedience to God's laws. Christianity brings forth agape, self-sacrifice, and forgiveness. Islam reminds one of the gap between God and humans, and of the total surrender to God's will demanded of the contrite believer.[8]

Wholeness

The goal of unitive religion is wholeness. "Each one of us," Raymond Panikkar observes, "may be aware of the whole under one particular aspect, and not just that we see only a part of it. The whole is what is wholesome for us. Something is complete when it has inner harmony. The root *kail* from which the word 'whole' derives, suggests both beauty and goodness. One must have reached a certain religious insight, poise, wisdom, and even inner peace and harmony within one's being, without which intellectual discourse about religion will be marred from the outset." For example, in watching an American Indian dance, "if we have not at least a glimpse both of the transforming effects of the dance and of the inner relationship between dance and the rest of life, we shall not be able to make much headway in interpreting the religious phenomenon of the dance. Religion is the symphony, not the soloist."

Separateness will no longer suffice, Panikkar believes. "No single human or religious tradition is today self-sufficient and capable of rescuing humanity from its present predicament. Hinduism will not survive if it does not face modernity. Christianity will disappear if it does not meet Marxism. Technocratic religion will destroy itself if it does not pay heed to the Amerindian tradition. Humanity will collapse if we do not gather together all the fragments of the scattered cultures and religions." What is required is not uniformity but common trust. Both the many and the One are needed for pure symphonic effect. "Concord is neither oneness nor plurality. It is the dynamism of the many toward the One."[9]

John V. Taylor, the Anglican Bishop of Winchester, delineates the role of interfaith dialogue in building religious unity. Taylor says that "we should think of every religion as a people's particular response to the reality which the Holy Spirit of God has set before their eyes. Human beings can use religion as an escape from God just as much as an approach to Him. And both the obedience and the disobedience get built into the tradition which is passed on to later generations. So every living faith is in a continual process of renewal and purification. The Ultimate Reality in every religion is the same. All religions express an awareness of human alienation and need for healing and deliverance, and in all religions people experience an inward liberation, a sense of being made new. Though rituals vary, yet the sense of oneness and communication with a gracious Divinity is common to them all, as is the hunger of the heart for such communion."[10]

Arthur Schopenhauer believed that persons in all ages have validated mankind's unity. "In all individuals," he said, "there is manifest only one Being, ever the same in all, and with us through all time. Friedrich Schelling, he said, united "deftly in a single system the doctrines of Plotinus, Spinoza, Kant, and Jacob Boehme, combined with the findings of modern science." As the distinction between self and neighbor dissolves, the foundation of a universal ethical code is provided, said Schopenhauer, "that one individual should recognize in another, himself in his own true being."[11]

Wilfred Cantwell Smith feels that future historians will look back on the outstanding event of this century, not as any of the scientific achievements, but rather on the fact that it was the period when planet earth became a single community. The music of French composer Oliver Messiaen epitomizes the unification. Messiaen, who has "an extraordinary rapport with the spiritual values of all religions," employs "Tibetan ritual music, ancient Hindu rhythmic cycles, animist birdsong, and the synesthetic use of color vibrations as sound" to get across his deeply religious messages.[12]

Pope Pius XII believed in the concept of world community. Mankind's common origin and equality in God's sight makes us a unity, he taught. "In the light of this unity of all mankind, which exists in law and in fact," he said, "individuals do not feel themselves to be isolated units, like grains of sand, but united by

Religion: Bane into Blessing

the very force of their nature and by their internal destiny, into an organic, harmonious mutual relationship. And nations, despite a difference in development, are not destined to break the unity of the human race, but rather to enrich and embellish it." We should be good citizens of our country, but never "close our eyes to the all-embracing nature of Christian charity, which calls for consideration of others in the pacifying light of love. To consider the state as something ultimate to which everything else should be subordinate cannot fail to harm the true and lasting prosperity of nations."[13]

"'No man is an island' applies not just to Christian believers," George Knight declares, "but to adherents of all religions. Thus it might be cruel and un-Christlike to try to make an individual cut himself off from the total world view in which he has been reared. Such an act is proselytism, something quite distinct from evangelism." Knight cites Christ's castigation of the scribes and Pharisees (in Matthew 23:15) for attempting to make proselytes but instead turning persons into "children of hell" like themselves. "In other words," says Knight, "you insist on his losing the degree of *shalom* he knew when he fitted into the context of his own faith."[14]

Joseph Campbell asserts that mythology demonstrates the unity of the human race. "What appears to be diverse religious traditions," he states, "are actually different expressions of a unitary experience that is shared across all cultures." The mystical function of mythology, Campbell feels, is to connect our waking consciousness with the whole mystery of the universe. Mythology also has a moral function, giving us ethical standards by which to live. We tend to think of other people's religion as mythology, But realizing that all religion is mythological, meaning that it refers not so much to actual historical events as to abstract meanings which grow out of specific events, what is needed, he says, is "remythologization, recapturing the mythological meaning," since this "reveals a common spirituality of mankind."[15] For Christians, Campbell says, the cross is a crossing, a meeting place, where God (through Christ) comes to humans, and where humans (through Christ) return to God.

Ken Wilber detects many signs of an emerging worldwide wisdom culture. These signs include the fact that people are beginning to see beyond color to recognize the family of man.

Other signs are the revolt of the younger generation against purely pecuniary values, and the growing merger of science and religion. Also encouraging is the nascent acceptance of the transcendent unity of all major religions, rejecting any system that insists that it is the only true path to God. The time might even come when voters will demand that candidates be mentally and spiritually mature in order to hold public office. The ultimate goal is the expansion of consciousness to where every person is seen to be an equal member of the mystical body of Christ/ Krishna/Buddha.[16]

Overcoming Divisiveness

Adrio König asks, When dogmatic churches clash, where is God to be found? "The lack of unity and catholicity among churches," he feels, "constitutes one of the greatest problems in trying to identify positively the work of God." Vatican II refers to the church as "the place where the universal brotherhood of man has already taken shape. In this sense the church then has the task of exhibiting itself to the world as an example of what God's ultimate goal for all mankind is, and to call the world and inspire it to work towards this goal."[17]

A lopsided religion, König says, preaches eternal salvation minus the social gospel, or the social gospel without the salvation message. True religion is neither faith alone or works alone, but faith made real by works. Not to love one's neighbor is not to love God, since God dwells within one's neighbor.

Anne Fremantle provides a necessary antidote to religion's male chauvinism: "The word for *Spirit* is female in Arabic, Hebrew, and Sanskrit, so that in Genesis the Spirit of God that brooded over the waters is feminine, as is, in Islam, the Spirit of God, *Ruh'Allah.*"[18] In the Nicene Creed in the original Greek, the word for the Holy Spirit is feminine.

The Bhagavad Gita describes "a royal road to hell" traveled by demoniac people who "want to make a show of religion, although they do not follow its principles. They are always arrogant, proud of possessing some type of education or wealth. Desiring to be worshipped by others, they grow very angry over trifles, and speak harshly, not gently."[19] They like to build big cathedrals where they worship Mammon, not God. The Hindu scriptures give an accurate account of many modern American television evangelists.

The Gita also describes another type of demons on that path to hell. They are politicians who, despite a gaudy show of false leadership, lack the intelligence and compassion to govern capably, and are primarily engaged in self-worship. They put their trust in purely material things, such as weapons, with "the result that the people are growing more and more cruel and violent."[20] Ultimately they invent or use weapons of great destruction, because of their godlessness. They lie when they say that the weapons are for the peace and prosperity of the world.

If lying is a personal flaw, can it be a public virtue? This would seem to be the outlook of a schizophrenic society. In a recent poll 69% of American voters indicated that they thought their leaders consistently lied to them. Persons with so little integrity that voters would not want them as friends manage to get elected as leaders persistently. Unitive religion has a role to play in cleaning up political morality in the United States.

Religion is often based upon fear, Radhakrishnan reminds us. In Christianity, he says, "the Fall symbolizes the disintegration of the harmony, the lapse into division, from a unitive life into a separate self-centered one. A reintegration of human nature is the meaning of salvation. So long as religions themselves are an expression of fear, the security they afford is purchased at a terrible price and ends in distorting human life. The dogmas lead to mutual destruction.

What we need is a religion of freedom, which stimulates faith not fear, spontaneity not formalism. To be religious is to apprehend the reality of other souls. 'What sorrow is there for him who perceives this unity?' asks the Upanishads. He who realizes the universal self sees all human beings as belonging to a kingdom of ends. Spirits in unity with themselves must in the end be in unity with one another."[21]

The ancient religion of Taoism has some very practical applications in the modern world. The doctrine of *wu-wei* might be called "creative non-action." It has been used successfully by Mahatma Gandhi, Martin Luther King, Jr., and other civil rights leaders. It poses genuine humility in opposition to the "king of the hill" philosophy of cutthroat competition. It is, says Holmes Welch, a survival philosophy. After the Type A hustlers have atom-bombed themselves into ruins, Welch predicts, those who practice *wu-wei* will live together in simple peace.

Reconception in Modern Religion

There is scarcely any religion which does not have lamentable quantities of divisive religion. But all religions also possess considerable amounts of unitive religion. What the world needs is not conversion from many faiths into one, but rather for each religion to reconceive itself in terms of its fundamental strengths, which ordinarily are similar to those of the ideals of its founder.

Mordecai Kaplan has a number of suggestions on how Judaism must reconceive itself so as to be a more vital force in the modern world. "The only way in which Jews will ever be able to coordinate their own mode of life with the life they must share with their neighbors," says Kaplan, "will be by rethinking their beliefs, reorganizing their institutions, and developing new means of self-expression as Jews. For Judaism to become creative once again, it must assimilate the best in contemporary civilization. Not separation must henceforth be the principle of living as a Jew, but otherness. Separation is the antithesis of cooperation, and results in ingrown and clannish stagnation. Otherness thrives best when accompanied by active cooperation."

"True to his historic tradition," Kaplan continues, "the Jew should throw in his lot with all movements to further social justice and universal peace, and bring to bear upon them the inspiration of his history and religion. Such a program calls for a degree of honesty that abhors all forms of self-delusion." Mutual toleration of religions can only come about, Kaplan feels, through recognition "that each religion must strive to have its beliefs and practices meet the universal needs of human nature, and that each religion must cultivate its uniqueness" within that framework. "Jewish civilization cannot survive without the God-idea as an integral part of it," Kaplan concludes, "but it is in no need of having any specific formulation of that idea authoritative for all Jews."[22]

Christianity, like all modern religions, is in a crisis. When business ethics conflict with Christian teachings, the public watches to see if the church will stand up for Christ's values. Walter Rausenbusch said that "if the church cannot Christianize commerce, commerce will commercialize the church." Albert

Schweitzer felt that "Christianity can become the living truth for successive generations only if thinkers constantly arise within it who, in the spirit of Jesus, make belief in him capable of intellectual comprehension in the thought-forms of the world-view proper to their time."[23]

Most Christians cannot imagine a time when Christ cannot save sinners. Despite all technological change, political strife, economic competition, and revolutions in communications, humans will always sin and thus need a savior. Christ will never be obsolete, but many of the outward forms of the rituals associated with his worship will undergo radical change, the better to reveal his spirit of love and redemption at work in a world badly needing both.

Kosuke Koyama contrasts three hands: the clenched fist of Lenin says "I will fight you for my rights"; the open palm of the Buddha represents the compassionate peace of a spiritual teacher; and the pierced palm of Christ stands for the agape which caused him to sacrifice his life to save humans from their own hatred and violence.

Ken Wilber finds symbolic meaning in Christ's death and resurrection. His death stands for the death of the separate selfish self in all of its forms. His resurrection was the prototype of rising to ultimate unity consciousness, to the point where he could truly say, "I and the Father are One." Christ evolved to the highest level of being, the causal level, Wilber states, and thus he was crucified by those at the lower levels, who, being unable to understand the causal level, feared and thus hated it. Christ's teaching was that all humans can achieve the causal level, that is, recognize themselves as sons and daughters of God.

The modern media can hasten unity consciousness, says Marshall McLuhan: "Psychic communal integration, made possible at last by the electronic media, could create the universality of consciousness foreseen by Dante when he predicted that men would continue as no more than broken fragments until they were unified into an inclusive consciousness. In a Christian sense, this is merely a new interpretation of the mystical body of Christ; and Christ, after all, is the ultimate extension of man."[24]

J. Leslie Dunstan speculated on the future of Protestant Christianity. As a religious movement stressing individualism and self-government, Protestantism would seem to have a secure future, Dunstan opined, for there are ever more democracies in the world. Protestantism also provides for meeting the spiritual needs of a wide variety of dissimilar people. But there are also some ominous signs. Spiritual anarchy always threatens such a centrifugal system. Also, the Bible cannot serve as the complete source of ultimate authority, as envisioned by the early Protestant reformers. And since the Roman Catholic Church has largely cleansed itself through internal reform, there is now little left that needs a "protest."

Modern Contemplation

"What we have to realize," said Alan Watts, "is not the getting of union with God, but the not being able to get away from it." The Holy Spirit, says Thomas Merton, "often tells us to sit still. He delivers us from ambition. He inspires obedience and humility. No one really knows Him who has not tasted the tranquility that comes with the renunciation of our own will, pleasure, and interests, without glory, notice, or approval, for the interests of some other person."[25] Because of the Holy Spirit we are happy to know God but remorseful at what we have been. Knowing God cannot help but make us dissatisfied with ourselves. But the believer has the assurance that the Spirit who united Christ with the Father is the same Spirit which unifies all believers with God.

What is the value of contemplation in the modern world? Raymond Panikkar answers that "we need the contemplative for a very important corrective in the encounter of religions and cultures, since harmony does not imply uniformity, and metaphysical oneness does not imply administrative union. The contemplative has a priestly-prophetic role: he mediates between issues irreconcilable until now, and he anticipates an age by realizing in his inner being what one day may also be a common condition. Action and contemplation have to join hands. No person, no religion, has the right to set the rules of this ultimate game of the human encounter in depth. From all sides we have to recognize our insufficiency, welcoming any contribution from whatever corner it may come. This attitude makes the inter-religious dialogue and the common search for truth one of the purest religious acts today."[26] This attitude entails love, understanding, and faith in God.

Frithjof Schuon says that the core of religion is to realize that God entered into man so that man might be able to return to God. Ibn 'Arabi called this "the religion of love." "It is not we who know God," says Schuon, "it is God who knows Himself in us. If we want the truth to live in us, we must live in it. Reality has entered into man's nothingness, so that nothingness might become real. Since God loves the world, man must love his neighbor, thus repeating on the human plane God's love for the world. Man must 'lose his life' because God sacrificed Himself for him."[27]

Carl H. Voss quotes an anonymous poem:

In thee, in me, in all men
There dwelleth the One God;
In all He suffers, and He suffers for all.
In all everywhere, see thyself.
Abandon this, thy ignorant conceit,
Which holds that thou art separate from others.[28]

Fyodor Dostoevsky advised, "Love all God's creation, the animals, the plants. If you love each thing you will perceive the mystery of God in all, and once you do, you will grow every day to a fuller understanding of it, until you come at last to love the whole world with a universal love."[29]

Leo Tolstoy stated that "religion must define the relation of man to the Source of all, the destiny of man, and the rules of conduct from this destiny. The universal religion, the fundamental principles of which are identical in all faiths, entirely satisfies these demands. The spirit of God lives in man. I believe that it is His will that we love one another. We must grow in love. This growth will contribute more than any other force to establish the Kingdom of God on earth—to replace a social life in which division, falsehood, and violence are all-powerful, with a new order in which humanity, truth, and brotherhood will reign."[30]

All of the beauty in nature responds in gratitude to the hand of the Creator, says Schuon. "A noble animal or a lovely flower is 'intellectually' superior to a base man. God reveals Himself to the plant in the light of the sun. The plant irresistibly turns itself towards the light; it could not be atheistical or impious."[31] Man, presumably gifted with a higher intellect, can be considered higher only when his misguided reason does not betray him to alienate himself from his Maker and his fellow man.

Creative Forgiveness

Like Hosea's, God's love is a forgiving love. "If society is imperfectible because man is sinful," says Peter Hinchliff, "then forgiveness is the primary way to deal with it." All great religious leaders understood the crucial necessity of forgiveness. We need to forgive not only individuals and groups which have offended us, but we must also be ready to forgive ourselves for unseemly conduct. Moreover, our striving will always outdo our achieving. "God forgives," says Hinchliff, "in spite of betrayal, infidelity, cowardice, lack of integrity, hatred, cruelty, political intrigue, and mockery. Morality is partly a matter of picking oneself up out of the dust of each day's failure and doggedly, penitently asking for the grace to make another attempt. Forgiveness enables us to accept the reality of imperfect human nature without lowering our standards of what human beings ought to be."[32]

We can learn from Christ, says Hinchliff, how to make our forgiveness creative. "All the hatred of Christ's enemies was flung at him, was gathered up and held to himself, not passed on in hurting others, but formed into a great creative and self-giving act of love. If the church is to be an alternative to a sinful world, a redeemed humanity, then it ought also be a paradigm of what human community should be."[33] Christ's faithfulness, integrity, self-sacrifice, and love, says Hinchliff, are the marks of his true church.

Taoists teach that by "letting go" (of one's ego, desires, vanity, and selfishness) one enters the world community, where every man is a gentle man, and then indeed the Kingdom of God comes to earth.

Persons imbued with unitive religion have peace and harmony both within and without. "For those who are opposed to us are our brothers," said Radhakrishnan, "from whom we happen to be estranged, and they can be won over by love and understanding. A Gandhi who declares that 'if untruth and violence are necessary for furthering the interests of my country, let my country go under' shows himself to be more religious than the so-called religious who tells us that it is sometimes our religious duty to kill. When religion succeeds in making us spiritual, our conflicts are resolved. Nothing human is alien to us. We have the primary patriotism which is the love of humanity. The unity of all life, which is the intellectual assumption of science, becomes the consuming conviction of the sage."[34] This person has the profound peace that passes understanding which enables him to say, like Christ, "I have overcome the world."

Reverence for Life

A German proverb states that "man's emergency is God's opportunity." Mankind's survival crisis, brought about by the development of nuclear weapons, might force us back to fellowship with God. History will probably reveal that, greater than America's ingenuity in developing atomic weapons, was America's remorse over having used them. It takes a great nation to lose a war rather than use atomic weapons on Vietnamese civilians and soldiers. For all the lies about Jews spread by anti-Semitic persons, the fact remains that Jewish-Americans, who constitute 3% of the American population, comprise fewer than 1/10 of 1% of Americans imprisoned for crimes of violence, such as assault, rape, and murder.

Albert Schweitzer's concept of Reverence for Life unites a religious affirmation of life with an ethical philosophy. "Through ethical acceptance of the world and of life," Schweitzer says, "we reach a power of reflection which enables us to distinguish what is essential in civilization and what is not. With so much progress in knowledge and power, true civilization has become not easier but harder. We all have to struggle with circumstances to preserve our humanity. Sooner or later there must dawn the renaissance which will bring peace to the world."[35]

"The world can be saved," said Radhakrishnan, "only if men and women develop a heart that will make it impossible for them to witness with equanimity the mutual slaughter and suffering of people."[36] Dietrich Bonhoeffer saw no return to a more pristine primitive life. Positively conceived, he said, the secularization of the world amounts to God teaching man to grow up, to be mature (which means to be interdependent). Bonhoeffer recalls Yahweh telling Ezekiel: "Son of man, stand upon your feet, and I will speak to you." Man has a new responsibility, along with God, for what happens in the world. In Galatians 4:1-7 Paul describes this condition as freedom with responsibility, as he differentiated sonship from slavery. In liberation theology, Latin Americans are showing that a concern for current freedom "is an essential part of becoming a child of God and an inheritor of the kingdom of heaven." As President John F. Kennedy said, "Those who make the peaceful revolution impossible make the violent revolution inevitable."[37]

Hans Küng answers the question of "What is demanded today of a basic Christian attitude toward the other world religions? Let there be more indifference toward the alleged orthodoxy that makes itself the measure of the salvation or damnation of human beings, and wishes to make good its truth claim with instruments of power and force. Let there be more sensitivity for allowing every religion to be seen within its own web of relationship." Religious freedom means "a positive freedom for new responsibility towards one's fellow human beings and God."[38]

Paul Tillich envisions an ultimate spiritual unity of mankind, with religions playing an evanescent role. "A particular religion," he says, "will be lasting to the degree in which it negates itself as a religion. In the depth of every living religion there is a point at which the religion itself loses its importance, and that to which it points breaks through its particularity, elevating it to spiritual freedom and with it to a vision of the spiritual presence in other expressions of the ultimate meaning of man's existence."[39]

Christianity needs to spend less time trying to convert people and more time loving people, George Knight asserts, who adds that believing in Christ means more than accepting him as one's savior. "Those who stay aboard this onward-moving activity of the living Christ, taking up their cross daily, and 'emptying themselves' in love and compassion for their neighbor, find themselves actually enjoying eternal life, beginning here and now. They also find themselves imparting that life to those whom they are seeking to serve in love. The whole notion of converting individuals from one 'religion' to another has gone with the wind. The racial tensions and dogmatic superiority of one culture and religion over against another are manifestations of the chaos that has been present in human life since the foundation of the world."[40] The chaos of divisive religion is no older, however, than the great unitive force of agape, God's sacrificial love.

Man's spiritual goal is God, not conformity to a prescribed set of religious rules. "Man begins to be adequately religious," says Wilfred Cantwell Smith, "only when he discovers that God is greater and more important than religion." Mankind's hope is that believers will learn to put faith in God ahead of faith in religion. It is only by this means that the blessings of unitive religion can continue to have the upper hand over the bane of divisive religion. "God," says Mordecai Kaplan, "is the life of the universe, immanent insofar as each part acts upon every other part, and transcendent as the Whole acts upon each part."

Religion, says John Hick, is not a set of mutually exclusive systems but a dynamic continuum, with new fields of force constantly appearing. Thus, religions are not true or false, any more than are the civilizations which produce them. Religions are expressions of the diverse ways humans use as they try to reach God. Invariably they develop a bureaucracy somewhat at odds with the intent of the founder. Part of this institutionalization is an effort to set up boundaries so that "we" who are inside can feel superior to "those" who are outside the boundaries. This is understandable in terms of human psychology, but false from God's standpoint, since "those" who are outside are "we", His children. Reconception in each religion needs to eradicate exclusiveness and demonstrate God's unity and our oneness as His children.

"The holy man of our time," says John Dunne, "is not a man who could found a world religion, but a figure like Gandhi, a man who passes over by sympathetic understanding from his own religion to other religions and comes back again with new insight into his own faith. Passing over and coming back is the spiritual adventure of our time."[41]

James, the brother of Jesus, insisted on the necessity of applying one's faith in a living context. He said, "You believe there is but one God; you do well, but the devils also so believe and tremble. Know, O vain man, that faith without works is dead" (James 2:19-20). My first college president, in greeting me, said, "I don't know what church you belong to, but whatever your faith, if you live up to its best teachings, you will be a better man than I am."

In his "Essay on Man" Alexander Pope presented the case for unitive religion:

For modes of faith let graceless zealots fight;
His can't be wrong whose life is in the right.
In faith and hope the world will disagree,
But all mankind's concern is charity.
All must be false that thwart this one great end,
And all of God, that bless mankind or mend.

Religion is too important a part of human life for it to be scrapped because of its misapplications. Any activity that can produce, in addition to the scriptures of the world, such great works as Gothic cathedrals, Handel's *Messiah,* and the great Hindu and Buddhist art deserves mankind's undying gratitude. The world would be incomparably poorer without Moslem art and architecture, Dante's *Divine Comedy,* Hebrew psalms and prophecy, and Michelangelo's frescoes on the ceiling of the Sistine Chapel.

Divisive religion leaves humankind with an opposite heritage. One conjures visions of 20,000 human hearts being torn out allegedly to appease an Aztec god. Many religious wars described in the world's scriptures are cruel, inhuman, and ungodly. The Christian Crusades are a monument to man's misguided faith, just as is modern Moslem terrorism. The slaughter of Christians by Christians in Ireland, ostensibly for political goals but suffused with religious bigotry on both sides, is a patent insult to Christ and to all sensitive believers in a loving God. The Spanish Inquisition reveals how far afield fanaticism can lead from the essence of true religion. Mankind's horrible record of anti-Semitism reached its gruesome climax in the Nazi holocaust, probably the lowest point ever achieved in human conduct. The splintered faiths produced by divisive religion have caused untold heartaches, split homes, suffering, and death.

On the other hand, unitive religion continues to be mankind's best hope for progress towards spiritual maturity. One measure of the excellence of unitive religion is the praise given across religious boundaries. Everyone can praise an Emperor Asoka for his humaneness and kindness, or a St. Francis for his tender love of all creation. Leaders like Moses Maimonides and Thomas Aquinas earn virtually unanimous respect because of their devotion to God, and their service in helping lead others to God. It is hard to imagine a better code of values than that given to our species by the Sufi masters. In the current century giants like Dr.

Tom Dooley, Mahatma Gandhi, Pope John XXIII, Frank Laubach, Albert Schweitzer, and Mother Teresa serve as monuments to the great gains to mankind when unitive religion is recognized and supported. It is the purpose of this book to make clear the awesome difference for the future history of the human race if unitive religion can replace divisive religion wherever possible.

References

[1] Altizer, pp. 172-74.
[2] J. Herman Randall & J. Gardner Smith, eds., *The Unity of Religions* (Crowell, 1910), pp. 355, 362.
[3] Kennedy, pp. 186-88.
[4] Hick, pp. 106-07.
[5] W.C. Smith, *Towards a World Theology,* p. 168.
[6] Ibid., pp. 112, 121, 192.
[7] Randall, p. 156.
[8] Ibid., pp. 323, 327-28, 333-34.
[9] Swidler, pp. 139-40, 143, 145.
[10] Hick & Hebblethwaite, pp. 217, 232.
[11] Campbell, *Creative Mythology,* pp. 73-75.
[12] Raphael Mostel, *New York Times,* 11 December 1988, 2:25, 38.
[13] Brantl, pp. 219-22.
[14] George A.F. Knight, *I Am: This is My Name* (Eerdmans, 1983), p. 79. Knight is a New Zealand biblical scholar.
[15] Kennedy, pp. 71, 84.
[16] Wilber, *Up From Eden,* pp. 325-26.
[17] König, pp. 162-63.
[18] Fremantle, p. 41.
[19] Bhaktivedanta, p. 236.
[20] Ibid., pp. 237-38.
[21] Radhakrishnan, pp. 44-46.
[22] Mordecai M. Kaplan, *Judaism as a Civilization,* rev. ed. (Thomas Yoseloff, 1957), pp. 331, 513-15, 522.
[23] Albert Schweitzer, *The Mysticism of Paul the Apostle,* 2nd ed. (Adam & Charles Black, 1953), p. 377.
[24] Thompson, p. 43

[25] Merton, p. 186.
[26] Ibish, pp. 99-102.
[27] Schuon, pp. 95, 116, 442.
[28] Voss, p. 232.
[29] Ibid., p. 255.
[30] Ibid., pp. 151, 262-63.
[31] Schuon, p. 115.
[32] Hinchliff, pp. 59, 200.
[33] Ibid., pp. 53-54.
[34] Radhakrishnan, pp. 46, 52.
[35] Schweitzer, *Out of My Life and Thought*, p. 127.
[36] Radhakrishnan, p. 113.
[37] Robinson, pp. 87-88.
[38] Swidler, p. 237.
[39] Paul Tillich, *Christianity and the Encounter of the World Religions* (Columbia University Press, 1963), p. 97.
[40] Knight, p. 87.
[41] Robinson, p. 22.

BIBLIOGRAPHY

Adler, Mortimer J., ed. *The Great Ideas*. Vol. 2. Chicago: Encyclopedia Britannica, 1952.

Albright, William F. *From the Stone Age to Christianity* 2nd ed. Garden City: Doubleday, 1957.

Allen, Richard. *Imperialism and Nationalism in the Fertile Crescent*. London: Oxford University Press, 1974.

Altizer, Thomas J.J. *Oriental Mysticism and Biblical Eschatology*. Philadelphia: Westminster, 1961.

Angus, S. *The Mystery Religions*. 2nd ed. New York: Dover, 1975.

Bainton, Roland H. *The Medieval Church*. New York: Van Nostrand, 1962.

Barstow, Anne Llewellyn. *Witchcraze*. London: HarperCollins, 1995.

Berdyaev, Nicholas. *Slavery and Freedom*. New York: Scribners, 1944.

Bhaktivedanta, A.C. *Bhagavad Gita As It Is*. Los Angeles: Bhaktivedanta Book Trust, 1975.

Blakney, Raymond B. *Meister Eckhart: A Modern Translation*. New York: Harper, 1941.

Bohm, David. *Wholeness and the Implicate Order*. London: Routledge & Kegan Paul, 1980.

Brantl, George, ed. *Catholicism*. New York: Braziller, 1962.

Browning, Don S. *Generative Man: Psychoanalytic Perspectives*. Philadelphia: Westminster, 1973.

Campbell, Joseph. *Creative Mythology*. Harmondsworth: Penguin, 1984.

—— *Occidental Mythology*. New York: Viking, 1971.

—— *Oriental Mythology*. New York: Viking, 1971.

—— ed. *Spiritual Disciplines*. Princeton: Princeton University Press, 1960.

—— & Charles Musès, eds. *In All Her Names.* HarperSanFrancisco, 1991.

Carlston, Kenneth S. *Law and Organization in World Society.* Urbana: University of Illinois Press, 1962.

Cell, Edward, ed. *Religion and Contemporary Western Culture.* Nashville: Abingdon, 1967.

Cousins, Norman, ed. *In God We Trust.* New York: Harper, 1958.

Cragg, Kenneth. *The Wisdom of the Sufis.* New York: New Directions, 1976.

Crim, Keith, ed. *Abingdon Dictionary of Living Religions.* Nashville, Abingdon, 1981.

Das, Bhagavan. *The Essential Unity of All Religions.* 2nd ed. Wheaton, IL: Theosophical Press, 1966.

Davies, Paul. *God and the New Physics.* New York: Simon & Schuster, 1983.

Dietl, Wilhelm. *Holy War.* New York: Macmillan, 1984.

Dimont. Max I. *Jews, God, and History.* New York: New American Library, 1964.

Driver, Tom F. *The Magic of Ritual.* HarperSanFrancisco, 1991.

Dunstan, J. Leslie, ed. *Protestantism.* New York: Braziller, 1962.

Durant, Will. *The Age of Faith.* New York: Simon & Schuster, 1950.

—— *The Life of Greece.* New York: Simon & Schuster, 1939.

—— *Our Oriental Heritage.* New York: Simon & Schuster, 1954.

—— *The Reformation.* New York: Simon & Schuster, 1957.

—— & Ariel Durant. *The Age of Louis XIV.* New York: Simon & Schuster, 1963.

—— & Ariel Durant. *The Age of Reason Begins.* New York: Simon & Schuster, 1961.

Eliade, Mircea. *From Primitives to Zen.* New York: Harper & Row, 1967.

—— *The Myth of the Eternal Return.* Princeton: Princeton Univ. Press, 1974.

—— *The Sacred and the Profane.* New York: Harcourt Brace Jovanovich, 1959.

Falk, Richard A. *A Study of Future Worlds*. New York: Free Press, 1975.

Ferguson, Marilyn. *The Aquarian Conspiracy*. Los Angeles: Tarcher, 1980.

Ferm, Vergilius, ed. *Living Schools of Religion*. Ames: Littlefield, Adams, 1956.

Finegan, Jack. *The Archeology of World Religions*. Princeton: Princeton University Press, 1952.

Fisher, Joe & Joel L. Whitton, *Life Between Life*. New York: Warner Books, 1988.

Forbush, William B., ed. *Fox's Book of Martyrs*. Philadelphia: Universal Book & Bible House, 1926.

Frankfort, Henri et al., eds. *Before Philosophy*. Harmondsworth: Penguin, 1949.

Frazer, James G. *The Golden Bough*. New York: Macmillan, 1951.

Fremantle, Anne. *Pilgrimage to People*. New York: David McKay, 1968.

Fromm, Erich. *You Shall Be As Gods*. New York: Holt, Rinehart & Winston, 1966.

Gandhi, Mohandas K. *An Autobiography*. Boston: Beacon, 1957.

Gandhi on Non-Violence. Ed by Thomas Merton. New York: New Directions, 1965.

Gard, Richard A., ed. *Buddhism*. New York: Braziller, 1962.

Ghirsman, R. *Iran from the Earliest Times to the Islamic Conquest*. Harmondsworth: Penguin, 1961.

Gibbon, Edward. *The Decline and Fall of the Roman Empire*. New York: Harcourt Brace, 1960.

Glassman, Bernard. *Anti-Semitic Stereotypes Without Jews*. Detroit: Wayne State University Press, 1975.

Goble, Frank. *The Third Force*. New York: Pocket Books, 1971.

Harmsworth, Alfred & S.S. McClure, eds. *The World's Greatest Books*. Vol. 13. New York: McKinley, Stone, & Mackenzie, 1912.

Haught, James A. *Holy Horrors*. Buffalo: Prometheus Books, 1990.

Heard, Gerry C. *Mystical and Ethical Experience*. Macon: Mercer Univ. Press, 1985.

Heaton, E.W. *The Hebrew Kingdoms*. London: Oxford University Press, 1968.

Heim, Karl. *The Transformation of the Scientific World View*. New York: Harper, 1953.

Heisenberg, Werner. *Physics and Philosophy*. New York: Harper, 1958.

Hertzberg, Arthur, ed. *Judaism*. New York: Braziller, 1962.

Hick, John. *God and the Universe of Faiths*. Rev. ed. London: Collins, 1977.

—— & Brian Hebblethwaite, eds. *Christianity and Other Religions*. Philadelphia: Fortress Press, 1981.

Hinchliff, Peter. *Holiness and Politics*. Grand Rapids: Eerdmans, 1983.

Hixon, Les. *Coming Home*. New York: Anchor, 1978.

Hocking, William E. *The Coming World Civilization*. New York: Harper, 1956.

Hoffman, Edward. *The Way of Splendor*. Boulder: Shambhala, 1981.

Homage to Mahatma Gandhi. New Delhi: Ministry of Information, no date.

Humphreys, Christmas. *Buddhism*. Harmondsworth: Penguin, 1954.

Huxley, Aldous. *The Perennial Philosophy*. New York: Harper, 1945.

Ibish, Yusuf & Ileana Marculescu, eds. *Contemplation and Action in World Religions*. Seattle: University of Washington Press, 1978.

Jacobs, Louis. *Jewish Mystical Testimonies*. New York: Schocken, 1977.

James, William. *The Varieties of Religious Experience*. New York: Modern Library, 1936.

Jones, Rufus M. *Spiritual Reformers in the 16th and 17th Centuries*. Boston: Beacon, 1959.

Juliana of Norwich. *Reflections of Divine Love*. Garden City: Doubleday, 1977.

Bibliography 363

Kaplan, Mordecai M. *Judaism as a Civilization*. Rev. ed. New York: Thomas Yoseloff, 1957.

Katz, Steven T., ed. *Mysticism and Religious Traditions*. New York: Oxford University Press, 1983.

Keddie, Nikki R., ed. *Scholars, Saints, and Sufis*. Berkeley: University of California Press, 1972.

Kennedy, Eugene. *The Now and Future Church*. Garden City: Doubleday, 1984.

Klaaren, Eugene M. *Religious Origins of Modern Science*. Grand Rapids: Eerdmans, 1977.

Knight, George A.F. *I Am: This is My Name*. Grand Rapids: Eerdmans, 1983.

König, Adrio. *Here Am I*. Grand Rapids: Eerdmans, 1982.

Küng, Hans. *Christianity and the World Religions*. Garden City: Doubleday, 1986.

—— *On Being A Christian*. New York: Doubleday, 1976.

Loisy, Alfred. *The Origins of the New Testament*. New York: Collier Books, 1962.

Louth, Andrew. *The Origins of the Christian Mystical Tradition*. Oxford: Clarendon Press, 1981.

Maraini, Fosco. *Meeting with Japan*. New York: Viking, 1960.

Marechal, Joseph. *Studies in the Psychology of the Mystics*. Albany: Magi Books, 1964.

Marty, Martin E. *The Pro and Con Book of Religious America*. Waco: Word Books, 1975.

Merton, Thomas. *The Ascent to Truth*. New York: Harcourt Brace Jovanovich, 1951.

Moore, R. Laurence. *Religious Outsiders and the Making of Americans*. Oxford: Oxford University Press, 1986.

Müller, F. Max, ed. & tr. *The Upanishads*. New York: Dover, 1962.

Newell, William L. *Struggle and Submission: R.C. Zaehner on Mysticism*. Washington, D.C.: University Press of America, 1981.

Nicholson, Reynold A. *Studies in Islamic Mysticism*. Cambridge: Cambridge University Press, 1967.

Niebuhr, Reinhold. *The Self and the Dramas of History*. New York: Scribners, 1955.

—— *The Structure of Nations and Empires*. New York: Scribners, 1959.

Norman, E.R. *Anti-Catholicism in Victorian England*. London: Allen & Unwin, 1968.

Norman, Edward. *Christianity and the World Order*. Oxford: Oxford University Press, 1979.

Noss, John B. *Man's Religions*. 3rd ed. New York: Macmillan, 1963.

Otto, Rudolf. *Mysticism East and West*. London: Macmillan, 1932.

Padover, Saul K. *Thomas Jefferson on Democracy*. New York: Penguin, 1939.

Pagels, Heinz. *Perfect Symmetry*. New York: Bantam, 1986.

Panikkar, Raymond. *The Unknown Christ of Hinduism*. London: Darton, Longman, & Todd, 1964.

Parrinder, Geoffrey. *Jesus in the Qur'an*. New York: Barnes & Noble, 1965.

—— *Mysticism in the World's Religions*. New York: Oxford Univ. Press, 1976.

—— *Religion in Africa*. New York: Praeger, 1969.

Phillips, Dorothy B. et al., eds. *The Choice is Always Ours*. Wheaton, IL: Re-Quest Books, 1982.

Phillips, J.B. *God Our Contemporary*. London: Hodder & Stoughton, 1960.

Piggott, Stuart, ed. *The Dawn of Civilization*. New York: McGraw-Hill, 1961.

Progoff, Ira. *Depth Psychology and Modern Man*. New York: McGraw-Hill, 1973.

Radhakrishnan, Sarvepalli. *Eastern Religions and Western Thought*. 2nd ed. London: Oxford University Press, 1940.

Randall, J. Herman & J. Gardner Smith, eds. *The Unity of Religions*. New York: Crowell, 1910.

Reiser, Oliver L. *Cosmic Humanism and World Unity*. New York: Gordon & Breach, 1975.

Renou, Louis, ed. *Hinduism*. New York: Braziller, 1962.

Robinson, John A.T. *Truth is Two-Eyed.* Philadelphia: Westminster, 1979.

Roth, Cecil. *A History of the Jews.* New York: Schocken, 1961.

Rousseau, Richard W., ed. *Christianity and the Religions of the East.* Scranton: Ridge Row Press, 1982.

Scholem, Gershom G. *Major Trends in Jewish Mysticism.* Rev. ed. New York: Schocken, 1946.

Schuon, Frithjof. *The Essential Writings of Frithjof Schuon.* Warwick, NY: Amity House, 1986.

Schweitzer, Albert. *The Mysticism of Paul the Apostle.* 2nd ed. London: Adam & Charles Black, 1953.

—— *Out of My Life and Thought.* New York: New American Library, 1953.

Sears, William. *Release the Sun.* Wilmette, IL: Baha'i Publishing Trust, 1960.

Siegel, Bernard S. *Love, Medicine. and Miracles.* New York: Harper & Row, 1986.

Slater, Robert L. *World Religions and World Community.* New York: Columbia University Press, 1963.

Smart, Ninian. *Beyond Ideology: Religion and the Future of Western Civilization.* San Francisco: Harper & Row, 1981.

Smith, Huston. *The Religions of Man.* New York: Harper & Row, 1958.

—— *The World's Religions.* HarperSanFrancisco, 1991.

Smith, Wilfred Cantwell. *Faith and Belief.* Princeton: Princeton University Press, 1979.

—— *Islam in Modern History.* New York: New American Library, 1959.

—— *Religious Diversity.* New York: Harper & Row, 1976.

—— *Towards A World Theology.* Philadelphia: Westminster, 1981.

Spencer, Sidney. *Mysticism in World Religion.* New York: A.S. Barnes & Co., 1963.

Stace, Walter T. *The Teachings of the Mystics.* New York: New American Library, 1960.

Stone, Merlin. *When God Was A Woman.* New York: Dorset Press, 1976.

Suzuki, Daisetz T. *Zen and Japanese Culture.* New York: Pantheon, 1959.
Swidler, Leonard, ed. *Toward A World Theology of Religion.* Maryknoll, NY: Orbis Books, 1987.
Talbot, Michael. *Mysticism and the New Physics.* New York: Bantam, 1981.
Teilhard de Chardin, Pierre. *The Phenomenon of Man.* 2nd ed. New York: Harper & Row, 1965.
Thompson, William Irwin. *Passages About Earth.* New York: Harper & Row, 1981.
Tillich, Paul. *Christianity and the Encounter of the World Religions.* New York: Columbia University Press, 1963.
—— *Dynamics of Faith.* New York: Harper & Row, 1958.
Tolstoy, Leo. *My Confession: My Religion: The Gospel in Brief.* New York: Scribners, 1929.
Torjesen, Karen Jo. *When Women Were Priests.* HarperSanFrancisco, 1995.
Toynbee, Arnold. *An Historian's Approach to Religion.* 2nd ed. Oxford: Oxford University Press, 1979.
—— ed. *Half the World.* New York: Halt, Rinehart & Winston, 1973.
Tulloch, John. *Chekhov: A Structuralist Study.* New York: Macmillan, 1980.
Underhill, Evelyn. *Mysticism.* 16th ed. New York: Dutton, 1948.
Vaillant, George C. *The Aztecs of Mexico.* London: Penguin, 1950.
Van Doren, Carl. *Benjamin Franklin.* New York: Viking, 1938.
Voss, Carl H., ed. *The Universal God.* Cleveland: World Publishing Company, 1953.
Watts, Alan. *The Way of Zen.* New York: New American Library, 1959.
Whitaker, Donald P. & Rinn-Sup Shinn, eds. *Area Handbook for the People's Republic of China.* Washington, D.C.: American University, 1972.
Wilber, Ken, ed. *The Holographic Paradigm and Other Paradoxes.* Boulder: Shambhala, 1982.
—— *No Boundary.* Boulder: Shambhala, 1981.

―― ed. *Quantum Questions.* Boulder: Shambhala, 1984.
―― *The Spectrum of Consciousness.* Wheaton, IL: Theosophical Publishing House, 1977.
―― *Up From Eden.* Boulder: Shambhala, 1983.
Williams, David Rhys. *World Religions and the Hope for Peace.* Boston: Beacon: 1951.
Williams, John A, ed. *Islam.* New York: Braziller, 1962.
Woods, Richard, ed. *Understanding Mysticism.* Garden City: Doubleday, 1980.
Zaehner, Robert C. *Mysticism, Sacred and Profane.* New York: Oxford University Press, 1961.
Zimmer, Heinrich. *Philosophies of India.* New York: Meridian Books, 1960.